The Funny Parts

ALSO BY
ANTHONY BALDUCCI

*Lloyd Hamilton: Poor Boy Comedian of
Silent Cinema* (McFarland, 2009)

The Funny Parts

A History of Film Comedy Routines and Gags

ANTHONY BALDUCCI

McFarland & Company, Inc., Publishers
Jefferson, North Carolina, and London

To my sister, Joanne DeFeo

LIBRARY OF CONGRESS CATALOGUING-IN-PUBLICATION DATA

Balducci, Anthony, 1958–
The funny parts : a history of film
comedy routines and gags / Anthony Balducci.
     p.   cm.
Includes bibliographical references and index.

ISBN 978-0-7864-6513-2
softcover : acid free paper ∞

1. Comedy films — History and criticism.
I. Title.
PN1995.9.C55B35 2012   791.43'61709 — dc23   2011043814

BRITISH LIBRARY CATALOGUING DATA ARE AVAILABLE

© 2012 Anthony Balducci. All rights reserved

*No part of this book may be reproduced or transmitted in any form
or by any means, electronic or mechanical, including photocopying
or recording, or by any information storage and retrieval system,
without permission in writing from the publisher.*

Front cover image: Stan Laurel, Oliver Hardy and
Jimmy Aubrey in *That's My Wife*, 1929 (author's collection);
background element © 2012 Shutterstock

Manufactured in the United States of America

*McFarland & Company, Inc., Publishers
Box 611, Jefferson, North Carolina 28640
www.mcfarlandpub.com*

Table of Contents

Preface		1
Introduction		3
1	And Then There Were Pies	7
2	Mannequins and Other Dummies	16
3	Animals	34
4	Adventures in Eating	77
5	Attack of the Vamps	99
6	Indecent Exposure	107
7	Spooky Apparitions	118
8	Bombs and Burglars	130
9	How to Disguise Yourself as Furniture and Fool Your Friends	135
10	The Amazing Trapdoor Chase	145
11	Science and Magic	151
12	Tooth Extraction and Laughing Gas	158
13	Into the Looking Glass	162
14	Sleepless Nights	168
15	Fathers to *Sons of the Desert*	178
16	The Big Jangly Box, the Sliding Ladder and Other Comic Props	183
17	The Buster Keaton Variations	192
18	The Harold Lloyd Variations	222
19	Hysterical History	229
20	Bugs	241

21	Scared Black Servants, Dice-Playing African Cannibals, and the Most Racist Comedy in Silent Cinema History	245
22	Other Variations	259

Chapter Notes   299
Bibliography   303
Index   305

Preface

I initiated work on this book with a visit to New York City, where I spent three days screening films at the Museum of Modern Art. It was my objective at the time to write a book that made readers aware of important film rarities that cannot be viewed outside of a major archive. The working title of the book was *A Visit to the Archives*. Steve Massa, a well-versed authority on silent film comedy, invited me to his home to view DVD transfers of other rare archive acquisitions. I managed to keep my wits and enthusiasm intact as I watched nearly 70 short films in four days. Much to my surprise, I never found myself short of a laugh no matter how many films I watched in a single day. These performers had been stars in their day, and their mastery of comedy remained evident decades after their passing.

Being exposed to a variety of comedians, one after another, brought out the differences in their styles and approaches. I came to notice that the comedians often made use of common gags, routines and subjects. It fascinated me to see the juxtaposition of these assorted comedians performing the same routines or making use of the same gags. The extensive law classes that I took in college trained my mind to analyze similar cases through the method of compare and contrast. I found that, by employing this method with these similar comedy scenes, I could better understand the essence of these comedians.

The process of writing this book never got complicated. My strategy, simply, was to watch films. I sat down in front of a screen, whether the screen was in my living room, on my computer monitor or mounted on the wall of a screening room, and I watched a steady succession of films. I obtained these films from many different sources. Some were ordered on Amazon, while others came from faraway archives in Paris and Amsterdam.

I was nervous at first about viewing films in a screening room. As great an opportunity as it was to be able to see high-quality prints of rare motion pictures on a large screen, it concerned me that I might have a hard time scribbling notes in the dark while a silent film comedy, filled with chases and sight gags, zipped across the screen before me. I turned to modern technology for assistance. I worked out a system which allowed me to keep my eyes fixed on the screen while I spoke my observations aloud into a digital voice recorder. I later used speech-recognition software to create a transcript of my remarks. The fact is, technology carried me through the research and writing of this book. I played DVDs on my big-screen television. My Kindle made it easy for me to review my manuscript. Photo contributors sent me stills by way of email. My iPod soothed me with music as I worked my way through rewrites (the album I played most often was Duffy's *Rockferry*). I was even able to watch a 1918 Larry Semon comedy streamed by YouTube onto my iPod. I never lost sight of the fact that I was creating a study of old films (some dating back 110 years) using high-tech modern technology. Hi-tech meets hijinks. But I came to realize that the technology, old or new, did not matter. The true revelation was that, while a great deal of technology has come and gone in the last century, these films never got old. Semon's film *Romans and Rascals* once made people laugh in the 3,300-seat Strand Theater in New York City and that same film, in its appearance on my iPod, had no trouble at all making me laugh. Film archives may one day post their holdings online and that may bring about a rebirth of these films. I hope that this book will prepare readers for that possibility.

A valuable source of information was the trade journal *Moving Picture World*, which filled in the gaps regarding films that have become lost in the decades since their release.

I was pleased by the assistance and hospitality extended to me during my visit to the Museum of Modern Art's Department of Film. My thanks goes to the curator, Charles Silver, and his assistant, Ron Magliozzi. I also must thank former curator Eileen Bowser, who acquired the majority of the museum's silent film comedy holdings in the 1970s and 1980s.

I also extend my gratitude to Steve Massa, Ben Model, Serge Bromberg, Bruce Lawton, Cole Johnson, Robert Arkus, Bill Sprague, Pat Cashin, Jerry Murbach, Annette D'Agostino Lloyd, Tom Reeder, Steve Rydzewski, Greg Hilbrich, John Townsen and the Filmmuseum in Amsterdam for their valuable contributions to this book.

In closing, I must express gratitude to my son Griffin for his steadfast support and encouragement. He watched many of these films with me and, I must say, he developed into an enthusiastic advocate of the weird and underrated Larry Semon.

Introduction

The objective of this book is to trace the history of popular comedy routines and gags, some of which developed for hundreds of years as they made their way through theaters, circuses, film and television. This book will attempt to trace gags to their beginnings and follow them up through the years as they pass through the hands of a diverse group of comedians. These routines, after a variety of remakes, revivals, recycles and revamps, became accepted as conventions of the genre.

Early film comedy appears, on the surface, to be chaotic. Throwing pies at a fancy dinner party is presented as unapologetic dysfunctionality. But it is, at some level, a demonstration of convention and order. To this day, this form of entertainment adheres to basic rules that came to be established at the beginning. The comedy tradition possesses its own unique purposes and definitions. When one takes a closer look, one can detect distinct patterns beneath the stylistic flourishes and surprising variations.

As classic comedy routines addressed a finite number of conventional subjects, it was left to the creativity of a comedian to take the conventional and make something unconventional out of it. A comedian could make a routine his own by emphasizing his personal perspective, style and approach. The best interpretations of a routine told the viewer something about the comedian. The comedian also had the option of springing a twist on the audience to turn existing expectations on their head.

As this book will show, gags tended to be expanded and embellished when different writers, directors and comedians took charge of the material and made their own contributions. This was a productive process which allowed an idea (as simple as a man falling down a hill, for example) to develop into something surprisingly intricate and meaningful. Scores of professionals were able, through their individual visions, to contribute collectively to a routine. Author Gerald Nachman wrote, "If you follow the paths long enough, you will find that all comedians are linked in some way, consciously or unconsciously feeding, or playing, off one another. The DNA of jokes, routines, and premises ... can be traced back across decades from comic to comic to comic."[1] This gag genealogy will provide a study of the ancestry of gags and routines, from original forms through developed forms, and, finally, to degenerated forms.

Just as gags and routines were adapted to suit the style and personality of different comedians, they were also adapted to conform to their given time periods. There came a time, however, when this community ("It-Takes-a-Village-to-Raise-a-Gag") methodology changed. Modern audience find that magicians may be willing to share secrets to their tricks

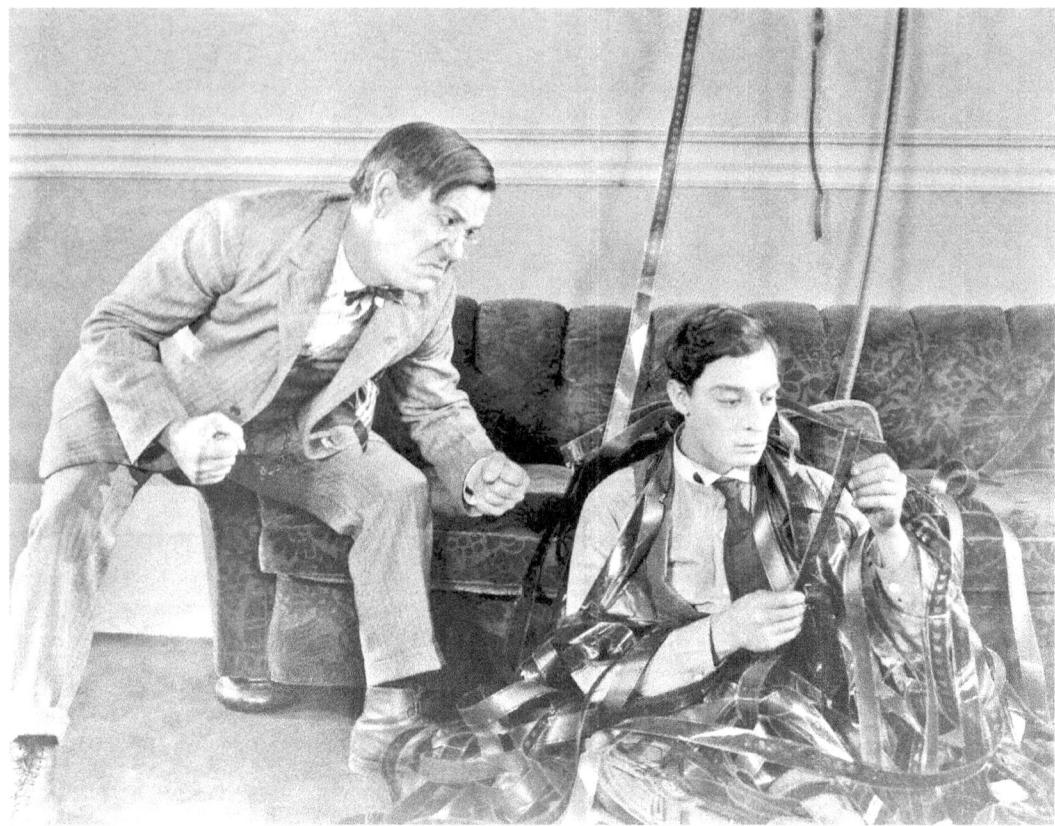

Buster Keaton is wrapped up in his work as a projectionist in *Sherlock Jr.* (1924). On the left is Ford West (courtesy www.doctormacro.com)

and singers are willing to share their songs, but comedians are dead set against sharing their jokes.

George Carlin and Bill Cosby were friends when they were each starting out their stand-up comedy careers in the early 1960s, but their relationship quickly grew chilly when Cosby appropriated one of Carlin's routines. At the time, Carlin devoted much of his act to poking fun at television commercials. Audiences responded particularly well to a segment of the routine in which the comedian acted as an inarticulate football player stumbling through a product endorsement. Cosby saw a way to make the routine funnier and believed that this justified him introducing his own version of the routine. The routine turned up on Cosby's 1963 debut album *Bill Cosby Is a Very Funny Fellow Right!* under the title "Little Tiny Hairs" (a reference to a line in a razor blade pitch). It was another three years before Carlin was able to secure his own recording deal and preserve his television commercials routine on vinyl for *Take-Offs and Put-Ons*. By then, he had conceded ownership of the inarticulate football player concept to Cosby and all traces of the character had been excised from the routine. Carlin remained resentful of Cosby for taking his material. For nearly 45 years, the two comedians continued to run into each other at various functions, but Carlin always managed to rush off before Cosby had a chance to talk to him.

In more recent years, a number of comedians have come under attack for joke-stealing. The endless stories about Robin Williams's joke-stealing have become legendary among stand-up comedians. A debate has carried on for years as to whether or not Denis Leary stole his act, including style, attitude and jokes, from Bill Hicks. The worst attack was waged against Carlos Mencia, who was exposed for stealing material from a variety of sources. Hostilities reached a fevered pitch with a 2009 episode of *South Park* episode entitled "Fishsticks," in which Mencia's theft of a joke was resolved with the comedian's bloody beating and ultimate beheading.

It was not always like this. Harold Lloyd was not shunned, mocked or burned in effigy for reworking a Buster Keaton gag. Reusing material was not considered joke-stealing. It was, for lack of a better term, joke-*sharing*. Silent film comedians were part of a brotherhood that was willing to make use of common routines. These performers were still very much competitors, but they competed in their efforts to accomplish the best version of a routine. The comedian's code was that a routine should belong to the comedian who could perform the funniest and most timely version regardless who came up with the idea first. In this way, delivery was more important than the routine itself.

This book addresses a number of specific routines. The chapter "Into the Looking Glass" is a study of a famous mirror routine performed by Charlie Chaplin and the Marx Brothers, among others. But other chapters deal with instances where a routine served as a basis of an all-out trend. For instance, a simple routine featuring a bear chasing a hunter up a tree led to a multitude of comic bear attack routines and this, in turn, led to a much broader trend of animal rampage comedies.

Routines will be deconstructed to outline the manner in which filmmakers modified material to suit different performers and different eras. Many of these gags and routines survive to present day due to one plain fact: a good routine is indestructible. It can be transferred, altered, rearranged, extended and updated, but it can never be wiped out. In the process, the book identifies links between early comedy and contemporary comedy, taking readers from *Tillie's Punctured Romance* to *Zombieland*.

A number of routines selected for discussion in this book are still turning up regularly in movies and television programs. I can say that, as of this writing, I have seen well-established routines in the latest episodes of *30 Rock*, *Chuck* and *Breaking Bad*. A television sitcom celebrated for its surreal humor, *30 Rock* tends at times to have the sort of outlandish gags that could be found in a silent film comedy short. The latest episode of *30 Rock* included three individual silent film comedy routines: a vicious dog creates a panic by invading a party; a character is chased by a peacock; and a cardboard cut-out of a person is mistaken for a real person. *Breaking Bad* made use of one of the oldest recorded comedy routines, "Lazzo* of the Fly," for an episode titled "Fly."

Today, silent film comedy is vaguely perceived by the general public. Even a silent film comedian as illustrious as Buster Keaton receives little attention. Keaton was a comedy star in a time so distant from our own that it hardly seems that his films could be relevant to our own experiences. Take, for instance, the comedian's 1923 feature *Our Hospitality*. Could this sweet and funny satire dealing with the Southern code of honor possibly matter to a modern audience? Yes, it can. Keaton's films are still guaranteed to awe and amuse an audience, and they continue to inspire new generations of filmmakers. Buster Keaton was, in fact, a major inspiration behind the Pixar film *WALL-E*, which grossed more than a half billion dollars worldwide in 2008. Without question, the Keaton canon remains a valid one in the examination of film comedy. Keaton and his highly creative pratfalling brethren

---

*The word "lazzo" (plural "lazzi") is Italian for a joke or comic action.

shaped film comedy for all time. The proof of their lasting value can easily be found in many modern films.

Film comedy is a vital part of our culture. The best way to understand a cultural development is to look closely at its past. It is my hope that, by looking at the history of gags and routines, older comedy forms will be freed from their current vacuum and given the prominence in our culture that they deserve.

1

And Then There Were Pies

At an early time in their history, comedy films came to be dominated by a large number of recurring gags. An example is the ill-prepared pancake that is so hard it breaks a plate. Al St. John, as a newlywed subjected to his bride's bad cooking, confronts a plate-breaking pancake in *Live Cowards* (1926). Shanghaied galley cook Paul Parrott serves up a leaden pancake to ill-tempered sea captain Kalla Pasha in *Deep Sea Panic* (1924). Lige Conley cooks up the worst of these pancakes while demonstrating department store cookware in *Fast and Furious* (1924). The Conley film offers justification for the pancakes being so hard — Conley has confused a sack of cement mix for a sack of flour. His pancakes do more than break a plate. After bending a fork, a pancake slips off the plate, flies across the room like a missile, and bursts apart a barrel upon impact. Another plate drops off the table and creates a massive hole in the floor.

A gag can gain depth and definition by repeated use, a gag can develop into something more elaborate and more expansive through various passages, and a gag can be adapted to define the specific personality of a comedian. In *Oh, Doctor* (1917), Roscoe Arbuckle acquires patients for his medical practice by deliberately plowing his car into a crowd of pedestrians. Arbuckle calmly approaches the people lying injured to distribute his business card. In *Never Weaken* (1921), Harold Lloyd wants to create business for the osteopath for whom his girlfriend works. He pours soap powder on a walkway at the same time that a street cleaner is coming up the street spraying water. Soap powder and water mix together to create a slippery surface. People lose their footing as they cross the street; no sooner do they hit the ground than Lloyd is handing them business cards. *Hey Doctor!* (1918) features Alice Howell working as a receptionist for a doctor whose practice is failing. Steve Massa, who viewed a rare print of this comedy, described a scene where Howell sets out to direct business to the practice. Massa wrote, "[Alice] walks down the street dropping banana peels on the sidewalk. As the pedestrians begin slipping and falling, Alice distributes cards for the doctor."[1] Roscoe Arbuckle is aggressive. Harold Lloyd demonstrates planning and forethought. Alice Howell, tossing around banana peels, is just plain silly.

This concept had turned up earlier in the Keystone comedy *A Healthy Neighborhood* (1913), which featured Dr. Noodles (Ford Sterling) sending his assistant around a hardy community to scatter banana peels. Another Keystone comedy, *Pills of Peril* (1916), revolved around rival doctors causing accidents to increase business. This routine could go back even farther. The gaps in the film record make it difficult, if not impossible, to trace the exact genesis of certain gags and routines. Howell, herself, had previously enacted a variation of

Ben Turpin calls for a cease-fire during the pie fight in *Keystone Hotel* (1935). He is accompanied by Vivien Oakland (right) and another (unknown) actress (courtesy Steve Rydzewski).

this routine in *Alice in Society* (1916). This time, Howell was tailor's assistant who walked down the street ripping and cutting people's clothing just prior to handing them her boss' business card.

Variation was not always necessary. Some gags were so plain, precise and impersonal that they were freely recycled without change. In *Good Night, Nurse!* (1918), Roscoe Arbuckle appears to be traveling down a hospital corridor atop a stretcher. But then the sheet draped over Arbuckle falls off and it is revealed that he is in fact walking down the hall holding out a pair of crutches with shoes affixed at the ends. The gag remained intact twenty five years later when it was faithfully recreated by Lou Costello in *Hit the Ice* (1943).

Comic staples were many. Common among the staples were banana peels, seltzer bottles, custard pies, mud puddles, bombs, cactus, glue, hoses, automobiles, flowerpots, and limburger cheese.*

The depiction of a person slipping on a banana peel has been a staple of physical comedy for generations. In its retooling for film, this gag needed to function within the context of a story. A banana peel played a pivotal role in the Biograph comedy *The Passing*

---

*The earliest-known limburger cheese gag can be found in *Oh! That Limburger: The Story of a Piece of Cheese* (Vitagraph, 1906), in which mischievous boys hide a piece of limburger cheese in their father's coat pocket. The smell is so irritating to the father's co-workers that they gang up on him and give him a beating. Limburger cheese routines were performed by a variety of comedians — Charlie Chaplin (*Shoulder Arms*, 1918), Harry Langdon (*The Strong Man*, 1926), Our Gang (*Bear Shooters*, 1930), the Three Stooges (*All the World's a Stooge*, 1941), and Abbott and Costello (*Who Done It?*, 1942).

of a Grouch (1910), in which a man becomes irate after slipping on a banana peel and treats other people badly because of his ill mood. The banana peel now had to put more at stake for a character. Sid Smith slips on a banana peel while walking across a girder. In *For Heaven's Sake* (1926), Harold Lloyd tumbles out of the top tier of a runaway double-decker bus and manages to catch his feet on the front bumper just as he is about to fall into the road. He is attempting to climb back up when a banana peel tossed onto the hood by a drunken passenger causes him to slip and nearly fall under the wheels of the bus. This is the slipping-on-a-banana-peel gag at seventy miles per hour. The banana peel could be used with a strategic purpose. In *Waiting* (1925), Lloyd Hamilton scatters bananas across the floor to cause angry pursuers to lose their footing. Hamilton then lifts a corner of a rug, watches as these people go sliding underneath, and nails down the rug to trap them. In the climactic football game of the Marx Brothers' *Horse Feathers* (1932), Chico and Harpo trip up opposing players by throwing banana peels in their path. It was also possible to increase the scale of this gag. Woody Allen slips on the peel of a hydroponically produced giant banana in *Sleeper* (1973). In *Billy Madison* (1995), a bus driver (played by Chris Farley) throws a banana peel onto a highway and a car driving over the banana peel loses traction and drives off a cliff.

Pies go back to the days of the Commedia dell'Arte. Weber and Fields are credited with introducing the pie-in-the-face gag to vaudeville. An early pie-in-the-face gag appeared in the 1905 comedy *The Coal Strike*, in which a charwoman becomes so angered by a small boy stealing a pie that she rubs the pie in his face. According to Sennett historian Brent Walker, the Keystone Studio's first patented pie-throwing routine appeared in *A Noise from the Deep* (1913), in which Roscoe Arbuckle hits Nick Cogley in the face with a custard pie. The scale of a pie fight was soon expanded, as shown by *A Quiet Little Wedding* (1913), in which a wedding party is broken up by a pie fight.

The pie fight has never left us. The Three Stooges kept the pie fight alive for decades. Pie fights also turned up periodically in feature films, including *Hollywood Cavalcade* (1939), *Man of a Thousand Faces* (1957), *The Great Race* (1965), *What's Up, Doc?* (1972), *Blazing Saddles* (1974), *The Shaggy D.A.* (1976) and *Bugsy Malone* (1976). The pie fight then morphed into a food fight with *Animal House* (1978). In a unique twist, a food fight in the *Animal House*–inspired *H.O.T.S* (1979) involves pies being tossed from a hot-air balloon. The food fight is still around, as evidenced by a food fight that recently broke out in an episode of the NBC sitcom *Community*.

Seltzer bottles figured prominently into film comedy at an early stage. The Edison comedy *Getting Evidence* (1906) features a scene in a restaurant where a customer, irritated by an inept waiter, sprays the waiter in the face with seltzer.

Mack Sennett introduced a number of seltzer-bottle episodes into his comedies. The time was always right for someone to get sprayed in the face with seltzer. A slapstick seltzer battle could even occur during a funeral, as proven by the Keystone comedy *Among the Mourners* (1914).

Charlie Chaplin found that, at times, less was more. In *The Adventurer* (1917), Chaplin exploits a seltzer bottle as a comic prop in two separate scenes. The plot has an escaped convict (Chaplin) posing as a refined gentleman at a fancy dinner party. He starts out using the seltzer bottle to mix a drink and, while he acts as if he know what he is doing, he manages to squirt the seltzer everywhere but in his drink. Later, he sneaks a spritz of seltzer in the direction of a romantic rival (Eric Campbell), who is spying on him and his lady love through a doorway. Chaplin is able to use the seltzer bottle to advance the story and develop characters and, more important, he is able to earn laughs while avoiding an obvious all-out seltzer battle.

Stan Laurel takes a fall as Oliver Hardy looks on with displeasure in *Berth Marks* (1929) (courtesy Bruce Lawton Collection).

The Three Stooges, less concerned about being obvious, waged seltzer-bottle wars in a number of films, including *No Dough Boys* (1944), *Three Loan Wolves* (1946), *Three Little Pirates* (1946) and *Love at First Bite* (1950). These were comedians who operated on a different level: they were at their funniest when dripping wet, coated in mud, or smeared with cake frosting.

Early filmmakers recognized the humor of a person falling into a mud puddle. This is evident in the 1904 comedy *Three Little Maids*, in which a group of rambunctious little girls roll down a grassy slope unaware that a mud puddle is waiting for them at the bottom. The mud puddle routines got more fantastic as time went on. In *Out of Place* (1922), Al St. John lays his coat over a puddle so that a woman can walk across. The woman plunges into the puddle and disappears without a trace. The valiant lad does not hesitate to dive into the puddle to rescue the woman. He is smiling when he finally pokes his head back out of the water. But where is the woman? St. John brings out his hand to show he has a hold of the woman by her foot. Oversized puddles later became an important comic device in Roach comedies. In *All Wet* (1924), Charley Chase assumes that he can drive across a puddle, but the puddle proves considerably deeper than he anticipated and manages to swallow up his car. Chase spends much of the film wading around in the puddle trying to extract the car. In *Accidental Accidents* (1924), Chase falls into a puddle and reemerges with his pants outlandishly bloated with water.

In *Mud and Sand* (1922), Stan Laurel steps out of a cart and falls into a mud puddle.

Later, Laurel teamed up with Oliver Hardy and let Hardy take most of the spills into mud puddles. Hardy, from the beginning of his partnership with Laurel, fell down regularly into deep puddles, as evidenced by *Putting Pants on Phillip* (1927), *We Faw Down* (1928), and *Angora Love* (1929). Hardy and others fall victim to this comic device in *Should Married Men Go Home?*, in which a climactic battle takes place in a sprawling mud puddle on a golf course. Hardy is riding in his car with Laurel and a traffic cop (Edgar Kennedy) when their car sinks into a mud puddle in *Leave 'Em Laughing* (1928). By the time that Hardy fell into a mud puddle in *Towed in a Hole* (1932), the mud puddle had developed a special significance for his character. Falling into a mud puddle most often served as comeuppance for Hardy's foolish arrogance. Other times, it served as the crowning blow in a series of mishaps. In either case, it removed that last remnant of dignity to which Hardy so desperately clung.

Cecil Hepworth, a British filmmaking pioneer, realized that the havoc created by a speeding car could be good for laughs. Hepworth's *How It Feels to Be Run Over* (1900) features a car speeding directly towards the camera. The passengers are waving their arms frantically as if to warn people that the car is out of control and that they need to get out of the way.

Georges Méliès developed this idea further with *An Adventurous Automobile Trip* (1905). Méliès designed his lead character as a parody of King Leopold II of Belgium, who had become notorious for his recklessness as a motorist. He devised a road trip plot — the motorist has 17 hours to travel from Paris to Monte Carlo. He embellished the action with lively

A quieter moment between Stan Laurel (right) and Oliver Hardy, in *Towed in a Hole* (1932) (courtesy www.doctormacro.com).

crowds, colorful sets and special effects. The effects start off with a miniature shot of the automobile crossing mountains. Additional effects depict a series of car accidents. The motorist runs down an old man, who is literally flattened under the weight of the car. He soon strikes another man, who explodes on impact. The film climaxes with the car crashing through a building.

Stop Thief! (1901) has the first-known chase scene in films. It is no more than a brief footrace, but it qualifies as a chase nonetheless. A longer and more vigorous chase appears in *Desperate Poaching Affair* (1903). These were serious cops-and-robbers films involving desperate fugitives and deadly gun battles. The comedy chase was not introduced in film until 1904. That year, funny chases appeared in a number of French films, including *The Bath Chair Man*, *The Escaped Lunatic* and *Personal*. The main character of *The Bath Chair Man*—a bath attendant named Pierre—is pushing an old man with gout in a wheelchair when he sees his wife with another man. He rushes after his wife and her lover while still pushing the wheelchair. He travels with the wheelchair across town and eventually storms into a building and maneuvers the wheelchair up several flights of stairs.

The automobile came to be integrated into the comic chase in 1906. This year, film pioneer Robert W. Paul produced *The '?' Motorist*, which incorporated elements of *An Adventurous Automobile Trip* with an imaginative chase scene. A rich, arrogant motorist is recklessly driving his automobile through the countryside. He does not hesitate to run down a police officer who gets in his way. The officer, who neither flattens nor explodes, stands up and chases after the motorist. The motorist, determined to escape the officer, drives up the side of a building and heads into outer space, where he drives his car around the rings of Saturn. André Deed remained earthbound in the comic car chase depicted in *Les Débuts d'un chauffeur* (1906). According to the Internet Movie Database (IMDB), the plot is as follows: "The proud owner of a new car ... gets behind the wheel for the first time and weaves down the street, hitting everything from lamp-posts to market stalls and baby carriages. An ever-increasing crowd of incensed pursuers chases after him."[3]

André Heuzé, the scenarist of *Les Débuts d'un chauffeur*, came to specialize in chase comedies. One of his more curious chase comedies was the 1906 Pathé Frères comedy *La Course à la perruque*, known in America as *The Wig Chase*. Film historian Richard Abel described the film as follows: "Boys attach a bunch of balloons to the hat of an old woman sitting on a park bench, and the balloons sail off bearing not only the hat but her wig as well.... With the furious woman and a crowd in hot pursuit, the hat and wig fly over woods and fields, cross the Seine, enter an apartment window, and finally escape up a fireplace chimney."[4] The crowd also chases the wig up the Eiffel Tower and takes charge of a boat to chase the wig across a lake. A Heuzé film that was to have a strong influence on Keystone's comedy car chases was the 1907 French short *Le Cheval emballé*, or *The Runaway Horse*. The horse-drawn wagon at the center of the action creates as much destruction and chaos as a motorized vehicle. The wagon knocks workmen off a scaffold, smashes through vendor stands, and pulls a wheel off another wagon.

Mack Sennett's Keystone Cops made their first appearance in *Hoffmeyer's Legacy* (1912), but slapstick police had been around from the earliest days of film. This is demonstrated by the Edison comedy *Chinese Laundry Scene* (1895). The plot is simple. A laundry worker has an altercation with a cop and strikes the cop with a laundry basket. The cop becomes irate and chases the laundry worker through a revolving door. The silent film comedian was to learn quickly that their most serious adversary was the man in blue.

Aggressive police officers were a vital element of silent film comedy. In *Fatty and Mabel at the San Diego Exposition* (1915), a cop is making sure that the crowd stays behind a rope while watching a parade. Arbuckle, who is being shoved forward, cannot stop his oversized stomach from straining against the rope. The cop, looking to get Arbuckle back in line, offhandedly batters him over the head with his club. The cops may have used their clubs less in the coming years, but they never lost their menacing disposition. In *Hello, Baby!* (1925), Charley Chase has an encounter with police more familiar to a modern audience. A grim-faced traffic cop, who has stopped Chase for having a headlight out on his car, has at the ready his ticket book, which Chase regards as more intimidating than a club.

The police raid was a recurring event in silent film comedy. In *Fatty's Reckless Fling* (1915), a plainclothes detective raids an apartment to break up a friendly poker game. As police prepare to raid a party in *Mighty Like a Moose* (1926), an officer tells his partner, "There's nothin' wrong with the party—but the chief says arrest everybody for practice." In *Sweetie* (1923), the cops raid a posh party reportedly in search of bootleg alcohol. In truth, the raid has no justification except to bring the film to a lively finish.

Officers can usually be seen in comedies patrolling a park or main street. This actually had its origins in the real world. Most states had broad vagrancy, loitering and disorderly conduct laws. The police had a great concern about people wandering around from place to place without a lawful purpose. Strict vagrancy laws were designed to control the migration of the unemployed. The police, who walked the beat at the time, were in the thick of activity, prepared to arrest anyone who breached the peace—rogues, vagabonds, beggars, drunkards, prostitutes, pickpockets, muggers, lewd persons, lascivious persons, gamblers, railers, and common brawlers. The general public agreed that riotous conduct needed to be controlled. Considering that slapstick comedy was in every sense riotous conduct, it only made sense for the police to be employed to get it under control.

Comedy films of the period reflected the public's mistrust of the overall law enforcement system. In *The First Execution* (1913), dignitaries arrive for drinks and lunch before an execution. The inmate escapes and the officials, unwilling to reveal their incompetence or spoil a good celebration, knowingly put an innocent man in the electric chair in his place. This became a recurring premise. A grand-scale version was Lloyd Hamilton's *A Waiter's Wasted Life* (1918).

A comic staple more unusual than banana peels, custard pies and funny cops was exploding spit. Men spewed exploding spit for a variety of reasons. Lige Conley's salvia has mixed with a powerful alcoholic brew in *Below Zero* (1925). Larry Semon has eaten biscuits baked with gun powder in *The Suitor* (1920). In *Broken Bubbles* (1920), Hank Mann begins a visit to Hell by drinking potent water from the river Styx. These gags were not restricted to the human species. A rooster who has consumed nitroglycerin spits out flames in Larry Semon's *The Show* (1922).

Tough women were loaded with exploding spit simply as part of their perverse nature. Gang leader Notorious Nora raises a dark puff of smoke when she spits on the ground in Larry Semon's *Oh, What a Man!* (1927). Betty Boyd, as a bold military chief in Lupino Lane's *Battling Sisters* (1929), manages with a drop of spit to split a rock in half.

Routines never changed more than when they were transferred from one gender to another. With a woman at the center of the action, the emphasis could be shifted from slapstick violence to womanly charms. The 1908 Pathé Frères comedy *Contagious Nervous Twitching* revealed Max Linder to be afflicted with a nervous disorder that causes him fits of twitching. The twitching proves contagious to the people who come into contact with him. People suddenly overtaken by the twitch lose control of themselves and suffer accidents.

A bicyclist crashes. A construction worker falls off a ladder. Everyone in a wedding party is seized with the tic and are left with their heads jerking uncontrollably. Even a statue is made to twitch. A sexual aspect was added to the routine when it was adapted to a female character in *Mrs. Simpson's Attractiveness* (1909). This time, a nervous tic causes a woman to smile involuntarily. Her smile distracts passing men, who assume that the woman is flirting with them. Complications and chaos ensues. The routine was later returned to its original twitchy form in a 1913 film entitled *Nervous Leo*.

Violence was at a minimum when a woman was at the center of a routine. In *Ella Cinders* (1926), Colleen Moore seeks to get past a studio guard by concealing herself inside a wrap and balancing a mannequin bust on top of her head. The disguise is exposed when a dog yanks off the wrap. Moore, panicked, sprints away. This routine was distinctly different when enacted by Billy Dooley in *Campus Cuties* (1928). Dooley's disguise is exposed by a trigger-happy security guard, whose barrage of bullets causes the mannequin head to shatter into pieces. Other examples are more about characterization than situation. In *The Wizard of Oz* (1925), Larry Semon disguises himself as a scarecrow and hangs himself off a yard stake. When a pair of men show up, Semon cannot resist taking advantage of the situation. He waits for the men to turn their backs and then he gives them each a hard kick. Semon eventually manages through his aggressive antics to make himself known. A woman, though, was not perceived as being capable of kicking people for no good reason. In the Sennett comedy *The Bull Fighters* (1927), Madeline Hurlock disguises herself as a scarecrow to avoid her guardian and the sheriff (Andy Clyde and Barney Hellum). The lady, more docile than Semon, is only exposed when a cow comes along to eat the straw that makes up her disguise.

Film cameras allowed comedians to expand the scope of their stunts, which also meant expanding their risk for physical injury. When a clown falls down in a circus ring, the pain that he expresses is fleeting and inconsequential. He grimaces, rubs his bruised backside, and moves on. The silent film comedian engaged viewers by putting himself in much greater peril.

At first, the pratfalling comedian simply made use of the expanded territory. In *Love and Sour Notes* (1915), Billie Ritchie head-butts Fatty Voss, who is sent tumbling down a lofty hill. But the fall developed in time into something more. In *Seven Chances* (1925), Buster Keaton slides down a hill while an avalanche of boulders are pursuing him. The scene introduces a variety of dangers and surprises as larger and larger boulders become dislodged on the hill. At one point, Keaton climbs a tree, only to have a boulder knock the tree down. It is a masterfully choreographed epic of comedy that is equally funny and thrilling.

The slapstick revivals of recent years have been regressive, as is suggested when Chris Farley slides down a hill in *The Black Sheep* (1996). Farley is not endangered by boulders. He does not climb a tree. The scene, nothing more than a long and dusty pratfall, is a crude example of slapstick comedy. It is, in effect, Fatty Voss rolling down a hill all over again.

Classic slapstick comedy was rarely so artless. As stated in the introduction, an idea as simple as a man falling down a hill could develop into something intricate and meaningful. In *Tramp, Tramp, Tramp* (1926), Harry Langdon climbs a fence to get away from police without realizing that fence is built on the edge of a cliff. A nail that catches on his sweater prevents Harry from falling. Harry, terrified by the steep drop, pries nails out of the fence so that he can use the nails to further secure his sweater, along with himself, to the fence. However, the removal of the nails causes the fence to break apart. Harry goes sledding down

Silent film comedy often relied on danger and tension, as shown in this scene from *The Soilers* (1923). The combatants are Jimmy Finlayson (left) and Stan Laurel (courtesy Robert Arkus).

the side of the cliff while sitting on top of the fence boards. Boulders roll down the cliff after him but he seems to be able to anticipate each boulder and dodge them with minimal movement. He leans to the left, allowing another boulder to pass, and he leans the right, which allows a boulder to pass. At one point, he lifts up his backside and a boulder passes through his legs. This is a carefully developed routine that builds up tension, conveys character, and evokes laughter.

Tension was vital to this form of comedy. Two gold prospectors (Charlie Chaplin and Mack Swain) find their lives endangered in *The Gold Rush* (1925) when storm winds carry their cabin to the precipice of a cliff. As the cabin teeters over the edge, the men slide across the floor towards an open doorway, ready to deliver them to certain death. Chris Farley and David Spade performed a similar scene in *The Black Sheep* with an avalanche releasing a massive boulder, which knocks the pair's cabin at a tilt. The lack of a cliff in this reworking removed all of the comic tension from the scene and simply made the scene about Farley rolling across the floor and ultimately getting tossed through a window.

The pressure to outdo one another within the conventions of comedy motivated Keaton, Langdon and Chaplin to make their work as creative and thrilling as possible. Those who are not compelled by this sense of competition are content to adopt the conventions without improving on the original gag.

2

Mannequins and Other Dummies

In *Run, Fat Boy, Run* (2007), Simon Pegg, a security guard in a lingerie store, is having trouble concentrating on his duties now that chafing from his new running routine has caused an itchy rash to break out on his inner thighs. Pegg notices the sharp fingernails of a scantily clad mannequin and sneaks behind the mannequin to rub his thighs against its hand for relief. A group of teenage girls notice Pegg's activity and assume that he is humping the mannequin for sexual gratification. Pegg quickly pulls away from the mannequin, accidentally pulling down its nightie and exposing its sculpted breasts.

Frottage with an artificial woman is not necessarily a modern idea. An early Edison comedy, *Rube's Visit to the Studio* (1902), involved a man making a visit to an art studio and becoming overly fascinated with a statue that resembles a real woman. The man tries to embrace the statue, but the statue disappears before he can get his arms around it and it reappears magically on the opposite side of the room. The man dives after the statue repeatedly, but it keeps disappearing from one spot and reappearing in another. The man's wife catches her husband trying to embrace the statue and gives him an unrestrained thrashing.

A trend in early films showed objects with human likeness to be secret protectors of mankind. The 1908 Gaumont fantasy *The Good Playthings* features toys in a nursery coming to life when a fire breaks out and endangers the life of a child. The toys launch an ingenious operation that succeeds in extinguishing the flames. A statue of the Madonna comes to life to rescue a young woman from the Devil in Méliès's *The Devil and the Statue* (1902). A statue comes to life to aid a homeless little girl in *The Waif and the Statue* (1907). This, however, was not a trend that would last. Mannequins were destined to serve a greater purpose.

A perusal of *Moving Picture World* issues from 1913 show mannequins turning up regularly in both dramas and comedies. In Thanhouser's *The Wax Lady* (1913), a fairy brings dummies to life in a tailor's window to attack the tailor, who has been cheating his customers with inferior goods. In Gaumont's *The Living Doll* (1913), a doll maker seeks consolation from his daughter's death by dressing up a life-sized doll in his daughter's clothing. Later, a girl accidentally breaks the doll and dresses in the doll's outfit to fool the doll maker. In *Funnicus Is Tired of Life* (1913), students steal a tailor's dummy and throw it off a bridge into a river. Paul Bertho dives in after the dummy thinking that it is a man trying to drown himself. It was easy (in the context of a silent films, anyway) for a mannequin to come to life and be mistaken for a man. Conversely, it was just as easy for a man to freeze in a dull pose and be mistaken for a mannequin.

Louise Fazenda uses a dress dummy to fool a criminal (Glen Cavender) in *Her Screen Idol* (1918) (courtesy Steve Rydzewski).

Many routines were based on the idea that a mannequin, or other facsimile of the human form, could easily be confused for a man. In the Georges Méliès comedy *Robert Macaire and Bertrand* (1907), a soldier hangs his hat and coat on a stake in the yard. A fugitive, mistaking the arrayed stake for a soldier, is quick to pull out a knife and attack it.

A boxing dummy has a key role in the Keystone comedy *Mabel's Married Life* (1914). A husband (Charlie Chaplin) gets drunk in order to find the courage to fight a masher who has offended his wife (Mabel Normand). Meanwhile, Mabel has bought Chaplin a boxing dummy so that he can build up his muscles. Mabel, struck by the dummy's resemblance to a man, finds herself embarrassed to be in front of the dummy wearing nothing but her pajamas. Later, her drunken spouse mistakes the boxing dummy for the masher and launches an attack on the bold intruder. Chaplin shoves the dummy, which causes it to list backwards and then spring forward with sufficient force to knock its inebriated opponent off his feet. In his comic battle, Chaplin manages to make the dummy appear to have a life of its own. In *Fraidy Cat* (1924), Charley Chase gives a reasonable explanation for a dress dummy's combativeness — it turns out that the dress dummy is his romantic rival in disguise. Chaplin, though, saw no need to offer an explanation. He was confident that the audience could accept an inanimate object as a disagreeable creature. After all, one of his most popular routines to date had the comedian waging war with a Murphy bed. The same principle was at play when Chaplin became contentious with a folding chair in *A Day's Pleasure* (1919). The fact is that inanimate objects often had a life of their own in the world of silent film comedy. This certainly applies to Billy Bevan, who finds himself thwarted by a tricky water pump in *By Heck* (1921). Lupino Lane has an even harder time in *Only Me* (1929) when he gets into a shoving match with a theatre sign able to pitch back and forth on its rockers. In *Chop Suey Louie* (1923), Joe Rock is unable to pass through a wrought iron gate as the fickle gate opens and closes at will. In *Salute* (1925), Lee Moran is a military cadet assigned to raise the flag outside of his academy, but the flag will not stay where Moran puts it and it slides up and down the flagpole repeatedly until the cadet is thoroughly flustered.

While training in a gym, Curly Howard has trouble with a boxing dummy bouncing back up and clobbering him in the Three Stooges short *Grips, Grunts and Groans* (1937). This is Chaplin's boxing dummy routine except that Curly, aided by sound technology, is able to express his growing frustration with comic groans and squeals. Shemp Howard, performing the same routine in *Fright Night* (1947), beats out his predecessors with his fancy footwork, his flyaway hair, and his generally exaggerated reactions. Boxing with a dummy does not call for subtlety.

Mannequins could easily confuse a person who did not have their wits about them. This was proven by Chaplin's boxing dummy routine along with a number of other routines. In *Mr. Jinks Buys a Dress* (1913), a drunken man goes to buy his wife a dress but ends up leaving the tailor shop with a dress dummy, which he is delighted to stand alongside himself at the neighborhood bar. In *Fighting Fluid* (1925), Charley Chase drinks water from an office cooler without realizing that the water has been spiked with alcohol. It is while intoxicated that he momentarily confuses a mannequin for his girlfriend. When the mannequin's leg falls off, he picks it up and later puzzles his girlfriend when he tries to return it to her.

While it took alcohol to confuse Mr. Jinks and Mr. Chase, it was not necessary for alcohol to be involved in these situations. Some comic characters were simply confused by nature. Harry Langdon's screen persona possessed a decidedly poor sense of reality. In *The Strong Man* (1926), Langdon is carrying an unconscious woman upstairs to her apartment. He becomes entangled with a ladder on the landing and drops the woman. When he goes to retrieve her, he mistakenly picks up a carpet roll instead. He carries the carpet into the apartment and sets it down gently on a sofa before he realizes his mistake. An individual who cannot tell the difference between a woman and a carpet roll can hardly be expected to tell the difference between a man and a mannequin. Langdon had much in common with the Commedia dell'Arte clown Pierrot, a trusting fool often hindered by his naïveté. Like Pierrot, he was moonstruck, distant and oblivious to reality.

Langdon expressed a great deal of confusion with mannequins. In *His First Flame* (1927), Langdon emerges from a window of a burning building carrying a mannequin, which he believes to be a woman. He holds onto the mannequin tightly as he scrambles down a ladder. Once he has progressed a safe distance, Langdon turns to the mannequin to offer comfort. It should be obvious to him that this is not a real woman, but Langdon, though suspicious, is not really sure. He does not come to a definite conclusion until he taps the mannequin's wooden cheeks, then presses his hand against the mannequin's cold brow, and finally pokes his finger into the mannequin's painted eyes.

Langdon's confusion is even greater in *Feet of Mud* (1924). Langdon does not see that a dummy has gotten latched onto the broom that he has resting over his shoulder. He has a growing sense that he is being followed. He turns his head slightly and sees a figure of a man out of the corner of his eye. Langdon snaps around and pounces on the dummy. He

Mannequins leave it to Al Cooke (right) and Barney Hellum (left) to work out their troubles with the police. The porter is unidentified. The scene still is from a 1928 Standard Photoplay series; the film's title is unknown (courtesy Robert Arkus).

falls to the floor with the dummy and the two of them roll around vigorously. Langdon thinks he has a hold on the mannequin's leg but he has, in fact, grabbed his own leg. He is twisting so hard that his leg becomes racked with pain. He grumbles to the dummy, "Let go of my leg or I'll knock your block off." He swings his arm with all his might and knocks off the mannequin's head. As film historian James L. Neibaur wrote of this scene, "[Langdon] stops, stares, ponders what has occurred, offers a worried look, tentatively approaches the severed head, carefully lifts and examines it, and finally realizes that he has been fighting with a mannequin."[1]

A common routine involved a comedian mistaking a mannequin in a police uniform for an actual police officer. It took no more than a uniform to transform a man into a symbol of law enforcement, and the uniform had much the same effect on a mannequin. The mannequin in a police uniform served as an effective scarecrow to the troublemaking comedian. Billy Franey enacted an early, bare-bones version of this routine in *The Water Plug* (1920).

If a mannequin in a police uniform was funny, why not have multiple mannequins in police uniforms? In *Pay or Move* (1924), Monty Banks is trying to collect rent from a couple of tough deadbeats who have made a sport of beating rent collectors. Banks realizes that he needs to come up with a strategy to get the toughs to pay. He comes back from a costume shop with a dozen mannequins dressed in police uniforms. He lines up the mannequins against a fence and nails them securely into place. He then rigs up the fence so she can turn a crank and flip the fence around to the other side, thereby keeping the mannequins out of sight until they are needed. When the toughs go to attack him, Banks gets working on the crank and brings his police squad into view. The toughs are frightened at first and pay Banks the money they owe him. They do not remain fooled for long, however, and chase after Banks to get their money back. Meanwhile, real police officers come along and line up in front of the fence. The toughs, who are circling the fence, assume that the policemen are mannequins and push their way past them, knocking a couple of the officers to the ground. The policemen are enraged. They swarm around the toughs and give them a merciless pummeling. In the midst of the beating, a jump-cut allows the filmmakers to switch the toughs with dummies, which are tossed in the air and finally thrown over the fence. In the course of this scene, real people have been substituted with fake people, first by the fictitious hero and then again by the real-life director. It shows that, on multiple levels, people in this world remained interchangeable with mannequins.

Langdon enacted the most impressive version of the mannequin-in-a-police-uniform routine in *Long Pants* (1927). Langdon is trying to smuggle his escaped convict girlfriend (Alma Bennett) to safety when he sees what he believes to be a police officer sitting on a crate across the street. The presumed officer is, in fact, a mannequin that a costume shop owner has dressed in a police uniform. Langdon attempts various tricks to lure the officer away. He starts out by simply calling out to the officer and cannot understand why he is not getting a reaction. Langdon spends more than five minutes of screen time trying to get the mannequin to respond to him. He backs out of a doorway with his hands in the air to make it look as if he is being robbed. He rolls around on the ground pretending to be having a seizure. He is bewildered that the officer has not moved the entire time. Finally, a man comes out of a shop, lifts up the mannequin, and carries it inside. Langdon is astounded. While Langdon's back is turned, an actual police officer comes along and sits down on the crate. Langdon, turning back around, is angry to see that this mannequin who fooled him has returned. He picks up a brick and hurls it across the street, knocking the police officer from the crate. The officer leaps to his feet and chases Langdon down the street.

Easy Curves (1927), released eight months after *Long Pants*, has Billy Dooley in the same basic situation. Dooley, though, holds no deference for the mannequin in the police uniform. Dooley, a comic gremlin, enjoys making trouble. He runs in a circle, mocking the officer and daring him to chase him. The mannequin does not respond. Dooley then, in a taunting manner, folds his hands on his hips and skips away. Still, no response. Finally, he skips directly towards the mannequin. At this point, he accidentally bumps into the mannequin, which springs back up at him and knocks him on the floor (a reminder of Chaplin's boxing dummy). This makes Dooley angry. He picks up an Indian club, swings it, and knocks off the mannequin's head. This dervish, lacking Langdon's patience, is much quicker to attack the mannequin.

For certain, Dooley's perception was less reliable than that of Langdon. The fact that Langdon is viewing the mannequin from across a street gives him a reasonable excuse for mistaking the mannequin for a real person. But Dooley is standing inches away from the mannequin and still fails to realize that this is not a real person. If Langdon was a dim bulb, then Dooley, the embodiment of action without thought, was a blackout.

It has to be the height of confusion for Dooley to mistake a mannequin for his own girlfriend, which is something that the comedian does in *Easy Curves*. Dooley is invited to a fashion show by his girlfriend (Vera Steadman), who is modeling outfits in the show. Dooley causes such problems in the audience that the management calls in the police to eject him. After being chased backstage by the police, Dooley discovers Steadman in her dressing room and asks her to escape with him out of a window. Dooley climbs out of the window first and, once he is down on the sidewalk, he stands under the window and holds out his arms to catch Steadman. However, the police swarm around Steadman before she can get out of the window. A dummy, attired in a copy of Steadman's dress, gets bumped out of the window. Dooley catches the mannequin, which he assumes is Steadman, and quickly carries it into a cab. The mannequin is made up with an excessive amount of eye shadow, rouge and lipstick and has a goofy blank expression very similar to Dooley's own goofy expression. Dooley cuddles up to the mannequin and, while hugging the mannequin around the neck, he causes its head to pop off. Appalled, he stares into the camera, screams, and faints.

Larry Semon did not meet a mannequin he didn't like, as indicated by the number of mannequins he used in his films. He used every type of mannequin routine, from having his character confuse a mannequin for a police officer in *Horseshoes* (1923) to having his character chased by a volatile Oliver Hardy through a large stock of mannequins in *The Gown Shop* (1923). However, his most elaborate mannequin routine appeared in *The Stunt Man* (1927), in which Semon took the subtle, gradual mannequin scene from Langdon's *Long Pants* and converted it into a wild, high-energy action scene. In this film Semon, who has been hired as a stunt man for actress Gloria Rampage, shows up on a movie set dressed in a billowy checkered skirt and a floppy hat with a long feather sticking straight. Semon makes repeated blunders in his effort to perform stunts. At one point, he loses control of a car and crashes it through a set. Up to this point, the film is much like the Ben Turpin comedy *The Daredevil* (1923). Turpin, an inept stunt man, mistakenly fires off a prop gun, the impact of which knocks walls of scenery on top of the crew. The action then veers off in a different direction. The infuriated director chases after Semon, who is desperate to find a place to hide. Semon finally climbs inside the passenger compartment of a biplane. It is only moments later that the plane takes off. It is revealed (through a conversation between the director and a visitor to the set) that the plane is being operated by remote control. The director plans to film the plane being blown out of the sky by a battery of guns. Semon emerges meekly from his hiding place. He sees what appears to be a pilot in the front seat of the plane, but a change in the camera angle reveals that it is a mannequin occupying the pilot's seat. When the guns blast at the plane, Semon begs the pilot to take the plane down, and he becomes puzzled when the pilot fails to respond. He suddenly notices that the pilot's arms are hanging limply. He lifts one of the arms and sees that it is made of plastic. Semon flies into a panic. Suddenly, with a look of anguish, he clutches the mannequin as if hoping to receive comfort. The plane suffers a direct hit and splits apart. The mannequin's parachute opens and Semon, still looking absurd in his drag outfit, clings to the mannequin on the way down.

Semon mistakes a dummy for a figure of authority and seeks to communicate with it before realizing that it is not really a person. This is essentially the same setup as the Langdon scene, except that Semon intensifies the situation by having himself and the dummy flying high above the ground while missiles are being fired at them. The most intriguing part of the scene is that Semon, an inhuman character in many ways, seeks to make an emotional connection with his artificial companion.

Curiously, a reworking of this routine in *Abbott and Costello Meet the Keystone Kops* (1955) uses every element of the scene except the dummy. Costello is a stunt man dressed in drag. He takes off in a two-seater biplane with partner Abbott. The plane loses control when struck by live rounds of ammunition. Abbott puts on a parachute and bails out. Costello exits the plane without a parachute and manages a safe descent by clinging to Abbott's legs.

The *Long Pants* routine had to be altered to make it work in a sound film, where it was less plausible for a mannequin to be mistaken for a man. This was demonstrated by the approach to the routine in the Three Stooges comedy *A Plumbing We Will Go* (1940). Curly does not see the mannequin at first. He backs up into it and, startled, reaches back and feels around. He feels the outline of a human figure, the uniform and, most important, the badge. He no sooner turns around than he realizes that he is dealing with a mannequin. Annoyed, he castigates the fake police officer and then gives it a hard shove.

Reality is relative in the context of art. An altered state of reality certainly existed in silent films, as exhibited in *The Goat* (1921). Buster Keaton, waiting at the end of a bread line, does not realize that he has gotten behind a couple of mannequins on display outside of a men's clothing store. He grows so impatient that he brings out a pin and sticks it into the mannequin's backside to get this character moving. He is mystified when he gets no reaction. Just then, the shopkeeper comes out of his shop to take the mannequins back inside. Keaton is left slack-jawed, unable to believe what he has just seen.

It is hard to imagine Keaton's sharp-witted character being unable to tell the difference between a man and a mannequin. Even the fact that Keaton did not have the opportunity to confront the mannequins face-to-face should not have made too much of a difference. He should not have been fooled as easily as Langdon. However, we can believe that the mannequin resembled a man to Keaton only if we accept that the rules and perceptions are different within this dreamscape, which was void of dimension, color and sound. In this universe, a real person has little more substance than a mannequin. This was proven in *Robinet boxeur* (1913). Marcel Perez, on a rampage smashing porcelain statues to bits, just as easily smashes the statues' seller to bits. It does not matter in this strange world that a mannequin does not produce a sound, neither breath nor heartbeat, for no one here, not man or mannequin, makes a sound. When all is said and done, flesh has no place in a land of dreams.

A fantasy film, *Legend of Ponchinella* (1906), does well in demonstrating this point. Evil aristocrats abduct a young woman and whisk her off to their storybook castle, where they turn her into a mechanical doll and have her dance for their amusement. Max Linder, in the role of a Harlequin, leads an army of dwarfs up a mountain to rescue the woman. The dwarfs use their torches to set the castle on fire. A ceiling damaged by flames collapses on the heroine, causing her to break into pieces. Linder gathers up the body parts and stuffs them into a sack. Linder sees a number of life-size dolls hanging from the ceiling. He waves a magic wand, which causes the dolls to drop off the ceiling and perform a festive dance. It is through a noticeable jump cut that the dolls transform into flesh-and-blood chorus girls. Linder sets down the mountain with his sack. When he comes to a gap, he waves his magic wand to create a bridge. Once he is off the mountain, he spills the body parts out the sack and waves his magic wand over them. The heroine instantly reassembles and falls lovingly into Linder's arms. The rebirth of this young woman was able to effortlessly transpire in this enchanted world.

The actors in a silent film — nothing more than light and shadow — were not real.

These mere images were more phantom than man. With apparent ease, Méliès was able to transform people into inanimate objects. In *The Famous Box Trick* (1898), he turns a boy into a sheet of paper and then tears the paper into pieces. In *The Hilarious Posters* (1906), illustrated characters come to life and leap out of a poster. Police chase after them and end up becoming trapped inside the poster themselves. The plain and simple fact is that a person in a film frame is no more real than a person in a poster frame, and replacing one with the other is no great feat. Under these circumstances, a mannequin can attain parity with a man.

Later, in *The Goat* (1921), Keaton scratches a match against a cigar-store Indian, only to have the Indian come to life and attack him. Keaton acknowledges in this way that human facsimiles have great power in this universe and that their status can, under conducive circumstances, rival that of human beings. Just because the prick of a needle fails to jolt a clothes dummy to action does not mean that a prick of a match cannot at a later time rouse a cigar store mannequin to violence.

It was not uncommon in early films for a human replica — a mannequin, a statue, a doll or a scarecrow — to suddenly come to life to create mischief. It could be no more than a fleeting gag or it could form the basis of a number of amusing complications. The title says it all in the case of the 1901 Pathé Frères comedy *The Statues on a Spree*. The figures were often provoked to life by a bad act. Typical was a 1903 Pathé Frères comedy entitled *Mannequin vivant* (translated as *Living Dummy*), in which two men having fun beating up a mannequin are startled to find that the mannequin is willing to fight back. The Comica comedy *Zigoto à la fête* (1912) shows Lucien Bataille tickling a statue, which comes to life as quickly as Keaton's cigar store Indian to defend itself.

The Goat takes the parity issue further in one of its final scenes. Keaton has to find a way to elude a police officer. He climbs atop a clay model of champion thoroughbred Man O' War and assumes a pose to make it look that he is part of the figure. Spectators accept him as a clay jockey until the horse buckles under his weight.

The comedians certainly saw themselves as interchangeable with dummies. Ben Turpin replaces a dummy to be near the lovely Juanita Hansen in *A Clever Dummy* (1917). Lupino Lane pretends to be a prop dummy to conceal himself from a studio security guard in *Movieland* (1926). Harold Lloyd pretends to be a mannequin to outwit robbers in *Next Aisle Over* (1919). Lloyd later helps out a football team by standing in for their tattered tackling-dummy in *The Freshman* (1925).

A variety of routines came out of the idea of a comic character switching places with a mannequin. In *Homer Joins the Force* (1920), Fred Ardath hides in plain sight of a police officer by posing as a mannequin. The officer is ready to give up his pursuit of Ardath until Ardath's pants fall down and the comedian's bony knees are exposed. Billy Bevan has a trickier time keeping his lower extremities covered when he pursues the same ruse in *Be Reasonable* (1921). Bevan has managed to fool police by blending in with the mannequins outside of a men's clothing store. He just needs to keep still until the police move past the store and go looking for him elsewhere. But a man approaches the shop owner to purchase the coat that Bevan is wearing. Bevan remains perfectly still while the shop owner removes his coat and passes it on to the customer. The man then points to Bevan's hat, which the shop owner quickly removes. It is when the customer offers to buy Bevan's pants that Bevan has taken all that he is willing to take. Bevan, choosing to take his chances with the police, breaks out of his pose to ward off the clutching hands of the shop owner. Before the police can act, he bolts off down the street.

Buster Keaton varies this ploy while eluding the police in *Daydreams* (1922). He is able, by kneeling on a podium and covering himself with a sheet, to make himself look like a mannequin bust. Bevan was able to fit himself in among a group of similar-looking mannequins, but Keaton was willing to distort his appearance to take his deception even further. This was not the only time that Keaton posed as human figure without complete body parts. A famous portrait of Keaton has him without arms in the pose of the Venus de Milo.

Harold Lloyd engaged in his own physical distortion as a mannequin in *Safety Last!* (1923). Lloyd arrives late at his job at a department store. He takes notice of a clerk unloading mannequins from a truck and he seems (by his pleased expression) to have come up with an idea. In the next shot, a clerk is shown lifting a mannequin dressed in a fur-trimmed woman's coat and a big, floppy-brimmed hat. The mannequin has a thin metal stand in place of legs. It stiffly bobs when it is lifted. It in no way suggests a living person. But then, after the clerk carries the mannequin into the building and approaches the time clock, the mannequin suddenly raises its head and we can see, hidden under the floppy hat, that it is Lloyd. He moves the minute hand back on the clock, punches his time card, then moves the minute hand back to the correct time. He remains still while the clerk carries him onto the retail floor. He reveals, as he climbs down off the stand, that he has been keeping his legs folded up underneath the long skirt of the coat.* Lloyd, unlike Keaton, cheated in the way that he executed this scene. An actual mannequin appears in most of the shots in which it is supposed to be Lloyd in disguise as a mannequin. Just as much as he deceived the store manager, Lloyd deceived everyone watching the film. A simpler, and more straightforward, version of the gag was performed by Pierre Étaix in *Le Soupirant* (1962). Étaix, determined to visit a pretty singer in her dressing room, poses as a wardrobe mannequin and is promptly carried backstage by a stagehand.

Charlie Chaplin, ever sly, turned this situation to his advantage at an amusement park in *The Circus* (1928). A pickpocket, unnerved by the presence of a police officer, slips a stolen wallet into Chaplin's pocket. This soon gets Chaplin in trouble with the officer,

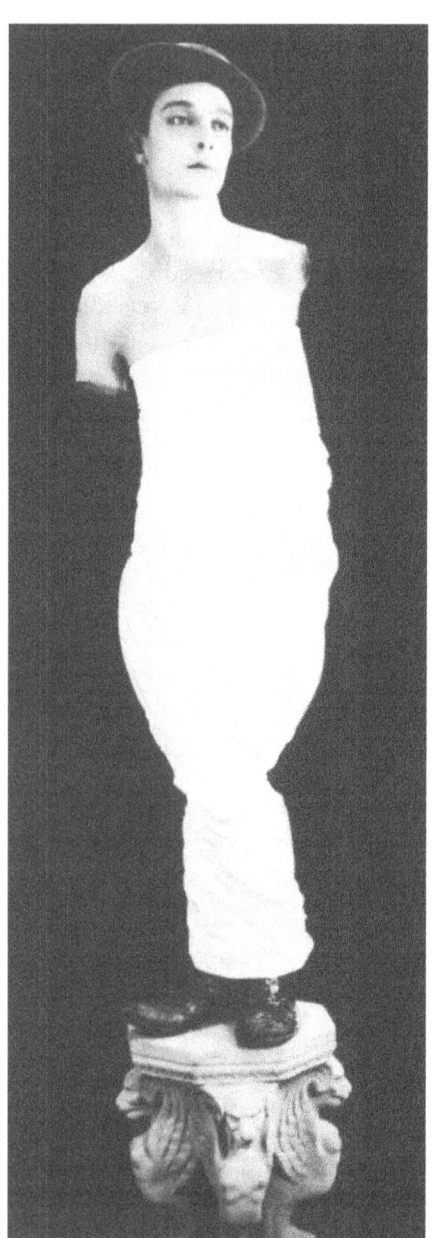

Buster Keaton as the Venus de Milo (publicity photograph) (courtesy www.doctormacro.com).

---

*This gag was derivative of a gag from *Bumping into Broadway* (1919), in which Lloyd hid from view by curling up inside of a coat hanging off a coat rack.

who chases both Chaplin and the pickpocket into a funhouse. Chaplin, posing as an automated mannequin, pretends that it is part of his mechanical routine to repeatedly slam the pickpocket on the head with a club. After each blow, he swivels forward and then jerks back his head in a merry robotic chuckle.

Larry Semon reasoned that, just as pursuers can be made to see a man as a mannequin, they can also be made to see a mannequin as a man. This ploy was used by Semon to dark effect in *Dummies* (1928). Semon must find a way to escape a gang of thugs about to break down a door to get to him. He pretends to be so distressed that he is willing to resort to suicide. After making it sound as if he is killing himself, he arranges a mannequin under a sheet to look as if it is his corpse. This gag is far too morbid to be funny.

Lucille Ball revived this statue-impersonation routine more than 30 years later in the *I Love Lucy* episode "The Ricardos Dedicate a Statue" (1957). Ricky is scheduled to unveil the statue of a Revolutionary War hero, but, only hours before the ceremony, Lucy backs her car into the statue and smashes it into pieces. Distraught, she staggers back into her home holding the head, the musket and a foot. Lucy, afraid to own up to the mishap, turns up at the unveiling ceremony disguised as the statue. The crowd is unaware of the ruse until a dog licks Lucy, who responds by opening her eyes. This is not much different than the plot presented in 1908 by *The Living Doll*.

The tradition has been carried on in recent years. Miley Cyrus pretends to be a mannequin in a 2006 episode of *Hannah Montana* entitled "It's a Mannequin's World." Dany Boon acts as a mannequin in the French comedy *Micmacs* (2009).

A helpless mannequin was susceptible to more terrible abuse than a comedian. A burly villain could grab Clyde Cook by the leg and twist it into the shape of a pretzel, but filmmakers needed a mannequin to escalate the slapstick violence. Despite the amazing physical talents of a comedian like Cook, only a mannequin could have its leg yanked off or its head knocked across the room.

The idea that a person's head could be removed with ease, and even continue to function in a disembodied state, was popularized in early films by Georges Méliès. Méliès turns a woman's head into a bouncing ball in *Jack Haggs and Dum Dum* (1903); he saws off a woman's head as part of an outrageous medical procedure in *Sure Cure for Indigestion* (1902); and he conducts four detached heads singing in union in *Four Heads Are Better Than One* (1898). Comedian André Deed was disassembled and reassembled in his earliest known film, Méliès's *An Extraordinary Dislocation* (1901). He performed other variations of this trick in *Cretinetti che bello!* (1909) and *Cretinetti e le donne* (1910). The latter film featured Deed being torn to pieces by ardent female admirers. Filmmakers other than Deed eventually came to follow Méliès's example. *Le Bon Invalide et les enfants* (1908) is a highly unusual park comedy. After tiring of playing with a ball, a group of boys approach an old man sitting on a bench. Following a brief discussion, the old man obligingly removes his head and hands it over the boys, who proceed to toss it around to each other. The boys then pluck off the limbs from the headless old man and, as described by film historian Richard Abel, they "stand the body parts up like pins and bowl them over with the head."[4] In the Eclipse comedy *Polycarpe Wants to Shoot at Targets* (1912), Charles Servaès plays a trigger-happy boob who accidentally shoots off a waiter's head and then desperately replaces it with a pig's head. In *Robinet boxeur* (1913), Marcel Perez is so encouraged by a boxing lesson that he proceeds to deliver uppercuts to everyone in sight. Perez, in his exuberance, literally knocks off a man's head in the gym. He chases after the head as it rolls across the floor. He then takes hold of the head like a volley ball and wallops it from one end of the room to the other. The decapitation gag was still showing up in European comedies as late as 1913, when it was the focus of the Cines comedy *Kri Kri Headless*.

After 1913, films were no longer so surreal that a comedian could go around decapitating other people nor could disembodied heads be floating around in mid-air. Filmmakers now had to settle for the next best thing: bringing forth a bloodless surrogate to lose its head. A simulated man allowed for simulated violence. It could be comforting to enjoy the violent action while realizing that, even in the fictional context, the objects of the attacks were not really being hurt. A viewer was, more to the point, free to laugh without feeling sadistic. In *Ambrose's Little Hatchet* (1915), the shadow of dressmaker Mack Swain taking apart a dummy looks to onlookers like a bloodthirsty killer savagely dismembering a woman. Similar action is conveyed in *Poor Simp* (1920), which featured a shadow of a man with a large knife cutting an arm and head off a dummy. Lupino Lane, masquerading as a stunt dummy in *Movieland* (1926), is horrified to see dummies having their heads and arms sawed off by a prop man, who looks to have the same plan in mind for him.* In *Oh, What a Man!* (1927), Larry Semon is a police detective on the trail of Notorious Nora (Gertrude Astor). Semon pursues Notorious Nora and her gang into a nightclub. The lady gangster spots Semon spying at her from another table. Enraged, she pulls out a revolver and opens fire on him. The hail of bullets blows off Semon's head, except that it is really a mannequin head made to look like Semon's head. Semon's actual head pops out of the collar in place of the lost head. The comedian has, in this way, been able to lose his head and keep it, too.

Semon's decapitation gag turned up more than 30 years later in a slightly more credible form in *The Court Jester* (1955). Danny Kaye is garbed in full armor for a joust to the death with a brawny, vicious knight. The knight charges up to Kaye, swinging a mace with a great deal of force, and strikes Kaye hard enough to apparently knock off his head. The headless rider is trotted across the arena by his horse. But then, suddenly, Kaye's head pops out from inside of the chest armor, where it has been safely tucked away.

Other variations of this gag appeared now and then. In *The Rummy* (1933), Ben Blue reacts to the sight of a mummy by retracting his head down inside his collar, which makes it look to co-star Billy Gilbert as if the man has lost his head.

Buster Keaton was aware that these make-believe people were capable of causing either delight or fright. In *Seven Chances* (1925), Keaton has only hours to find himself a wife to qualify to be the heir to his grandfather's fortune. He is proposing to every female that moves — even one that doesn't move, a deceptively shapely mannequin he encounters in a barbershop. He recoils in horror when the barber comes along and pops off the mannequin's head. Keaton is not, at any point, delighted when he stumbles upon a fake person in *Steamboat Bill, Jr.* (1928). Keaton, seeking refuge from a hurricane, enters a theatre and observes a ventriloquist's dummy sitting on a table. The wind blows through a window and causes the table to shift. The dummy shifts with the table and his face turns towards Keaton, which is creepy enough to make Keaton run away. This is Langdon in reverse. Keaton assumes that this figure is inanimate and then is surprised to find that his assumption might not be correct. Keaton said that this scene was based on a real-life experience. As a child working in vaudeville, he developed a fascination for a ventriloquist named Trovollo. Tro-

---

*The scene is similar to the Commedia dell'Arte routine "Lazzi of the Sack," which originated in Bavari in 1568. Slaughtered pigs are being stuffed inside of sacks to be delivered to the butcher shop. Pantalone, hidden inside one of the sacks, is promptly hauled off to the butch shop, where he becomes frightened at the sound of the butcher sharpening his knives. Woody Allen performed a variation of this routine in *Sleeper* (1973). Allen, posing as a robot, has to flee from a repairman trying to remove his head with a gargantuan pair of pliers.

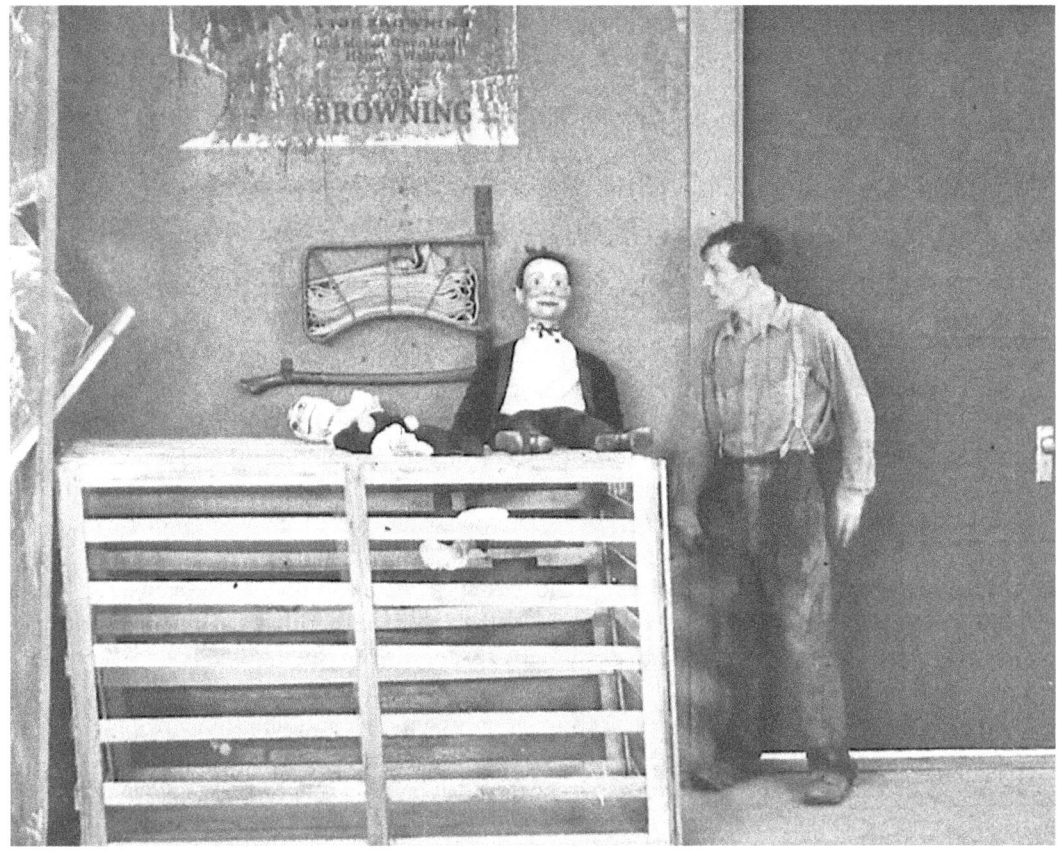

Buster Keaton is unnerved by a ventriloquist dummy in *Steamboat Bill, Jr.* (1928).

vollo discovered that Keaton was coming into his dressing room when no one else was around to have conversations with his dummy, Red Top. One night, Trovollo hid inside his dressing room and, when Keaton sat down to talk to Red Top, he caused Red Top to move. Keaton was so frightened that he ran out of the theatre. The idea of soulless imitation of a human being was spooky indeed.

The biggest collection of mannequins appeared in *Who's Afraid?* (1927), in which Lupino Lane becomes trapped in a museum with spooky mannequins after nightfall. The film was likely designed to capitalize on the frights of *Waxworks* (1925), a popular Paul Leni horror film in which a museum's scary wax figures come to life. During *Waxworks*'s climax, a wax model of Jack the Ripper stalks a man through the museum and, in the end, raises up a knife and plunges it into the man's chest. It is at this point that the man awakens and realizes that it had all been a dream. The mannequins in *Who's Afraid?* never actually come to life, but they are threatening nonetheless. Lane is awkwardly making his way through the dark and shadowy museum when he bumps into a mannequin, which topples forward into a second mannequin. The shadow cast by the entangled mannequins looks to be a shadow of a man strangling a woman. Lane, panicking, runs to find help. He looks relieved to come upon a mannequin dressed as a cop. He grabs the mannequin by the hand, thinking to lead this fellow to the attacker, but instead he pulls off the mannequin's hand. Later, as he crawls across the floor, his boot spur becomes tangled up in a rope attached to a dolly, on top of which stands a likeness of an Indian warrior. He unknowingly drags this mannequin along behind him. Revealed in a wide-shot is Lane crawling across the floor as the Indian follows behind him, looking all too ready to bring down his tomahawk. At that moment, the wax figure looks to be as dangerous as *Waxworks*'s Jack the Ripper. *Who's Afraid?* anticipates *Night at the Museum* (2006), in which a night watchman played by Ben Stiller is frightened to find that a museum's exhibits come to life at night.

A mannequin film that could make a person laugh and feel unsettled at the same time is the 1908 Centaur release *The Doll Maker's Daughter*. Minnie, desperate for something to wear to a party, steals an outfit from one of her father's life-sized dolls. Minnie is coming to return the outfit when her father suddenly enters the workshop. The room is dark enough for Minnie to fool her father into thinking that she is the doll. The old man, though, has a big surprise for his daughter. He applies a galvanic battery to the supposed doll on the theory that a surge of electricity will be able to bring the doll to life. When the daughter jumps around in reaction to the electrical current, the doll maker assumes that the doll is performing a dance for him, and he is so overwhelmed with joy that he dances along with her.

The creepiest of all mannequins is the one that stalks Max Linder through a haunted castle in *Help!* (1924). The tricky mannequin freezes in its path just as Linder turns around. Linder is puzzled as he tries to understand how this mannequin could have moved. He brings up the flame on his lighter and holds it under the mannequin's finger, which proceeds to melt away. The mannequin springs back to life, angrily shoving Linder down a flight of stairs.

Mannequin legs and heads, on their own, created more confusion for comedians than mannequins in their entirety. It was common for a mannequin's leg sticking out of a car window to make a passerby assume that a backseat dalliance was in progress. Comic business in this area could get even more elaborate.

Mannequins provided, as their key comic feature, body parts that could pop off instantaneously. In *Picking Peaches* (1924), Langdon is working as a store clerk and he goes to bring out shoes for a woman to try on. While waiting, the woman sees stockings displayed on a mannequin leg and rests the leg under the hem of her skirt to see how the stockings would look with her dress. Langdon returns at this point and takes hold of the mannequin leg, which he presumes to be the woman's leg, and is startled when the leg comes off in his hand.* *Fast and Furious*, a Lige Conley comedy produced the same year, offers Langdon's mannequin gag in reverse. A clerk sets a mannequin leg off to one side while he helps a woman to try on shoes. Another woman moves the leg out of the way to sit down. The clerk, preoccupied, reaches over to retrieve the mannequin leg and grabs the woman's leg by mistake.

Larry Semon provides an extended version of Langdon's mannequin leg routine in *Dummies* (1928). Semon, a theatre magician, is sitting on steps outside of a dressing-room door. A girl appears in the doorway and shows Semon that the heel of her shoe has been broken. Semon removes the shoe to repair it and, while he is hammering the heel back into place, the girl steps away and a dummy resembling the girl (even wearing an identical polka-dotted dress) is set down in the doorway in her place. Semon finishes fixing the shoe. Unaware that the girl has been replaced by a mannequin, he tries to squeeze the mannequin's foot into the shoe and manages in the process to pull off the mannequin's leg. It was the same payoff with a longer setup.

Stray body parts, real or fake, can also provoke deep-seated anxieties. This is evident

---

*Lou Costello performs the same gag in a 1954 episode of *The Colgate Comedy Hour*.

in *Roaming Romeo* (1928), which casts Lupino Lane as a runaway slave in ancient Rome. Lane, in flight from soldiers, collides into a marble statue. He is in a daze when he sits up in the rubble, which includes a number of the statue's body parts. It is shocking to the slave when he tries to cross his legs and a marble leg, which he has taken to be his own leg, suddenly falls away. The fear of losing body parts arose in other ways in comedy films of the period. In *Creeps* (1926), Lou Archer gets trapped in the rumble seat of a car. He is thrown about so much that he emerges with both of his legs in the same pants leg. At first, he thinks he has lost his leg and flies into a panic.

During this same period, director Tod Browning displayed an obsession with missing limbs in his horror films, none more so than *The Unknown* (1927). Browning biographer David J. Skal attributes this morbid fascination to the many veterans of World War I who had returned home with missing arms and legs.

Amputation phobias did, in fact, return to films in the wake of World War II. This is evident in dramatic films such as *Kings Row* (1942) and *The Best Years of Our Lives* (1946). Comedy films of the period also followed suit. In *Nervous Shakedown* (1947), an escaped convict posing as a doctor wraps a blood-pressure cuff around Hugh Herbert's leg. He heavy-handedly pumps the bulb to inflate the cuff's bladder, which grows to the size of a basketball before it explodes. Startled by the explosion, the convict bumps into a table and knocks a medical model of a leg to the floor. Herbert screams in panic, thinking the model leg is his own leg, presumably blown off in the explosion.

In *Burstup Holmes' Murder Case* (1913), a husband needs to find a way to play poker with his friends without letting his wife know about it. He uses a mannequin's head to create the illusion that he is sleeping in bed. He is trimming the wig to make it look just right when he cuts his finger and gets blood on the bed sheet. After the husband has climbed out of the bedroom window, his wife comes into the room intending to rustle him awake. She screams in terror when the head drops to the floor. She finds the blood on the bed sheet and assumes that a maniac has chopped off her husband's head.

Severed mannequin heads became a means for comedy in Three Stooges films. In *Dizzy Detectives* (1943), the Stooges are poking around a dark and dusty storeroom when Curly gets his head trapped in a guillotine. The blade drops at the same time that a mannequin's head comes rolling across the floor. Moe, assuming that this is Curly's head, cries out and faints. The fact is that the guillotine blade is made of rubber and Curly was never in danger at all. *Shivering Sherlocks* (1948) climaxes with a ghoulish hunchback chasing Shemp with a meat cleaver. The hunchback swings the meat cleaver at Shemp's head but he misses Shemp and chops off the head of a dummy instead. Shemp sees the fake head drop to the floor and becomes hysterical thinking that this is his own head.

These comic characters realized that, if a mannequin could fool them, they could be used in schemes to fool other people. *Her Dummy Husband* (1915) involved an old maid who becomes so concerned about a rash of burglaries that she dresses a dummy in a man's overcoat and sits it in an armchair in her front room. Harold Lloyd also saw that a dummy could be an imposing figure. In *Speedy* (1928), Lloyd is riding a horse-drawn trolley across Manhattan in a desperate race against time. A mannequin, dressed in a police uniform, topples off the back of a parade float and lands in the path of the trolley. The astute Lloyd is quick to recognize this figure as a mannequin and gets an idea of how he can use this object to his advantage. He sets up the mannequin beside him on the trolley and rigs up a rope that allows him to control the mannequin's arm. Now, as he makes his way through the city, he is able to make the mannequin salute at motorists, who react by quickly clearing out of the way.

In *Fluttering Hearts* (1927), Charley Chase cannot gain access to a private club unless he is accompanied by a woman. He has a mannequin pose as a date to bluff his way into the club. Once inside, he takes the mannequin out on the dance floor. Oliver Hardy, playing a drunken patron, becomes involved in a flirtation with the mannequin. This proves useful to Chase, who needs to obtain an incriminating letter from Hardy. He covers himself up in a cloak, sets the mannequin down in his lap, and extends his arms to make them look as if they belong to the mannequin. The ruse ends up being ruined when the mannequin loses its head. Chaplin had performed essentially the same routine nine years earlier in *A Dog's Life* (1918), except that it was an unconscious thug that he propped up like his own personal puppet. The routine, in fact, originated as a Commedia dell'Arte routine known as "Lazzo of the Hands Behind the Back."

In *Don't Be a Dummy* (1926), Arthur Lake hopes to make a young woman jealous by using a mannequin to create a shadow of a woman on his window shade. The Kansas Board of Review censored footage in which it was suggested by the shadow that Lake was removing his shapely new companion's panties. Essentially the same gag was used years earlier in Vitagraph's *What One Small Boy Can Do* (1908). In that instance, a mischievous boy manipulates cardboard cut-outs of a man and a woman behind a window shade to make it look to his mother as if father is inside the house kissing another woman. The premise was used yet again in the "The Boy Friends" comedy *Ladies Last* (1930). The "boyfriends" (David Sharpe, Grady Sutton and Mickey Daniels) refuse to attend a fancy dress party with their girlfriends (Gertrude Messinger, Mary Kornman and Dorothy Granger). To make the boys jealous, the girls obtain mannequins in dress suits and set them up by the windows during the party. The boys, who have come to spy on the girls, are quickly persuaded that the girls have found themselves a better class of boyfriends.

Writer/producer John Hughes combined elements from these various scenes (the rope-operated mannequin from *Speedy*, the shadow of the mannequin on the window shade from *Don't Be a Dummy*, and the mannequin party guests from *Ladies Last*) for a crowd-pleasing scene in *Home Alone* (1990). Macaulay Culkin, an eight-year-old boy home alone (as per by the title), needs a plan to frighten away burglars attempting to break into his home. The burglars are, in fact, deterred when they see evidence of a lively party underway in the home. Guests, as suggested by the shadows on the window curtains, are drinking and dancing as music blares from a stereo. However, this is a cleverly designed ruse on the part of Culkin, who has set up mannequins near the windows and is pulling on ropes to make the mannequins move. Harold Lloyd arranged for a mannequin to raise a salute while Culkin has arranged for a mannequin to raise a beer. The popularity of the scene motivated Hughes to devise a variation of the routine in a sequel, *Home Alone 2: Lost in New York* (1992). This time, a Bozo, the Clown blow-up doll set up behind a curtain in a shower stall creates the illusion of a man taking a shower.

An exceptionally lively mannequin is the source of confusion in *Taxi Dolls* (1929). At a vaudeville theater, a stagehand accidentally activates Beatrice the Mechanical Doll, who steps out of the theater and climbs into the back of Jack Cooper's cab. An identical woman, who happens to be the wife of Cooper's boss, later gets into the same cab and Cooper mistakes her for the doll. This was a rare instance where a doll was played by an actual person (in this case, Virginia Vance).*

---

*This robot comedy was predated by *The Mechanical Doll*, a 1901 Urban-Eclipse comedy, in which a valet must stand in for a robot broken by his clumsy tampering.

Mannequins appeared far less often in comedies of the sound era. They had lost their magic in this noisy, realistic new world. Buster Keaton next encountered a cigar-store Indian in a sound short, *The Gold Ghost* (1934). Keaton, startled, punches the Indian, but the figure fails to come to life. Still, the mannequins continued to be good for quick chills and fleeting misunderstandings. In *Seal Skins* (1932), ZaSu Pitts gets frightened when a mannequin falls out of a closet on top of her. In *A Gem of a Jam* (1943), a night watchman (played by Dudley Dickerson) becomes frightened when he backs up into a mannequin in a spooky storage room.

In the sound era, only the statues retained the power to come to life. A pair of statues suddenly draw revolvers on Harpo Marx in *Animal Crackers* (1930). Curly is kicked by a statue in the Three Stooges comedy *Three Sappy People* (1939).

A mannequin played a more crucial role in the Three Stooges' comedy *Three Pests in a Mess* (1945). The Stooges rush into an office to hide and, when they slam the door shut, a rifle comes loose from the wall and drops into Curly's hands. Curly accidentally discharges a ready round into a mannequin, which topples forward and lands flat on its face. The Stooges assume that the mannequin is a man. They never bother to turn over the figure to get a look at its face, they merely assume that the figure's stiffness is due to a swift onset of rigor mortis. They quickly stuff the mannequin in a sack and haul it to a pet cemetery to bury it. Curly is creeping through the cemetery with the sack over his shoulder when the mannequin's arm flops out and strikes him in the face.* Earlier versions of the mannequin-in-a-sack routine were performed by Max Davidson in *Dumb Daddies* (1928) and Ben Blue in *Wreckety Wrecks* (1933). Blue thinks that he has crashed his taxi into a man, but the figure splayed across his radiator grill is, in fact, a dummy from a tuxedo-rental store.

Harry Langdon continued to associate with mannequins in his sound films. *The Big Kick* (1930) centers around bootleggers smuggling liquor across state lines inside of mannequins. Harry decides that it is his civic duty to round up the liquor-filled mannequins, which he calls "booze-leggers." He struggles to stand up the mannequins in a row while holding a gun on them to deter them from fleeing. *The Hitchhiker* (1933) opens with Harry watching a movie being filmed in the park. He turns to a prop dummy to ask for the time and becomes confused when he fails to get an answer. Mannequins are abundant in *Knight Duty* (1933), which includes a poor recreation of the mannequin routine from *Long Pants*. This version of the routine looks more like Billy Dooley's rough and impatient version, ending with Harry smacking off the mannequin's head. Langdon reprised this routine yet again in *Counsel on De Fence* (1934).

Langdon is older and wiser in *Misbehaving Husbands* (1940), and now it is the perception of others that is wrong. Langdon breaks a mannequin while setting up a display in a department-store window. He puts the mannequin in his car to take it to a repair shop, but a friend of his wife sees Langdon and assumes that the store manager is on a date with another woman. Gossip about this scene gets back to Langdon's wife, who becomes convinced that the gossip is true when she finds the mannequin's high-heel shoe in the backseat of her husband's car. The woman is so upset that she files for divorce.

Andy Clyde also showed an interest in mannequins in sound films. In *A Maid Made Mad* (1943), dress-shop owner Clyde is surrounded by mannequins. In one scene, he gets

---

*This scene originates from a Commedia dell'Arte routine known as "Lazzo of the Living Corpse," in which Arlecchino carries off a slumbering man that he has mistaken for a corpse. The man secretly awakens and pokes Arlecchino in the backside with a sword.

a whim to dance around his shop with one of his prettier mannequins. Later, Clyde goes out to the front of his store to remove shoes from a mannequin, but he confuses a woman for the mannequin and snatches off her shoes before she has time to protest. In *The Blonde Stayed On* (1946), Clyde comes into contact with another mannequin as a manager of a department store. Clyde is adjusting the wig on the mannequin when his wife comes along and thinks her husband is getting romantic with a woman.

Baby dolls, like mannequins, were mistaken for real people, which also caused comic confusion, misunderstandings and mayhem. In *One Good Joke Deserves Another* (1913), John Bunny is fooled into thinking that a baby doll thrown into a lake is an actual baby. A doll that has fallen into a lake is mistaken for a little girl again in *Just Kids* (1913). A cop searching for a missing girl mistakes a doll for the girl in *The Inventor's Secret* (1911).

Preservation work is currently under way for the Triangle comedy *His Baby Doll* (1917). The plot centers on small-town tensions. Malcolm St. Clair is making preparations for his wedding when he receives a surprise visit from his sister, who has come to show him her new baby. St. Clair ends up looking after the baby for his sister and takes the baby for a stroll through the neighborhood. St. Clair is spotted by a friend of his fiancé, who quickly spreads rumors that St. Clair is harboring a secret love child. Later, St. Clair is visited by friends who are planning his bachelor party. The friends present St. Clair with a baby doll as a gag gift. The baby doll later creates trouble for St. Clair when his fiancé and her father mistake it for the rumored love child. This is similar to a "Hall Room Boys" comedy called *Oh, Baby!* (1920). The film starts out with Neely Edwards and Hugh Fay walking along the boardwalk at the beach. The pair stops to play a ball-tossing game at a booth and win a life-size baby doll as a prize. Their friend, Miss Millionbucks, requests that they bring the doll to a reception that she is holding. Before the reception takes place, however, a real baby is left outside the pair's door. The aforementioned confusion, misunderstandings and mayhem so inevitable in the comedy world, dominate the remainder of the film.

It was standard for a baby carriage to get knocked over during a slapstick chase and a doll meant to represent a baby to come flying out of said carriage. A baby is roughed up even more in the Cecil Hepworth comedy *Blood and Bosh* (1913). Clumsy kidnappers mishandle the little one, including tossing him into the air, trampling on him, and dropping him out of a window. These scenes are inoffensive as the baby is obviously not real.

A shocking scene from the war melodrama *The Heart of Humanity* (1918) featured Erich von Stroheim, as an evil Prussian lieutenant, tossing a crying baby out of a window. Lupino Lane set out to recreate this scene for comic effect in *Only Me* (1929). The scene takes place in a theatre, where Lane is playing the wicked landlord in a hokey melodrama. Lane snatches a baby away from his mother and tosses him straight out of a window. The baby, like a boomerang, comes flying back at him and knocks him flat on the floor. Lane then throws the baby out of the window a second time. Later, when he opens the door to leave, the baby comes flying through the door and strikes him again. The father arrives home and gets into a fistfight with the villain. During the ensuing scuffle, the pair manages to trample the baby.

Nearly three decades later, in the *I Love Lucy* episode entitled "Pregnant Women Are Unpredictable," mom-to-be Lucy (Lucille Ball) practices diaper-changing on a baby doll and manages, in her clumsy manner, to grossly mishandle the doll. Lucy, after dropping the doll upside down into a bath basin, plucks the doll out of the water by its foot. She then squeezes the doll's stomach and a stream of water squirts out of its mouth. After roughly toweling off the doll, the expectant mom means to finish her practice by applying talcum powder, but she squeezes the container so hard that she shoots the doll in the face with a potent blast of powder.

The baby doll remained a comic prop for years after. *The Untouchables* (1987) is presented as a historical crime drama, and yet it is often lacking in serious drama and historical accuracy. No better example of this can be found than the famed train station sequence in which Kevin Costner intercepts a baby carriage rolling down a staircase in the middle of a frenzied shoot-out. As a way to up the ante, the spoof-filled *Naked Gun 33⅓* (1994) features four baby carriages in jeopardy. Leslie Nielsen, as the film's comic hero, fails to stop the carriages from crashing to the bottom of the staircase and the impact sends a quartet of obvious baby dolls springing out of the carriages. By this time, many decades had passed since a baby carriage rolled into the thick of a comic riot in *Les Débuts d'un chauffeur* (1906), *Le Cheval emballé* (1908) and *The Curtain Pole* (1909). The abuse of a doll is still used today for comic effect. This is evident in *Scary Movie 4* (2006), which features an actor walloping what is obviously a doll made up to look like a ghost child.

After all these years, mannequins are still being abused in the interests of comedy. In 2010, *Tonight Show* host Conan O'Brien generated publicity for shooting wax figures of Tom Cruise and Henry Winkler out of a circus cannon. But it wasn't the firing of the cannon that got the biggest laugh of the night. The audience clearly enjoyed it more when, following the cannon blasts, stagehands rolled out the wax figures on gurneys and a close-up showed that the wax figures retained their big grins even though their faces had been cracked and partly melted.

In the modern world, mannequins are icons of consumerism. A department-store mannequin possessed by an ancient spirit comes to life in *Mannequin* (1987). The mannequin's charming presence in window displays draws hoards of shoppers to the store. In *Confessions of a Shopaholic* (2009), CGI mannequins talk to Isla Fisher to tempt her into buying clothing and fashion accessories.

Mannequins have also become an important part of tourist attractions. This fact helped to inspire *A Night at the Museum* (2006), in which museum mannequins are brought to life by a magical Egyptian tablet. Behind the scenes, the work of the magical Egyptian tablet was performed by CGI (computer-generated imagery).

CGI has, in general, allowed the film industry to come full circle, returning to the heady and headless ways of Méliès. Often, an actor is no more than a body with detachable parts in a magically surreal world. Eddie Murphy said in a 2010 interview, "More and more I find myself doing scenes by myself. Now you can do an action sequence where you just stand there and say your lines and they take your head and put it on some other body."[9]

3

Animals

Animal Antics

The Hal Roach comedy *Roughest Africa* (1923), which features Stan Laurel and Jimmy Finlayson as explorers tramping around Africa in search of wildlife, is a three-reel comedy loaded with animals.

In the opening scenes, Finlayson is awakened by a bear licking his bald head. The bear wrestles with him for awhile and eventually chases the explorer up a tree. In the meantime, a large ostrich chases Laurel across the Africa plain (actually, a plain on Santa Catalina Island). Laurel is dwarfed by the ostrich, who probably has a 20-pound weight advantage on him.

Soon after, Laurel encounters a cute, playful elephant. Unaffected by the elephant's charms, Laurel uses explosives to blow the elephant sky high. The hunter has to scurry out of the way to avoid the elephant's carcass crashing down on him. The fact that the sweet-natured pachyderm is now a carcass, and a fairly realistic carcass, makes this scene somewhat shocking and morbid.

Laurel, intending to lure a wild African lion, sits down on a log to play a bass violin. A lion bursts out of the brush. The jungle king then pounces into the middle of camp, breaking up a dice game among the natives. Laurel is too preoccupied playing the bass fiddle to notice when the lion jumps up on the log next to him. The lion has to thrust his snout forward, snap open its jaws and let out a fierce roar before the slow-witted explorer finally notices him. It ends up that this lion is part of a pride of lions. Laurel is chased down a narrow dirt path by as many as ten lions, which are scrambling over one another to get up the path. This audacious scene rivals the best of the comic lion attacks so prevalent in films of this period. The lions chase Laurel into an alligator-infested river. Laurel emerges on the other side of the river with a baby alligator latched onto his backside. The explorer no sooner escapes in a car than he discovers that a skunk has come along for the ride.

Bear, ostrich, elephant, lions, alligator, skunk. That is, without question, a well-stocked animal comedy. Comedy makers had by now learned the value of all creatures great, small and silly.

Animal acts were plentiful in vaudeville. Cliff Berzac's Circus was well received wherever the act played. Berzac would bring a mule onstage and challenge audience members to try riding the ornery creature. A stooge would come out of the audience and climb on top of the mule, at which point the mule would buck and give the stooge a tumultuous ride. Rhinelander's Pigs was a comedy act that featured the trainer dressed as a butcher. He had

Roscoe Arbuckle hugs a favorite co-star, Luke the dog (courtesy Steve Rydzewski).

his pigs perform silly acts — they played on a see-saw, they stood on top of one another to form a pyramid. The pigs, as trained, made it look as if they were hesitating to perform tricks so that the trainer had an excuse to take out a big butcher knife and start sharpening it on a whetstone. When this happened, the pigs would immediately hop to it and perform the trick at hand. Another animal act, Dick the dog, had a fountain pen tied to his paw so that he was able to draw pictures. The star of Barnold's Dog and Monkey Pantomime was Dan the drunken dog, who got laughs performing an act called "A Hot Time in Dogville."

Apes were even bigger stars in vaudeville than dogs, mules or pigs. Trainer Belle Hathaway performed in a popular vaudeville act with monkeys and a baboon. The act went under a number of different names, including Belle Hathaway's Jungle Comedians and Belle Hathaway and Her Simian Playmates. The jungle comedians did not have to do much to entertain crowds. The crowd-pleasing part of the act had the baboon catching plates thrown at him by Belle. Another popular vaudeville act featured a chimp named La Bella Pola who danced the Charleston. Gillette's Dogs and Monkeys had monkeys that performed a funny bowling routine. Still, the most famous ape in the theatre was Consul the Great, a chimp who was able to smoke a pipe and attend to a meal with a knife and fork. The act of eating food with common utensils may not sound as sensational as catching plates, or bowling, or dancing the Charleston, but Consul was so natural and relaxed that he seemed more human than ape. Consul started out performing in English music halls but he eventually toured through Europe and made a highly publicized visit to the United States in 1909. Consul was received as a celebrity on his arrival in New York. He performed tricks for the reporters who greeted him at the dock. A camera crew obtained footage which was later used in a film called *Consul Crosses the Atlantic*. Consul's act was imitated by other chimps, including Peter the Great, Consuline the Great, the Great Alexander, and Alfred the First. Buster Keaton, disguised as a chimp, performs Consul's routine in *The Playhouse* (1921). Topping Consul, Keaton also puffs on a cigar and rides a bicycle.

It was only a matter of time before these chimps were able to take Hollywood by storm. The Great Alexander was the first to arrive. He brought his table manners to the screen as the star of a restaurant comedy in 1915. The following year, a chimpanzee couple named Napoleon and Sally did a number of short comedy films for E & R Jungle Films.

The Fox Film Corporation featured the Fox Chimps in a series of comedies. The opening shot of their short *Monks a la Mode* (1923) reveals a chimpanzee in a checkered sports jacket and a derby sitting at a desk and puffing on a cigar. The brassy ape looks like Abbott & Costello's Bingo the Chimp. Much of the film's humor comes from showing an ape involved in activities usually reserved for people — driving a car, talking on a phone, etcetera.

The film includes a large amount of slapstick. Two chimps get into a fight and break up furniture. One chimp lifts a vase over its head and smashes it against the floor. A girl chimp beats a boy chimp over the head with a purse. A chimp riding on roller skates slips and performs a pratfall.

A key scene centers on a fashion show in which monkeys model clothing for rich women, as if high fashion is accentuated by hairy little models. The fashion show is being hosted by Jean Arthur. (Yes, this is the same Jean Arthur who would go on to star in the 1939 Frank Capra classic, *Mr. Smith Goes to Washington*.) Arthur becomes so impatient with one of her clothes monkeys that she snatches her by the ear and drags her off the runway.

Grief in Bagdad (1925) was the Fox Chimps' spoof of *Thief of Bagdad*. This is the best-known entry in the series because it was included on a 2001 DVD release of *The Thief of Bagdad* (1924). The film has received additional exposure by being posted on YouTube.

The chimp hero, like his human counterpart in *The Thief of Bagdad*, has a predilection for stealing. The hungry chimp gets to demonstrate his prowess as a thief when he goes after a bowl of noodles set out on a balcony to cool. He approaches a man sleeping against the building and succeeds in snatching off the man's turban without rousing the man. The turban, once unraveled, is now able to serve as a rope. The chimp throws one end of the rope over an outcrop of a sign and ties the other end to the tail of a donkey. Once the rope is in his grasp, he hurls a rock at the donkey's rump and the donkey becomes incensed and bolts forward. As the donkey tows the line at the one end, the weight of the chimp is raised at the other end and the chimp finds himself, in one lightning-fast movement, delivered up to the balcony. However, the little thief's troubles have only just begun. A burly man comes out onto the balcony, sees the chimp trying to steal his food, and draws out a saber ready to slice the chimp in half. Just then, a swami chimp causes a rope to magically rise into the air. This gives the chimp a quick means of escape.

The chimp becomes entranced when he sets his eyes on a princess chimp, who is being carried through the city in a lectica. It is obvious that his heart is beating strongly because a visible bulge beneath his shirt is rising and falling. The chimp, determined to meet the princess, works hard to avoid guards and get inside the palace. First, he hangs onto the bottom of the lectica to pass through the gates. Then, he jumps inside a big vase to hide. Along the way, he stumbles upon the henchmen of an evil prince, who overpower the princess and take her captive. Douglas Fairbanks rode to the rescue on a flying horse, and our heroic chimp, in the same spirit, rides to the rescue on a flying donkey. The chimp, through cleverness, courage and climbing skills, manages to get the princess out of the evil prince's castle. Palace guards fire a cannon at the couple as they flee on a magic carpet. The chimp is hit in the backside by a cannonball. He catches further cannonballs in his arms and throws them down at the guards pursuing them on horseback.

The chimp, though not as graceful and charismatic as Fairbanks, manages to perform a number of clever tricks and gets around surprisingly well in the comic chases.

Fox announced plans for a feature with the Fox Chimps, but the feature never came to fruition. Lewis Seiler, the director of the series, went on to direct numerous Tom Mix westerns, in which he only had to wrangle dogs, horses and cattle.

Chimpanzees continued to earn top billing in comedies. In 1926, a series of college comedies produced by J.R. Bray Studios teamed juvenile Buddy Messinger with a chimpanzee named Mr. X.

Monkeys turned up in various comic situations. A monkey plays a tambourine in a band in the Fox Sunshine comedy *The Heart Snatchers* (1920). In *Sweetie* (1923), Jennie the Monkey stands on a street corner dancing the shimmy for loose change. A monkey sits in auditorium rafters, spilling ink on Lloyd Hamilton's head in *Good Morning* (1924). A monkey slams Buster Keaton in the head with a cocoanut in *The Navigator* (1924).

Strangely, an organ grinder's monkey came to play a pivotal role in one of Keaton's most sentimental films, *The Cameraman* (1928). Keaton is assisted in his duties as a newsreel cameraman by a cute, scene-stealing monkey known in real life as Josephine. Keaton comes into possession of the monkey under morbid circumstances. The cameraman, in a hurry to film a parade in Chinatown, rushes down the street lugging his bulky camera equipment. He collides with an organ grinder and his camera drops squarely on top of the organ grinder's monkey. The monkey appears to be dead, and a cop forces Keaton to give the organ grinder cash as compensation. The cop then tells Keaton that he has, in effect, bought the dead monkey and it is his responsibility to properly dispose of the creature. Keaton slips down

Laurel (on the floor) and Hardy are in a fine mess with a horse in *Wrong Again* (1929).

an alley and dumps the monkey on a trash can, but the monkey regains consciousness and leaps onto Keaton's shoulders to evade a barking dog. The monkey develops an immediate attachment to Keaton. The animal is still clinging to Keaton's shoulder as the dauntless cameraman films a tong war in Chinatown. The monkey makes herself useful, starting with firing a Gatling gun at tong thugs. When a tong stalks Keaton, the monkey grabs a knife, hops onto the tong's back, and jabs him repeatedly with the blade.

The monkey, having bonded with her new master, seeks to model herself after the cameraman. She wears a cap backwards, like Keaton. She tries to operate the camera like Keaton. At first, her tampering with the camera sets up an 11th-hour crisis for Keaton. Keaton returns to the newsreel office unaware that the monkey has removed the filmbox from the camera. The boss assumes that Keaton neglected to load his camera prior to shooting. Infuriated, the boss ejects Keaton from his office. Keaton takes his camera out on a lake in a rowboat in hope of capturing newsreel-worthy footage. The monkey, as Keaton's assistant, operates the rudder of the boat while Keaton gets ready to load the camera. It is while sorting through his filmboxes that Keaton discovers the film reel with the lost tong-war footage. Before he can decide what to do with the reel, he sees a rowboat overturn in the middle of the lake. The rowboat's passengers, now thrashing about in the water, are Sally (Marceline Day), a woman who has captivated Keaton from the start of the film, and Harold (Harold Goodwin), a rival cameraman who has been competing with Keaton for

Sally's affections. Harold desperately abandons Sally to save himself. Sally is unconscious by the time that Keaton rescues her and she remains unaware of Keaton's heroics when Harold later takes credit for saving her. But the monkey, who took charge of the camera after Keaton dived into the lake, managed to record Keaton's rescue of Sally. Sally gets to see this footage, which succeeds in both exhibiting Keaton's heroism and exposing Harold's fraud. So, in the end, Josephine's monkeying with the camera has brought Keaton both crisis and victory. This monkey mischief had, all in all, a much greater effect than a monkey slamming a cocoanut onto the comedian's head.

Josephine was a talented animal. It is the same monkey that clings onto Charlie Chaplin's head as the Little Tramp crosses a tightrope in *The Circus* (1928), and she is the same monkey who misdirects the bad guy pursuing Harold Lloyd through a ship by clomping around in man-sized boots in *The Kid Brother* (1927).

Harold Lloyd and Josephine the monkey in *The Kid Brother* (1927) (courtesy www.doctormacro.com).

Actors had a hard time working with animals. Dorothy Devore, who worked with a monkey in *Hold Your Breath*, said, "This monkey was in many scenes, and he would get excited and bite me — the poor thing. I felt so sorry for the monkey, but quite often I was all cut up and bitten."[1] She also did a scene in which she had to slide off a horse, but the horse lost patience and became feisty. They had to use ropes to control the horse. Devore was surprised that she was able to get through the scene without breaking both of her legs.

A chimp named Joe Martin starred in a series of comedies for the Victor Film Company from 1916 to 1917. Series installments included *What Darwin Missed* (1916) and *Making Monkey Business* (1917). Martin moved to Universal, where he remained a popular star for nearly five years. The chimp was featured prominently in trade magazines. A double-page advertisement, dated April, 1920, featured Martin in a cowboy outfit — chaps, gun belt, and ten-gallon hat. The series was so successful that Universal launched a second chimp series starring a chimp billed as "Mrs. Joe Martin."

Martin had been trained by Curly Stecker and his wife, who trained a wide variety of animals. The ill-tempered ape once escaped from the studio and broke into someone's home, causing much destruction before he was finally recaptured. Diana Serra Cary, the former child star known as Baby Peggy, once had to pose for publicity photos with Martin. Cary wrote, "My skin crawled whenever the chimp put his hairy arms around my shoulders."[2] According to Cary, Joe Martin bit Mrs. Stecker in the arm while she was strapping him into a dentist chair for a scene. Stecker, enraged, beat the chimp with a crowbar. He had ended up knocking out a number of the chimp's teeth before he stopped. Cary recognized the sad twist of the scene — a movie star chimp known for his big grinning teeth got his teeth bashed out by his trainer. This, though, was not the end of the attack. Cary wrote, "[A]s though emerging from a trance, the trainer realized what he had done. Looking into the animal's pain-crazed eyes, he knew if he ever let him free now, the murderous chimp was capable of tearing any man to pieces."[3] Stecker, who carried a gun in case an animal got out of control, removed his gun from his belt and shot Martin while onlookers stared in horror and disbelief.

Stecker did not generally have good relationships with his animals. He had to keep a safe distance from Charley the elephant, who remained hostile towards the trainer for an instance when Stecker beat him with a chain. Press accounts of the day indicated that the elephant had crushed the trainer by accidentally sitting on him and the studio responded by retiring the elephant to a zoo. Cary, though, insists that this story was untrue. She provided a graphic account in her autobiography of the elephant getting loose and intentionally going after Stecker, who screamed for his life before the elephant stomped him to death. The elephant, according to Cary, was shot to death on the scene.

Snooky the Chimp was another popular comic ape. Snooky is up to his usual mischief when he smokes cigarettes and plays with a gun in the company of a baby in *A Tray Full of Trouble* (1920). The man in charge was William Campbell, a director who became one of the foremost specialists of animal comedies. Campbell developed a particular fondness for monkeys. His other chimp comedies included *Jazz Monkey* (1919), *Monkey Stuff* (1919), *Prohibition Monkey* (1920) and *Monkey Shines* (1922). Campbell was also responsible for the controversial gorilla-centric exploitation feature *Ingagi* (1931). The film's producers at Congo Pictures purported that *Ingagi*, which featured a tribe of gorilla-worshiping women, was the result of a documentary crew following an expedition to Africa. The truth, though, was that the action was staged entirely by Campbell.

Monkeys, chimps and orangutans continued to be useful to comedy makers. A monkey shoots bullets out of a meat grinder in the Three Stooges comedy *Goofs and Saddles* (1937). In *Tricky Dicks* (1953), a monkey gets hold of a gun and shoots Shemp Howard in the backside. In *Bedtime for Bonzo* (1951), a psychology professor (Ronald Reagan) raises Bonzo the chimp to test his heredity theories. Bonzo creates chaos in the professor's household. He tears opens a pillow and scatters feathers around the room. He makes a mess again trying to operate a vacuum cleaner. Bonzo went on to become the star player of a college football team in his next film, *Bonzo Goes to College* (1952).

The success of *Every Which Way but Loose* (1978), which showed Clint Eastwood clowning with a drunken orangutan, led to a spate of simian comedies. *Going Ape* (1981) has Tony Danza inheriting three mischievous orangutans from his uncle. The orangutans mostly make funny faces and smash furniture. One orangutan steals a floppy hat from co-star Jessica Walter. When Walter gets angry, the orangutan waits for her to turn around and then grabs her backside. Eventually, Danny DeVito shows up looking more ape-like than the orangutans.

The producers of *Air Bud* (1997), a film about a dog that can play basketball, traded the canine for a simian with *MVP: Most Valuable Primate*, which followed the adventures of a chimp that joins a junior league hockey team. Next, the producers introduced a chimp spy in *Spymate* (2003). Much like the Fox chimp using wire effects to climb a magic rope and ride a magic carpet, this chimp uses CGI effects to demonstrate a series of amazing skills — skiing, skateboarding, fencing, kung fu fighting. The spy chimp riding on a skateboard is not much different than the Fox chimp riding on roller skates. A film that used the same premise but replaced the steady stream of special effects with a steady stream of pratfalls was *Funky Monkey* (2004), the story of a sympathetic trainer (Matthew Modine) who frees an experimental spy chimp from a CIA laboratory.

Jason Alexander, playing a nervous hotel manager, pursues an orangutan trained to steal jewels in *Dunston Checks In* (1996). A set-piece of the film, featured prominently in the trailer, has a matronly woman lying on her stomach on a massage table without being aware that the individual massaging her back is none other than the orangutan. The woman, aroused by the massage, shrieks with joy when the orangutan smacks her backside. "More," she demands, "I like it rough!" Joe Martin, for all his flaws, was never so rude as to resort to smacking, groping or fondling a woman's buttocks for a laugh.

In recent years, capuchin monkeys have acted as scene-stealers in a number of major comedy films. In *Ace Ventura: When Nature Calls* (1995), Jim Carrey is accompanied on a perilous mission to Africa by a capuchin monkey named Spike. Spike, as combative as Keaton's capuchin monkey in *The Cameraman*, tasers a villain who is withholding information. A capuchin monkey has contributed much to the comic relief of *Pirates of the Caribbean* (2003) and its three sequels. The monkey, adopted by pirates as a ship mascot, becomes invulnerable when the pirate crew is doomed to a joyless immortality for stealing an ancient Aztec chest. The monkey becomes a nuisance for stealing the pirates' personal effects, ranging from a medallion to a glass eye, and the pirates vent their frustration by habitually shooting the undead little fellow. Ben Stiller is abused by a mischievous capuchin monkey named Dexter in *Night at the Museum* (2006). The monkey repeatedly slaps Stiller in the face, bites him on the nose, and urinates on him. The monkey in *The Navigator* only brained Keaton with a cocoanut. This supports the view that, without censorship, comedy has gotten less creative and more puerile. The capuchins have, nonetheless, been a lucky charm for these contemporary film franchises, which have earned a combined total of $4 billion in worldwide box-office receipts.

Even more popular than apes in silent comedy films were dogs. Pal the Dog proved to be an excellent babysitter in *Mind the Baby* (1924). Pal pushes the baby around in a carriage, carries the baby, puts him in a crib, and gives him a bottle. He protects the baby from kidnapper Fred Spencer. He even rescues the baby from an alligator. A tight shot shows the alligator and baby in the same frame together. Astonishingly, this is no composite shot or split-screen. The baby is crying as the alligator has a hold of him by his shirt tail. It looks as if the alligator's jaw has been wired shut and the baby's garment has been affixed to its mouth by the same wires. The dog clenches his teeth around the alligator's tail and drags him away from the baby. Steve Massa and Ben Model, struck by the outrageousness of *Mind the Baby*, presented the film at a Museum of Modern Art exhibit in 2009.

In 1923, Hal Roach featured a variety of animals, including cats, ducks, a dog, a monkey and a goat, in the "Dippy Doo-Dads" series. The animals, supplied by trainer Tony Campanaro, were typically dressed up in costumes and placed in scaled-down sets to perform in spoofs of then-current movie melodramas.

Universal's Century comedies featured a number of animals. Maude the Mule was showcased in *The Kickin' Fool* (1922), *Me and My Mule* (1922) and *Hee! Haw!* (1923). Queenie the Horse was featured in *Horse Tears* (1922) and *Bath Day* (1922). Sally the Horse was featured in *A Dark Horse* (1922). Diana Serra Cary had vivid memories working on the Century lot. She wrote, "The disconsolate roars and rank odors emanating from the big cats' cages and the elephant's corral gave ample warning to anyone approaching this corner of the lot that danger and even stronger odors lay ahead."[4]

Universal also put the trained animals to use in their serials. Jacko the chimpanzee led Elmo Lincoln to a damsel in distress in the "Elmo the Fearless" serial. The heroes of "The Lion Man" serial plunge off a roof and drop inside a cage with a man-eating lion.

The ostrich is without the beauty of the peacock or the regalness of the eagle. This tall, noodly necked, round-bellied bird, with its outrageously large physique, grotesque features and restless temperament, is a funny bird. If Mack Swain had been a bird, he would have been an ostrich. A very early film amused audiences simply by showing an ostrich eating the flowers out of a woman's hat. It is no wonder that the clownish bird seemed ideally suited to early slapstick comedies. Ostriches turned up in farm comedies along with cows and chickens. In *Poor Policy* (1915), Billie Ritchie grapples with an ostrich that has swallowed a bracelet he bought for his girlfriend. Similarly, an ostrich swallows a valuable locket in the Keystone comedy *The Surf Girl* (1916).

The problem is that an ostrich has little sense of showmanship and absolutely no sense of humor. Claire Luce routinely rode an ostrich onstage for a dance number in a *Ziegfeld Follies* show. Some nights, when the ostrich wasn't in the mood to stop on cue, the singer was carried off stage and the musical number had to carry on without her. Allegedly, W. C. Fields decided one night to pluck out one of the ostrich's feathers and the bird responded by chasing Fields into the street. Fields later did a scene in *You're Telling Me!* (1934) where, after a bout of heavy drinking, he stumbles home with an ostrich on a leash. The comedian and the bird, with their similarly rotund forms, were an ideally suited pair.

The ostrich, despite its laugh-provoking abilities, was a consistently dangerous and unpredictable animal. In 1916, Lillian Peacock was injured while filming a comedy scene with an ostrich. Cast and crew gathered at an ostrich farm at the San Diego Exposition, where Peacock was expected to ride atop an ostrich known as General Funston. The ostrich proved to be unfriendly and resisted letting the actress climb on its back. She finally was able to sit on the ostrich for a few minutes before it became agitated and threw her to the

Billy Bevan with an ostrich friend.

ground. *Universal Weekly* reported, "Miss Peacock wrenched her leg in the fall and was laid up for several days following her accident."[5] The actress was not intimidated by the experience. A few months later, she sustained internal injuries while leaping between automobiles during a chase scene. She died as a result of her injuries little more than a year later.

In 1933, Shirley Temple had a similar experience with an ostrich during the production of *Kid in Africa*. Temple was riding in a carriage pulled along by an ostrich when the ostrich became startled by the lights and bolted forward. Temple was thrown from the carriage but was fortunately unhurt. Less fortunate was Billie Ritchie, who was severely injured (and later died from internal injuries) when attacked by ostriches on the set of *A Twilight Baby* (1920). Joe Rock, as sturdy a comedian as he was, knew better than to roughhouse with an ostrich. A scene in *Chop Suey Louie* (1923) called for Rock to grab an ostrich around its neck to squeeze out a valuable watch consumed by the feathered pest. A real ostrich was alternated in shots with a puppet ostrich to allow Rock to engage in rowdy play without the risk of injury. The puppet, fairly convincing in its design, is thoroughly abused. Rock, pressing its neck with all his might, watches intently as a bulge created by the watch slips up and down the puppet's long, skinny neck. Of course, special effects have improved over the years. It was much easier by the time that Ben Stiller had to face an attack by ostriches in *Night at the Museum* (2006). Stiller never had to deal with so much as an ostrich feather as his ostriches were entirely CGI.

Animals of many varieties were unpredictable and dangerous. In *The Flower Girl* (1924), Baby Peggy leads around a jackass with two baskets of flowers draped over its back. Diana Serra Cary explained that the jackass was mean-spirited and, when an actress plucked a flower out of a basket, the animal "laid back his ears, bared his teeth and turned on her."[6] He chased her through the stages. She figured to escape by climbing an electrician's ladder but the jackass bit her on the backside before she was able to climb out of range. The actress was fuming mad when she found the producer and demanded that he get rid of "that goddamned fire-breathing dragon."[7]

A wide variety of animals got their chance in the spotlight. This included pinnipeds. A sea lion commanded a submarine in the Sennett short *The Summer Girls* (1918). Louise Fazenda and Sydney Chaplin acquiesced to supporting roles opposite a trained seal in the feature comedy *The Galloping Fish* (1924).

Animals provided wholesome fun for the entire family, although the Kansas Board of Review objected to a scene in the Hal Roach comedy *South of the North Pole* (1924) in which a man put a corset on a donkey. Also, the New York censor board excised a scene in *Snooky's Fresh Heir* (1921) in which Snooky the Chimp was given a diaper change.

Animals were less dominant in comedies after silent films ended. Directors cast the critters in brief roles for the purpose of throwaway gags. A prop duck shows up just long enough to nip Andy Clyde on the nose in *Old Sawbones* (1935). In *In Walked Charley* (1932), a horse's main job is to strut through a posh mansion dressed in a satin evening gown.

Animals can provide that extra zany touch needed to get a rise out of an audience. *Roars and Uproars* (1922) opens on a pit bull smoking a pipe. Andy Clyde is seen playing checkered with Puzzums the cat in *His Unlucky Night* (1928). People laughed at the pipe-smoking pit bull or the checkers-playing cat in 1920s, and they would laugh at these funny animals today if someone put them on YouTube. Benjamin Svetkey, a college professor, has recently conducted research to understand the popularity of funny cat videos on YouTube. To understand funny cats, the professor would do well to look back into the history of film comedy.

Animal Rampages, Part 1

The climax of the 1917 Fox comedy *Roaring Lions and Wedding Bells* featured lions getting loose at a wedding reception and the bridal party and guests fleeing in terror. Panic

A mallard advises Charley Chase (right) to duck as Tiny Sanford gets ready to swing in *Movie Night* (1929) (courtesy www.doctormacro.com).

stimulates impulsive reactions, irrational behavior and poorly thought-out decisions. In other words, panic stimulates comic behavior. To a large extent, slapstick comedy depends on elements of fear, peril, confusion, excitement and surprise. A man-eating lion making an unexpected visit to a wedding reception was certain to provide all of those elements. The lion was a frightening, anarchic figure which breached normal order and removed social controls. *Roaring Lions and Wedding Bells* proved to be a major success at the box office and inspired a long-lasting trend of lions-on-the-loose comedies.

By the time that *Roaring Lions and Wedding Bells* was produced, it was already a familiar comic premise in American comedies to have a wedding party disrupted in a devastating manner. *A Quiet Little Wedding* (1913) has a disappointed rival (Charles Inslee) break up a wedding with a pie fight. In *A Muddy Romance* (1913), a couple is getting married in a rowboat out in the middle of a lake when a rival drains the lake and leaves the couple stuck in mud. A rival (Syd Chaplin) swallows the engagement ring at an engagement party in *Hushing the Scandal* (1915). In *On Her Wedding Day* (1913), the groom's friends think that it would be fun to sprinkle red pepper on the bride's bouquet. The wedding is thrown into disarray when the guests, irritated by the red pepper, erupt into a mass sneezing fit. The 1908 Georges Méliès comedy *Le Mariage de Thomas Poirot* (released in America as *Fun with the Bridal Party*) involves a pair of pranksters who sneak into a wedding reception uninvited. First, the pranksters attach ropes to the chairs so that they can pull chairs away from guests as they try to sit down. Then, the pranksters disguise as ghosts and scare away the bridal party and guests. In *The Fatal Note* (1915), a wedding dinner nearly goes off without a hitch until a rival shows up. The groom (Billie Ritchie) intercepts a note that the rival tried to pass to the bride and he writes back for the rival to meet him across the hall. The rival rushes off expecting to rendezvous with the bride but is surprised to find himself face-to-face with the irate groom. This confrontation results in a large-scale battle involving various paraphernalia, including dumbbells and a fire hose. Injured in the process are wedding guests, including an old man with gout. This premise continued throughout the following decade. *Shot in the Getaway* (1920), a Universal Rainbow comedy, is a good example. A father demands that his daughter wed a man named Percy even though she loves another man. The girl is relieved when an escaped convict breaks up the wedding and scares Percy away. In *Cutie* (1928), Glen Cavender, a defeated rival, sabotages Dorothy Devore's wedding to Earl McCarthy by tying their car to a truck. This causes the car to be pulled to pieces when the couple tries to drive off.

Independent of the wedding disruptions, comedy films also featured big, scary carnivores invading benign human environs or disturbing leisure activities. *The Bull and the Picnickers* (1902), an Edison comedy, starts out with a group of men and women enjoying a picnic under a shade tree. Suddenly, a large bull comes along and the picnickers go into a panic. According to the Edison Catalog, "The girls jump up and climb a fence, and in doing so there is a great display of hosiery."[8] All except one man runs for cover. The man tries to chase the bull away but he is repeatedly knocked down for his effort. He eventually realizes that he doesn't have a chance and flees the vicinity. At this point, the bull reaches up and undoes his head, which is merely part of a costume. Emerging from the costume are Happy Hooligan and Gloomy Gus, who proceed to eat the food that the picnickers have left behind.

One of the earliest animals to cause a comic riot was a common dog. In *Help! Help! Hydrophobia!* (1913), a dog is fed a new milk formula that leaves a white foam around its mouth. While making its way through town, the dog panics residents who assume the dog is rabid.

Wild animals, rabid or not, did not belong in the company of civilized people. That was the message of the 1908 Pathé Frères comedy *Cumbersome First Prize*, in which a man unexpectedly wins a llama in a lottery. The man is trying to get the llama home when the clumsy dromedary bumps into a tradesman, causing the man's provisions to spill into the street, and knocks a pair of women to the ground. The man takes the animal into a park and causes a panic among the visitors. This is not much different than the 1912 Gaumont comedy *Zigoto, policier, trouve une corde* (translated as *Zigoto, police officer, finds a rope*), in which Lucien Bataille grabs a rope without realizing that it is attached to a bull and then proceeds to walk the dangerous animal along the avenue.

A large-scale, multi-species animal rampage occurred in the 1915 Victor comedy *Joe Martin Turns 'Em Loose*. A woman accepts a crate as part of an inheritance without realizing that the crate contains orangutan Joe Martin. Martin climbs out of a window and makes his way to the circus, where he sets about letting the animals loose. Elephants and camels launch into a stampede that nearly takes down the circus tent while a variety of big cats, including lions, tigers, leopards and pumas, terrorize the residents of a nearby neighborhood.

Of course, men also intruded on the domain of wild animals. One simple comic situation — a man encounters a bear in the woods and he climbs up a tree to evade it — has sustained as a stock comedy premise for American filmmakers for nearly one-hundred years. The earliest known version of this routine appears in *The Brave Hunter* (1912), a Biograph comedy in which a bear chases future comedy king Mack Sennett up a tree. As of this writing, a great big bear is presenting a comic threat in a movie release, *Did You Hear About the Morgans?* (2009). It is inevitable when city slicker Hugh Grant moves to a cabin in the woods that he will encounter a bear. Grant acts mildly upset and mentions his wife's affiliation with PETA before he runs for cover. Grant had no real reason to be afraid as he was separated from the bear by a strong wire barrier, which the filmmakers were able to digitally remove in post-production. Sarah Jessica Parker tries to spray the bear with mace but she misfires and sprays the mace into Grant's face. A police officer arrives at the cabin. He shoots at the bear and the bear runs off. The script called for a gun to be fired at the bear to scare him off, but the film crew did not want to actually scare the bear on the set and made a point to add the gunshots in post-production. The mace was new, the PETA reference was new and the now-you-see-it-now-you-don't wire barrier was new, but everything else had been done before.

Years before the Keystone Cops went into action, bears had been performing comedy antics and rough stuff on vaudeville stages and circus tents. Moxey the Bear wrestled his trainer in front of breathless crowds. Big Jim was an amusing bear who sped across the stage on roller skates. This was a talent pool well suited to slapstick comedy.

The earliest-known bear comedy is the 1911 Lux comedy *Patouillard et l'ours policier* (loosely translated as *Policeman Patouillard and His Bear*), in which an animal trainer employed by the police uses a dancing bear to track down a pair of master pickpockets.

Marie Prevost is wary of a bear's intentions, while Ben Turpin (left) and Heinie Conklin are simply terrified in *When Love Is Blind* (1919) (courtesy Steve Rydzewski).

The bear attacks the fugitives just as they are about to get away in a rowboat. The men leap into the lake to escape, but the bear clambers into the water and drags them back to shore.

In the Biograph comedy *The Brave Hunter* (1912), Mabel Normand comes across a circus bear on the loose in the woods. Mabel, unafraid, gets chummy with the bear and teaches it tricks. The bear could not be more docile. The two playfully wrestle with each other, the bear stands up on its hind legs to beg for food, and Mabel rides out of the woods on the bear's back. Mabel's charm and beauty continued to attract bears. In *Oh! Those Eyes* (1912), Mabel manages to befriend a bear after her father and two suitors have fled the vicinity. In the Keystone comedy *Mabel's Bear Escape* (1914), Mabel is out for a picnic when a pair of bears come along and chase after her.

The bear became a standard comic threat. Bear attacks, in fact, were more common in Keystone comedies than pie fights. *A Bear Affair* (1915) focuses on a hunting party that encounters an unfriendly bear in the mountains. Two bears chase Roscoe Arbuckle up a telephone pole in *Mother's Boy* (1913), and a single bear chases Arbuckle into a pond in *He Would a Hunting Go* (1913). *When Hazel Met the Villain* (1914) is also when Hazel met the bear. Hazel, tied to railroad tracks by the villain, is fretting about getting flattened by a locomotive when a bear shows up to frighten her further. In *A Bear Escape* (1914), a fugitive (Ford Sterling) overpowers two detectives (Mack Sennett and Fred Mace) and ties them to a tree in the woods. The detectives are struggling to free themselves when a belligerent bear shows up. Ford Sterling uses a bear to ward off creditors in *A Landlord's Troubles* (1917). Among Sennett's other bear comedies were *Homemade Movies* (1922), *One Cylinder Love* (1923) and *Honeymoon Hardships* (1925).

Other comedy producers introduced bears into the action. Dorothy Devore fled from a bear in the Christie comedy *Her Bear Escape* (1919). A bear invaded a campsite in the Vitagraph comedy *Billy the Bear Tamer* (1915). Our Gang encountered a bear while hunting in the woods in *It's a Bear* (1924). A reviewer with *The Moving Picture World* noted of the Pathé comedy *A Bear Escape* (1913), "There is a bear in the picture, and he trees the nearly bare professor."[9] A colleague who viewed the Imp comedy *A Pair of Bears* (1913) observed in his analysis: "A couple of live bears and some burlesque actors furnish the chief amusement in this number. The bears get loose and have many exciting experiences."[10] More in line with *Roaring Lions and Wedding Bells* was *Caught with the Goods* (1915), an L-KO comedy that climaxed with a bear escaping from a menagerie and invading a town.

Bears were not all bad. The hero of Sennett's *Her Circus Knight* is Bruno the Bear, who takes off in a chariot after the bad guys, rescues the girl, and chases the bad guys up a telephone pole. A true professional, Bruno worked on a consistent basis. By now, the bear had become a familiar player in the Sennett comedies. He regularly followed the crew to various locations. *The Snow Cure* (1916), a slapstick farce set at a snowbound mountain resort, features Bruno chasing a group of men down a toboggan run. The animal also co-starred opposite Gale Henry in *Her Week-End* (1919). He teamed up with Brownie the Bear to torment Larry Semon in *Bears and Bad Men* (1918). Bruno and Brownie also had competition from Bessie the Bear, who starred in the Triangle comedy *It's a Bear!* (1919).*

Bears could just as easily be cute as they could be vicious. A bear cub named Cubby found work at Sennett. Cute little Cubby was not about to scare anyone. Cubby, when introduced in the Sennett circus comedy *When Summer Comes* (1922), is wearing oversized

---

*It is an indication of the popularity of this trend that, between 1913 and 1924, seven live-action comedies were released with the title *It's a Bear!*

Elton John–style eyeglasses and dining with the rest of the circus folk at a table. Mildred June affectionately feeds the bear cub milk from a baby bottle. Later, Cubby is shown playing on a lawn with a dog. In *Mabel's Wilful Way* (1915), Fatty Arbuckle and Mabel Normand casually feed their ice cream cones to a bear at the zoo. At one point, Arbuckle feeds the bear by holding the tip of his cone between his teeth and sticking his head between the cage bars.

In *The Gold Rush* (1925), Chaplin is walking casually along a mountain ledge, unaware that he is being followed by a bear. The bear ducks into a cave in the mountainside without ever having made his presence known. This bear-on-the-loose routine, as established, depended on a confrontation between a bear and a man and the man having a frightened response to the bear. Chaplin plays against expectations, turning the situation on its head — the man has no confrontation with the bear and the man, having failed to confront the bear, cannot have the anticipated frightened response.

Still, the bear does return later, at which time it ambles through the back door of Chaplin's cabin. By this time Chaplin has befriended another prospector (Mack Swain). The pair has been trapped in the cabin due to a blizzard. The men are suffering from starvation and need a meal quickly if they are to survive. An actual bear is used for the establishing shot, but a man in a bear suit acts as the bear for the remainder of the scene. Chaplin hides under his bed sheets, but he gets knocked out of bed as Swain scrambles past in flight from the bear. Chaplin, trying to hold the bear back from getting to Swain, tightens his arms around the bear's legs as the shaggy creature's ample backside slams into his face. Chaplin is thrashed about while he grapples with the bear. The bear turns on him, at which point Chaplin leaps on the bed and backs into a corner. He looks horrified, as if he is certain that he is about to be killed, when the bear suddenly turns away and wanders out the front door. Chaplin picks up a rifle, points it through the doorway and fires off a shot. The starving prospectors now have meat to eat. The scene is mostly meant to be dramatic, although the fakery of the bear suit undermines that purpose.

Keaton performed a fairly standard bear scene in *Hard Luck* (1921). The comedian, trying to lasso a horse, tosses his rope out of range of the camera frame. He pulls on the rope with all of his might, at which point a bear (with the lasso tight around its neck) emerges angrily from the brush. Buster runs off with the bear in furious pursuit.

More inventive than the *Hard Luck* scene was Keaton's encounter with a pair of brawny bears in *The Balloonatic* (1923). Keaton, hunting rifle in hand, crawls after a squirrel without realizing that a bear is following closely behind. As Keaton gets ready to shoot the squirrel, a second bear pokes its head out of a pit in front of him. Keaton is nose-to-nose with the bear. He cautiously backs away while, at the same time, raising his rifle. He finally slams the rifle butt down on the bear's head, which simultaneously causes the rifle to fire and kill the bear behind him. The two bears, one on either side, go down at the same exact moment. In this case, Keaton created a well-structured gag sequence which put his character in grave danger and then had him rescued by way of an astonishing twist of fate. The scene ends with bulky prop animal carcasses lying on the ground, much like exploding elephant scene in *Roughest Africa*, but the scene is marked more by cleverness than gruesomeness. The bears, sacrificed to the comedy gods, did not die in vain.

Before *The Balloonatic*, it had already become a stock routine to have a hunter led from his pursuit of a harmless furry creature (a rabbit or a squirrel), into a surprise encounter with a frighteningly large predator (a bear or a lion). In *Free and Easy* (1921), Lige Conley is calmly preparing to shoot a rabbit poised at the peak of an incline, but just then a lion

Buster Keaton is visited by a curious bear in *The Balloonatic* (1923) (courtesy Robert Arkus).

clambers onto the incline and displaces the rabbit. Conley leaps to his feet and flees the scene. In a wide-shot, Conley can be seen running for his life, unaware that nothing but the rabbit is following him. In *A Friendly Husband* (1923), Lupino Lane is getting ready to shoot a squirrel when a bear appears out of nowhere. Lane, his legs trembling, turns to look at the camera as the bear licks the barrel of his gun. The distraught hunter finally bolts to avoid being mauled to death by the bear. He is stopping to catch his breath when a rabbit jumps out of the bushes and nearly scares him to death.

Keaton ran into a bear one last time, in *The General* (1926). The comedian is hurrying through the woods on a stormy night when a burst of lightning illuminates a great big bear. It is like a scene out of a carnival's haunted house ride where flashing lights momentarily reveal a frightening tableau.

Lige Conley is not a very sporting hunter in *Wild Game* (1924). He turns a special lever that extends the barrel of his gun several feet until it is nearly touching his helpless rabbit prey. He pulls back on the trigger, at which point the barrel breaks in half. This is just the start of his bad karma, for just then a brown bear clambers into view and chases after him. The fact that Conley is on a tropical island, not a known habitat for brown bears, suggests that the bear came through a time/space rift like the polar bear on *Lost*. Conley comes across a quaking bush. His frightened valet (Spencer Bell), who has been hiding from the bear, emerges cautiously from the bush.

Bears continued to come after Bell in other films, including *Below Zero* (1925) and *Creeps* (1926). In *Below Zero*, Bell is out in snowy wilds of Canada when he bumps into a bear. Bell, terrified, runs off with the bear in hot pursuit. The bear, amazingly, scrambles up a tree after Bell. Bell loses his grip and falls from the tree. The bear slides back down after him.

In *Smith's Vacation* (1926), Mr. Smith (Raymond McKee) is bathing *au naturale* in the hot springs of Yellowstone National Park when a bear comes along and chases after him. This scene, like the aforementioned *Bear Escape*, was more about the bare than the bear. Mr. Smith, who often found himself in embarrassing situations, was not so much worried about the bear catching up to him as he was worried about other tourists seeing him without clothing. He is able to find temporary cover behind a geyser.

An appropriate sound debut for the comedy bear occurred in *The Rogue Song* (1930), in which Laurel & Hardy go inside a cave to take refuge from a storm. The camera does not follow the comedians into the cave, it instead remains trained on the dark mouth of the cave. The comedians can be heard in conversation. Hardy asks Laurel where he got the fur coat. Laurel responds that he doesn't have a fur coat. A bear's roar is heard, at which point the comedians come scrambling out of the cave. By now, the audience had seen so many bear scenes that they had no need to see the actual bear.

Bears continued to plague comedians in the sound era. During the 1940s and 1950s, the bears appeared most often onscreen with Abbott & Costello. The shaggy beasts, invariably portrayed by men in bear suits, terrorize the duo in *Ride 'Em Cowboy* (1942), *Hit the Ice* (1943), *The Naughty Nineties* (1945), *Abbott and Costello Meet the Killer, Boris Karloff* (1949), *Jack and the Beanstalk* (1952) and *Lost in Alaska* (1952). Most times, these were fleeting episodes with no clever twist and no importance to the plot. In *Abbott and Costello Meet the Killer, Boris Karloff*, Costello accidentally lights a stick of dynamite and gets rid of it by tossing it into a cave. The dynamite explodes, which rouses a bear from hibernation. Costello sees the bear, screams, and runs off. The bear is never seen again. Costello spends even less time with a polar bear in *Lost in Alaska*. A chase scene in *Ride 'Em Cowboy* shows the team driving through a cave and coming out the other side with a bear at the steering wheel. Costello, in a panic, shoves the bear out of the car. In *Hit the Ice*, Costello is skiing downhill to get away from gangsters when a bear hitches a ride on the back of his skis. This prompts Abbott to shout, "You have a bear behind." Costello, believing that Abbott is saying that he has a "bare behind," becomes embarrassed and attempts to cover his backside. *The Naughty Nineties* made more elaborate use of a bear. The pair is desperate to get their drunken friend out of a casino before he loses all of his money. Abbott tries to create a commotion by entering the casino wearing a bear costume. Abbott is putting on the costume just as a real bear gets loose in the casino. The comedy in the scene is meant to come from Costello assuming that the bear is merely his partner in disguise, and smacking the vicious bear for failing to stick to the plan. The scene fails to generate the appropriate excitement as the real bear and the fake bear look no different from one another in their respective bears suits.

Bears ran their full, if limited, gamut with Abbott & Costello and they managed to do little else in other films. Just as Costello is chased by a bear in *Abbott and Costello Meet the Killer, Boris Karloff*, hunter Andy Clyde is chased by a bear in *Just a Bear* (1931). Bears got to ride in car with comedians other than Abbott & Costello. In *Idiots Deluxe* (1945), The Three Stooges drive off in a car, unaware that a bear has climbed into the backseat. The Stooges, once they see the bear, leap out of the car, leaving the bear to crash into some trees. In *The Love Bug* (1968), David Tomlinson picks up a bear as a passenger during a car race through the Sierra Nevada Mountain Range. Lively bear skin rugs also turned up on a number of occasions. In the "Our Gang" comedy *Night 'n' Gales* (1937), a rainstorm forces the gang to spend the night in the home of dithery Johnny Arthur. As the children take over his bed, Arthur finds refuge on the living room couch, where he finds warmth under a bear skin rug. The gang sees Arthur covered in the rug and mistake him for an actual bear. The most original use of a bear occurred in *The Life and Times of Judge Roy Bean* (1972), in which a bear turns up as the bailiff in the frontier court of the legendary Judge Bean (Paul Newman).

Bears were still chasing men up into trees, but the esteemed writing team of Ben Hecht, Nunnally Johnson and Charles Lederer found a way to elaborate on this idea for the "Ransom of Red Chief" segment of *O. Henry's Full House* (1952). Kidnappers Fred Allen and Oscar Levant find themselves in possession of an evil brat of a boy. One night, the boy lays down a trail of bread crumbs to lead a bear into camp to terrorize the kidnappers. Once the bear has chased the kidnappers up a tree, the boy bargains to chase away the bear if the terrified men give him their watches. This scene is purely derived from film comedy traditions and is not even suggested in the original O. Henry short story.

The bear even had a place in the 1970s college sex comedies. A bear is introduced in *H.O.T.S* (1979) as the mascot of a college football team. After being kidnapped by a rival team, the bear takes up residence in a sorority house, where it is allowed to roam free and make the place a real animal house. During the course of the film, the bear gets drunk swilling alcohol from a still, rides in a hot-air balloon, and performs laps in a swimming pool.

Bart the Bear, a 1,700-pound Alaskan Kodiak brown bear, was an extraordinarily talented bear who worked regularly in major motion pictures in the 1980s and 1990s. By all accounts, Bart was the sweetest animal offscreen, but he was able to act ferocious on cue. He is the bear who terrorizes John Candy in *The Great Outdoors* (1988). In their first encounter, Candy fires a shotgun at the bear. The shotgun pellets graze the bear's scalp, removing a strip of hair down the middle. The bear, at this point, becomes known as the "Bald-Headed Bear." Later, the bear returns to chase Candy through the woods. Candy runs inside his cabin and slams the door shut. He is standing with his back pressed up against the door when the bear breaks open the door. The door, along with the bear, comes toppling down on Candy. Candy grabs a shotgun and fires at the bear. This time, the shotgun pellets burn away a large patch of fur on the bear's backside. Prosthetic buttocks are used to show the bear running off with a bald backside.

Bart the Bear died in 2000, but his trainer adopted a new bear which he also named Bart. The new Bart made his film debut in the Eddie Murphy comedy *Dr. Dolittle 2* (2001) and has continued to make a career for himself in comedy. In an episode of *Scrubs*, Zack Braff drives out to the woods with a girlfriend and is getting ready to have sex in the car when Bart suddenly arrives to break up the action. In *Without a Paddle* (2004), Bart charges out of the woods to chase after three hapless campers (Seth Green, Matthew Lillard and Dax Shepard). The bear runs fast enough to catch up to Green, who responds by rolling up in the fetal position and sobbing uncontrollably. The bear smells this small, helpless creature and assumes it is an infant in need of protection. He carries off Green to his lair and tries to feed him a dead, mangled squirrel. Green eventually escapes and joins his friends, who promptly climb up a tree to stay out of the bear's reach. Green must have enjoyed the experience because he has a similar scene in *Old Dogs* (2009), during which he sobs uncontrollably while a gorilla cradles him in his arms and rocks him. Bart is also the bear who appears opposite Hugh Grant and Sarah Jessica Parker in *Did You Hear About the*

Morgans? (2009). Grant said that he and Parker got jealous of the haughty superstar bear. As Grant explained, "He wouldn't come out of his trailer until he had 12 cans of iced tea and had been hosed down from head to foot. The crew had to applaud and say, 'Yay, Bart, you're so great.'"[11]

Bart does not have a monopoly on funny bear roles. It was Miz the Bear who had a wrestling match with Sacha Baron Cohen in *Borat* (2006). The bear who got loose in a sports arena in *Semi-Pro* (2008) was Rocky the Bear. Bart's greatest competition has come from a Syrian grizzly bear named Cheyenne. In 2008, Cheyenne had a memorable role in an episode of Spike TV's "A Thousand Ways to Die." The episode features a sex group that has gathered in the woods, dressed in animal pelts for a "furry orgy." A bear that has wandered into camp catches the attention of an intoxicated man, who assumes that the bear is a woman in a pelt. The man is attempting to mount the bear for intercourse when the bear becomes enraged and mauls him. (Just one of the thousand ways to die.) It was only a matter of time after this stunning performance that Cheyenne moved on to big-screen roles. The bear chases "stoner" bikers down a hill in the Boy Scouts comedy *Adventure Scouts Honor* (2008). In *Fired Up* (2009), the bear comes across a group of campers who are skinny-dipping and is overtaken by a mischievous impulse to swipe their clothing.* In *Furry Vengeance* (2010), the bear chases after Brendan Fraser, who takes refuge in a Port-A-Potty. The bear tips over the Port-A-Potty with Fraser inside and then jumps up and down on the structure in a fit of rage. When the bear finally leaves, Fraser emerges from the toilet, covered in excrement. Later, at the climax of the film, the bear arrives at a groundbreaking ceremony and the attendees flee in terror.

Evidently, modern filmmakers and television producers are convinced that the old-fashioned bear attack is best updated with orgies, bestiality, drugs and excrement. After all, this is the era in which Brownie the Bear was replaced by *Late Night*'s Masturbating Bear. The "dirty bear" trend reach its peak in a Comedy Central series *Nick Swardson's Pretend Time*, in which a bear foraging in a woman's cellar rapes a hapless pest exterminator ("Monday Morning Meltdown," 2010).

A debate has arisen as to whether trainers are taking sufficient precautions with the bears. On the set of *Furry Vengeance* (2010), a trainer restrained a bear by chaining it to a three-foot pipe. The brawny beast became attracted to a berry bush planted by the green dresser and managed with ease to rip the pipe out of the ground to free itself. Shortly after *Semi-Pro* wrapped, Rocky the Bear attacked and killed his trainer at the Predators in Action training facility. The California Department of Fish and Game considered having Rocky euthanized, but PETA and other animal rights groups convinced officials to spare the bear.

Film crews have had to learn to be more sensitive and cautious with animals. *Ace Ventura: When Nature Calls* (1995) placed comedian Jim Carrey in an African jungle filled with a variety of wild animals, which was not much different than the situation that had been confronted by Stan Laurel in *Roughest Africa*. But times had changed. Carrey's actions may have looked wild and crazy onscreen but much preparation went on behind the scenes to make sure that no mistakes were made. A scene called for Carrey to join a family of chimps in a grooming session. The actor was made to spend time with the animals in advance of shooting so that they would feel comfortable having him sit among them to pick nits out of their fur. Concealed tethers tied down lions for a scene in which Carrey and the lions

---

*As the result of reshoots, the finished film features a raccoon in place of the bear. Cheyene's trainers at Amazing Animal Productions were contacted to determine the reason for the change, but the company failed to provide a response.

appear together eating a dead zebra. In the film's climax, Carrey had to ride an ostrich to the rescue. The ostrich was trained to sprint a total of 30 feet with weights on its back. The weights were gradually increased to match Carrey's weight to make sure that the animal was conditioned to perform the stunt and would not find it startling to suddenly have to carry the weight of the actor on its back.

Rivaling the bears for movie roles were the elephants. Elephants had also performed successfully in vaudeville. Power's Dancing Elephants, a vaudeville act in the late teens and early twenties, featured elephants that danced, fenced, and played baseball. This immense animal proved to be impressive when projected on a big screen. An elephant raced against an automobile in *A Unique Race* (1899). *Elephants Shooting the Chutes at Luna Park* (1904) showcased a pair of elephants going down a water slide. It was reported in the Edison Catalog, "[The elephant] strikes the water with a tremendous splash, remains under the water for a short time, enjoying his cool bath. It takes considerable coaxing on the part of his Arabian keeper to get him to come out of the water."[12] Bobby Burns and Walter Stull played tramps who adopt an escaped elephant in *The Tramp Elephant* (1912). Vitagraph featured elephants in a number of comedies produced at their Brooklyn facility in 1912. These titles included *Diana's Legacy*, *Mammoth Life Savers* and *An Elephant on Their Hands*. *An Elephant on Their Hands*, which was screened at the Museum of Modern Art's Cruel and Unusual Comedy exhibit in 2009, involves an old man who gets drunk and wanders home with a baby elephant. The following year, Al Christie produced a comedy called *An Elephant on His Hands*, which had to do with a circus going broke and the owner asking his nephew (Eddie Lyons) to take care of the elephant. Eddie's wife, Ramona, is so fond of animals that she will not allow her husband to refuse his uncle's request. Jon C. Mirsalis did research on this lost film because it included an early appearance onscreen by Lon Chaney. Mirsalis wrote, "Eddie has to pay a $300 shipping bill and then the stable he has rented does not allow him to keep the elephant there. When they try to keep the creature in the yard, the neighbors complain and the authorities order it removed. The last scene of the beast shows him dragging a furniture van with Ramona sitting on top and Eddie leading."[13]

Some 84 years later, in 1996, a similar plot was used to team Bill Murray with an elephant in *Larger Than Life*. Murray unexpectedly inherits the elephant and has the executor of the will demanding he pay a sizable bill for the feeding and boarding of the elephant. The elephant has been boarded in a yard but has occasionally broken loose and made forays into the community. The elephant is loose again as Murray goes to take possession of it. Murray observes a broken awning, a smashed fruit stand, and other wreckage that the elephant has left in his wake. He confronts an angry mob, which demands that he take his elephant and get out of town.

Christie produced an elephant-on-the-loose comedy called *His Friend, the Elephant* in 1916. In *Rastus Loses His Elephant* (1913), an elephant gets loose in town and, according to *Moving Picture World*, chases a "crowd upstairs and downstairs."[14] Other elephant comedies include *An Elephant Sleuth* (1912), *Come 'Round an' Take That Elephant Away* (1915), *Too Much Elephant* (1917) and *Cupid's Elephant* (1922). In *Open House* (1926), Johnny Arthur gets involved in the Be-Kind-to-Animals charity and opens his home to a variety of animals, the most troublesome of which is an elephant.

A series of elephant comedies starring Hughie Mack was produced in 1920. The series consisted of six comedies, all of which had the same basic story. The series debut, *Elephants on His Hands* (1920), was written and directed by Vin Moore, who had directed several lion comedies for Century Film. Film historian Cole Johnson calls this film "the *Citizen Kane* of berserk elephant movies."[15] In the opening scene, Mack learns that his uncle has sent him a gift from India. The gift is contained in crates waiting for him down at the pier. A freight man slides open a shed door to reveal a pair of elephants. "These are your little pals," he says. The elephants, on their introduction, snatch away Mack's cigarette and snatch away the missus's hat. Mack ties the elephants to the rear bumper of his car, but the rope breaks during the drive and the elephants go wandering through town. The elephants converge on a fruit stand and gorge themselves. Eventually, Dot Farley, Mack's eccentric maid, catches up to the elephants. She latches the rope onto a door of a building, hoping that this will keep the elephants from getting away, but the animals take the entire wall with them as they march off to explore downtown. They barge into a hotel and break down walls to get inside rooms. An elephant knocks a guest into his rolling bed. An elephant takes a gun away from a hotel detective to shoot Mack in the backside. The elephants invade the showers in the hotel gym, at which point girls, wearing nothing but towels, come running out of the showers. An elephant sprays water into Farley's face. An elephant chases a man into a suite. The man falls onto a bed and the elephant shoves the bed through the wall, leaving the man hanging off the bed several stories above the street.

Comedians found elephants to be useful stooges. Most comedians climbed trees, fences, flagpoles or buildings to elude police, but Max Linder manages in *Seven Years Bad Luck* (1921) to climb on top of a zoo elephant to put himself out of the reach of the police.

In *Smith Family's Candy Shop* (1927), four-year-old Bubbles Smith (Mary Ann Jackson) feeds candy to an elephant at the zoo. The elephant likes the candy so much that it breaks loose from a leg restraint and follows after Bubbles. People on the street panic and run inside shops. The elephant strolls up behind a woman, sitting on her windowsill attempting to clean her window. The elephant pokes its trunk into the woman's backside, which causes her to tumble into her apartment. The elephant has walked off by the time the woman returns to the window. The woman sees a man who has come around the corner and, assuming that he was the one who goosed her, she batters him mercilessly with a broom. The elephant continues to wreak havoc, including shoving cars into a brick wall. Then, the elephant walks into a barbershop. Everyone runs off except for a man leaning back in the barber's chair waiting for a shave. The elephant curls its trunk around a straight razor and proceeds to give the man a shave. The elephant then sticks its nozzle into a jar of powder, sucks up the powder, and blasts it into the man's face. (This is similar to the scene in Buster Keaton's *Go West* [1925], in which cows invade a barber shop.) Later, the elephant catches up with the villainous Andy Clyde and shoots a stream of water at him. Clyde, however, is not to be outdone. He sidles up alongside the elephant with his mouth filled with water. After glancing furtively from side to side, he spits the water out at the elephant and then scurries off before the elephant has time to retaliate.

French comedian Pierre Étaix, a student of silent film comedy, well understood the principles and devices of the genre. It was under his staging that an elephant breaks into a lavish party and incites a riot among the guests in *Yo Yo* (1965).

The adopted elephant premise was revived periodically, although it was not always received with enthusiasm. *Ethel Is an Elephant*, an unsold 1980 pilot, starred Todd Susman as a photographer who adopts an abandoned baby circus elephant and moves the animal into his Manhattan apartment.

In more recent years, an elephant was central to the plot of *Operation Dumbo Drop* (1995). An elephant, as part of a wide assortment of animals, also appeared in *Evan Almighty* (2007).

A popular early film was *Lion, London Zoological Garden* (1895), which featured a zoo attendant antagonizing a lion so that the animal would growl and claw at the camera. This was a preview of things to come.

The lion comedy originated in Europe. In *Cretinetti nella gabbia dei leoni* (1910), André Deed argues with a lion tamer, who takes revenge by tossing Deed into a lion's cage. Deed succeeds in escaping the cage, but he is so upset by the experience that he is haunted by visions of lions. Deed is sitting in a movie theatre watching one of his own films, when actual lions get loose in the theatre. Theatergoers flee for the doors while the lions, fascinated by the comedian's antics onscreen, sit down to calmly watch the film. As the story comes to a close, Deed is relieved to have the lions as fans and sits down next to them to enjoy the rest of the film.

French filmmaker Alfred Machin produced travel films about big-game hunting prior to supervising comedy productions at Pathé's Comica Studios. Machin, who knew that a large-fanged predator could thrill an audience, cast his pet panther Mimir in a number of comedies, including *Babylas vient d'hériter d'une panthère* (1911), *Madame Babylas aime les animaux* (1911) and *Little Moritz chasse les grands fauves* (1911). The protagonist of *Babylas vient d'hériter d'une panthère*, played by Louis Boucot, inherits a panther straight from the wilds of Africa. The panther upsets residents of Boucot's apartment building while in pursuit of a rabbit. The scene climaxes with the panther chasing the rabbit down a chimney flue and bursting out of a fireplace in the bedroom of Boucot's neighbors. The animal creates an even worse commotion when it goes on a rampage in a dress shop. Mimir is later responsible for similar problems when the animal gets loose at a banquet in *Little Moritz chasse les grands fauves*. The final shot of the film, according to film historian Richard Abel, is the panther "licking its paws contentedly among scattered hat and coats."[16]

The trend continued with the Éclair comedy *Gavroche fait une riche marriage* (1912), in which a suitor seeks to impress a rich American woman by showing up at her house with a pair of pet lions. The same year, the Gaumont comedy *La Maison des lions* (released in America as *House of Lions*) depicted lions escaping from a private menagerie and invading a fashionable party.

The earliest American lion comedy that turned up in research for this book was *The Amateur Lion Tamer* (1913), a Vitagraph comedy in which Hughie Mack attempts to dominate a lion. A critic for *Moving Picture World* wrote, "There are some sure-enough lions and they have a lean and hungry look as well as a decidedly ferocious aspect. The escape of the lions from their cage is convincingly carried out. The recapture of one of the lions is a rare bit of realism in which there is no trace of comedy."[17] Mack was not the first funnyman to try to use a whip and a chair to elicit laughs while using a real lion. In 1905, the famous clown Marceline became a Broadway sensation for a comic lion-taming act he performed with real lions in the New York Hippodrome musical extravaganza "A Society Circus." Later, in 1913, Vitagraph released a second lion comedy, which was called *Betty in the Lions' Den*.

Other films of the period relied on fake jungle cats. The Kalem short *Minnie the Tiger* (1915) used an actor in a tiger costume to relate the humorous tale of a man (Bud Duncan) who forms a friendship with a fugitive tiger from the zoo. A still from the Mutual Vogue comedy *Bugckin the Tiger** (1917) shows Ben Turpin locked in a cage with an actor in a tiger costume.

---

*The title was a spoof of the bestselling novel *Bucking the Tiger*, which came out the same year.

Lions were not initially welcomed on a Keystone set. *Gussle Tied to Trouble* (1915) was being filmed in Mt. Baldy when a mountain lion showed up and threatened the crew. The director, Charles Avery, acted swiftly to dispose of the mountain lion with his personal firearm. But this boycott was soon to end.

In 1909, Col. William Selig, president of the Selig Polyscope film company, took notice of the widespread news coverage of President Theodore Roosevelt's African safari and set about to capitalize on the publicity by creating a film dramatization of the event. The film, titled *Hunting Big Game in Africa*, was a big success for Selig and inspired the filmmaker to produce further jungle adventures with lions, elephants and other wild animals figuring prominently in the action, enhancing the drama. In Selig's *Alone in the Jungle* (1913), Bessie Eyton is riding her horse through the jungles of Africa when she sees that a lioness has been shot. She gets off her horse to help the lioness when another lion comes along and attacks her horse. The scene brought audiences to the edge of their seats. Selig's most popular animal was an elephant named Toddles, who was shown to have great empathy for her human co-stars. This is especially evident in *A Wise Old Elephant* (1913), in which Toddles helps a young mother by toting her baby around in a cradle. In the poignant climax, the elephant steps in to settle a family rift. She approaches the woman's grumpy old dad and, after grasping his hand with her trunk, leads the man to his estranged daughter to compel a reconciliation. Selig's animals had no problem making an audience gasp or cry. By 1913, Selig had gathered a large collection of animals and created a zoo to house them. When the studio closed in 1917, he maintained the zoo and rented out the animals to Fox and other studios.

Brothers Charles and Muriel Gay, French circus performers, founded Gay's Lion Farm as a breeding facility and tourist attraction in Los Angeles in 1914. The farm's exhibition of African lions attracted film producers, who put Gay's lions in jungle dramas. The Centaur Film Company featured Gay's lions in a number of films, including *The Woman, the Lion and the Man* (1915), *Avenged by Lions* (1916) and *The Lion's Nemesis* (1916).

Gay's Lion Farm was regarded as the Disneyland of its day. Residents became comfortable with Gay's lions, which appeared at barbeque socials and high school football games. One of Gay's lions became a mascot for El Monte High School, whose football team was named the Lions.

In 1914, the British military were in need of extra space and evicted the Bostock Animal and Jungle Show from its London exhibition rooms. The manager of the show sold the animals to David Horsely, who immediately transported the menagerie to Los Angeles. Horsley constructed a new park where he could display the animals, which would come to include 58 lions and two elephants. When park admissions failed to pay for the upkeep of the park, Horsely built a film studio on the site and featured the animals in films. An early success for Horsley's film company, Bostock Jungle Films, was his " Stanley the African Explorer" serial.

Rural comedies, which were common in the early film era, were filled with horses, cows, chickens and roosters. *Educated Roosters* (1915), an L-KO comedy, showcased the tricks of a pair of roosters, Banty and Billikens. Banty performed a tightrope walk. Billikens pecked out answers to intricate arithmetic problems. But farm animals were, obviously, limited in their entertainment value. The best that a comedy director could expect was a mule launching a comedian into a puddle of mud. Now, with the introduction of the Selig Zoo, Gay's Lion Farm and Bostock Animal and Jungle Show, a wide variety of exotic animals had become available to filmmakers.

Characters in films were no longer safe from carnivorous creatures. This is made clear when a lion suddenly roams out of the jungle and invades a railroad office in the Lux drama *The Man Eater* (1913).

The new surplus of lions was used for comedy purposes early on. The Selig Polyscope comedy *The New Woman and the Lion* (1912) features a lion in its climax. The lion, ghoulishly named "Bloody," breaks out of its cage at an animal show and leaps out at a terrified crowd. A panic ensues and everyone scrambles for safety. A brave group, including police, firemen, cowboys and militia members, get the meat-eater cornered in a butcher shop, but they are driven back by the lion every time they try to capture it. The stalemate is broken by a woman walking past. The woman, emboldened by a victory at her ladies club, takes a hatpin in hand and marches into the shop. A few moments later, she reemerges leading out the bratty lion by its ear.

One of Gay's lions provided a comic threat to the heroes of *A Sunshine Dad* (1916), a five-reel serial spoof written by Tod Browning. An international thief (Chester Withey) has stolen sacred jewels from a Hindu shrine. Mystic seers (led by Max Davidson) suspect that the jewels were given as a gift to Mrs. Marrimore (Fay Tincher). Mrs. Marrimore cannot convince them that she doesn't have the jewels. The mystic seers drag her off to their shrine, where they tie her to a stake outside of a lion's cage. Davidson raises the cage door to release the lion but, before the lion can get to Mrs. Marrimore, her boyfriend Fred (Eugene Pallette) arrives and whisks her away to safety.

The Lion and the Girl (1916), a Keystone comedy, used a real lion for a scene in which Claire Anderson falls into a lion's cage. By the time Joe Jackson unlocks the cage to free Claire, he finds her petting the lion as if it were a kitten.

Less formidable animals had upset festivities before *Roaring Lions and Wedding Bells*. A mouse gets loose at a wedding and panics the guests in *Their Social Splash* (1915). Crocodiles create problems at a lakeside party in *Crossed Love and Swords* (1915). This, though, was not a situation in which the predators escaped their habitat to intrude on the gathering. The toothy reptiles are only riled after two men jump into the lake to retrieve a poodle that has drifted away in a rowboat. It took free roaming lions, more fearsome than a mouse, an escaped convict, a disgruntled rival or water-logged crocodiles, to really turn a wedding upside down.

The king of the jungle became the king of comedy upon the release of *Roaring Lions and Wedding Bells* in 1917. French filmmakers had let lions loose at parties in *Little Moritz chasse les grands fauves* (1911) and *La maison des lions* (1912), but never had these gatherings achieved the grand scale of the wedding reception of *Roaring Lions and Wedding Bells*.

A Lion's Alliance (1920), a Century comedy, features a cage of lions getting released in a beauty parlor and athletic establishment. The Century Lions starred in 29 comedies from 1919 to 1921. The combination of beautiful women, romantic affairs and wild lions was promised by most of the series titles, including *Looney Lions and Monkey Business* (1919), *Lonesome Hearts and Loose Lions* (1919), *Daring Lions and Dizzy Lovers* (1919), *Frisky Lions and Wicked Husbands* (1919), *Howling Lions and Circus Queens* (1919), *African Lions and American Beauties* (1919), *Loose Lions and Fast Lovers* (1920), *Naughty Lions and Wild Men* (1920), and *Lion Paws and Lady Fingers* (1920). *Naughty Lions and Wild Men* is propelled forward by the heroine's promise to marry the bravest of hunters. Billy Engle, determined to marry the fair lady, contends with lions and cannibals to prove his worth as a hunter.

The lion comedy could be adapted to all sorts of comedians. Chris Rub (also spelled Rube), who portrayed a dimwitted Swede in Universal's "Okeh" series, can be seen mouthing malapropisms as he flees a lion in a typical entry, *In the Soup* (1920). The plot has Rub courting the daughter of an old African lion hunter, who insists that the daughter may only marry a brave hunter. Rub, after many mishaps, catches a lion in a barrel. This was a routine previously performed by Lloyd Hamilton in *Hungry Lions in a Hospital* (1918). The "Okeh" series did not last long. Rub is better known today for having provided the voice of Geppetto in Disney's *Pinocchio* (1940). Rub allowed animators to study his likeness, expressions and movements. Geppetto, in every aspect of his design, is Rub, whose slapstick roots are evident in the woodcarver's pratfalls and his comic interaction with a lesser cat named Figaro.

Lions turned up in a variety of comedies. Larry Semon accidentally locks himself in a dungeon with lions in *The Wizard of Oz* (1925). *Sherlock Sleuth* (1925) includes a scene in which Arthur Stone, disguised as a lion, confronts an actual lion but assumes that it is his own mirror reflection.

Even veteran silent film comedian Max Linder got caught up in the phenomena. Linder gets trapped in a lion's cage in *Seven Years Bad Luck* (1921). A lioness climbs onto Linder's back and Linder playfully wrestles with the animal. Linder does not treat this situation in the conventional way. Contrary to the panicked response that audiences had come to expect, he decides to lounge around with the big cat. Getting ready to light a cigarette, he nonchalantly scratches a match against the lion's head.

In *Ella Cinders* (1926), Colleen Moore is unable to get out of a burning building because a lion is blocking the door. A lion joins Al St. John on a bicycle in *Pink Elephants* (1926). Lions became so associated with Hollywood that, in the Hollywood spoof *The Extra Girl* (1923), Mabel Normand cannot help but encounter lions while hanging around a movie set.

Some parties protested the lion comedies. The lion scenes in *Hungry Lions in a Hospital* (1918) were disturbing to the Kansas Board of Review, which demanded the shortening of a scene featuring lions biting patients.

Buster Keaton, a fiercely independent artist, thumbed his nose at the lion trend. In *The Three Ages* (1923), Roman soldiers throw him down into a lion's den. The audience most likely expected that, at this point, the comedian would have a frightening encounter with a lion. Instead, Keaton encounters a man in a baggy lion's costume. Not only is the costume patently fake, the man in the costume makes no attempt to act like a lion. He responds to Keaton with familiar human gestures. The scene is inspired by "Androcles and the Lion," the fable of an escaped Christian slave who befriends a lion by removing a thorn from his paw. Keaton does Androcles one better by manicuring the lion's nails. The lion seems pleased as he holds out his nails and examines them. When Keaton finds a way out and prepares to leave, the lion shakes his hand and waves goodbye.

Keaton has a fleeting encounter with lions in *Sherlock Jr.* (1924). Keaton, a projectionist, magically walks inside of a movie scene on the theatre screen. A series of quick cuts transitions Keaton from one scene to another, including a scene where the comedian appears stranded in a jungle meadow, flanked by lions.

It wasn't until nearly 40 years later that Keaton shared more than a passing scene with an actual lion. The film was *The Adventures of Huckleberry Finn* (1960), in which Keaton played an old-time lion tamer unable to get much action out of his broken-down lion, Orville. Keaton went on to star in a more traditional lion comedy in 1964, when he appeared in a television commercial for Ford, driving in a van with a lion as a passenger. The commercial, fashioned like a Keystone comedy, climaxes with Keaton losing control of the van and driving perilously down the street. The van is on the verge of crashing when the lion, who has been abruptly substituted by a man in a lion costume, gestures frantically and throws a paw over his eyes. This is a funny costume, very much like the one used in *Three Ages*.

Sennett produced a number of lion sagas, including *When Summer Comes* (1922), *The Lion and the Souse* (1924), *Scarem Much* (1924), *The Hollywood Kid* (1924), *The Lion's Whiskers* (1925), *Circus Today* (1926) and *The Lion's Roar* (1928). Lions overrun a home in *When Summer Comes*. They jump through windows and vault through transoms. One lion climbs up to the roof and drops down the chimney, just as the panther did in *Babylas vient d'hériter d'une panthère*. An exciting point-of-view shot was obtained by having the cameraman lie on the floor as the lion leaps over him. Edgar Blue unknowingly gets into bed with a lion, at which point a flurry of feathers erupts. In *Circus Today*, Billy Bevan is transporting a crate of lions in a horse cart when he crashes the cart and the lions get loose. *The Hollywood Kid* features a lion paying a visit to Mack Sennett at his office. A lion, in the style of the bears, chases Billy Bevan and Johnny Burke up a tree in *The Lion's Roar*.

Gay found that, of his 200 lions, one in particular was adept at performing comedy scenes. Numa, named after the lion in the Tarzan books, was an amiable, even-tempered creature who did not get agitated by the antics of slapstick comedians, and could do a funny trick or two not appropriate for a serious jungle adventure. For instance, Numa had a trick that he developed at the farm where he laid across Gay's wife as she reclined on the ground. He performed this trick on camera with Madeline Hurlock in *Circus Today*. The good-natured lion made a number of other memorable appearances. Numa gets loose at a movie premiere in *The Lion and the Souse* (1924). Billy Bevan panics when he discovers that he is

Mack Sennett has a meeting with a lion in *The Hollywood Kid* (1924) (courtesy Steve Rydzewski).

driving in a car with Numa in *The Lion's Whiskers*. Numa, paired with another lion named Duke, made additional appearances in *The Extra Girl* (1923), *Scarem Much* (1924), *Wandering Willies* (1926) and *The Girl from Everywhere* (1927).

The highlight of Numa's career came when he appeared opposite Chaplin in *The Circus* (1928). Chaplin again defies expectations. His Little Tramp panics when he finds himself locked in a cage with a sleeping lion. Very carefully he opens a trapdoor leading into another

Charlie Chaplin in a lion's cage in *The Circus* (1928) (courtesy www.doctormacro.com).

cage. Poking his head inside, he sees that it is occupied by a vicious leopard. He decides to stay where he is and figure out another means of escape. Just then, a playful dog comes up the cage and barks loudly at him. Chaplin struggles to shoo away the dog before his barking wakes the lion. It walks up to Chaplin, sniffs him, and, disinterested, he saunters away. The lion then lies down and goes back to sleep. The female circus rider (Merna Kennedy), the object of Chaplin's affections, comes along and sees Chaplin trapped inside the cage. She quickly opens the cage door to let him out, but he now regards the lion as harmless and thinks that he can impress the girl by nonchalantly approaching the lion. The lion responds by roaring at him. Terrified, he sprints out of the cage and climbs up a pole. Chaplin did not use the lion to create chaos. He did not have the lion go on a rampage (the lion sleeps through most of the scene). He patiently made use of the lion to build up a situation, create tension and develop characterization.

Harold Lloyd was not known for animal comedy, but he certainly indulged in the genre with *Among Those Present* (1921). In that three-reeler he has a tumultuous ride on a bull. He gets trapped in a log with a bear. He is chased by a dog. He has a bird land on his head and refuse to leave. He is butted in the backside by a goat. He is terrified by a snake. He contends with a bucking bronco. He is pecked mercilessly by a flock of ducks. As if this is not enough, he also tangles with a fox, a skunk and, of course, a lion. The lion shows up in a fantasy scene as Lloyd tells dinner party guests a tall tale about his adventures as a big-game hunter. The scene opens with Lloyd sneaking up behind a lion and pulling the animal's tail. The animal's mild reaction suggests that the animal was heavily sedated prior to filming. Lloyd plays out the remainder of the scene with a stuffed lion, pouncing on the defenseless prop and wrestling it with the greatest of vigor.

Lloyd did not again co-star with a lion until the sound feature *The Milky Way* (1936), in which he enjoys sudden riches and buys himself a pet lion. Lloyd causes a commotion when he walks the lion through a hotel lobby. In his final film, Lloyd again found himself walking a pet lion into a building lobby in *The Sin of Harold Diddlebock* (1947). This more elaborate sequence ended with the comedian and his lion co-star, Jackie, trapped together on the ledge of a skyscraper. Director Preston Sturges, who intended for this film to be a tribute to the old silent clowns, no doubt combined dangerous height with dangerous beast to recall the thrills of silent film comedy. Offscreen, the pitch of Lloyd's voice irritated Jackie, who decided to take a bite out of the comedian. Fortunately, the lion's teeth only made contact with a prosthetic glove worn by Lloyd, who had long ago lost part of his hand in a 1919 accident with a prop bomb.

It was clearly recognized in Hollywood by the time of Lloyd's incident with Jackie that lions were dangerous creatures. In 1928, three lions got loose in Gay's Lion Farm when a trainer failed to close a door while he was moving the lions between cages. John Rounan, the farm manager, was killed before trainers could move into action to round up the lions. One walked into an open cage and was promptly locked inside by the trainers. A second lion was put down with a single bullet to the head. A third was wounded by a shot in the leg and went on a rampage through the park.

The lion comedy passed its prime by this time. Numa, the comic lion, was 18 years old when he died of cancer in 1930.

Sennett used lions in three films in 1932. Lions get loose on an ocean liner in *Hypnotized* (1932). A lion parachutes out of a plane in *The Lion and the House* (1932). In *Bring 'Em Back Sober* (1932), Arthur Stone flirts with a lion trainer's wife and he soon has the lion trainer setting his prize lion after him.

The Old Bull (1932), a Roach comedy, involves Thelma Todd and ZaSu Pitts encountering an escaped lion in the country. The script called for the lion to climb up on Pitts's character as she is getting into her car, but the scene was staged with an actor stand-in who kept her back turned to the camera so that her face was never visible. Filmmakers were no longer brazen enough to put lions and actors in the same shot like Sennett had done with Madeline Hurlock in *Circus Today*. A simple shot in which the lion has to walk past Pitts's character also makes use of an obvious double. Later in the film, Todd and Pitts are getting ready to drive off when the lion climbs into the backseat of the car. This entailed a composite of two different shots.

The script for the Three Stooges comedy *Hold That Lion!* (1947) called for Shemp Howard to meet up with a lion who has gotten loose in the baggage car of a train. Howard made it clear before filming started that he would not have contact with a lion. Jules White and his crew came up with an effect more convincing than a composite shot — a sheet of plate glass was placed between their actor and the toothy beast.

Abbott & Costello recycled the bear-in-the-casino routine from *The Naughty Nineties* for *Africa Screams* (1949). Costello needs to pass himself off as a lion tamer. Abbott gets the idea of disguising as a lion and letting Costello crack a whip at him. But Abbott is run off by a real lion, and Costello — thinking the lion is Abbott — gets into a cage with the animal and tries to boss him around. The lion is inserted in the scene with Costello by way of rear-screen projection.

Charles Barton, the director of *Africa Screams*, later reworked this routine for an episode of *The Gale Storm Show* called "Singapore Fling" (1957). An absurd series of events lead Storm to volunteer to be the assistant in an animal act. Bruno the Dancing Bear is brought onstage to follow a few simple commands. The bear is then led offstage, where a man in a bear suit is waiting to take his place for a dance routine. But Bruno has taken a liking to Storm and is unwilling to be put back into his cage. He knocks down the man in the bear suit and saunters back on stage. Storm dances with the bear, thinking that it is the man in the bear suit. She doesn't know she is in danger until the bear becomes irritated and roars at her. Barton threw out technology, including composite shots and rear-screen projection, and created his bear by putting an actor in an old-fashioned bear suit. Storm's sidekick, ZaSu Pitts, rushes onstage to rescue Storm and beats the bear vigorously with her purse. Pitts was able to be braver and funnier with this patently fake bear than she was with a real lion. In the end, the scene is bland and empty without a real bear present to offer a plausible threat.

The Monty Python troupe did a sketch, "Scott of the Sahara," that used stock footage of a lion along with a trashy stuffed lion, which is thrown into the frame at Michael Palin. By the 1970s, animal-attack scenes had become so fake that they had become subject to ridicule.

Old lessons at times need to be reinforced. The plot of a 1966 *Gilligan's Island* episode entitled "Feed the Kitty" had a lion washing ashore in a crate. The lion was supposed to act as if it was sleeping in bed as Gilligan (Bob Denver) snuck past it. However, the lion suddenly stood up and took a leap at Denver. The fact that the bed was unstable and moved as the lion pushed off threw off the lion's balance and caused it to fall short of the actor. The trainer had time to grab hold of the lion before it could continue its attack.

This is not to say that fakery did not go on in the earlier lion comedies. Often, a lion was filmed on its own while its trainer stood off-camera, provoking the animal to roar and claw at the air. This was not so different than the zoo attendant provoking the lion in *Lion, London Zoological Garden*. This footage was later combined with a shot of an actor being cuffed with a fake lion's paw which was manipulated off-camera by a stagehand. *Special Delivery* (1922) included multiple scenes in which a lion was represented merely by a prop paw. In *Wild Game* (1924), a fake paw is poked into the frame to knock off explorer Lige Conley's pith helmet. In *All Wet* (1924), a fake lion's paw extends out of a cage and tears off Charley Chase's pants. In *Roars and Uproars* (1922), a fake paw enters the frame and grabs a comedian by the seat of his pants. The film closes with a paw entering the frame, grabs three men sitting in a row and drags them out of the frame as they look directly at the camera and doff their hats. The fake lion's tail also formed the basis of a number of gags. In *Ella Cinders* (1926), Colleen Moore mistakes a lion's tail for a power cord and tries to plug it into an electrical socket. In *The Lion and the Souse* (1924), the lion's tail wilts when the lion comes into contact with a skunk.

It was sometimes necessary to rely on tricks to make a scene more sensational. In *Skylarking* (1923), a scene in which lions attack a car made use of an articulated dummy set up in the driver's seat. The dummy, looking smart in a fashionable straw hat, has its string-automated arms flailing, making it look like a panicked motorist. The same dummy is later roughed up when a lion leaps into the air and plucks it down from a rope. A trainer stands in for the lead actor, Harry Gribbon, for other portions of the scene. *His Musical Sneeze* (1919) includes a scene in which actors are chased around a field by a dog dressed up to look like a lion.

No Fare (1928) did the lion-on-the-loose act without a live lion. The premise has Big Boy (child actor Malcolm Sebastian) walking his dachshund on a leash. When he is not looking, a bratty boy unhooks the dachshund and attaches the leash to a stuffed lion on display outside of a taxidermist shop. Big Boy unknowingly drags the stuffed lion behind him down the street. When he finally turns around and sees the lion, he becomes terrified and walks faster. The lion remains close behind until Big Boy lets go of the leash and the lion glides into a crowd of people at a train station. The crowd panics. A train attendant grabs a rifle. The taxidermist, who is bending over to recover his lion, catches the first shot in his backside.

Others made use of the lion-on-the-loose formula using smaller, less threatening animals. Substituting for a lion in the Billy Dooley comedy *Sailor Beware* (1927) was a guinea pig. The plot is set in motion by a newspaper headline warning the public that a guinea pig carrying a deadly contagious disease has escaped from a local laboratory. The same day, Dooley shows up in town with a guinea pig that he has brought back from New Guinea. Everywhere the little rodent shows up, people scream hysterically and run for their lives. Later, filmmakers found that they did not need to create a threat of deadly germs to have a small furry mammal to create a panic. A skunk gets loose in a college dormitory and causes a riot among the residents in *The Night Watchman's Mistake* (1929).

Jerry Lewis found an interesting way to create a lion-on-the-loose scene without using a lion. In *Ladies Man* (1961), Lewis runs around in a panic upon hearing a lion's roar. He is relieved when he finds out the source of the roar is a beagle. (This is comparable to the bear scene that Laurel & Hardy performed inside of a dark cave, where the bear was reduced to a mere roar.) Later, Lewis stages a second scene in which a crowd is panicked by a lion's roar. This time, as people scream and run past him, Lewis tries to tell them that the roar is coming from a harmless little dog. Then, suddenly, a full-fledged lion enters the frame and strides past Lewis. Lewis rushes up to the camera in a panic. "That's a big pussycat!" he cries. Lewis got a great deal of action out of this scene even though the lion appears for no more than two seconds.

Buster Keaton proved that he could stage the ultimate animal rampage without a claw or fang. He reserved his animal rampage for passive, cud-chewing cows stampeding through downtown Los Angeles in *Go West* (1925). The cows prove intimidating by their sheer mass. Jim Kline, author of *The Complete Films of Buster Keaton*, described the cattle "disrupting traffic, panicking the populace and overrunning local establishments."[18] Keaton's father, Joe Keaton, is seen sitting in a barber's chair waiting to get a shave when a cow comes along and licks shaving cream off his face.

This impressive scene was bound to inspire imitators. The cattle stampede was most faithfully recreated for a Rowan and Martin western parody called *Once Upon a Horse* (1958). A more aggressive variation of the scene was featured in the opening of *Jackass Number Two* (2006), during which bulls stampede through a picturesque middle-class neighborhood. The sequence is pure silent comedy. The hellbent bulls jump through windows, crash through fences, wade through a backyard pool, and smash down a gazebo. A man hides inside a trash can, only to have a bull ram the can with his horns sending the can flying. Classic slapstick abounds in the rest of the film. The Jackass team races down a hill inside tractor tires, which is a gag that Lupino Lane performed in *Howdy Duke* (1927). Various cast members are electrocuted, slammed in the face by a rake, get caught in an animal trap, crash while skiing down a ramp, and get caught inside a limousine with a swarm of bees. This was guerrilla filmmaking, without actors and the luxury of stand-ins or special effects. A rake in the face was a rake in the face. *Jackass* is a product of the YouTube age. The improvised stunts, self-injuring pranks and caught-on-tape mishaps regularly presented on YouTube represent the new wave of slapstick.

New and old tricks are used today to bring together the big comedian and the big cat. In *Talladega Nights* (2006), race-car driver Ricky Bobby (Will Ferrell) develops a fear of driving after he gets into a fiery car crash on the track. His father believes that one way to make his son face up to his fear is to have him drive around in a car with a cougar. Ferrell is reasonably frightened to see the cougar inside the car gnawing on the upholstery, and it takes him awhile to muster the courage to open the door. As soon as the door is ajar, the leopard springs on top of him. However, Ferrell was never put into real danger. The actor ended up on the ground wrestling with a stuffed leopard, not different from what Harold Lloyd had done at one time in *Among Those Present*.

The script for *Year One* (2009) called for a cougar to attack Michael Cera. A cougar (the same one used in *Talladega Nights*) was hired to jump out of a tree and pounce on top of a stunt man. But, on the day of shooting, nothing went right. It took a great deal of effort to coax the cougar into the tree, and then the animal refused to jump onto the stunt man. The trainer's excuse was that the cougar was constipated. The director, Harold Ramis, became frustrated and sent the cougar and his trainer home. "Because the cougar wouldn't do anything," he explained in the DVD commentary, "we had to CGI that baby."[19] In the end, neither the CGI cougar nor the stuffed cougar were very convincing. The scenes could not drive audiences to the laughter and excitement that *Roaring Lions and Wedding Bells* had more than nine decades earlier.

A tiger was used in a number of scenes in *The Hangover* (2009). For the main scene, the filmmakers trapped their leads in a car with the big cat. It was a scene staged for a number of silent films, including *Hungry Lions in a Hospital* (1918) and *The Lion's Whiskers* (1925). But the scene had never been staged like this before. A great amount of effort was made to minimize risk. The press material explained, "Four tigers were trained for different and specific tasks onscreen, while the film's cast and crew were similarly trained to a strict

Long before *The Hangover* (2009), Madeline Hurlock and Billy Bevan had to deal with a big jungle cat in their car in *The Lion's Whiskers* (1925) (courtesy Steve Rydzewski).

protocol about sharing space with them."[20] Production designer Bill Brzeski said, "Tame or not, working with wild animals is serious business, and tigers, in particular, don't like surprises. The facility was fully locked down whenever they were present, and non-vital personnel were kept off the set. Those remaining were cautioned to avoid sudden movements or hiding themselves from view."[21] Brzeski learned that tigers, which depend on traction, prefer firm surfaces (ask the lion who tried to pounce on Bob Denver). This meant that they had to remove the seat cushions from a plush Mercedes and replace the cushions with hard, solid material. "Hey," said Brzeski, "we wanted the tigers to be as comfortable as possible."[22] But the car scene also featured a life-size animatronic tiger that came out of the Jim Hensen Creature Shop. Some 30 servo motors in the eyebrows, cheeks and mouth controlled the animatronic tiger's facial movements. A concoction made from K-Y Jelly served as saliva on its impressive fangs.

As with bears, the big cats are used today in a highly careful and restrained PETA-friendly manner. The PETA philosophy is prevalent on the minds of the writers scripting these scenes. In the *Chuck* episode "Chuck Versus Role Models," geek spy Chuck has to steal microfilm stored for safekeeping in the collar of a Bengal tiger. The simple solution would be to shoot the lion, or even use Stan Laurel's patented dynamite to blow it sky high, but Chuck expresses his reverence for this "rare and majestic animal" and refuses to do anything that will harm the animal.

The Hangover expresses an undeniable screwball comedy influence. The film in many ways resembles Preston Sturges' *The Sin of Harold Diddlebock* (1947), which involves a man who gets drunk on a potent cocktail and cannot remember in the morning where he went or what he did the night before. The man retraces his steps to solve the mystery of his blackout and, in the process, discovers that he has gotten married and come into possession of a lion. *The Hangover*'s main tiger scenes, including a scene where Zach Galifianakis discovers the tiger in the bathroom and the aforementioned scene where the tiger sits in the back seat of a car chewing up the upholstery, are scenes directly out of Howard Hawks' screwball classic *Bringing Up Baby* (1938). *Bringing Up Baby*, the climax of which finds Cary Grant wielding a chair to fend off an ill-tempered leopard that has wandered away from a circus, falls squarely into the category of When-Predators-Attack comedy. The film, which was named one of AFI's Top 100 Films, gleefully delivered this uproarious old comedy routine to an unprecedented level of prestige and sophistication.

A Rubber Fish, a Wooden Horse, a Stuffed Goat and Animated Bees

The willingness of actors to work with real lions proved these men and women were daring in spirit and committed to thrilling audiences, but this does not mean that the animals in these early films were always real. *Giddap!* (1925) resorts to animation for a scene in which a polo horse kicks Billy Bevan over goal posts. Animation also comes into play in *Yukon Jake* (1924) to show a bear rolling down a snowy hillside. The bear keeps gathering snow until it is fully wrapped inside a giant snowball. *Below Zero* (1925), set in Canada's frigid north, has a scene in which a horse goes skating down a hill on snowshoes. The horse passes through a large tent and takes the tent along with it. It is obviously a wooden prop horse, but the fakery only adds to the silliness of the scene.

Moving Picture World reported that the title character of *Billy Whiskers* (1920) was played by "an unusually intelligent goat actor, who has been cleverly trained and directed."[23] Billy's lively antics included ringing doorbells at midnight, dancing the hula, and sauntering on a dining-room table. Detlef Eickemeyer, who viewed a pristine 35mm print at the Library of Congress, wrote, "[Billy] tries driving a taxi, but finds that it doesn't suit him. He finally finds his niche as a fireman, and becomes a hero by rescuing a baby from a burning house."[24] Eickemeyer observed that the filmmakers used a stuffed goat in many scenes, including a scene in which the goat comes sliding down a firehouse pole. A prop goat had to be created to deliver storybook feats beyond the capability of a real goat.

Rubber fish turned up in many silent film comedies, never more prominently than in *The Flirts* (1919). A fountain in a hotel lobby is a feeding ground for a hostile fish, which is periodically leaping out and biting guests. Presumably, the fish is in the pond to serve the hotel's decor and ambience, but this fish has other ideas. Jimmie Adams lures the fish gone amok into a basin and batters it into submission with a giant mallet. Adams, proud of his victory, steps forward towards the camera, unaware that he is putting a foot in the basin, and strikes a boastful pose for onlookers. This is pure absurdity. Amok fish had shown up before, but they showed up in places where a fish was more likely to be found. It raises no question for Arbuckle to be chasing a flopping fish around a kitchen floor while working as a chef in *The Waiters' Ball* (1916). A viewer could suspend disbelief when, in *Sea Scamps* (1926), the passengers on a cruise ship take up axes and pails to catch a flying fish that has come on board. However, the absurd fish in *The Flirts* bent and stretched reality into an unrecognizable state.

Creatures as ravenous as they were rubbery sprang out of the murky depths of a river, lake or ocean. Aquatic life forms are certainly a danger in *Coney Island* (1917), in which Arbuckle falls into the ocean and is attacked by a sizable fish. Al St. John fights a squid under water in *All Wet* (1922). A shark leaps out of the ocean looking to make a snack out of Lupino Lane in *The Pirates* (1922). A whale carries Harry Gribbon out to sea in *Skylarking* (1923). Ford Sterling panics to find that he has caught an alligator on his fishing line in the Keystone comedy *A Fishy Affair* (1913). According to *Moving Picture World*, Sterling "rushes away and plunges into the midst of a score of alligators."[25] Not all of the alligators were rubber. According to Brent Walker, the split-reel comedy was likely filmed at the California Alligator Farm. The magazine's reviewer was happy to report that Sterling managed "a narrow escape from the snapping jaws."[26]

It was typical, as in *Roughest Africa*, to use alligators for their rump-biting expertise. This was a tradition that carried on for many years. An ideal example would be Curly Howard getting bitten on the backside by an alligator in the Three Stooges comedy *We Want Our Mummy* (1939). It is a straightforward form of comic backside injury.

This gag, though, had a more elaborate context in *Long Pants* (1927). Harry Langdon removes a crate outside of steamship company, thinking it is a crate in which his escaped-convict girlfriend has hidden inside. Instead, an alligator is stored inside the crate. Langdon has just cracked open one corner of the crate when a policeman arrives on the scene. Langdon whispers into the crate that he cannot finish opening the crate until the cop goes away. He, unlike the viewers, cannot see the slimy snout of the alligator poking through the crack. Langdon quickly sits down on the crate in the effort to conceal his girlfriend. The alligator bites his backside, but Langdon, who assumes that his girlfriend is playfully pinching him, reacts by merely giggling. The alligator takes further bites out of Langdon's backside as Langdon, who is afraid to arouse the cop's suspicions, struggles to maintain his composure.

In *Some More of Samoa* (1941), the Three Stooges find themselves in a situation in which they need to retrieve a rare African plant that has been swallowed by an alligator. Most times, comedians are motivated to get far away from an alligator's jaws, but the Stooges must manage with the greatest of care to delve between this alligator's jaws. At first, Curly uses a stick to prop the alligator's mouth open but the alligator easily snaps the stick by half. Then, Moe manages to pry open the alligator's mouth using his belt while Curly reaches inside to pluck out the plant. The prop alligator, with its snapping jaws, is ridiculously fake. It is the sheer audacity of the scene that makes it funny, and the Stooges are able to get the most out of the silly prop.

Prop alligators are considerably more realistic now than they were in the days of the Three Stooges. Vince Niebla, a distinguished special-effects make-up artist, is particularly proud of the accurately detailed alligators that he constructed for comic gator attacks in *Ace Ventura: When Nature Calls* (1995) and *Gone Fishin'* (1997). His *Ace Ventura* alligator, with its hundreds of scales, was sculpted with great care and precision out of couch-foam material. As good as this model was, Niebla made an even more elaborate model for *Gone Fishin'*, the script of which called for a pair of bumbling fishing buddies (Joe Pesci and Danny Glover) to be attacked by a super-gator named Mad Maggie. This time, the effects artists were able to elevate the realism of the alligator by using silicone as skin.

The plot of *Gone Fishin'* has Pesci and Glover entering a swamp to retrieve a suitcase filled with money and jewels. The alligator rushes out of the water and snatches the suitcase between its jaws. The men punch and kick the alligator to get it to release the suitcase. This scene, which is neither silly nor inventive, has none of the humor of the *Some More of Samoa* scene despite its highly realistic alligator.

Bulls continued to show up as a threat to comedians. Billy Bevan and Eddie Quillan become trapped in a pen with a bull in *The Bull Fighter* (1927). A comic bullfight was the highlight of *Bull and Sand* (1924). But *A Roman Scandal* (1919) proved that a fake bull can be funnier than a real bull. A theatrical company performs a Roman scene wherein warrior Urus entertains Emperor Nero by wrestling a bull. The bull, portrayed by a cow outfitted with fake horns, does not put up much of a fight. Later, when the Humane Society limits the theatre company's use of the cow to one performance per week, a stagehand travels to a ranch to get a real bull for the show. He grabs the bull by the tail and, when the bull turns on him, he jumps over the fence to get out of its way. Rodeo clowns do this stunt all the time, but the bull's reaction is so vicious that it is likely to produce fear, not laughter. In the climax of the film, Earle Rodney wrestles with two stagehands dressed as a bull. In the struggle, a diminutive stagehand falls out of the back end of the costume. Moments later, the actor playing Nero gets knocked out of his spectator stand. *This* is funny. A fake bull was also used for comic effect in *Mud and Sand* (1922), which had star matador Rhubard Vaselino (Stan Laurel) swaggering into a bull ring and tossing a bull over the fence.

Using a dummy animal was not only about eliminating risk. It could be quicker and easier to use a dummy rather than the real thing. A fake horse's head was employed for a scene in which a horse eats Lige Conley's straw hat in *What a Night!* (1924). A horse could have been coaxed to eat a straw hat, but this would have taken more time and effort than the director was apparently willing to spare. Also, a prop man blasts steam out of the fake horse's nostrils, which may have been considered a big laugh-getter.

The dynamism that characterized silent film comedy came to a quick end in the sound era. Once upon a time, real lions got loose from a baggage car on a train and attacked passengers in *Roaring Lions on the Midnight Express* (1918). Animals now got loose from the baggage car of a train in *One Track Minds* (1933) but it failed to generate the same amount of excitement when those animals turned out to be animated bees. The animals on the loose in the sound era tended to be non-predatory animals that were more a nuisance than a threat. In *Sunk by the Census* (1940), Edgar Kennedy buys a milking cow and keeps it in his backyard. When the temperature gets low, Edgar's father-in-law brings the cow indoors, where the animal eats the stuffing out of a couch.

The fakery became more common during this period. In *The Kid from Spain* (1932), Eddie Cantor runs away from an angry bull, unconvincingly generated by rear-screen projection. Comedians now had stunt men in wigs and padding take their pratfalls for them. The funnymen were no longer willing to jeopardize their backsides for the purpose of comedy. In *His Bridal Fright* (1940), a German shepherd chases Charley Chase up a wall and goes to take a bite out of his backside. In this case, the dog is real, but the backside isn't. The dog ends up sinking its teeth into an obvious pillow, stuffed into a pair of trousers.

Where has this all led us? *Babe* (1995) returned animals to prominence in comedy films, but *Babe*'s state-of-the-art effects changed the way that animals were depicted. Often, animals were now shot on their own, against a green screen, to allow the actors to be inserted into the action later at the director's convenience. More significant, a combination of CGI and animatronics was used to enhance the range of the animals' expressions and body movements. The animals' eyes and mouths were freely animated to make the performances funnier and more meaningful. It was not an entirely novel idea. Traditional hand-drawn animation had been used to display animals moving their mouths to talk as a recurring gimmick of

Bob Hope and Bing Crosby's "Road" comedies. These new enhancements, though, were much more elaborate and convincing. These impossibly expressive animals followed their debut in *Babe* with appearances in *Doctor Dolittle* (1998), *Cats & Dogs* (2001), *Good Boy!* (2003), *Racing Stripes* (2005), *Nanny McPhee* (2005), *Charlotte's Web* (2006), *The Beverly Hills Chihuahua* (2008) and *Furry Vengeance* (2010). Totally CGI animals have been incorporated into live-action settings for *Stuart Little* (1999), *Scooby-Doo* (2002), *Garfield* (2004), *Alvin and the Chipmunks* (2007), *G-Force* (2009), *Marmaduke* (2010) and *Yogi Bear* (2010). Ben Stiller is attacked by a ferocious pack of CGI lions in *Night at the Museum* (2006). Robin Williams and John Travolta are attacked by CGI penguins more aggressive than any pack of lions in *Old Dogs* (2009).

Today, it is no longer just about live animal actors. Clever editing seamlessly melds the work of many partners, including the animals, trainers, puppeteers, animators, designers, compositors, sculptors, and visual-effects technicians. The animatronic models, which have been built to capture animals down to their musculature and skeleton, are manipulated by a team of well-rehearsed puppeteers to move realistically. Mr. Tinkles, a power-mad Persian cat out to overthrow the human race, provides an artful performance in *Cats & Dogs*. According to the American Humane Association, this was "a flawless composite that begins with the live animal, moves to its puppet double, and into a CGI 'cyber' double and back to the real thing."[27] CGI, in all its versatility, is able to enhance an animal's performance in unexpected ways. A dog had to be shown urinating in *Old Dogs* (2009). All the dog had to do was lift its leg on the trainer's cue and technicians digitally added a stream of urine to the scene in post-production. One of the greatest accomplishments for CGI animators has been their success in capturing the dynamics of fur, which will continue to be important in their line of work.

Animal Rampages, Part 2

Pathé Frères exploited the anxiety created by Darwin's theories with *The Monkey Man* (1908) and *An Apish Trick* (1909), which suggested that a man could develop ape-like tendencies by accepting a blood transfusion or organ transplant from an ape.

The murderous orangutan of Edgar Allan Poe's "The Murders in the Rue Morgue" later inspired the introduction of the killer ape in feature films, including *Go and Get It* (1920) and *The Leopard Lady* (1928). *Go and Get It*, directed by Marshall Neilan, featured a gorilla that goes on the rampage after having his brain replaced with a human brain. It is the commands of a demented animal trainer that drives gorillas to kill in *The Leopard Lady*.

In *The Covered Schooner* (1923), comedian Monty Banks is thrown into a gorilla's cage by a romantic rival. Banks manages to befriend the angry gorilla by teaching it to shoot craps. Banks, determined to stop the rival from marrying Lois Boyd, gets the gorilla to help him to escape and then uses the gorilla to break up the wedding. It is a retread of *Roaring Lions and Wedding Bells*, a film in which Banks also appeared. Unfortunately, the poorly designed gorilla costume makes the actor look more like a missing link than a gorilla.

A scene-still from *Scared Stiff* (1926), a lost Roach comedy, shows Clyde Cook in a mad scientist's lab with a hairy ape arm reaching out of a cage to grab him. For several decades, the comedy cliché was a mad scientist who lived in a creepy mansion and kept a gorilla caged in his laboratory. Our Gang had trouble with a laboratory gorilla in a lost silent comedy, *The Holy Terror* (1929). The scientist, in this case, is Mary Ann Jackson's uncle. Mary Ann lets the gorilla out of the cage, and the gorilla proceeds to stalk the kids around the house. Farina comes face to face with the gorilla. Farina, worried that a sudden movement could agitate the gorilla, pretends not to be afraid and stands perfectly still. Allen Hoskins, who played Farina, was an extraordinarily talented child actor. He always played fright scenes in a "slow-build" manner. He tries desperately to act cool and casual but it is obvious from his facial expressions that he is getting more terrified by the moment. He will ultimately scream and run off, but not before he has built up the tension — and the laughs.

The gorilla-in-a-haunted-house premise, as limited as it was, was not only employed in short subjects but in a number of low-budget features, including *Crazy Knights* (1944), *Gildersleeve's Ghost* (1944), *Spook Busters* (1946), *Who Killed Doc Robbin?* (1948), *The Bowery Boys Meet the Monsters* (1951), *The Ghost in the Invisible Bikini* (1966), and *Hillbillies in a Haunted House* (1967).

Charles Gemora, who played the gorilla in *The Leopard Lady*, found himself in demand to play gorillas. His gorilla costume, which he had personally created, was a vast improvement over the gorilla costume worn in *The Covered Schooner*. *The Circus Kid* (1928) featured Gemora in a key dramatic role as a circus gorilla who befriends a boy (Frankie Darro). Next, Gemora was a gorilla in the horror comedy feature *Seven Footprints to Satan* (1929), which involved a couple (Thelma Todd and Creighton Hale) who become prisoners in a haunted castle. After his stellar comedy debut, Gemora mostly played his gorilla roles for

Stan Laurel (right) shares a secret with Ethel the Chimp (Charles Gemora, in a gorilla suit) in *The Chimp* (1932). Oliver Hardy feels left out (courtesy Robert Arkus).

laughs. He went to the Christie studio to play an ape opposite Bobby Vernon in *Why Gorillas Leave Home* (1929). He periodically found work on the Roach and Sennett lots for the next couple of years. In Our Gang's *Bear Shooters* (1930), Gemora plays a bootlegger who disguises himself as a gorilla to frighten away the gang, whose hunting expedition in the woods has brought them poking around his hideout. The gang mistakes the gorilla for a bear and set out to capture him. The gang proves to be formidable hunters. Wheezer hits the gorilla in the head with rocks, Mary Ann strikes him with a board, Spud tricks him into stepping into a bear trap, Chubby opens fire on him with a shotgun, Farina shoots arrows into his backside, and Jackie hurls a highly active beehive in his direction. Farina repeats his routine with the gorilla from *The Holy Terror*. Farina, who is sitting on a boulder, smiles nervously at the gorilla while trying to get up to leave. "Well, I guess I'll be going," he says politely. Every time that he tries to stand, the gorilla shoves him back down. Gemora went on to play Jocko the Boxing Gorilla in the Todd & Pitts short *Seal Skins* (1932), Ethel the Chimp in the Laurel & Hardy short *The Chimp*, and Mr. Chadwick in the Charley Chase short *Nature in the Wrong* (1933). Mr. Chadwick is the most unique of these gorillas in that he wears a top hat, speaks in an English accent, and is able to treat the Chase family to a rendition of "Chopsticks" on the piano. The Sennett studio had Gemora climb into his gorilla suit to chase Andy Clyde around a haunted house in *Ghost Parade* (1931), rattle a pair of

Bobby Vernon plays hide-and-seek with a gorilla (Charles Gemora) in *Why Gorillas Leave Home* (1929) (courtesy Cole Johnson Collection).

detectives on an airplane in *Hawkins & Watkins, Inc.* (1932), and help Bing Crosby and Florine McKinney elope in the musical short *Sing, Bing, Sing* (1933).

The demand for comedy gorillas got even greater, and Gemora found himself a member of a guild of gorilla impersonators, including Fred Humes, Emil Van Horn, Art Miles and Steve Calvert.

The torch, or the banana, was eventually passed to Columbia. Walter Catlett encounters a gorilla in *You're Next!* (1940). Hugh Herbert gets a shave from a gorilla in *Tall, Dark and Gruesome* (1948). A gorilla chases after Joe Besser and Jim Hawthorne in *Fraidy Cat* (1951) and its remake, *Hook a Crook* (1955). The Three Stooges had to deal with gorillas in a number of films. In *Three Missing Links* (1938), Curly is hired to play a gorilla on location in a jungle movie. Curly battles a real gorilla thinking that it is just another actor trying to take his job. Although the two gorilla suits are identical, Curly is able to easily distinguish himself with his inimitably comical body language. In the end, "love candy" causes Curly to fall in love with the gorilla, which becomes horrified and runs off. The Stooges encounter a gorilla while investigating a burglary in *Dizzy Detectives* (1943). In *Bubble Trouble* (1953), a cranky old man (played by Emil Sitka) consumes an excess amount of the Stooges' new youth elixir and, as a consequence, is transformed into a gorilla. Other "gorilla" comedies from the Stooges included *A Bird in the Head* (1946), *Crime on Their Hands* (1948), and *Spooks!* (1953).

The comedy gorilla, as hokey as it was, appeared in feature films with every popular comedy act — Laurel & Hardy (*Swiss Miss*, 1938), the Marx Brothers (*At the Circus*, 1939), W. C. Fields (*Never Give a Sucker an Even Break*, 1941), and Abbott & Costello (*Africa Screams*, 1949). Fields, upon meeting a gorilla, flippantly remarks, "Last time it was pink elephants!" Groucho Marx was unwilling to hang upside down on a trapeze in *At the Circus*, but a stunt man in a gorilla suit was willing to swing tirelessly on the trapeze for the film's climax. Hope and Crosby contended with a gorilla in two "Road" pictures. Hope wrestles with a gorilla in *Road to Zanzibar* (1941) and he flees from a love-starved gorilla in *Road to Bali* (1952). The Ritz Brothers spent an entire feature film tracking down a gorilla in a film, appropriately titled *The Gorilla* (1939). Even RKO's comedy-short division, which specialized in domestic comedies, had an escaped gorilla show up at Edgar Kennedy's home in *No More Relatives* (1948).

Men in gorilla costumes were losing their ability to get laughs by the time they appeared in *Hold That Monkey* (1950) and *Bela Lugosi Meets a Brooklyn Gorilla* (1952). It failed to make it any more interesting when Buster Keaton danced a minuet with a gorilla in a 1951 episode of his television series. Emil Van Horn, a gorilla impersonator who once raised a flask to W. C. Fields in *Never Give a Sucker an Even Break* and chased Lou Costello around a carnival in *Keep 'Em Flying* (1941), was no longer able to find steady work as a gorilla in motion pictures. His bio on "The Gorilla Men" blog reads, "Once cinema work dried up, Van Horn continued to work the clubs in his decaying suit until it was stolen."[28]

In the sixties, George Barrows appeared dressed as a gorilla in several television series, including *The Jackie Gleason Show*, *The Beverly Hillbillies* and *The Addams Family*. The actor had a recurring role on *The Addams Family* as Gorgo the Gorilla.

The comedy gorilla returned as a pure camp figure in *The Magic Christian* (1969) and *The Kentucky Fried Movie* (1977). Both films relied on a rampaging gorilla to disrupt the proceedings. For a transitional scene in *Monty Python and the Holy Grail* (1975), director Terry Gilliam filmed a woman's hand turning the page of a storybook. Gilliam later decided that he needed to do something to make the scene funny, so he added a gorilla's hand coming into the frame and snatching the woman's hand.

It was due to the influence of *King Kong* (1933) that gorillas were sometimes depicted as amorous creatures apt to carry off beautiful young women. *Rat Pfink a Boo Boo* (1966), which includes a hodgepodge of movie clichés, has a gorilla show up randomly to kidnap a woman. *One Million AC/DC* (1969), a softcore sex romp written by Ed Wood, features a gorilla defiling a cave woman. *Pussycat, Pussycat, I Love You* (1970), which was written by Rod Amateau and Woody Allen, involves a man who consults with a psychiatrist to cure himself of a sex addiction. The man recounts many of his sexual exploits and also tells the psychiatrist about a recurrent nightmare in which he is being pursued by a sex-starved gorilla. The therapy session, along with the entire film, is brought to an abrupt conclusion by the gorilla climbing into a window of the psychiatrist's office. A gorilla wearing a bra was prominently featured on the movie poster. More recently, Jim Carrey had to contend with an amorous silverback gorilla in *Ace Ventura: When Nature Calls* (1995).

An actor in a gorilla costume had, in time, lost its ability to scare anyone, even children. In the Saturday morning live-action comedy series *The Ghost Busters*, which ran from 1975 to 1976, the gorilla is no longer on the side of the sinister forces spooking houses. The resident ape, Tracy (Bob Burns), has devoted himself to helping Forrest Tucker and Larry Storch to rid old homes and castles of supernatural squatters.

In 1986, a five-year-old boy fell into the gorilla enclosure at Jersey Zoo. A large male silverback gorilla named Jambo stood guard over the boy, keeping away agitated younger gorillas, until the zookeepers could remove the boy. A video that captured the incident was broadcast on news stations across the world. Jambo, nicknamed "The Gentle Giant," instantly changed the perception of gorillas. Following this incident, gorillas were depicted in motion pictures as gentle, childlike creatures, able to engage in loving relationships with humans. This was the situation depicted in *Baby's Day Out* (1994), *Born to Be Wild* (1995), *Buddy* (1997), *Fierce Creatures* (1997) and *Mom, Can I Keep Her?* (1998). *Baby's Day Out* included a scene in which a baby crawls into a gorilla cage and finds himself in the protective arms of a loving gorilla. Sophisticated animatronic gorilla costumes were used in most of these films. The gorillas were now more expressive and sympathetic. The gorilla in *Baby's Day Out*, with his animatronic dimples, was perfectly cute. The truly fierce creatures in *Fierce Creatures* were John Cleese and his fellow humans. Still, in spite of their gentleness, the gorillas were able to create an uproar in public. The gorilla in *Mom, Can I Keep Her?* causes a riot when it runs loose through a restaurant. The gorilla in *Born to Be Wild* panics a cashier when it pops its head out of a car while riding through a restaurant drive-thru.

A gorilla named Bollo, represented by an actor in an old-fashioned gorilla suit, is a regular character on the British cult comedy series *The Mighty Boosh*. Bollo, the animal familiar of shaman Naboo, is a talking ape with human abilities, including the ability to play Jimi Hendrix riffs on an electric guitar. But Bollo is inept and cowardly. His catchphrase, recited warily at the start of every adventure, is "I've got a bad feeling about this." The gorilla, in acknowledgment of Darwin's theories, is finally treated as one of us.

In *All Work and No Pay* (1942), Andy Clyde becomes stranded on a lifeboat with a gorilla. Andy doesn't see the gorilla at first. He speaks aloud to express his relief to have gotten away from dangerous criminals on board the liner. The gorilla, piping up in a friendly human voice, agrees wholeheartedly with Andy. Andy turns around, sees the gorilla, and dives off the boat. This is nearly identical to the scene in *Abbott and Costello Meet Frankenstein* (1948) when Bud and Lou escape from Dracula's castle in a rowboat and discover that the Invisible Man has come along for the ride.

Abbott and Costello Meet Frankenstein replaced the animals-on-the-loose comedies with monsters-on-the-loose comedies. The new comic threat involved vampires, werewolves and ghouls. In the 1960s, the "mysterious and spooky" Addams Family sent people running in accelerated silent comedy mode on a weekly basis. The family's pet lion, Kitty, was the least of a person's concerns when they found themselves caught in the Addams mansion. *Ghostbusters* (1984) added ghosts and demons into the mix.

An American Werewolf in London (1981) climaxes with a werewolf causing a riot while rampaging through Piccadilly Circus. This chaotic finale includes plenty of gruesome slapstick action, including multiple car crashes, a man flying headfirst through a windshield, and people falling through a plate-glass window. The underlying fear in a lion comedy was that a lion would use its fangs and claws to tear a person apart. In this film, a police detective marches into the chaos to take charge, only to have the werewolf pounce on him and rip off his head.

The werewolf also creates havoc in a movie theatre, which is an ideal setting for a monster rampage. A group of people huddled together in a dark building to enjoy the week's entertainment is unprepared for the attack. It makes the shock much greater for the monster to finally show up to shatter their sense of security. This was already seen in horror classics *The Blob* (1958) and *The Tingler* (1959) and it was also shown in the earliest-known lion comedy, *Cretinetti nella gabbia dei leoni*.

The comic tone of the film is established early when the lycanthropic hero awakens naked in a zoo the night after a transformation and covers his body with a bunch of balloons before he rushes home.

A trend of "nature strikes back" thrillers, which had predatory animals wreak vengeance on humans, started up in the sixties with *The Birds* (1963) and reached a fevered pitch in the seventies after *Jaws* (1975). The animals in these films were not merely zoo animals that had slipped out of their cages. Arriving to threaten the populace were monstrous mutant beasts, created by rampant pollution and amoral scientific experiments. Lions crashed a wedding in *Roaring Lions and Wedding Bells*, but now, in *Alligator* (1980), nuptials are disrupted by a 36-foot mutant alligator. The alligator knocks down banquet tables and swallows up servers like hors d'oeuvres. The ravenous fish that once attacked hotel guests in *Flirts* now had a bold relative in a ravenous shark that attacks beach tourists in *Jaws*. Gags were reworked to achieve a more chilling effect. In *Roars and Uproars* (1922), a lion creates an explosion of feathers while attacking a man in bed. Now, in a grisly scene in *Prophecy* (1979), a bear ravages a camper curled up in a sleeping bag, and the air becomes filled with feathers torn loose from the padding. Lloyd Hamilton was funny when fending off a frenzied flock of birds in *The Optimist* (1923) but, now, Rod Taylor and Tippi Hedren look like bloody wrecks having to cope with ferocious avian attacks in *The Birds*. Just like prop lion paws and tails were used in the lion comedies, a fake bear claw was poked at actors in *Grizzly* (1976) and actors were whacked by a rubber alligator tail in *Alligator*.

The Birds director, Alfred Hitchcock, used his feathery cast members in much the same way as the comedy makers had used their animals. He explained that the role of the birds was, simply, to destroy complacency. The birds, according to the director, represented "the catastrophe that surrounds us all."[29]

The latent comedy elements came to dominate these films. A slew of tongue-in-cheek monster-rampage films, including *Tremors* (1990), *Arachnophobia* (1990), *Lake Placid* (1999) and *Eight-Legged Freaks* (2002), had the citizens of quiet, remote communities suddenly terrorized by giant killer spiders, a man-eating 30-foot-long crocodile, and strange carnivorous worm-like creatures called Graboids.

Gremlins (1984) used gremlins in their true manifestation to create comic mischief and chaos. The malignant little creatures overrun a Mayberry-like town and send the residents into a full-blown panic. Slapstick ensues — car crashes, buildings exploding, and a crabby old woman being launched out of a window. Just as resourceful as Lloyd Hamilton is in trapping a lion in a barrel in *Hungry Lions in a Hospital*, Frances Lee McCain is resourceful in trapping a gremlin in a microwave oven.

Whether silent or sound, animals have always been a part of the comedy canon. And this trend will most likely continue. There will always be someone trying to turn man's best friend into a comedian's best gag.

4
Adventures in Eating

A restaurant setting was used in a number of Commedia dell'Arte routines, the best known of which is "Lazzi of the Waiter." The Three Stooges were among many film comedians inspired by this routine. In *Wee Wee Monsieur* (1938), when Curly casts a fishing line out of his apartment window to snatch a halibut off a fish peddler's cart, he is reworking a part of the routine in which a hungry waiter made use of a fishing rod to steal a roasted duck from a customer's table.

The restaurant comedy stood in good stead in early film with its standard characters — the harried waiter, the fussy customer, the arrogant chef, the apprehensive proprietor, and the pretty cashier. The characters were not so much characters as individual personality traits drawn together in controversy.

The Chef's Revenge (1915), a Sterling comedy, was a restaurant farce starring Lloyd Ingraham as the chef, Emma Clifton as the cashier, and Arthur Tavares as the proprietor. The restaurant is crowded with hungry patrons and the proprietor is frantic that his chef, Debean, is late, as usual. Debean arrives unapologetic and takes time to flirt with the pretty cashier before he gets to work. Mr. Millions, a grouchy millionaire, enters the café. Debean takes special care in preparing a steak for Millions, but Millions is a finicky diner and decides that the steak does not meet his high standards. Debean and Millions get into an argument and strike each other with the steak. The steak gets thrown around the restaurant and wallops a number of diners. In the end, Millions is ejected from the restaurant and Debean quits. The chef, who has gone into a jealous rage after learning that the cashier has gone off with the proprietor, sneaks back into the kitchen to plant a bomb in the boiler. He accidentally locks himself in the kitchen with the bomb and, when it explodes, he is sent flying along with the kitchen's full stock of pots and pans.

Similar comedies were produced by a number of companies. It became monotonous after awhile. The *Moving Picture World*'s description of *A Waiting Game*, a 1916 restaurant comedy produced by Essanay, summed up the general attitude: "[Ben Turpin] becomes a waiter in a swell café, and the usual things happen with dishes, guests, chefs, etc."[1] Waiters competing for the affections of a girl tossed eggs and cream puffs at each other in Kalem's *Rival Waiters* (1915). *His Private Wife* (1920), a Sunshine comedy starring Chester Conklin, showed a restaurant service being ruined by the cook and the proprietor engaging in a bout of dough slinging. *The Waiter's Ball* (1916), a Keystone comedy, centers on a cook (Roscoe Arbuckle) and a waiter (Al St. John) vying for the attention of a pretty cashier (Corinne Parquet). The men knock each other to the ground. They hit each other with brooms. At one point, St. John chases Arbuckle around the restaurant with a butcher knife. In the end, the pair's disruptive rivalry angers the manager, restaurant patrons and other employees.

Bill's New Pal (1915), an L-KO comedy, featured Billie Ritchie as the waiter, Henry Bergman as the chef and Gertrude Selby as the cashier. Ritchie's "new pal," as suggested by the title, is the chef, but friendships cannot withstand a lady as fair as Selby. The rivalry between these men interferes with business, annoying the proprietor and the patrons. The chef throws a number of kitchen utensils at Ritchie. A knife strikes Ritchie, seemingly killing him. The chef, becoming desperate, hides the body in a barrel. Meanwhile, the proprietor, patrons and waiters descend upon the kitchen to attack the troublesome chef. The chef falls down a cellar, and his pursuers follow. In the meantime, the revived waiter seeks safety in the oven and is almost incinerated before being rescued by Selby.

A knife is used as a deadly weapon. A man is almost incinerated in an oven. An apparent corpse is stuffed into a barrel. A seedy character is chased by a mob through a dark, dank cellar. This grungy restaurant, with its knives, ovens, barrels and cellar, has all the props needed for rough and low-down slapstick, but these same props would be just as much at home in a slasher thriller. A thin line separates slapstick and slasher, both of which depend on characters with dark and violent tendencies and the looming threat of fatal injury. No comedy demonstrates this better than *False Roomers* (1921). At the film's climax, a frustrated hotel manager drags his inept janitors (Sid Smith and Harry McCoy) into an office and ties

Charlie Chaplin is ready to enjoy an extravagant meal in *Modern Times* (1936) (courtesy Bruce Lawton Collection).

them to a table. A sharp-edged pendulum that swings back and forth above the men threatens to slice them by half. The pendulum was in fact introduced as a murder device in *False Roomers* before its lethal potential was famously demonstrated in *The Raven* (1935).*

Along with the violence of restaurant comedies came many silly routines having to do with food preparation. Roscoe Arbuckle comically juggles utensils in *The Cook* (1918). He bounces eggs off the floor. He flips pancakes in the air and catches them behind his back. In *A Flyer in Flapjacks* (1917), Lloyd Hamilton gets a rhythm going by flipping burgers in the air and catching them on a plate. One burger does not come down as expected. Hamilton looks puzzled as he stands holding out the plate and waiting for the burger to arrive. He is turning back to the grill as if he has given up on the burger when, suddenly, he spins around and sticks out the plate exactly in time to catch the burger. Carrying on the tradition in the sound era was Curly Howard, who turned food preparation into high comic art. Curly's kitchen skills are on display in a number of films, including *Playing the Ponies* (1937), *An Ache in Every Stake* (1941), *Busy Buddies* (1944) and *Crash Goes the Hash* (1944).

Today, the most recognizable of the restaurant characters is the chef, whose great arro-

Joe Murphy looks as if he is about to be filleted, in this unidentified restaurant comedy (courtesy Robert Arkus).

*This is not to deny an early depiction of the deadly pendulum featured in a French adaptation of "The Pit and the Pendulum" entitled *Le puits et le pendule* (1909).

gance makes him volatile and villainous. This character could recently be found in *Ratatouille* (2007) in the guise of Chef Skinner. John Cleese, as the chef in Monty Python's "Restaurant Sketch," exploited the idea of the testy chef better than anyone and, in the process, demonstrated that a madly volatile man with a big hat and a meat cleaver is indeed a threatening figure.

Other types of workplace comedies followed the same basic format. The hotel comedy, for instance, did no more than substitute the cook, waiter and cashier with a house detective, bellboy and a switchboard operator.

The tramps who were prevalent in silent film comedy were often obsessed with searching out their next meal. In *A Dog's Life* (1918), Charlie Chaplin has to be quick and furtive to steal food from a lunch wagon. In *The Vagrant* (1921), Lloyd Hamilton performs a routine in which he stares longingly at a diner enjoying a grand meal in a restaurant. But these scenes were as much sad as funny. Hamilton removes all trace of poignancy from the situation in *Breezing Along* (1927), in which he is introduced as a starving tramp seeking work at an unemployment office. Hamilton sits down next to a man chomping on an oversized hero sandwich, out of which is jutting a roll of salami. When the man is not looking, Hamilton steals the salami and replaces it with a rubber tube from the man's tool bag. As the man

A chef (Dave Morris, right) is prepared to grind a romantic rival (Fatty Voss) into hamburger. On the left is Vera Reynolds (courtesy Robert Arkus).

struggles to take a bite out of the rubbery sandwich, Hamilton comes to his assistance and grabs the other end of the sandwich. Securing his foot on the bench for leverage, Hamilton pulls back on the sandwich until the rubber is stretched out several feet. He gets distracted, lets go of the sandwich, and the rubber tube snaps forward, striking the man in the face.

A more elaborate and energetic routine develops out of the food theft premise in *Africa F.O.B.* (1925). Monty Banks is desperate for something to eat. He follows a baker holding up a tray of donuts thinking that he can snatch a donut without the baker noticing. He jumps up repeatedly to reach a donut, but the tray is out of his range. He eventually gets an idea. He opens his umbrella, raises it up to the level of the plate, and twirls it in a circle so that he catches the donuts on the umbrella's prongs. The plan works perfectly except that Banks stands with the umbrella next to a merry-go-round and children, thinking the donuts are brass rings, grab them off the umbrella as they come past. The last donut drops off the umbrella and Banks goes chasing it down a sloping street. He shoos away a pack of starving dogs that come racing alongside him to steal the donut for themselves. Even after he gets scooped up onto the fender of a streetcar, Banks still does not give up in his hungry pursuit. He holds steady on the fender while continuing to grab for the rolling donut, which is moving just fast enough to stay out of his reach. Finally, the donut sails into a lake, where it is promptly eaten by a duck. Banks had, in effect, crossed Chaplin's underfed tramp with Harold Lloyd's athletically daring go-getter.

Eating, even when food is available, is generally difficult in silent film comedy. The examples of this problem are many.

In *Free and Easy* (1921), Jimmie Adams and Lige Conley sit down for dinner at a hunting lodge. They start out having trouble keeping peas balanced on their forks. Nearby is a table of hunters consuming soup. Conley spills pepper on the table, which causes all of the hunters to list forward at the same time and sneeze into their soup. Soup erupts out of the bowls and splatters all over the diners.

The Cook (1918) sets out to make the point that spaghetti, with its slippery strands, is not the easiest food to eat. Roscoe Arbuckle and Buster Keaton are among a group of men who sit down at a table to eat spaghetti. The forks prove inadequate tools to manage the unwieldy meal. Arbuckle uses knitting needles to securely join sloppy strands together. He feeds spaghetti to another diner through a funnel. Keaton pours spaghetti into a coffee cup and uses a pair of scissors to trim off the excess spaghetti that hangs over the rim. He then settles back and genteelly drinks the spaghetti out of the cup. The other diners get hold of the same strand of spaghetti at opposite ends. The spaghetti strand stretches across the table into a single taut line, over which Arbuckle and Keaton hang their wet laundry.

Larry Semon found another solution to the spaghetti problem. He is able to eat it with great flourish through the aid of reverse photography in *Risks and Roughnecks* (1917).

Round food, which was able to roll off a plate, was not regarded as practical in silent film comedy. A dutiful valet stands by as his idle rich employer, Johnny Arthur, struggles to get a cherry on a fork in *Honest Injun* (1926). Arthur stabs at the cherry, but end up stabbing the valet in the leg instead. He stabs at it again and, this time, the cherry shoots off the plate and flies into the butler's mouth. A similar routine turned up in the Laurel & Hardy comedy *The Second Hundred Years* (1927). Stan Laurel is expected to use proper etiquette while pretending to be a dignitary at a dinner party, but his good manners are challenged when a cherry drops out of his fruit salad. He pursues the cherry around the serving plate in an effort to recapture it on his spoon. Eventually, the cherry springs off the plate and he has to chase it across the table. He is making an attempt to scoop up the cherry

Dick Sutherland (left), Ruth Hiatt and Lloyd Hamilton in a restaurant scene from *My Friend* (1924).

when it goes flying into the air and becomes stuck in the eye of the governor (Jimmy Finlayson). The team used the routine again the following year in *From Soup to Nuts* (1928). This time, it is Anita Garvin who has trouble with a cherry rolling off her plate. Garvin becomes frustrated from chasing the elusive cherry around the table while trying futilely to maintain her decorum. She is considerably funnier than Laurel, who acted as nothing more than a boob as he thoughtlessly pursued the cherry. Dick Van Dyke provided an affectionate recreation of this classic routine in *The Comic* (1969). W. C. Fields provided his variation in *Never Give a Sucker an Even Break* (1941). Fields, eating an ice cream soda, maneuvers two straws into the soda to lift out a cherry and deliver it to his mouth. He encounters a problem balancing the cherry, which keeps rolling up and down between the straws.

Convicts have difficulty eating peas in the Billy West prison comedy *A Rolling Stone* (1919). One inmate is on the verge of tears because he is unable to make his peas stay on his knife. He eventually gets the idea to mix them up in his mashed potatoes. West dumps his peas into a cup and drinks them, similar to Keaton's spaghetti gag in *The Cook* (1918).

Hank Mann made the struggle to eat peas a running joke. He continually came up with new and creative solutions to eat peas without having to balance them on a fork. In *When Spirits Move* (1920), Mann pulls out a needle and thread and threads the peas to create a pea necklace. He lowers the thread into his mouth and sucks off the peas. In *Junk* (1920), he inserts the peas into a device that looks like a pencil sharpener and he quickly rotates a crank on the side. The peas, which come out square-shaped, are unable to roll around. He turns over the device. A label reads, "Queer's Patented Peas Dicer." He was always finding creative ways to resolve the difficulties of eating food, as is shown when he dons earmuffs to keep his ears from getting wet while biting into a wedge of watermelon. He is, however, less successful eating a grapefruit, which repeatedly squirts juice into his eye.

A man trying to eat an inedible article probably was a comic scene for cavemen. This type of gag goes back at least to the Commedia dell'Arte. "Lazzi of the Waiter" involves a waiter mistakenly using oil from an oil lamp as salad dressing. Comic servant Arlecchino breaks his teeth by chewing on stones in a Commedia dell'Arte routine called "Lazzi of the Stones," which was introduced in Paris in 1766.

These routines continued on in motion pictures in direct and indirect forms. Charlie Chaplin, a comedian who greatly appreciated the traditions of the Commedia dell'Arte, had a galley cook using oil from an oil lamp as salad dressing in *Shanghaied* (1915). In a similar vein, Buster Keaton mixes gasoline into salad dressing in *The Timid Young Man* (1935). Keaton has a special appreciation of automobile fluids. In *The Garage* (1920), he manages to spice up his beverage by adding a shot of motor oil.

Usually, the consumption of inedible articles is unintentional. Hank Mann attends a fancy dinner party in *When Spirits Move* (1920). He sets out to eat spaghetti, but confetti is hanging down his face, and he accidentally wraps up the confetti in his fork and eats it by mistake. This was a gag repeated by Chaplin in *City Lights* (1931). Chaplin is tipsy, which is the reason it takes him longer to realize that he is eating the confetti.

Roscoe Arbuckle perpetuated the notion that fat people will eat anything. Arbuckle, as a hospital patient in *Good Night, Nurse!* (1918), impulsively eats a thermometer that a doctor places in his mouth. Suffering the ill effects of the mercury, Arbuckle is rushed into surgery. Arbuckle is posting playbills in *Back Stage* (1919) when he sees a small boy eating — and enjoying — the poster paste. Arbuckle is immediately curious to know how the paste tastes for himself. At first, he tentatively sticks a finger into his paste brush and licks the paste off his finger. He smiles at the camera to let viewers know that, much to his surprise, the paste does not taste bad. He is sufficiently encouraged at this point to plunge the brush greedily into his mouth.

For decades, screen comedians made it a habit to eat inedible objects for laughs. Those who were somewhat otherworldly shared this peculiar trait. Harpo Marx ate buttons off a bellman's vest, quenched his thirst by drinking ink, and snacked on a crunchy thermometer. Ben Blue eats oysters, shells and all, in *Taxi Barrons* (1933). In *Lost in a Harem* (1944), Abbott and Costello are hypnotized into believing they are termites and proceed to eat a wooden chair and table. In *High Society* (1955), Huntz Hall is offered a "cold plate" and acts overjoyed to take a bite out of the actual plate. Woody Allen, groggily emerging from a cryogenic state, eats a rubber surgical glove in *Sleeper* (1973). Even a lovely young woman could engage in these rough gnashings. In *The Bargain of the Century* (1933), Thelma Todd digs into a serving of ZaSu Pitts' homemade ice cream without knowing that a watch fell into the churn. She has a hard time chewing at first and then is appalled to drag a long mainspring out of her mouth.

Curly Howard cannot figure out how to get past the leafy wrapping of a tamale in *Three Sappy People* (1939).* Yet, he had no trouble eating a number of indigestible items. He mistakes a powder puff for a biscuit in the same short. He mistakes a potholder for pancakes in *Busy Buddies* (1944). This last routine was later expanded in *Uncivil Warbirds* (1946),

---

*An earlier variation of this routine appeared in the "Our Gang" comedy *The Pooch* (1932). Matthew "Stymie" Beard, peeling his way through artichoke leaves, famously remarks, "It might choke Arty, but it ain't gonna choke Stymie!"

during which Curly bakes a potholder into cake. The cake is served at a dinner party and soon, a roomful of people are coughing up feathers. This routine, alternately known as "coughing up feathers" and "feathers in the cake," also appeared in Abbott & Costello's *The Naughty Nineties* (1945) and the Three Stooges' *Three Hams on Rye* (1950).

In *Sons of the Desert* (1933), Stan Laurel is sitting in the Hardy living room by himself, reading. He reaches into a bowl of fruit to remove an apple. A label, revealed to the camera, indicates that the apple is made of wax. Laurel, however, does not examine the apple closely before he bites into it. Surely, he can be expected to find out his mistake soon enough. However, Laurel is no normal man. He is not deterred in the least, even though he is clearly having a hard time chewing and swallowing the apple. He is lacking the common sense given a small child to distinguish the taste and consistency of actual food. It takes Hardy to see what he is doing and to tell him that the apple that he is eating is not real. Hardy then tells his wife that he caught Laurel eating a wax apple. She fumes. "That's the third apple I've missed this week!" she exclaims. The idea that Laurel has made this same mistake several times before is the final and biggest shock for Hardy. Mrs. Hardy later refers to Laurel as "that wax-eater," as if this strange incident in many ways defines him.

In *Way Out West* (1937), Laurel and Hardy need to recover a deed stolen from them by Jimmy Finlayson. Laurel remarks to Hardy, "We'll get that deed or I'll eat your hat." After their effort to recover the deed fails disastrously, a disgruntled Hardy intends to hold his friend to his word. Laurel resists eating the hat at first. He insists, "Whoever heard of anybody eating a hat?" But Hardy will not change his mind. With Hardy looking on with intent interest, Laurel takes a timid bite out of the hat brim. The action is accompanied by a loud crunching noise and the song "Where Did You Get That Hat?" But then, suddenly, Laurel reacts as if he is not at all bothered by the taste. He pulls a handkerchief out of his pocket and ties it neatly around his neck in the fashion of a bib. Then, he pulls out a salt shaker and sprinkles salt on the hat. He is about to take a ravenous bite out of the hat when Hardy, aggravated, snatches the hat away from him. Moments later, when Laurel is not looking, Hardy steals a bite out of the hat for himself. He chews at the piece for a bit, looking increasingly nauseous. Finally, he spits out the piece in disgust.

In *Saps at Sea* (1940), Laurel and Hardy get trapped on a boat with escaped killer Nick Grainger (Rychard Cramer). Grainger demands at gunpoint that the duo "rustle ... [him] up some grub" and he will not listen to their excuses as they try to explain they have no food on board. Hardy gets the idea that, if they prepare him a synthetic meal out of indigestible items, Grainger might get sick and no longer be a threat. They fix up string, red paint and sponge together to look like spaghetti and meatballs. They top off this dish with soap shavings meant to look like grated cheese. The duo is so pleased with their efforts that they tell Grainger, with great assurance, that the meal is "better than mother used to make." However, the killer has gotten wise to the ruse and forces these proud chefs to eat the meal themselves. Hardy gags while trying to swallow the sponge meatball and Laurel gets nauseous forcing down the string spaghetti. Fans of Laurel & Hardy have complained that Laurel, "that wax-eater," should have had no problem eating a mere piece of string.

A connoisseur of inedible objects who leaves a lasting impression is Larry Semon, who takes this eccentricity to an extreme. In *The Show* (1922), Semon is working in a theatre as a property man. He is tantalized by the items in a make-up kit. The lipstick looks so appetizing that he proceeds to take a bite of it. Encouraged by the taste of the lipstick, he moves on to a powder puff, which he gleefully stuffs into his mouth as though it were a powdered donut.

Chaplin ate an old boot because he was starving. Laurel ate a wax apple because he thought it was real. Curly ate a pot holder because he mistook it for a pancake. True, Harpo had no excuse for his odd eating habits. Harpo, though, was being puckish when he ate buttons, which could be regarded as acceptable behavior. After all, a button looks as harmless as a piece of candy, and little children have been known to swallow buttons without incident. But Semon, who grins foolishly as he gobbles up obvious make-up supplies, looks to be inhuman. Eating a powder puff, with face powder spraying out of his mouth, is not so much puckish as it is freakish.

Other comedians tried their hand at recreating Semon's powder-puff routine. A version by Curly Howard, complete with teeth-rending sound effects, has already been discussed. A more tidy and polite version was performed by Harold Lloyd in *For Heaven's Sake* (1926). A pretty young woman (Jobyna Raltston) has baked several small cakes and arranged them on a serving platter. A powder puff, which resembles the cakes, accidentally drops on the platter without anyone noticing. Ralston offers a cake to Lloyd, who unwittingly removes the powder puff from the platter. Lloyd, intent on making a good impression on Ralston, struggles to be courteous, despite the difficulty of eating this improbable snack. He is straining to smile as he finally bites off a piece and gulps it down. Lloyd's version of the routine, which puts a lovely lady's affections at stake, provides the motivation and tension lacking in the other versions. It has to be said, though, that Curly, through the silliness of his gestures and expressions, makes his version the funniest even without motivation and tension. In the end, this routine depends more on the details provided by props and performance than the broader circumstances. Lloyd, though he provides a satisfying setup, is too subtle in the details. A puff of powder that bursts out of Lloyd's mouth is nothing compared to the mess produced by Semon. Semon manages by sneezing repeatedly to scatter the powder in several directions. Powder drizzles down his shirt front. His lips become coated in powder. The Semon scene is grotesque—grotesque but funny. *Uncivil Warbirds*, which multiplies the players and increases the emissions, ends with the scene obscured by a blizzard of feathers, which is much more memorable than the faint bit of powder that Lloyd produces.

Lloyd's version of the powder-puff routine was, in fact, a reworking of a routine from *Grandma's Boy* (1922). Instead of a powder puff dropped on a tray, it was mothballs dropped in a candy box. Again, the treat is offered to him by a pretty young woman (Mildred Davis) and Lloyd, who is trying to make a good impression, graciously accepts. Lloyd's reactions to the taste of the mothballs are more exaggerated this time. He grimaces painfully at the camera, then smiles at Davis to let her think he finds the candy to be delicious. The routine is developed even further upon the arrival of a romantic rival (Charles Stevenson). Stevenson eats some mothballs as well and he also does his best to conceal his disgust. At one point, the two men stare at each other with a look of sheer horror. The men are bonded by their mutual discomfort and act in unison as they nod and smile at Davis. The scene is well constructed and Lloyd is in top form.

The Sennett gag writers, in their own unique style, cooked up a more fantastic version of the powder-puff routine for Harry Langdon to perform in *Picking Peaches* (1924). Harry sits down for breakfast intending to eat a pancake, but he unwittingly grabs hold of his wife's powder puff instead. He is too busy to notice his mistake as he decisively works his knife to slice off a bite-sized piece. Harry's facial expressions as he eats this indigestible ball of cotton velour are exquisite. He first looks puzzled and then distressed. He turns to the side and coughs, which releases a plume of white smoke. This looks like a magician's trick, as if Harry is an illusionist pretending to be a smoke-breathing beast of old. He then covers his mouth, at which point powder explodes out of his ears. This is a type of routine that is not meant to be sensible or controlled. It should, by all means, be preposterous.

It is hard to find an action that is comparable to Semon's powder-puff-eating spectacle. Jim Carrey swallows a time bomb in *The Mask* (1994), which would seem at first glance to be more extreme than what Semon did. Still, context is always relevant. Carrey, endowed with super powers by an ancient mask, devours the bomb to save innocent bystanders from being killed. The bomb explodes harmlessly inside his stomach. In the end, Carrey had behaved reasonably under the circumstances and CGI effects have made his actions, apart from a fiery belch, neat and tidy. The simple stagehand's rapacious consumption of the powder puff did not save anyone's life. The consumption was for the consumer's own perverse pleasure. Semon, a fan of L. Frank Baum's "Oz" books, may have read in Baum's *Queen Zixi of Ix* about the ball-shaped creatures called the Roly-Rogues, who had "no judgment and consume[d] buttons and hairpins as eagerly as they [did] food."[2] Semon was a Roly-Rogue.

Semon, despite his wholehearted effort, does end up choking on the powder puff. He coughs, which sprays the white powder onto the face of a black woman. The black woman, who has now turned white, screams in horror. Semon, who was fond of using special effects to create cartoonish routines, would have enjoyed the many applications of CGI. It is fun to imagine Semon being alive today and eating a time bomb in his own version of *The Mask*.

Harold Lloyd, as a dinner party guest in *Among Those Present* (1921), is so smitten with a society girl that he is unable to pay attention to what he is doing. He thinks that he is removing food from a serving tray when he is, in fact, reaching into a centerpiece and collecting flowers. He remains oblivious of his mistake as he stuffs a particularly large flower into his mouth. Lloyd Hamilton is on the verge of starvation when he delicately nibbles a flower in *Move Along* (1927). In *Pardon My Scotch* (1935), Larry Fine ecstatically sprinkles salt on a flower and stuffs it into his mouth. Eating flowers was something a person did if they were ridiculously confused, sadly desperate, or outright kooky.

Circumstances changed in the 1950s. Obtaining food was not the issue in that prosperous decade. The issue had become maintaining a healthy and attractive weight by eating nutritious food. In the *Your Show of Shows* sketch "Health Food Restaurant," Sid Caesar is dragged by his wife (Imogene Coca) to one of those trendy establishments, where he is served a flower as an appetizer. The taste of the flower does not at all sit well on his palate. Other comedians, when having to eat something distasteful, act forlorn and nauseous. But not Caesar. Riled to anger, he violently spits out the repulsive item. He growls like a lion as he demands for the waiter to take away the flower and bring him a steak.

The free-spirited, "flower power" sixties introduced a new reason for eating a flower, as expressed by Peter Sellers after he blithely dines on one in *The Bobo* (1967). "I believe, you see," Sellers explains, "that, if a thing is beautiful to the eye and pleasant to the smell, why should it not be delicious to the taste?"

Comedians are no longer seen eating inedible items today, unless you count Jack Black snacking on animal dung in *Year One* (2009).

Arlecchino, who has become shipwrecked, is so hungry that he chews on his shoes in the Commedia dell'Arte routine "Lazzi of Hunger." This is not all that different than Chaplin, as a starving prospector, eating his boots in *The Gold Rush* (1925).

It was the failed Arctic expeditions of British explorer Sir John Franklin that inspired Chaplin to create *The Gold Rush*. Franklin led three expeditions to the Arctic between 1819 and 1847. Dominating historical accounts of the expeditions were stories of survivors

Harold Lloyd (right) and James T. Kelley prepare to eat in *Among Those Present* (1921) (courtesy www.doctormacro.com).

descending into madness and resorting to cannibalism. But it was not the madness or cannibalism that captured the public's imagination as much as it was the strange stories of the survivors eating their own boots to stay alive. Chaplin set out to turn the tragic tales into comedy. Mack Swain, Chaplin's partner in the snowy Alaska wilderness, descends into madness and tries to eat Chaplin, whom he imagines to be a big chicken. As funny as this was, Chaplin eating his boots proved to be the film's most memorable scene.

Food plays a major role in *The Gold Rush*, which explains the reason that the film includes a second classic food-related routine. This one has become known as the "Dance of the Rolls," wherein Chaplin creates a tabletop dance routine using a pair of forks with dinner rolls as feet. Joyce Milton wrote, "The routine was a variation on an old music hall turn attributed to the British comic, G. H. Chirwin, who made a pair of clay pipes 'dance' on a tin tray."[3]

Another comedian had performed the Dance of the Rolls on film before Chaplin. In *The Rough House* (1917), Roscoe Arbuckle is flirting with a pretty young maid who is serving him breakfast. He takes a fork in each hand and stabs them into a pair of dinner rolls. He proceeds to manipulate the forks to perform a dance routine, including high kicks and a shuffle. It is a silly little routine that ends almost as soon as it begins. By contrast, Chaplin's routine was more intricately designed, carefully timed, and gracefully executed. Also, Chaplin's scene assumes a sense of poignancy as the tramp character is imagining himself entertaining dinner guests who have, in fact, stood him up.

Charlie Chaplin's classic boot-eating scene in *The Gold Rush* (1925) (courtesy www.doctormacro.com).

Larry Semon's answer to Chaplin's Dance of the Rolls came in the World War I comedy *Spuds* (1927). Semon is an American soldier at a French café. A language barrier is making it difficult for him to communicate with his waitress. He decides, as a way to socialize with the waitress, to draw a cartoon of his fat sergeant. Once the drawing is complete, he cuts an apple in half and affixes one of the halves to the drawing in place of the sergeant's stomach. Then, he cuts two round holes beneath the stomach and sticks his fingers through the holes to create legs. Finally, he puts olives at the end of fingers as shoes. He proceeds to move his fingers around to make the cartoon sergeant perform a dance. This pantomime, which could well be called Semon's Dance of the Olives and Apple Half, lacks the elegance, charm and simplicity of the Chaplin routine.

Curly presents the Dance of the Rolls in *Pardon My Scotch* (1935). Moe, annoyed, sticks forks into a couple of dinner rolls and then pokes the rolls into Curly's eyes. This is a classic Chaplin scene done in the Stooges' style.

The Dance of the Rolls remains popular with present-day leading men. Robert Downey, Jr., performed the routine in *Chaplin* (1992) and Johnny Depp followed suit in *Benny and Joon* (1993).

Modern man does not hunt his own food and, in instances where he dines at a restaurant, he does not prepare his own food, either. This could create a degree of anxiety for a restaurant patron. In the Commedia dell'Arte routine "Lazzi of the Waiter," the waiter is at odds with his customers. When a customer complains about a dirty plate, the waiter cleans the plate by rubbing it on the back of his pants. This is not essentially different from a more recent scene in *Waiting...* (2005) in which cooks respond to a customer's complaint by mixing spit, dandruff and pubic hair into the customer's meal. The risk of finding a pubic hair in a restaurant meal is not only a vulgarity that arises in modern comedy. Sydney Chaplin, as a waiter in *A Submarine Pirate* (1915), has just finished setting a table for a party when he pulls a long loaf of French bread out of the front of his pants and lays it nonchalantly across the table.

Food safety, including restaurant hygiene, had become a major concern of the public at the start of the 20th century. *His Trysting Places* (1914) deals with the unhygienic table manners to be found at a greasy spoon lunch counter. Charlie Chaplin is the first to show bad manners by wiping his hands on an old man's beard. But then Chaplin has to contend with a diner who is too disgusting even for him. The diner, Mack Swain, sits next to Chaplin, crudely slurping soup. Chaplin finds the slurping to be so loud that he sticks his fingers in his ears to muffle the noise. Chaplin looks positively nauseated as Swain scratches his head with his fork. He has finally had enough when he is about to eat his meal and Swain sneezes into it. It is at this point that a slapping match erupts between the two men. It would be more than a decade before Swain's bad eating habits degenerated from soup-slurping to attempted cannibalism in *The Gold Rush*.

Elements of disparate routines were often patched together to form a new routine.

Laurel (left) and Hardy (center) get into trouble with a drunk (Jimmy Aubrey) while out dining in *That's My Wife* (1929).

Take, as one element, the elusive little critter that serves as a comic pest. In *Golf* (1922), Larry Semon takes to the fairways to play golf, only to be pestered by a mischievous squirrel. The squirrel pops out of a golf hole, snatches Semon's ball, and then vanishes back down the hole. Moments later, the squirrel emerges from another hole and drops the ball on the green. Semon is walking over to the ball when the squirrel makes off with it again. Semon becomes increasingly frustrated as the squirrel continues to move his ball back and forth. He draws a revolver and fires unsuccessfully at the squirrel. Semon rests the gun on the ground while he reaches down into the hole to rummage around for the squirrel. The squirrel comes out of another hole, takes the gun in hand, and fires a shot into Semon's backside. The squirrel stands as an antecedent of the gopher in *Caddyshack* (1980).

Lloyd Hamilton had similar problems as a hunter, having to contend with an aggressive rabbit in *His Musical Sneeze* (1919). The rabbit, hopping in and out of holes, bites Hamilton on the hand, the backside, and the face. The creature is a combination of Bugs Bunny and Monty Python's Killer Rabbit of Caerbannog (*Monty Python and the Holy Grail*, 1975). The routine had been such a success for Hamilton that he recreated it 12 years later in *Hello Napoleon* (1931).

Not even the dinner table is safe from pesky rodents, which was proven when a ship's captain discovered a mouse wriggling around in a bowl of soup in *Shorty Among the Cannibals* (1915).

A famous line from *Caddyshack*, delivered by Rodney Dangerfield, was, "This steak still has marks from where the jockey was hitting it." This brings us back to the anxiety that men have about eating food from unfamiliar sources. Man needs to be able to understand and dominate the prey beneath them in the food chain. This also means that they need to understand and dominate what is laid out on their plate and to be, at the very least, secure in their knowledge that it is dead.

The Three Stooges attempt to run a diner in *Playing the Ponies* (1937). Curly becomes angry at a dog who has pilfered sausages from the kitchen. A customer has just finished ordering a hot dog when Curly bursts out of the kitchen, chasing the dog with a meat cleaver. The customer quickly changes his order to eggs and toast. A similar misunderstanding arises in *The Naughty Nineties* (1945) when Lou Costello overhears a cook in the kitchen fussing with a cat. Later, when the cook serves Costello a grilled steak, Costello assumes that the steak was carved out of the cat. It furthers this assumption that the actual cat is hiding under the table and it cries out every time that Costello tries to cut into the steak. In the Three Stooges comedy *Malice in the Palace* (1949), Moe and Shemp get the idea that the café's hot dogs are made out of real dogs. Shemp hesitantly raises the hot dog to his lips, at which point the hot dog sprouts an animated tongue and fondly licks Shemp's face. The earliest known version of this routine was performed by Johnny Arthur in the silent comedy *Honest Injun* (1926). Over the years, the routine evolved from a simple misunderstanding, to a more elaborate misunderstanding, to a misunderstanding that turns out not to be a misunderstanding at all.

Other meals still had much life in them. *Short Orders* (1923) found Stan Laurel contending with a lively wedge of gorgonzola. Laurel has to stab the cheese with a knife to stop it from hopping around the table. In *Why Babies Leave Home* (1928), Ben Turpin accidentally mixes popcorn into pancake batter, which produces a pancake that bounces out the door. In *The Guide* (1921), Clyde Cook is content with his meal until he sets his attention on an asparagus stalk, a very lively vegetable that moves away from him every time he tries to take a bite. Cook, with a smug smile, lifts up his fork and plays it like a flute. The asparagus rises up obediently, much like a snake under the control of a snake charmer. It is only then that Cook is able to take hold of the asparagus and eat it.

Gale Henry sets off an intriguing scene in *The Detectress* (1919) when she sits down in a Chinese restaurant and orders a bowl of chop suey. The bowl is overflowing with indeterminable, unappetizing ingredients. Henry digs around in this tangle of debris and pulls out a variety of items, ranging from a piece of rope to a giant mosquito. She expresses a different emotion, including surprise, bewilderment and horror, in response to each new discovery. Finally, something wiggly pokes out of the noodles and vegetables. It is, she sees, a furry tail. Henry reaches into the lively bowl of food and pulls out a puppy. The humor in this routine largely comes from the eloquence of Henry's reactions.

This routine would have been ideally suited to Lloyd Hamilton, who was highly skillful at comic reactions. Director Eddie Sutherland described, with affection, a scene in which Hamilton sits down to dine on a trio of clams, but the clams are being uncooperative and appear to be conspiring to outsmart him. All three of the clams are open at first, but then they close, one by one, as Hamilton attempts to eat them. Unfortunately, Sutherland did not name the film in which this routine appeared and the scene cannot be found in any of the Hamilton films that have survived. Hardly a consolation is an insipid version of the routine performed by Snub Pollard in *Once Over* (1928). Pollard has trouble with a single

Eddie Nelson learns the dangers of making turtle soup in *Hot and Heavy* (1925) (courtesy Robert Arkus).

jumbo clam that closes tight whenever he moves in with his fork. When Pollard attacks the stubborn clam with a meat cleaver, it sprays a stream of water and leaps off the table. Pollard provides no array of subtle expressions. He is as restrained as a man can be brandishing a meat cleaver.

Another classic routine with difficult bivalve mollusks has survived in a wide variety of forms. The routine, known informally as the "oyster stew" routine, originated in *Wandering Willies* (1926), a Sennett comedy directed by Del Lord. Billy Bevan is served a bowl of oyster stew, which the waiter assures him is fresh. Bevan is dunking a cracker into his stew when a oyster pops out, steals the cracker from him, and disappears back into the milky depths. Bevan is not sure if he is seeing things and gets himself another cracker. This time, in plain view, the cracker is snatched out of his hand by the lively oyster. Bevan fashions a needle and thread into a miniature fishing pole and baits the hook with a cracker, which he proceeds to lower into the soup. The oyster grabs away the cracker without a problem. Bevan, in a frenzied effort to kill the pesky oyster, stabs his fork repeatedly into the soup. He gets a hold of the oyster's tongue, which stretches out a far distance before it snaps out of his hand. At this point, the oyster pokes out of its hiding place to squirt Bevan with soup. Bevan, determined that the oyster does not get the best of him, picks up a club and smashes it down on the bowl. The soup splashes onto a diner at a neighboring table. With the bowl now shattered into pieces, the oyster no longer has cover and is left to hop across the table to escape. Bevan continues to whack at the oyster and, at one point, delivers a blow to a man's head. Now, the restaurant manager and assorted patrons are chasing after Bevan, who is forced to flee the restaurant. In keeping with the Sennett style, it was necessary for the routine to degenerate into a food fight and a madcap chase. At the core of this routine is a simple goal, to establish the chowder's freshness and to take that idea to a humorous extreme. In time, Lord would move this routine away from that essential joke.

Lord had his first chance to recreate the routine in the Roach comedy *Thundering Taxis* (1933), in which it is Clyde Cook who is served the oyster stew. This is the first sound version of the routine, which meant that Lord had to decide what sort of sound a belligerent oyster should make. In the end, the choice was made for the oyster to emit a duck quack whenever it appeared. Lord recognized that the strength of the routine came from the comedian's reactions. The scene, as edited, spends much of the time on reaction shots from Clyde. Clyde starts out bewildered, then becomes apprehensive, and finally becomes angry. Clyde was a deadpan comedian who relied mostly on his eyes to express his emotions. This puts him at a disadvantage in a scene that demanded a wild demonstration of emotion. Cook ultimately responds in a fairly logical way. He picks up a heavy object, smashes it down on the bowl, and then storms out to have lunch elsewhere.

Charley Bowers may have been inspired by this routine when he used stop-motion animation to create elaborate beady-eyed comic mollusks in his comedies *He Done His Best* (1926) and *Whoozit* (1928).

A former Sennett writer, Vernon Smith, included the "oyster stew" routine in *The Cohens and Kellys in Trouble* (1933). The scene is not available for viewing, but it was, at least, funny to a *New York Times* critic, who wrote, "One of the high spots in the comedy occurs when a live lobster gets into Cohen's oyster stew while the two are drunk."[4]

The third time was the charm for Lord. In the Three Stooges comedy *Dutiful but Dumb* (1941), Curly Howard was not going to take this attack by an oyster lightly. Curly expresses a great deal of frustration, issuing grunts and squeals and smacking himself in the head. This time, the oyster sounds were more appropriate. The oyster now makes a loud snapping noise as it opens and shuts its shell. It also makes an unsettling crunching noise as it bites down on Curly's finger. Curly tries to lure the elusive oyster to the surface with crackers. He baits a thread with a cracker and dangles the cracker in the soup. The oyster is able to snatch away the cracker without getting caught on the hook. Next, Curly sprinkles an excessive amount of pepper on a cracker in an attempt to make the oyster choke. Instead, the oyster responds to the pepper with no more than a sneeze, which sends a wave of soup splashing onto Curly. As much as this irritates Curly, it gets even worse when the oyster reappears to spray a steady stream of soup into Curly's face. The routine ends with Curly pulling out a gun and firing wildly into the soup.

Lord got the most out of the scene by having Curly and the oyster remain together in the frame for most of their battle. After all, the scene was a comic match wherein the participants needed to play off each other with their various actions and reactions. The *Thundering Taxis* version of the routine had lost its rhythm and flow by focusing on lingering close-ups of Cook.

Lou Costello took on the "oyster" routine in *Here Come the Co-Eds* (1945). Costello starts out the scene in the standard fashion. He is putting a cracker in the stew when the oyster pops out of the stew, snatches away the cracker, and disappears back inside the stew. Costello makes himself into a pitiable victim in the scene. He wheezes and sobs in expressing perpetual distress. The scene is made even more surreal by the fact that Abbott, after being told by Costello about the oyster, swirls his fork throughout the stew and fails to find anything. Is the oyster a phantom that only Costello can see? In previous versions, the diner had randomly pulled out a needle and thread to use as a fishing line, but Costello comes up with the idea of sticking a pin through his tie and carefully bending it into the shape of a hook. He dangles the hook into the bowl, at which time the oyster grabs hold and yanks Costello's face into the stew. Director Jean Yarborough captures most of the action in a wide shot to include Abbott, who is reading a newspaper and remains oblivious to the oyster tormenting Costello. Abbott occasionally grumbles as soup splashes on him or Costello gets too loud. In the end, his presence weakens the scene by acting as an unnecessary distraction.

In the next ten years, Abbott & Costello and the Three Stooges both returned to the oyster stew routine on a number of occasions. These versions strayed far from the original concept of the routine and none of them were particularly funny.

The writers of *The Wistful Widow of Wagon Gap* (1947) tried to impose logic on this surreal routine. They had a mischievous boy slip a frog into Costello's soup. It takes longer in this scene for Costello to become aware that he has something alive in his soup. He is preoccupied by talking to Abbott the whole time that the frog is stealing his crackers. He does not even notice right away when he scoops up this bloated frog on his spoon. Costello finally sees the frog, panics, and drops the spoon back into the bowl. He lets Abbott know what he has just seen. Abbott does not believe him, but he is willing to humor his friend by switching soup bowls. When neither man is looking, the frog leaps from the soup into Costello's milk. Once the soups are exchanged, the frog climbs out of the milk and dives directly into Costello's new bowl. Again, the writers offer a logical explanation for Abbott not discovering the creature. Of course, they are willing to assume that the audience will accept that a frog can possess a high level of cunning. The routine ends with the frog poking out of the soup and blowing Costello a raspberry.

Moe Howard performs the routine in the Three Stooges comedy *Shivering Sherlocks* (1948). The writers are unwilling to have Moe deviate from his essential role as the irascible boss Stooge whose job it is to smack around the other two Stooges. Moe, who does not see the oyster swiping the crackers, assumes that it is Larry and Shemp who are the culprits. This gives him an ideal excuse to smack his partners. Moe, possibly as a homage to his ailing brother Curly, smacks his face and barks at the soup just as Curly had when he performed the scene. This is the most aggressive of all the mollusks featured in these routines. The oyster crunches down Moe's finger, then it chomps on Moe's nose, and then it clamps onto Shemp's finger. Larry, in an effort to dislodge the oyster from Moe's nose, picks up a rolling pin and slams it into Moe's face. At this point, the routine lapses into a standard Stooges routine in which the comedians hit one another with heavy tools.

The routine turned up again in *Abbott and Costello in the Foreign Legion* (1950). Abbott and Costello, newly recruited as Legionnaires, become lost in a desert in Algeria. They wander through the desert, desperate for food and water. Meanwhile, an old Arab man stops at an oasis to water his camel and collect water for himself. He is bending down into the water hole when his false teeth come loose and fall into the water. The old man is unable to retrieve his teeth before a ravenous fish comes along and takes them away. The man is frightened when the fish pokes out of the water, showing the false teeth affixed between its jaws in an oversized grin. Later, Abbott and Costello arrive at the oasis and decide to catch fish out of the water hole. Abbott catches his first fish, which he hands to Costello to clean. Costello is rinsing the fish off in the water when the toothy fish reappears and steals the fish out of Costello's hand. This business is repeated twice as Abbott, oblivious to his partner's troubles, hands Costello more fish. The fish, by snatching away Costello's fish, is no different than the oyster that snatched away Costello's crackers. Later, in the same manner as the oyster, the fish bites Costello's finger and squirts water in the face.*

In *Lost in Alaska* (1952), a whale steak seems to be so fresh that it still has an active blowhole. Every time Costello cuts into it, the steak sprays a forceful stream of water into his face. This is no different than Costello's experience with oyster stew.

Two variations of this routine were included by veteran comedy writer Felix Adler in the Three Stooges' *Income Tax Sappy* (1954). First, a hero sandwich snaps at Moe and squirts him in the face with mustard. Later, Larry is served lobster gumbo and a lobster claw repeatedly rises out of the gumbo to steal bread and attack Larry. A big, menacing lobster claw lacks the humor and charm of a mischievous little oyster.

Huntz Hall performed a loose variation of the oyster routine in the Bowery Boys comedy *Jungle Gents* (1954), which was the work of Stooges veterans Elwood Ullman and Edward Bernds. Hall is getting ready to cook oyster stew. Reaching into a bucket of snapping oysters, he lets out an ear-splitting scream. In the next shot, Hall comes running into the frame, struggling to shake loose a multitude of oysters clamped onto his face, arms and hands. This routine has violent oysters getting the better of a man who intends to eat them. Otherwise, it owes more to even older crab gags that appeared in silent comedies. In *Catch of Hard Shell Crabs* (1903), a mischievous boy empties a bucket of crabs into an old man's bed. The old man no sooner settles into bed than he jumps up with crabs clinging off various parts of his body.

Crab routines were something entirely different from those involving oysters. Invariably,

---

*This routine also has elements of a silly fishing routine performed by Buster Keaton in *Convict 13* (1920). Keaton has managed, in his ineptitude as a golfer, to hit a ball into a pond. He is about to swing his club at the ball when a fish rises out of the water and swallows the ball whole. Keaton, intent on recovering his ball, roots around in the pond and snatches up one fish after another. He eventually finds a fish with an unusual bulge and applies a hard squeeze to pop the ball out of the fish's mouth. Keaton lays the misbehaving fish across his knee and spanks it.

the comedian was slow to realize when he had a crab down the back of his pants. This is certainly the case in *Breezing Along* (1927). Lloyd Hamilton, a butler serving a crab entrée at a dinner party, has no idea that a mischievous boy has slipped one of the crabs into his back pocket. It is his assumption when the crab pinches him in the backside that a maid has jabbed him accidentally with her serving fork.

Harold Lloyd could not look more dumfounded when a crab first gets inside his pants in *Hot Water* (1924). He is wildly shaking his leg to rid himself of the pest when he kicks a man in the shin. Stan Laurel performed an exaggerated version of the same routine in *Liberty* (1929). Laurel's entire body convulses each time that the crab nips at him. He is not safe to be around due to the sudden, jerky movements of his arms and legs. Worse than kicking someone, he shoves partner Oliver Hardy to the ground, bolts threateningly towards the owner of a music shop, knocks over a record player, and shatters dozens of records. His panic escalates as these mysterious stabbing pains persist and he is unable to gain control of his body.

Lloyd transferred most of the action to the crab when he reworked the routine for *Speedy* (1928). The comedian is strolling through Coney Island with Ann Christy when a crab slips off a seafood stand and drops inconspicuously into his pocket. The rambunctious crab creates trouble with its various actions, which include pinching passersby, popping balloons, yanking off a woman's skirt, and stealing intimate apparel out of a woman's purse.

Writers mixed and matched components of routines in an effort to create something new. This was a continuing strategy of John Grant, who used his encyclopedic knowledge of old comedy routines to furnish Abbott & Costello with a steady stream of material. An example of his mixing and matching is evident in a 1954 episode of *The Colgate Comedy Hour*. Part of this new hybrid routine came from a haunted-house routine wherein an arm emerges from a sliding panel to steal a visitor's hat. Grant spliced this gag with gags from the stew routine, which shows that comedy can make strange bedfellows. Costello, disguised as the president of a politically unstable South American country, is warned that spies are out to kill him. He has just turned away from his soup when a hand rises out of a sliding panel in the table and sets out to pour poison into the soup. The arm retreats back down into the table as soon as Costello turns back around. In that split second Costello got a glimpse of the arm, but he is not certain of what he saw. He turns away again and the arm returns. He turns back and the arm retreats. This is much like the oyster being elusive with Costello. In the end, Costello battles with the arm, which grabs him and pulls his face down into the soup.

The "oyster stew" routine had a less than fond send-off in *Abbott & Costello Meet the Keystone Kops* (1955). In this instance it is not an oyster in soup that causes Costello problems but a squirrel that has burrowed inside a loaf of bread.

Food maintained a long-running truce with comedians until *Sleeper* (1973), in which Woody Allen is attacked by a blobby batch of instant pudding and needs to beat the pudding into submission with a broom.

Abbott & Costello's repertoire contained a number of food-related routines, including the "Turkey sandwich and a cup of coffee" routine.

Laurel and Hardy performed a less elaborate version of the routine in two films, *Should Married Men Go Home?* (1928) and *Men o' War* (1929). Laurel and Hardy want to impress two girls that they have met in a soda shop by buying them sodas, but there are four of them and they only have enough money for three sodas. Hardy has a solution. He tells Laurel to refrain from ordering a soda. All he has to do, explains Hardy, is say that he is not thirsty. When Hardy goes to order the soda, he goes through the pretense of asking Laurel what he would like to have. Laurel, confused by this apparent offer, orders a soda. Hardy frantically pulls him aside and reminds him about their scheme and their lack of funds. Laurel can not comprehend this and keeps making the same mistake again and again.

Abbott and Costello took this same routine to new, crazed heights in *Keep 'Em Flying* (1941). The duo arrives at a diner with only enough money to purchase a single sandwich. Abbott tells Costello that they can share the sandwich but it would be better if the waitress not know they are short on funds. He instructs Costello to pretend he is not hungry and simply tell the waitress that he "don't care for anything." Costello says that he understands. He agrees to let Abbott pretend that they are "big shots" rather than make a bad impression on the waitress. However, Abbott carries the pretense too far. When Costello tells the waitress that he doesn't care for anything, Abbott tells him, "Oh, go ahead. Have something." Costello says again that he doesn't "care for nuthin,'" but Abbott keeps after him. Costello, confused by Abbott's persistent coaxing, turns to the waitress and orders a turkey sandwich. Abbott violently grabs Costello and drags him off to the side. This routine keeps following the same pattern with Costello becoming increasingly resistant to ordering something while Abbott becomes increasingly insistent that he *does* order something. "Look," says Abbott, "you're in a restaurant. What do people go into a restaurant for?" Abbott tells him that, if he is not too hungry, he can order something small. Costello finally relents. "Okay," he says, "give me a small steak." Abbott smacks him across the face. The Laurel and Hardy version is about Laurel being too dimwitted to follow instructions. The Abbott and Costello version is about Abbott torturing Costello with a sadistic, schizophrenic mind game.

Abbott and Costello introduced a new food routine during a live performance of *The Colgate Comedy Hour* in 1953. Costello is unaware that a stolen necklace has been hidden under his burger bun. He is puzzled to hear a loud crunching noise whenever he bites down on his burger. Costello turns the routine into a duel with his sound-effects man, who must match his biting, chewing and swallowing with a variety of sound effects. The following year, the routine was reworked to have a bratty boy put caps from his cap pistol inside Costello's bologna sandwich. The sandwich makes popping noises as Costello eats it. The scene ends with the sandwich exploding. The routine was used one final time in *Abbott and Costello Meet the Mummy* (1955). This time, a cursed medallion winds up in Costello's burger. After he swallows the medallion, he is put under a fluoroscope by criminals who need to read the directions to a hidden treasure inscribed on the medallion.

Aunt Jane and the Tabasco Sauce (1902), a comedy produced by American Mutoscope and Biograph, shows a woman gasping for breath after eating a dish heavily seasoned with Tabasco sauce. Mack Sennett's comedies often featured dinner parties spoiled by adulterated food. In *Hot Stuff* (1912), Dell Henderson serves taffy at a dinner party without realizing that his rival (Sennett) has sprinkled hot sauce on the taffy. Guests at a birthday party are left with a bad taste in their mouths when lard is substituted for ice cream in *Baby's Birthday* (1929). Others freely made use of this premise. This is clearly evident in *The Cloudhopper* (1925) when Larry Semon has his romantic lunch disrupted by a mischievous boy who replaces the sausages in his sandwich with cigars.

A trend developed with alum-treated food and beverages. Alum powder, an acidic compound used as a food preservative, caused a person's mouth to pucker if taken in more than a small dose. The earliest-known alum routine appeared in *The Cockeyed Family* (1928). A farmer (Pinto Colvig) accepts a piece of alum from a mischievous boy thinking that it is a type of candy. Colvig, a former circus clown, distorts his rubbery face to make it look as

Joe meant to bake a birthday cake filled with party favors, but his kid sister's meddling has created a nightmarish cake, bulging with soap, tacks and old shoes. The film is the Our Gang comedy *Ten Years Old* (1927). The kids are (from left to right), Jay R. Smith, Jackie Condon, Joe Cobb, Bonedust Young, Allen Hoskins, Jannie Hoskins and Scooter Lowry (courtesy Bruce Lawton Collection).

if the alum is forcing his lips into an intense pucker. The first alum routine in the sound era, which involves a party at which the punch is spiked with alum, was featured in the Sennett comedy *The Bees' Buzz* (1929). In sound films, it now became the joke that a person's lips puckered so badly from consuming alum that they were unable to talk.

Alum routines came to be featured in numerous comedies in the thirties and forties. An alum routine ensues in Laurel & Hardy's *Tit for Tat* (1935) when Stan Laurel eats a marshmallow coated with alum. Alum accidentally gets mixed into a pitcher of water in *Alum and Eve* (1932). Curly mistakes alum for powdered sugar and mixes it into punch in the Three Stooges short *No Census No Feeling* (1940). Jimmy Durante adds alum to lemonade in *You're in the Army Now* (1941). In *Should Husband Marry?* (1947), a cook (Dudley Dickerson) is so preoccupied with a cake recipe that he fails to notice when he knocks over a canister of alum which spills in its entirely into his cake mix. The tainted cake has a severe effect on a dinner party hosted by Hugh Herbert. In real life, alum was eventually banned due to its adverse effects, which included death.

As is often the case, a thin line separates comedy from tragedy. In *Wedding Crashers* (2005), Owen Wilson spikes romantic rival Bradley Cooper's wine with eye drops to make him sick. In 2008, a 25-year-old Long Island woman, Kristine Anzalone, was inspired by this gag to put eye drops in a roommate's iced tea. It seems that she was angry with the roommate for smoking around her while she was pregnant. Unexpectedly, an ingredient of the eye drops, tetrahydrozoline, caused the man's blood vessels to contract. The man, who was vomiting and bleeding rectally, had to be rushed to the hospital. The man survived and sued Anzalone. The judge ordered Anzalone to pay the man's medical expenses, which amounted to $10,205.

Food is eaten to provide nourishment to the body in the form of carbohydrates, fats, proteins, vitamins, and minerals. It is assimilated by man to produce energy, stimulate growth, and maintain life. However, a comedian's one warped purpose in consuming a substance remains limited to producing laughs.

5

Attack of the Vamps

The vamp, a greedy and lustful woman who uses her sexual allure to manipulate men, was popularized by Theda Bara in the 1915 film *A Fool There Was*. Women with dangerously exploitive ways had been around in films and literature before Bara. This type of woman was described either as an adventuress or a *femme fatale*. But Bara's vamp gave a new dimension to this character. She attacked men like a vampire, leaching their strength and driving them to obsession and irrationality. Bara, often in the vamp mode, starred in close to three dozen features for Fox from 1915 to 1919. Her most lavish vehicles were historical epics, including *Cleopatra* (1917) and *Salome* (1918). If not for Bara's great popularity, the Fox organization would likely not exist today, which suggests that William Fox and many other men drew strength from this queen vamp.

Billie Brockwell played a comic version of Bara's vamp in at least two Keystone shorts, *Hogan Out West* (1915) and *The Village Vampire* (1916). Betty Compson, who normally played tender-hearted heroines, played a vamp in a 1916 Christie comedy called *Hist! At Six O'Clock*. Dora Rodgers played a Bara-like lead opposite Toto in the Rolin spoof *Cleopatsy* (1918). Other comedy vamps that came and went during the silent era were Alma Bennett, Carmelita Geraghty, Marion McDonald and Eugenia Gilbert. Bennett stands out the most in this group. The sultry, dark-eyed beauty played a vamp opposite Larry Semon in *Her Boy Friend* (1924). This evil lady knows how to get rid of a snoopy detective like Semon: she lights up an opium-laced cigarette and blows smoke in the pest's face until he passes out. Bennett played a series of comic vamp roles after this effective demonstration. She played a vamp opposite Ben Turpin in *The Jolly Jilter* (1927); Harry Langdon in *Long Pants* (1927); and Andy Clyde in *Midnight Daddies* (1930). She also played a vamp in the Colleen Moore vehicle *Orchids and Ermine* (1927).

Passionate, romantic seduction scenes were more than a fool could handle. In *Frozen Hearts* (1923), Stan Laurel resists the allure of Madame XXX (Mae Laurel) out of loyalty to his girlfriend, whose picture he clasps tightly in his hand. The vamp persists in hugging and kissing him until he can no longer resist and he ends up tearing up his girlfriend's picture into little pieces. In *Line's Busy* (1924), an amorous woman sidles up to Billy West on a sofa in a hotel lobby. West keeps scooting away from her, but the woman is undeterred and keeps moving closer. West is panicked. He gulps hard. He holds his hand to his heart. Just as he looks as if he is about to faint, the woman's husband comes along and drags her away. This couch confab between the comedian and the vamp came to be a standard routine.

George Ovey has fallen into the clutches of a vamp in *Jerry and the Vampire* (1917).

The more childish the comedian, the more terrifying the vamp. In *Careful Please* (1926), Lloyd Hamilton sits on a couch with a sultry young vamp. He gets nervous as she soon as she slides across the couch towards him. He expresses even greater discomfort as she places her hand over his hand and rests her other hand against his chest. When she lunges forward to kiss him, he recoils from her. As she persists in trying to lock lips, he hangs squeamishly off the end of the couch. Harold Lloyd looks less shocked hanging off a skyscraper. In *Time Flies* (1926), Lupino Lane is so desperate to avoid the embrace of vamp that he falls backwards off a couch and somersaults out of the room.

The most elaborate vamp scene was presented by Harry Langdon in *The Strong Man* (1926). Harry has just arrived in New York looking for Mary Brown, a minister's daughter with whom he corresponded while serving as a soldier in Belgium. Harry wanders the streets with a photo of Mary. He shows the photo to a doorman, who decides to have some fun with Harry. He assures Harry that Mary comes down this street every day, and all he needs to do if he wants to meet her is to wait on the street corner. Harry stands on the street corner looking at every woman who walks past. Nearby, a jewel thief named Dangerous Lil (Gertrude Astor) has a rendezvous with a fence to exchange a stolen necklace for a roll of cash. Lil, who sees that she has a cop on her trail, slips the roll of cash into Harry's pocket. After the cop frisks Lil and finds nothing, he has no choice but to leave her alone. Lil then tries to retrieve her bank roll, but she finds that it has fallen through a hole in Harry's pocket and has become trapped in the jacket lining. She has to find a way to get her money back without attracting attention. She convinces Harry that *she* is Mary Brown and invites him to accompany her on a cab ride to her apartment.

In the back of the cab, Lil secretly reaches around Harry with a knife to cut the money out of his jacket. However, Lil is not as subtle as she hoped to be. Harry becomes startled thinking that the minister's daughter is trying to grope an intimate area. As she continues to go after Harry, Harry curls up in a corner of the cab and begs this woman to keep her hands to herself. (A side-by-side comparison of the cab scene from *The Strong Man* and the drawing room scene from *Careful Please* would serve well to demonstrate the similarities between Langdon and Hamilton's characters.)

When the cab reaches its destination, Lil tries to drag Harry into an apartment building, but Harry is afraid what she will do to him once she has him inside and puts up an extreme amount of resistance. Lil realizes that she needs a different tactic: she faints. A doorman insists that Harry can't leave a woman lying on the street, so he has to carry her into her apartment. Harry has great difficulty carrying this woman up multiple flights of stairs. He finally gets her inside of her apartment, at which point Lil moves into action. The hardened jewel thief, determined that Harry not escape, locks the door and drops the key down the front of her blouse. Then, she saunters towards Langdon like a jungle cat. Langdon, moving back, steps on a bellows, which blows air into a fireplace and sends a flame shooting at his backside.

A scene with all the same vital elements is featured in a classic Laurel & Hardy feature, *Way Out West* (1937). Laurel and Hardy come to town looking for their late friend's angelic daughter, Mary Roberts, because they need to deliver a gold-mine deed to her. Lola Marcel (Sharon Lynn), a sultry saloon singer, learns about the deed. Larcenous Lola, looking to get her hands on the deed, pretends to be sweet Mary Roberts. This is not all that different from larcenous Lil, who pretends to be sweet Mary Brown to get her hands on the bankroll. In both situations, the woman locks herself inside a room with the comedian and proceeds to attack him for a valuable item. Lola tears open Stan Laurel's jacket and shoves her hand down his shirt. Laurel bursts out in a fit of laughter. Laurel is laughing hysterically as he and the woman roll around on a bed.

Unlike Laurel, Langdon never at any time laughs during his scene with the big, bad vamp. He acts utterly terrified. The actors' sizes account for differences in the scenes. Lynn, at 5'4", is petite compared to 5'9" Laurel. But Astor, at 5'8", is physically intimidating compared to the diminutive Langdon. This big, aggressive woman roughly handling Langdon's "grown-up baby" character makes this scene look like an act of child molestation. At one point, Lil pulls out her knife and chases Harry around the room. The *Way Out West* scene, in comparison, proves to be less frightening and more silly.

Langdon's *Strong Man* scene inspired many imitators. Jimmy Burke, who was groomed by Sennett as a Langdon imitator, finds himself in a similar situation with a female gangster named Necklace Nell in *Clunked on the Corner* (1929).

Lupino Lane copied the Langdon scene twice, first in *Fandango* (1928) and then in *Battling Sisters* (1929). While Langdon's seduction centered on characterization, Lane's *Battling Sisters* seduction centered on the bellows mishap and other gags. *Battling Sisters* showcases a future society where the women fight the wars while the men keep the home fires burning. Size, again, matters. Lane made a point to exaggerate the contrast in size between himself and his leading lady, Betty Boyd. Boyd, at 5'5", was two inches taller than Lane, but her military boots and headgear make her look even taller. Lane appeared so much smaller than his leading lady that it seemed plausible that she was able to lift him off his feet and bounce him on her knee.

Harry Langdon is attacked by a vamp (Natalie Kingston) in *Lucky Stars* (1925).

Lupino Lane is less than enamored of vamp Anita Garvin in *Roaming Romeo* (1928) (courtesy Cole Johnson Collection).

Boyd is not the only woman interested in Lane. A second female admirer, Violet Blythe, arrives on the scene as Count Van Violet, a military commander costumed with a white uniform and monocle like Erich von Stroheim's Count Karamzin from *Foolish Wives* (1922). The tough woman looks Lane up and down before effortlessly hoisting him into the air. She clearly likes what she sees. She throws off her jacket and undoes her gun belt. She leans longingly towards Lane, but he is quick to put a pillow between the two of them. She no sooner snatches away the pillow than he brings up another pillow. She snatches that pillow away and he produces yet another pillow. This is an embellishment on *The Strong Man* scene, wherein Langdon futilely shields himself against Lil with a lone pillow. Blythe is not looking for a gold-mine deed or a bankroll. Her interest is purely sexual. Langdon played the scene as if he was a virginal boy. Lane chose, instead, to play the scene as if he is a chaste woman. Lane's version is not as funny as Langdon's version, but it is certainly stranger.

It is astonishing that Lil's exploitation of Harry was closely duplicated with a wide range of other comedians. Harry Edwards, a former Langdon director, reworked these circumstances with little change for Walter Catlett. The bespectacled, cigar-chomping comedian was pompous, rambunctious and calculating. He was nothing like Langdon. Yet, these *Strong Man* scenes became the basis of a Catlett comedy *Blondes and Blunders* (1940). Under surveillance by a police detective, a jewel thief named Blondie (Marion Martin) sidles up to Catlett and slips a stolen necklace into his pocket. Blondie later pulls a gun on Catlett at his home and demands that he return the necklace. Catlett, helplessly sprawled across a divan, bursts out in a fit of laughter as Blondie frisks him. Columbia remade this film with the befuddled Hugh Herbert under the title *A Pinch in Time* (1948). Herbert adds nothing more to the scene except his trademark "hoo-hoo-hoo" cry as a gangster's moll searches him for the necklace.

Not every comic character put up much resistance. In *Briny Boob* (1926), the vamp sidles up to Billy Dooley on the sofa and thrusts his face to her bosom. Dooley looks uncomfortable at first, but he overcomes his shyness as soon as the beauty kisses him. Dooley becomes so excited that his pant legs roll up and down. He then lies down with the vamp on a bearskin rug. She kisses him again and his legs shoot straight up in the air.

In *Animal Crackers* (1930), Kathryn Reece cuddles up next to Harpo Marx, only to find that Harpo is too strange to seduce. "I like little boys like you," she coos. Harpo responds by trying to break her arm. He clarifies to Reece where his true affections lie when he reaches into his coat pocket and pulls out a picture of a horse. These comedy characters could make for strange little boys.

Bob Hope often found himself in this situation. *My Favorite Brunette* (1947) is reminiscent of *The Strong Man* in a scene when sultry Dorothy Lamour stalks cowardly Hope

A vamp (Madeline Hurlock) gets close to Billy Bevan in an unidentified Sennett comedy (courtesy Steve Rydzewski).

around a den with a knife while a fireplace log burns brightly in the background. In *My Favorite Blonde* (1942), Madeleine Carroll is a British spy traveling from New York to Chicago to deliver microfilm plans. She has the microfilm hidden inside a broach and, when she fears that Nazi spies are closing in on her, she makes a pass at Bob Hope and pins the broach to the back of his coat lapel. She later has to find Hope and get in his good graces to recover the broach. The broach, hidden on Hope's coat, now serves the same purpose as the bankroll hidden inside of Langdon's coat. However, Carroll is not as villainous as Dangerous Lil. In the early 1940s, a true vamp had no place in a wholesome mainstream comedy. Hope later found himself in a similar situation in *Paris Holiday* (1958), in which a criminal seductress (played by Anita Ekberg) plies her feminine charms on Hope while trying to snatch a key from his pocket. Hope is nervous at first, but his vain character believes that his charm is finally getting through to the fairer sex.

Lou Costello was more knowing in his portrayal of an overgrown boy. In *Hit the Ice* (1943), he proves to have greater cunning than vamp Ginny Sims. Sims asks him if he ever dated a girl before. He shyly explains that he is "too young" to be dating girls (he was 37). But it seems, when they finally kiss, that he has more experience with the opposite sex than he is letting on. At the conclusion of the kiss, smoke appears to rise from Costello's lips. In fact, he is standing against a heating vent and the seat of his pants have caught on fire. (This is somewhat like the fireplace-burning-Langdon's-backside gag.) Sims, like Carroll, is a

Eddie Cantor contends with vamp Gypsy Rose Lee in *Ali Baba Goes to Town* (1937).

wholesome girl at heart. She manages by the end of the story to repent from her evil ways and helps Costello to escape from her gangster cohorts.

In the Three Stooges short *Three Pests in a Mess* (1945), Christine McIntyre plays a golddigger who has come to believe that Curly is in possession of a fortune. She tries to cuddle up with Curly on a couch, but he slowly moves away from her. He finally drops off the edge of the couch and falls directly into oversized knitting needles, which become deeply embedded in his backside. The needles are, to the tool-obsessed Stooges, equivalent to the heat and flames that have burned the backsides of other comedians in this situation.

The vamp becomes literal in *Abbott and Costello Meets Frankenstein* (1948) as a seductive female vampire (Lenore Aubert) threatens the pudgy little comedian with teeth sharper than Dangerous Lil's knives. In another horror comedy, ghoulish femme fatale Christine McIntyre slips poison into Shemp Howard's drink in the Three Stooges' *Who Done It?* (1949).

Huntz Hall enacted these scenes in a number of films, including *Blues Busters* (1950), *Jalopy* (1953) and *High Society* (1955). Adele Jergens, who had already made a torrid pass at bashful Red Skelton in *The Fuller Brush Man* (1948), brought her great talents as a *femme fatale* to *Blues Busters*, but her efforts were lost on a man as strange and dopey as Hall. In *High Society*, Hall responds even less appropriately to being caressed by Amanda Blake, who is secretly frisking him to locate a valuable document in his coat pocket. Hall winces when the girl squeezes his bicep. "Not so hard!" he complains. When she runs her hands across his chest, he quickly pushes her away, telling her that he is too ticklish. It is a great achievement for the lovely Blake to finally plant a kiss on Hall. The real reason that Hall did so many of these scenes is mainly because they gave him the opportunity to do his trademark lip flutter.

In later years, spy comedies were filled with bloodthirsty vamps. A sexy Russian assassin played by Lesley Anne Down is hired to seduce Inspector Clouseau (Peter Sellers) in *The Pink Panther Strikes Again* (1976). Alexandra Paul plays a sexy assassin out to kill Leslie Nielsen in *Spy Hard* (1996).

In *Back to the Future* (1985), Michael J. Fox is understandably jittery when he time-travels to the past and meets up with the teenage version of his mother (Lea Thompson), who settles herself on the edge of his bed and makes overt sexual advances towards him. Fox, in backing away from her, falls out of bed in the much the same way that vamp-fearing comedians of the past had fallen off couches or somersaulted out of rooms.

The vamp, as is her specialty, will forever be drawing the fool out of a man.

6

Indecent Exposure

Comic actor Jason Segel spoke of a humiliating experience when he was dumped by a girlfriend while standing before her in the nude. But, as it is the way of the creative person to transform pain into art, Segel went on to recreate his naked breakup in *Forgetting Sarah Marshall* (2008). The scene remained true to life. Segel greets his girlfriend wearing nothing but a towel. He whips off the towel, planning to have sex, but his girlfriend promptly stops him to announce that she is breaking up with him. Segel is devastated. The spurned lover, in a state of full-frontal nudity, could not look more vulnerable and pathetic.

It was common in the long tradition of comedy for a man to suffer humiliation while in a state of undress in front of others. *The Misadventure of a French Gentleman Without Pants*, a 1905 Dutch comedy, features a man (Willy Mullens) losing his pants at the beach. But Mullens, as the many actors that followed him, was able to perform the scene without actually exposing himself to the audience. A scene in *Coney Island* (1917) features Roscoe Arbuckle visiting a bathhouse to change into swimming trunks. Arbuckle modestly gestures to the cameraman to raise the frameline before he removes his pants. Modesty of this sort is simply not to be found in today's films.

The 1910 comedy *Max Takes a Bath* (also known as *Max Embarrassed*) employs creative ways to suggest that Max Linder is naked without actually showing his bare essentials. The circumstances that bring about this spectacle are not something to which a modern audience can relate. Max purchases a new bathtub after his doctor prescribes a cold bath as a medical remedy, but his apartment lacks a water faucet from which he can directly fill the tub. Frustrated with trying to fill the tub with water from a vase, he drags the tub to a faucet on the landing outside his apartment. The tub quickly fills with water and he eagerly climbs inside. Max, not wanting to be seen, submerges himself under the water whenever anyone walks past. This trick, however, does not work for long. A woman, appalled to catch Max bathing out in the open corridor, summons police to arrest this man for indecent exposure. Max argues with the police and splashes water at them, but this does not deter them from taking him into custody. The police lift the tub with Max still in it and carry it aloft across town. Max squirms uncomfortably as a passing group of women peer over the rim of the tub to steal glances at him. But while these women have gotten a plain view of Max, the tub continues to block the audience's view of the naked man. The tub, in effect, functions as a portable modesty screen. No sooner does Max arrive at the station house than he flees from the police while hiding beneath the tub. All that can be seen of Max, jutting out from the bottom of the tub, are his pale, skinny legs skittering along the sidewalk. Max continues to

Jimmy Aubrey (center) has stolen Frank Alexander's pants in an unidentified Vitagraph comedy. In the pants with him is Helen Kesler.

wear the tub, looking like a snail inside a shell, as he scales a building to distance himself from the officers in pursuit. The dutiful officers react without hesitation to climb after the flasher. On the roof, Max conceals his naked body down inside a roof hatch before he lifts the tub over his head and tosses it down at the officers. The officers, like pins in a vertical bowling game, are knocked off the building and plummet to the ground. Max is now free to sneak back to his apartment.*

A bathtub was just one of many objects used to cover up a naked comedian's private parts. Peter Sellers shields himself with a guitar as a nervous guest at a nudist camp in *A Shot in the Dark* (1964). John Cleese covers his privates with a framed portrait in *A Fish Called Wanda* (1988). *Romance with a Double Bass* (1974), based on an 1886 short story by Anton Chekhov, allowed Cleese to offer an interesting twist on the premise. Connie Booth has her clothes stolen while she is skinny-dipping in a lake and a chivalrous musician played by Cleese returns her home hidden safely inside his bass case.

Buster Keaton finds himself stranded in a ghost town in *The Gold Ghost* (1934). He quickly settles into a routine, finding ways to look after himself. He strips off his dusty clothing to wash them in a horse trough. Keaton wants us to believe that he is naked behind

---

*Max Linder was more fortunate than Max Davison, who was left without cover when his defective bathtub split in half in *Call of the Cuckoos* (1927).

the trough. He displays the bare skin of his upper torso, his arms and his legs, the only parts of his body not blocked from view by the trough. Just then, a group of people unexpectedly drive into town. Keaton glances down at himself, expressing shame and dismay, and bolts for the nearest building. The expectation has been created that, by leaving the cover of the trough, Keaton will expose himself to viewers. It is quickly revealed that the comedian is, in fact, wearing boxer shorts.

A more elaborate version of this routine appears in *You Can't Cheat an Honest Man* (1939). W. C. Fields, as a circus owner, bathes in a shower set up in a common area on the circus grounds. He exits the shower and walks across the circus grounds presumably naked but, every time it looks as if he will be exposed to viewers, a pony walks past or a worker comes by carrying an object that hides Fields's body from view. Finally, an old woman gets a glimpse of Fields, who is bare as far as she can tell. The woman screams and faints, at which point Fields steps out and reveals that he is wearing pants. Fields, a misanthropic individual insensitive to social values, never seems particularly troubled by the fact that this old woman thought he was naked.

The routine was taken even further for a scene in *Austin Powers: The Spy Who Shagged Me* (1999) in which Michael Myers parades naked through a busy hotel lobby. View of Myers' bare body is blocked by a baggage cart and other items moved into his way. When he walks through the banquet room, parts of his anatomy are shielded by food items suggestive of the respective parts, including a rump roast and a banana. A man brings a walnut

Buster Keaton feels exposed in *Hard Luck* (1921).

into the foreground in time to conceal Myers's crotch area and, when the walnut is cracked open, Myers groans in pain. Times have changed. Myers's sexually liberated Austin Powers character shares neither Keaton's shame nor Fields' misanthropy. He sees his hairy naked body as something to share and celebrate with the masses.

In recent years, it has taken increasingly more to shock the viewer. In *The Cameraman* (1928), Buster Keaton realizes after he performs a high-dive into a public pool that he has lost his swimming trunks. A flash of Keaton's bare behind appears just at the end of the scene when he runs into the changing rooms. This was a bold routine for its day. Rowan Atkinson did a virtual frame-for-frame remake of the routine in *The Curse of Mr. Bean* (1991). The new scene, however, included multiple, sustained views of Atkinson's bare behind.

In 1929, author H. C. Witwer sued Harold Lloyd claiming that the plot of *The Freshman* (1925) was pilfered from his 1915 short story "The Emancipation of Rodney." Witwer claimed that he had visited Lloyd at his studio and discussed the details of this story with him. Lloyd insisted that he had never read the actual story.

The District Court judge identified significant similarities between the two works. Legal historian David P. Hayes wrote, "Both works concern a freshman college student who is not popular nor athletic but is fooled by other students and the football coach to think that he is on the football team."[1] Similarities are particularly evident at the climactic big game. According to the District Court decision, "[The] team is reduced to the last available man. He grasps the coach in appeal and argument to be allowed to enter the play. He forces his way into the game. By an extremely unusual play he wins for the home team. The girl justifies her faith in him.... He is the hero of the hour ... [and] attains [a] coveted nickname."[2] Witwer won a judgment against Lloyd but it was overturned on appeal. The Appeals Court discounted to what extent Lloyd and his company had been exposed to the Witwer story in the writer's meeting with Lloyd. Witwer admitted to discussing the story entirely from memory and that he could not recall the specific details that he offered to Lloyd.

Lloyd claimed that he knew before Witwer's visit that he wanted to make a college film. He wasn't sure what the plot would be, but he knew that he wanted the film's climax to be centered on a football game. Lloyd was able to provide evidence that, well before Witwer's visit, he had sent out a camera crew to shoot footage of a college football game to be used in the film.

The judge examined the works in greater detail and discovered substantial differences, including the central motives of the characters, the way in which a key romantic plotline develops, and the general attitude that the lead characters have towards their studies. This last difference is obvious. Rodney, a devoted student, is a math genius and history expert while Lloyd's character, Harold Lamb, is focused entirely on cultivating his popularity on campus and shows no interest at all in his studies. Harold is never seen in a classroom for the entire film. He never encounters a professor. The film has nothing to do with scholastic achievement.

The judge also did not see Lloyd as being stingy about paying writers for material. He ended up paying his writing staff a total of $40,000 for their work on *The Freshman*. Witwer was paid, on average, $1,000 for the screen rights to a short story, which would have been a relatively insignificant amount for Lloyd to pay if he had, in fact, used material from the "Emancipation of Rodney" short story.

The one disturbing aspect of this case was that Lloyd was enjoined from further exhibition, distribution or marketing of the film and, if he lost the case, he would have been forced to surrender the film to a marshal to be destroyed.

6. Indecent Exposure   111

One gag routine that Lloyd got out of his $40,000 had to do with Harold Lamb losing his pants at a gala. It did not seem to be unique idea. Previous films had involved a comic character attending a fancy dress party and experiencing a wardrobe malfunction that leaves him indecently exposed. This happened to Max Linder in a comedy titled, simply, *My Pants Ripped* (1908). In this French comedy, Max splits the seat of his pants while dressing for a

Harold Lloyd is arrested for indecent exposure in *Professor Beware* (1938). To the right is Chuck Hamilton. The other officers are unidentified.

party. He only has time to make a hasty repair of the tear before he leaves to meet his date. Later, Max escorts his date to the dance floor and his unsecured stitching comes undone. He attempts to look inconspicuous while covering his backside with a serving tray, but it is only a matter of time before another guest notices the gaping tear. Laughing hysterically, the guest points out the tear to others. Max is left mortified.

Linder's decidedly bourgeois character, dressed proudly in a dapper suit and a silk top hat, was unlike the rowdy and ragged buffoons that dominated early screen comedy. A tramp no more than bruised his posterior when he took a fall, but taking a fall was more a cause of embarrassment for Linder's respectable citizen. Linder, whether playing an elite family man or a sophisticated playboy, had a responsibility to maintain the regard of his peers and to uphold his social standing. But he could hardly do that when his pants tore and other mishaps befell him. This gave Linder's comedy a tension lacking in other slapstick burlesque.

Linder was not the only comedian who had to worry about keeping his pants intact at a party. A mishap of this sort befell John R. Cumpson twice, first in *Mr. Jones at the Ball* (1908) in which he split his pants, and then in *Mr. Jones Has a Card Party* (1909) in which he loses his pants entirely. Both films were written and directed by D. W. Griffith, who was at the time the lead director at American Mutoscope & Biograph. It was under Griffith's supervision that Mack Sennett further developed this premise in *The Tragedy of a Dress Suit* (1912). This time, Dell Henderson borrows a suit from his landlord to attend a fancy party. The landlord storms up to Henderson in the middle of the dance floor and forces him, in front of all the party guests, to strip off the suit. Sennett remade the film in 1914 as *Fatty's Magic Pants*, also known as *Fatty's Suitless Day*. In this one-reeler, Roscoe Arbuckle steals a rival's suit. Later, the rival shows up at a dance and sneaks up behind Arbuckle. He tugs on a loose pant thread, which undoes the stitching. Arbuckle no sooner stands than his pants come apart. Now you see it, now you don't — just as the title suggests.

Other companies saw merit in this premise. One film with many of the same elements was the Sterling comedy *The Fox-Trot Craze* (1915). Percy (Ernest Shields) steals a dress suit from his roommate, Harold (Arthur Tavares), to have an outfit to wear at a hotel dance. At the dance, Percy sits on a smoldering cigarette, which sets the seat of his pants on fire, and he has to remove his pants to douse the flames. Harold shows up at the dance wrapped in a curtain and demands that Percy give him his suit back. Harold loses his wrapping while fighting with Percy. The two men, exposed in their underwear, are forcibly ejected from the dance.

An even more violent version of the routine was concocted by famed screenwriter Anita Loos for *The Fatal Dress Suit* (1914). Sam (Edward Dillon) puts on a dress suit for a party unaware that his romantic rival, Walter (Tammany Young), sprinkled gun powder into the pockets and lining. When he learns about the gun powder, Sam makes sure not to make a sudden move on the dance floor to avoid blowing himself up. This dilemma is more anxiety-provoking than a split seam. Splitting the seams in a suit pales in comparison to a suit splitting the seams in you. Of course, Sam's suit ultimately explodes and leaves Sam in tatters.

Lloyd, himself, had lost his pants at a fancy gathering before, at least on the screen. His priority in *Among Those Present* (1921) is to make a good impression on the rich folk at a grand estate. Contrary to his plans, he has to climb under a barbed-wire fence to escape a bull. He loses his pants in the process. He has yet to notice his pants are missing when he is approached by a group of women. Scenes in which the comedian loses his pants are about the comedian's embarrassment, but the humor in this scene comes from the fact that Lloyd, who does not understand his predicament, is not embarrassed at all. He is being charming and nonchalant until it becomes obvious to him that he is not properly dressed. Lloyd then rushes to get back indoors while avoiding being seen. At one point, he is able to hide his bare legs behind the lower half of a barn door, but he does not see that a small dog has pushed the door aside. Again, he remains unaware of his exposure.

The gala scene in *The Freshman* did, in fact, turn into an original, well-structured and highly amusing routine. Lloyd goes to pick up his tuxedo for the gala and finds that the tailor, who has been suffering seizures, has been unable to finish the suit on time. Lloyd, in desperation, settles on wearing the tuxedo even though it is loosely held together by temporary basting stitches. The tailor volunteers to accompany Lloyd and try to insert permanent stitches at the party.

A man can split his pants at a party, become embarrassed, and run home. This is something that can happen in a matter of seconds. But Lloyd and his writers had found a way to build the comic tension. The audience knows the suit can fall apart at any moment, and the filmmakers sustain the premise with assorted reoccurrences of the same mishap. Lloyd no sooner splits a seam than his tailor, who is hiding behind either a potted palm or some curtains, gets to work to repair the seam. Lloyd has just gone out on the dance floor to dance with a young woman when his sleeve becomes snagged on the woman's belt and is torn off his jacket. He has to find a way to hide his arm while following the woman off the dance floor to retrieve his sleeve, which the tailor promptly sews back on. Still, Lloyd's persistence and ingenuity are not sufficient to get him through this predicament. He undergoes a series of mishaps that significantly stress the seams. The tailor cannot work fast enough to keep the entire suit together. In the end, Lloyd loses his pants and jacket, which leaves him standing on the dance floor in nothing but his underwear.

The routine received a crude, uninspired treatment in a low-budget Weiss Brothers comedy, *Holding His Own* (1928). The star of the two-reeler, Ben Turpin, simply has the misfortune to wear a poorly made tuxedo to a fancy dinner party. He shakes the host's hand, at which point his sleeve comes off, and he bows to the hostess, which causes his backside to burst out of the pants. The tear in Max Linder's pants was trivial compared to this spectacle.

It was a rite of passage for a status-conscious comic character to suffer the indignity of losing his pants in public. Charley Chase, whose character could not be more status-conscious, expresses excruciating embarrassment when he loses his swimsuit at the beach in *No Father to Guide Him* (1925) and panics even more when his pants are stolen by a feisty dog in *The Way of All Pants* (1927). Lloyd Hamilton's comic alter ego, even though he has fallen on hard times, finds it important to preserve his dignity. His "shabby gentleman," as Hamilton called him, was Linder's upright man in tramp clothing. Hamilton failed to keep hold of his pants in a number of films. At one time, a speeding car sideswipes him and in the process manages to tear off his pants. In *King Cotton* (1925), Hamilton is bathing in a drainage ditch to remove a skunk's stench when the ditch suddenly empties. He is then forced to flee before an approaching woman sees him unclad.

The embarrassment of being left bare to the masses was especially profound for Alec Guinness in *The Man in the White Suit* (1951). Guinness, playing a research chemist at a textile mill, is exuberant when he invents a glowing white fiber that can repel dirt and can never wear out. The management and employees of the mill become infuriated as clothing that never needs to be replaced is certain to make the textile industry obsolete. The film climaxes with Guinness, dressed in a suit made from the revolutionary fiber, running through the streets at night to escape angry mill workers. The mob begins to close in on him when the suit, the chemical structure of which is not as stable as Guinness believed, begins to come apart. The crowd tears away at loose clumps from the suit and leaves the chemist standing in his underwear. Guinness is humiliated, not because his legs are showing, but because his great invention has proven to be a failure. Seeing how profoundly sad Guinness is, a man steps forward out of the crowd to drape his coat over Guinness' shoulders. "Here, lad," he says, "wear this." The crowd, more hostile than the crowds in the prior films, actively participates in the undoing of the suit and, yet, this is the first time that a member of the crowd shows compassion and covers up the exposed man.

Linder, as a pioneer of "embarrassment" comedy, continues to exert an influence on today's comedians. Ben Stiller is a prime example. The fact that Linder starred in a number of "meet the parents" comedies, including *Max Gets Stuck Up* (1912) and *Max's Hat* (1913), is just one of many parallels that can be drawn between the old comic master and Stiller.

The polar opposite of Hamilton's riches-to-rags persona is the big-time Hollywood comedy writer that Larry David plays on *Curb Your Enthusiasm*. Hamilton possessed character without standing while David possesses standing without character. David, as much a member of the upper class as Linder was, manages to become embroiled in embarrassing breaches of social etiquette far stranger than the loss of one's pants at a trendy party. David's breaches can be major (he invites a prostitute into his car so that he can use the High Occupancy Vehicle lane on the expressway) or trivial (he gets into an argument over the acceptable amount of caviar one may put on a cracker at a house party). David is willing to lose his pants for a laugh, but it is not enough for him to simply lose his pants — he has to lose his pants and be revealed to be wearing women's panties ("Officer Krupke," 2009). On another occasion, David suffers his own uniquely embarrassing wardrobe malfunction while with one of his wife's girlfriends at a movie theatre. As he sits down, his loose-fitting pants bunch up in such a way that makes it look to the woman as if he has an erection ("The Pants Tent," 2000). This is a long way from *Fatty's Magic Pants*.

The average person finds that their clothing serves its function to cover them up and make them look fashionable, but comedians often found that their clothing was able to betray them. Harold Lloyd expected only to make a good impression in his tuxedo at the school gala. Ben Stiller had similar expectations when, in *There's Something About Mary* (1998), he dressed up in a ruffled taupe tuxedo to attend the senior prom. Unfortunately, a simple visit to the bathroom ends with Stiller getting his penis stuck in the pants' zipper. Stiller, with his tangled member, becomes a freakish sight to his girlfriend, his girlfriend's parents, paramedics, and the neighbors watching as he is loaded into an ambulance.

This premise of the comedian losing his pants at a social gathering was finally taken to its extreme in *Life of Brian* (1979). Graham Chapman, who has been mistaken for the Messiah, rises out of bed, naked, and throws open his window shutters only to greet a waiting throng of disciples. Chapman stands before the crowd, as well as the camera, in a state of full-frontal nudity.

True indecent exposure has become common among comedians in recent years. It does not take loose stitching for Will Ferrell to get naked at a party in *Old School* (2003). After a few drinks, Ferrell strips off all of his clothing and streaks naked out into the street. In *Cyrus* (2010), John C. Reilly drops his pants at a backyard party to urinate on a bush. Perhaps society has become too coarse to afford us modesty. People can hardly feel a sense of privacy about their bodies in a time when airport security measures require them to casually expose themselves to a brood of strangers.

An episode of *The Big Bang Theory* features Sheldon (Jim Parsons) buying a new suit to make a good impression at an awards gala ("The Pants Alternative," 2010). At the ceremony, Sheldon is on edge because he is due to accept an award and will be required to stand in front of the crowd to make a speech. He quickly downs a couple of drinks to settle his nerves, but he goes too far and becomes drunk beyond reason. Once onstage, he forgets his speech, insults people in the audience, and drops his pants to moon the crowd. Where Linder and Lloyd were once victims of fate undone by unfavorable circumstances, comic protagonists are now more likely to be undone by their own bad habits or bad judgment.

Women have also been able to make use of this premise. In *Bringing Up Baby* (1938), Cary Grant unwittingly steps on the train of Katharine Hepburn's evening dress as Hepburn is walking past him at a fashionable nightclub. The back of the dress is torn away, leaving Hepburn exposed, and Grant must walk closely behind her to keep her covered. (This comic business includes elements of a synchronized walking routine to be discussed in a later chapter.) At one point, Grant covers Hepburn's backside with his top hat, much as Linder once used a serving tray to cover his own backside.

Women today are freer than ever to engage in these boyish hijinks. This is made evident by an episode of the BBC series *Miranda* ("Date," 2009) in which Miranda Hart's hip-wiggling on the dance floor causes her pants to slip off. Hart figures that she can pull up her pants without being noticed if she simply keeps to the rhythm of the music. In an episode of *30 Rock*, Tina Fey subjects herself to embarrassment at a corporate dinner by tearing off her blouse and dancing in her bra as a way to distract attention from a flub by her boss Jack Donaghy (Alec Baldwin) ("Retreat to Move Forward," 2009). This exposure at least served a noble cause.

In 1942, veteran comedy writer Clyde Bruckman was in the throes of alcoholism and was having a difficult time coming up with new material. Instead, he recycled many of the old routines that he had written for Buster Keaton and Harold Lloyd. He rewrote the "loosely basted tuxedo" routine from *The Freshman* for the Three Stooges' short *Three Smart Saps* (1942) and a "magician's coat" routine from Lloyd's *Movie Crazy* (1932) for the Stooges' *Loco Boy Makes Good* (1942). It was not worth the effort. These routines were designed to put a shy and nervous character into socially awkward situations and derive tension along with comedy from the character's growing embarrassment. Curly, who took Lloyd's place in these scenes, was neither shy nor nervous. When he loses his pants, he struts around shamelessly in polka-dotted long johns and carries on as if nothing is wrong.

Bruckman was hired in 1943 by Universal to write a series of low-budget musical features. He continued to heavily recycle material for these features. *So's Your Uncle* (1943) included another reprise of the magician's coat sequence. *South of Dixie* (1944) borrowed material from Buster Keaton's *Our Hospitality* (1923). *She Gets Her Man* (1945) was a distaff version of Lloyd's *Welcome Danger* (1929). Joan Davis, in Lloyd's role, plays the daughter of a former police chief who is assumed to have her mother's crime-solving abilities and is brought to town to help out in a murder investigation. Unfortunately, Davis bungles her way through the investigation and turns up a number of false leads and wrong suspects. *Her Lucky Night* (1945) included a reworking of the "loosely basted tuxedo" routine. Noah Beery, Jr., is meeting with his rich uncle at a nightclub to have an important discussion about the family business. He learns that the tuxedo he ordered for the evening has not been completed because the tailor has gotten drunk. Beery takes the drunken tailor along with him hoping that he will be able to stitch the suit at the club, but the tailor has further drinks at the club and becomes increasingly drunk until he finally passes out. The Andrew

Sisters, who have befriended Beery, step in to lend assistance, but they lack sufficient skills to sew up the suit.

Bruckman and fellow comedy veteran Felix Adler were hired to work on the Abbott & Costello comedy *The Naughty Nineties* (1945) as gag writers. Adler and Bruckman were content to fill the film with numerous gags that they had used before at various times in their careers. Abbott & Costello were to perform gags that had previously been performed by the Three Stooges, Buster Keaton and Harold Lloyd.

The "iron bar" gag from Harold Lloyd's *The Kid Brother* (1927) made it into the film. In *Kid Brother*, a thug (Constantine Romanoff) strikes Lloyd repeatedly over the head with an iron bar. The pummeling has no effect on Lloyd, even though the bar is bent in the process. Lloyd steps away, revealing that he had been standing under a bracket that had protected his head. The gag helps to break up the tension of a harrowing fight scene. But the *Naughty Nineties* scene has no tension to relieve. Costello never, at any time, acts as if he is peril. As the villain is trying to crack his head with an iron bar, he smiles at the camera as if to let the audience know that the villain is being fooled. Costello's willingness to give away the surprise defeats the purpose of the gag. Lloyd, who was exceptionally proud of this gag, spoke about it at length in his autobiography and also brought it up in later interviews. He said, "[Romanoff] gives me this terrific blow, and all I do is blink my eyes. And he cannot imagine what's happened. So he hits again. And again I don't do anything — it should have killed me."[3] The scene is arranged so that, when the bracket is finally revealed, the audience realizes that they had been fooled just as much as the villain.

Lloyd referred to this specifically as a "surprise" gag.[4] It was a type of gag also favored by Buster Keaton and Lloyd Hamilton. In *His Musical Sneeze* (1919), Hamilton is among a party of hunters mounted on horses for a rabbit hunt. The hunters manage as they ride off to desert Hamilton, who is revealed to be sitting on a saddle rack. Keaton later used a similar gag in *The Goat* (1921). In the scene, Keaton expects to escape police by hitching a ride on the back of a car which is about to drive away. He grabs hold of what appears to be a tire carrier mounted on the rear bumper, but the car takes off without him. The tire carrier is, in fact, part of a sign that has nothing at all to do with the car.

The worst part of the reworked "iron bar" gag is that the shot meant to reveal a pipe (used in place of a bracket) fails dismally. Costello jumps out to attack the villain without it having been clearly established that this pipe had been over his head. The audience is supposed to notice the pipe in the background during Costello's tussle with the villain and make the appropriate connection on their own, but it is hard to believe that anyone could understand the point of the gag unless they were already familiar with the original.

Costello specifically asked Bruckman to redraft the magician's coat routine for the film. The scene was shot as scheduled. Costello mistakenly dons a magician's coat in a washroom. The coat is filled with animals. A pigeon flies out of the coat and lands on a woman's head. A mouse climbs up onto his shoulder. He suddenly pulls out a rabbit. Finally, the coat releases a bunch of mice on the dance floor. Later, when Lloyd threatened to sue, the scene was excised and replaced with a new scene where a bear disrupts the gathering instead.

Lloyd decided that Bruckman had gone too far. On March 7, 1946, he sued Columbia Pictures for the use of the magician's coat routine in *Loco Boy Makes Good*. The suit sought $500,000 in damages. At the same time, Lloyd filed a lawsuit against Universal for damages in the amount of $1.7 million. The suit exclusively related to *So's Your Uncle*, claiming that the film's appropriation of a key sequence from *Movie Crazy* destroyed the reissue and remake value of *Movie Crazy*. Even though Bruckman had included the drunken tailor as a new twist on the routine, it did not distinguish this version enough from the original version.

The District Court ruled in Lloyd's favor, but they were unable to award him the damages that he requested. The court calculated that the magician's coat sequence comprised 20 percent of *So's Your Uncle*, and Lloyd was, therefore, only eligible to receive 20 percent of the film's profits, which came out to the paltry sum of $4,000. Lloyd filed an appeal in 1947. The Appeals Court agreed that Lloyd had established that the value of his property had been lessened by Universal's infringement on his copyright. The court noted, "It is common knowledge that the repeated use of comedy detracts from its force as amusement."[5] Still, the Appeals Court denied increasing the award. It was their determination, based on precedent, that awarding a portion of the profits as worked out by the District Court "avoids an unjust course."[6]

It could be argued that Bruckman was the keeper of the flame. The writer is, in fact, the reason that many of these gags remained before the public for many years.

The lawsuits came full circle in 2000. It was at this time that Suzanne Lloyd Hayes, granddaughter of Harold Lloyd, sued Disney on behalf of the Harold Lloyd Trust, citing that the Disney film *The Waterboy* (1998) infringed on the copyright of *The Freshman*. The lawsuit claimed that a "substantial ... similarity"[7] existed between *The Freshman* and *The Waterboy*, including "similarity in plot, action, theme, mood, characters and setting."[8] The lawsuit went on to state, "Although some of those elements have been modified to please the Nineties audience and to employ the Nineties technology, reviews of *The Waterboy* in respected American publications immediately recognized and reported the defendant's film to be a Nineties copy of *The Freshman*."[9] Lloyd and *Waterboy* star Adam Sandler both play "nerdy" waterboys to a college football team while dreaming of becoming football stars. This, though, was not the limit of the similarities. A total of 56 common characteristics were cited in the lawsuit. (No scene in *The Waterboy* shows Adam Sandler losing his pants at a party, although the team's coach [Henry Winkler] pulls down his pants to show off a tattoo. Modesty has truly become a thing of the past.)

Disney was not caught with their pants down. In 2001, Disney's lawyers successfully moved for dismissal of the lawsuit. The U.S. District Court for the Central District of California found, as a matter of law, that there was no substantial similarity between *The Freshman* and *The Waterboy*. The Ninth Circuit Court of Appeals affirmed the District Court's judgment.

This book should make the point that a large amount of essential material is shared by a community of comedians, writers and directors. Comedy gags, routines and situations are, to a significant extent, codified by comedians.

7

Spooky Apparitions

Ghosts were not among the usual fare of silent comedy films. Georges Méliès depicted ghosts in several fantasy films, including *The Haunted Castle* (1896), *An Hallucinated Alchemist* (1897) and *Bluebeard* (1901). The Lubin drama *Burglar and Fairy* (1903) depicts a burglar strangling a woman to death, after which the woman's ghost rises out of her body and attacks the burglar. *Cave of the Spooks*, a 1908 Pathé Frères thriller, takes viewers inside a dark cave, where a pair of women come out of caskets and transform into skeletons. The skeletons proceed to dance around in fire and brimstone, accompanied by an assortment of other spooks. Ghosts, though, did not have a secure place in comedy during this period.

A "haunted hotel" trend was inspired by Méliès's *The Bewitched Inn* (1897), in which a hotel guest is plagued by poltergeist activity—his hat scuttles across the room, his pants climb up the wall, his candle explodes, his suitcase vanishes, and furniture stacks up on his bed. The supernatural forces would become more tangible in subsequent films. A country rube has a frightful encounter with a ghostly apparition in his hotel room in Lubin's *The Haunted House* (1899) and a hotel guest has his hat knocked off by a skeletal specter in *Uncle Josh in a Spooky Hotel* (1900).

Apart from this short-lived "haunted hotel" trend, actual ghosts were absent from the plots of haunted-house comedies. These comedies were largely centered on a phony spiritualist, a prankster hidden under a white sheet, or a person being mistaken for an apparition after stumbling into whitewash. It also applies in the case of *The Ghost of Bingville Inn* (1915) that the ghost is no ghost at all. The guests at the inn are unsettled by bumps in the night, but the sounds simply come from an unruly drunk stumbling around the hallways in search of his room.

A typical "ghost" comedy was Lyons & Moran's *With the Spirits' Help* (1916). A professor (Moran) comes to town and claims to have control over spirits. Emily (Priscilla Dean) becomes upset when her father, who is preoccupied with the spirit world, demands that she leave her boyfriend Jed (Lyons) to marry the professor. Her father, infuriated to find Jed loitering, forcibly ejects him and tells him never to return. That night, the professor is to give a sermon at Emily's home. The professor pretends to be summoning a ghostly Indian guide named White Bull at the same time that Emily and Jed are slipping out of the kitchen door to elope. Jed, not looking where he is going, knocks over pots and pans. The people in the living room think that the noises are the work of the Indian spirit. They go to the kitchen to investigate and find Jed hidden in the flour barrel. The group is startled when Jed springs out of the barrel, covered from head to toe in flour. The professor, who assumes

Jed is a spirit that he has unwittingly called to life, fearfully flees from the premises. Emily assures everyone that Jed is no spirit. Father, who now realizes that the professor was a fraud, gives Emily his blessing to marry Jed.

Ham and Bud (Lloyd Hamilton and Bud Duncan) turned out a number of ghost comedies, including *Lotta Coin's Ghost* (1915), *The Spook Raisers* (1915), *Midnight at the Old*

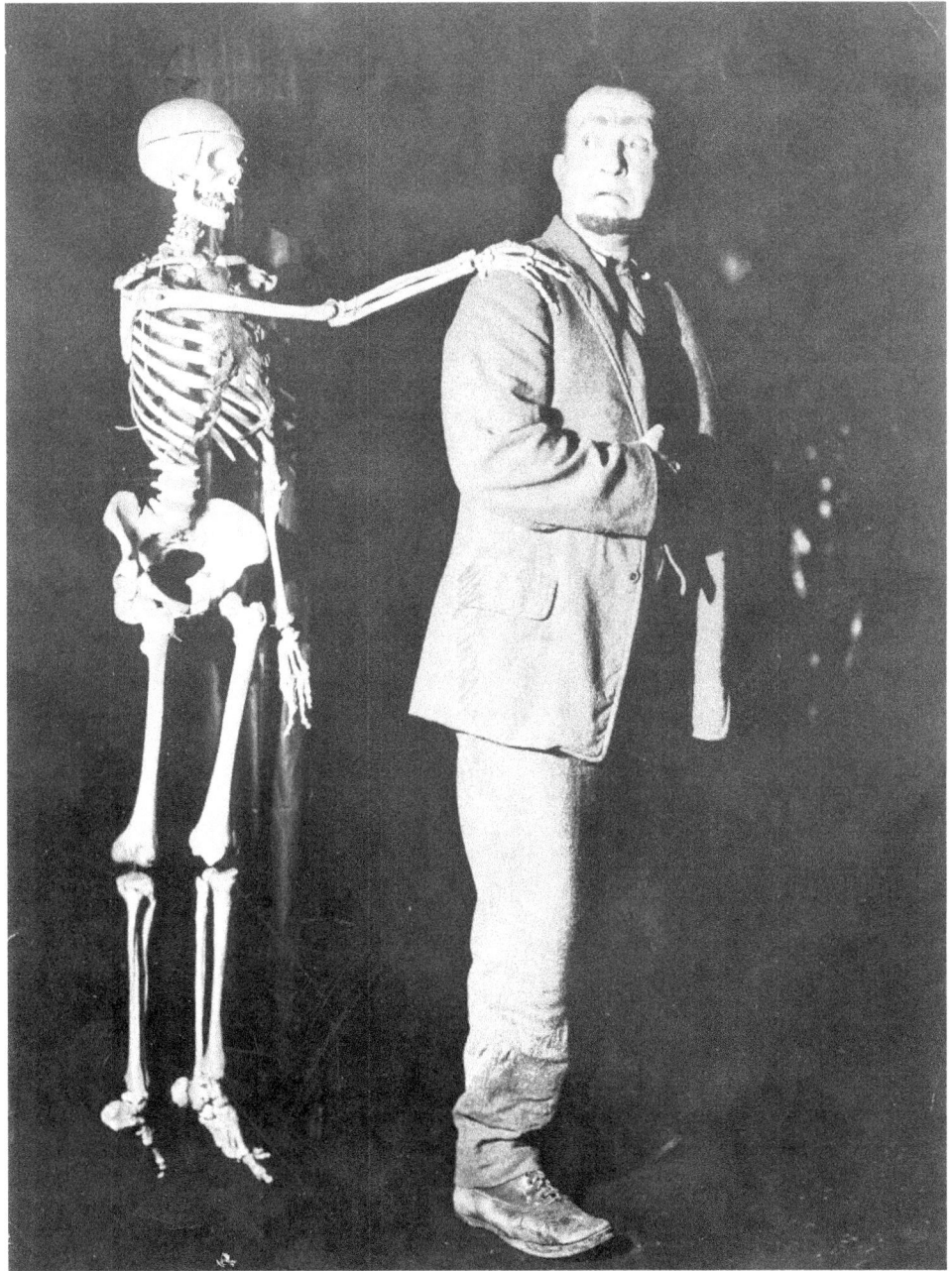

Charlie Murray pretends to be frightened by a stock haunted house prop in a publicity photograph (courtesy Steve Rydzewski).

Mill (1916) and *Ghost Hounds* (1917). However, not a single ghost appeared in these films. The plots did not stray far from "scare" routines popularized by the Commedia dell-arte. In *Lotta Coin's Ghost*, Ham and Bud's efforts to burglarize a mansion are thwarted when the owner dresses up as a ghost to frighten them off. This is much like "Lazzi of the Ghost" or "Lazzo of the Multiple Thief," in which a trickster dresses up as a ghost to frighten other characters. In *Midnight at the Old Mill* (1916), Ham is employed as an expressman for a surgeon who is practicing on corpses. Ham is fearful that a sack he is instructed to deliver to the doctor contains a fresh corpse. Bud, seeing this as an opportunity to frighten Ham, hides inside of the sack before Ham arrives. Ham is carrying the sack back to the doctor when Bud takes to tickling him in the ribs. This scene was closely modeled after a Commedia dell'Arte routine called "Lazzo of the Living Corpse." Aspects of these films also made use of material from "Lazzi of the Nightfall."

The Commedia dell'Arte gave performers a substantial number of gags and routines in this area. "Lazzi of Fear" was the basis of a popular routine from *Abbott and Costello Meet Frankenstein* (1948). The routine begins with Lou Costello unwittingly sitting in the lap of Frankenstein's Monster. It is while pondering the presence of an extra set of hands on the armrest that Costello's slow-witted character gradually comes to realize that he is not alone. A more intricate version of the routine was performed by Stan Laurel in *A Chump at Oxford*

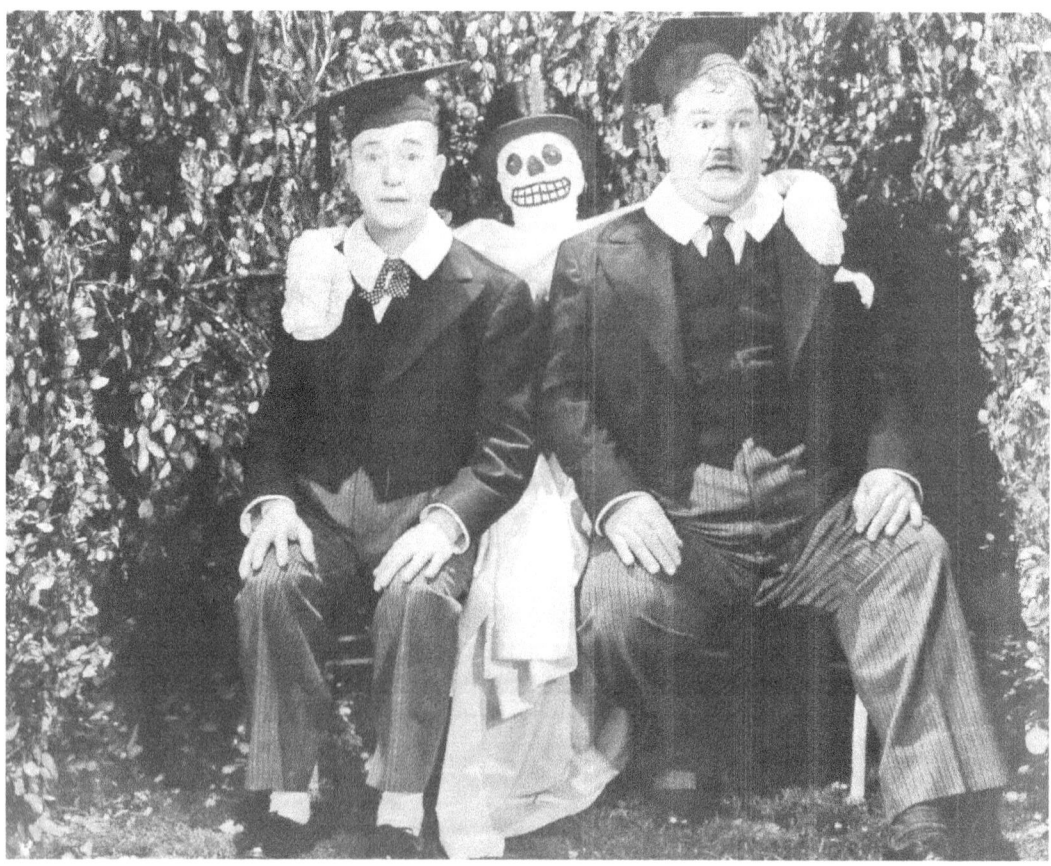

A phony ghost catches Laurel (left) and Hardy by surprise in ***A Chump at Oxford*** (1940) (courtesy www.doctormacro.com).

(1940). Laurel has just settled down on a bench to smoke a pipe when an arm mysteriously emerges from a hedge behind him and assists him in lighting the pipe. Laurel is slow to realize that he has suddenly attained a third arm. A rudimentary version of the routine, without an monster of iconic status or a pipe in need of a light, was performed by Ben Blue and Billy Gilbert in an earlier comedy called *Wreckety Wreck* (1933).

The most edgy ghost comedy of the silent era was *Help!* (1924), in which Max Linder accepts a wager to spend an hour alone in a haunted castle. Linder encounters a rapid succession of surreal apparitions, including bedeviled mannequins, slimy alligators and a battery of ghosts. An African statue festooned with snakes comes sliding across the room towards him. Ominous shadows can be seen outside the windows. One shadow, in the iconic shape of Nosferatu, comes crawling across a stained glass window. The weirdly nightmarish visions presented in the film are truly scary and the film features a surprisingly dramatic climax in which Max's girlfriend is attacked in her bed by a ghoulish brute. The film was written and directed by Abel Gance, who went on to direct the classic historical epic *Napoléon* (1927).

Ghost fantasies, a moviestaple of the late 1930s and early 1940s, furnished plenty of ghosts and ghostly activities. Still, these lighthearted films, which included *The Ghost Goes West* (1935), *Topper* (1937), *Heaven Can Wait* (1943), *The Canterville Ghost* (1944), *Blithe Spirit* (1945) and *The Time of Their Lives* (1946), offered little in the area of scares. *Young Frankenstein* (1974) launched a trend in horror movie spoofs. Later, *American Werewolf in London* (1981) spoofed the sheer carnage of horror films and offered graphic EC Comics–type depictions of the living dead meant to exploit man's most morbid fears. This began yet another trend, inspiring such corpse-ridden gore-fests as *The Evil Dead* (1982), *Creepshow* (1982), *Death Becomes Her* (1992) and *Idle Hands* (1999). Writer-director Tim Burton successfully combined many of these diverse elements in *Beetlejuice* (1988). Beetlejuice is a grotesque living corpse who, much like the Canterville ghost, prides himself on his stock of "scare" tricks.

"Scare" comedies in the sound era had spooky mansions with sliding panels and secret passageways, but none of those homes were as outlandish as the spooky funhouses to be found in silent comedies. A running gag in *The Haunted House* (1921) centers on Buster Keaton's impossible efforts to make it up a collapsible staircase. Keaton can never make it to the top before the stairs fold up and he is sent sliding back to the bottom. It is just the same in *Creeps* (1926) when guests at a spooky mansion must contend with a trick staircase that unexpectedly converts into a slick ramp. They try to make their way upstairs by climbing the banister, but the banister flips to one side and dumps them onto the floor. A strange and spooky home in *Nerve Tonic* (1924) is equipped with a variety of chutes and slides. A secret tunnel allows characters in ghoulish costumes to climb up into the home through the sofa. A hapless visitor (Jimmie Adams) becomes separated from his girlfriend when a wall suddenly drops down between them. Adams fares no better than Keaton in making his way to the top of the staircase. The problem for him is that the staircase is rigged with trapdoors that drop him down chutes and invariably deliver him back to the foot of the staircase.

Other threats came to be worse than a flipping banister or a collapsible staircase. The 1925 Broadway play *The Gorilla* featured a man murdering visitors of a dark old mansion while dressed as a gorilla. The play (by Ralph Spence) had an unmistakable influence on the Educational comedy *Goose Flesh* (1927), in which Lloyd Hamilton confronts a killer in a gorilla suit while poking around a spooky old house. In a 1927 film adaptation of the play, Sennett veteran Charlie Murray plays a bumbling detective on the hunt for a killer ape. Murray tiptoes through the dark house without realizing that the gorilla is tiptoeing directly behind him. A 1939 sound remake of this film replaced Murray with the Ritz Brothers. In this version, Harry Ritz thinks that he is leading his brothers Al and Jimmy through the dark, spooky house when, in fact, the gorilla has scared away his brothers and has taken their place directly behind Harry. When he turns and sees the gorilla, Harry performs a comic decathlon with his eyes — he bugs out his eyes, he rolls his eyes, he crosses his eyes. He also sputters a series of unintelligible sounds. If he had not been wearing a hat, he would have no doubt resorted to his stock trick of jerking his head to make strands of his hair flop around. The fright take, in all of its nuances, can be a truly artful endeavor, and few could do it as well as Harry Ritz. Harry's comical hysterics is one of the reasons that he had such a big influence on other comedians, particularly Mel Brooks, Jerry Lewis and Sid Caesar. Caesar uses a Harry Ritz–style take in a sketch where finds out how much his wife spent on a mink coat. According to author Gerald Nachman, Caesar "bellows, crosses his eyes, and weeps copious tears in close-up."[1] A drawback to Harry's performance is that he tries to sell unfunny lines in the script by delivering the lines in an increasingly loud voice. An unfunny line that is shouted does not magically become funny. It remains unfunny and also becomes annoying. Trav S.D. wrote in reference to *The Gorilla*, "[The Ritz Brothers] seem to be really exerting themselves, making a lot of random, aimless contortions to little effect. Rarely have so many faces been pulled in the production of so little laughter."[2]

The idea of a comedian creeping through a dark, spooky mansion as the unwitting escort of a gorilla or other monstrosity became a standard routine in "scare" comedies. Embellishments to the routine centered on interactions between the comedian and the monster before the monster is finally revealed. Moe Howard often found himself in this situation. In *A Bird in the Head* (1946), the gorilla edges closer to Moe, who tells the gorilla to stop breathing down his neck. In other instances, Moe tells his companion to stop crowding him, or wonders why his hand is so hairy, or reprimands him for neglecting to cut his nails, or asks him if he has been eating onions. Moe's fright take relied on a special effect that caused his hair to rise up. His hair rises up in at least nine films, the earliest examples appearing in *Spook Louder* (1943), *If a Body Meets a Body* (1945) and *The Ghost Talks* (1949).

The hair-raising gag may have originated with Max Linder in *Max and the Flirtometer* (1909). Linder becomes startled when a new scientific device known as a fidelity meter threatens to expose his unfaithfulness. He leaps to his feet and his hair stands straight up. The effect was greatly improved by the time that it was employed by Harold Lloyd in *Haunted Spooks* (1920). A close-up is used to fully capture the effect as Lloyd reacts to the appearance of a man disguised as a ghost. Lloyd liked the effect enough to use it again a few months later in *High and Dizzy* (1920). This time, the comedian's hair raises up when he looks down from a building ledge and sees how high up he is. The following year, Linder reclaimed the gag in its new and improved form for another one of his domestic farces, *Be My Wife* (1921). The effect was even depicted in posters for the film. Still, in spite of Linder's efforts of domestication, the standing-hair effect would remain in future a trusted stock gag of "scare" comedies.

A horizontal variation of the monster-escort routine occurs in the Three Stooge's short, *Hot Scots* (1948), when a ghoul climbs into bed beside Shemp. Shemp is reaching back for the covers when his hand brushes against a pair of distended fangs. "Hey," he chides, "you ought to see a dentist." Shemp, with his "eeb-bee-bee"' cries and his flopping hair, has more than a passing resemblance to Harry Ritz. This similarity is even more obvious when Shemp encounters a ghoul in *Shivering Sherlocks* (1948). Shemp, though, is even wilder than Ritz and gives this comic business his own unique flavor.

It amused audiences when an animal hid inside an inanimate object and caused the object to be mysteriously propelled forward, terrifying onlookers. In *The Haunted Hat* (1909), a entire town panics when a hat with a cat hidden underneath seems to be moving on its own up Main Street. Harold Lloyd executed the same gag to perfection in *High and Dizzy* (1920). It was a gag that was simple to set up. Lloyd fails to notice that he has set his derby on top of a puppy and becomes alarmed when he sees the derby suddenly moving across the floor. Lloyd provided a more unique variation of the gag in *Hot Water* (1924). This time, a mouse slips undetected inside a white glove. The glove crawling across the floor creates the illusion of a disembodied ghost hand, which is creepy enough to send Lloyd running for cover. In Abbott and Costello's *Hit the Ice* (1943), a dog gets inside a bearskin rug and moves around, startling bystanders into thinking that the bear has risen from the dead.*

The most common variation of this routine can be traced back to Lupino Lane's Fox comedy *The Pirates* (1922). The skeletal remains of the pirates' long-forgotten captives hang from chains in the bowels of their ship. The pirates have no qualms about their violent deeds until a cat gets stuck inside of a skull, and the skull — under the cat's power — comes skittering out onto the deck. The superstitious pirates, who take the lively skull to the ghost of a victim, are terrorized. This animal-in-a-skull gag became a staple of "scare" comedies. No other gag had more variations than this one. A cat is the driving force inside of a scary Mardi Gras head in *Creeps* (1926). A chicken flies through a room enclosed inside a skull in *That's the Spirit* (1924). The Sennett comedy *Cold Turkey* (1925) features a dinner party thrown into turmoil when a parrot stuffs itself into a turkey and then makes it appear, through its squirming, that the turkey being served has suddenly come back to life.

In *Public Ghost No. 1* (1935), Charley Chase re-adapted the idea for the sound era. Chase, who has been hired to haunt a house, figures that he can enlist his dog to play a ghost. He attaches a skull mask to the dog's face and, so that his ghost will make unsettling noises, he inserts a party horn into the dog's mouth. The animal-in-a-skull gag continued to be used for many years. A parrot crawling inside a skull and walking around scaring people was a routine used in a number of Three Stooges comedies, including *If a Body Meets a Body* (1945), *The Ghost Talks* (1949) and *Scotched in Scotland* (1954). Buster Keaton was frightened by a penguin trapped inside of a skull in *The Spook Speaks* (1940).

Larry Semon provided the most outlandish variation of this gag in *Dome Doctor* (1924), in which a monkey climbs inside a Jack O'Lantern. It is a strange sight when the monkey's furry, spindly legs sprout out of the bottom of the Jack O'Lantern. The Jack O'Lantern/monkey hybrid proceeds to hop around on counters and shelves. It eventually leaps down onto a man, leaning back in a chair. When Semon turns around, it looks as if the man has a Jack O'Lantern for a head. This becomes an even stranger sight when the monkey springs up and down making it look as if the head is attached by strange, hairy tentacles.

The Three Stooges turned out "scare" comedies on a frequent basis, and gags in these films were borrowed from a variety of sources. A prime source was *Super-Hooper-Dyne Lizzies* (1925), a Halloween-themed Sennett comedy, in which Billy Bevan spends the night in an inventor's workshop to guard secret plans. At one point, Bevan is awakened by the sound of prowlers. Before he has a chance to get out of bed, he unwittingly kicks a hat stand and knocks off a hat, which latches onto his foot and makes it look as if a prowler is

---

*This is similar to a scene in *A Submarine Pirate* (1915), wherein Sydney Chaplin causes a woman to faint while running around a hotel lobby concealed beneath a leopard-skin rug. Larry Semon performed the same routine with a bearskin rug in *The Gown Shop* (1923).

Harold Lloyd and Mildred Davis are frightened by a ghost in *Haunted Spooks* (1920). It's actually Wallace Howe, coming out from under the table.

lurking at the end of the bed. He picks up a gun and fires, accidentally shooting himself in the foot. Del Lord, the director of *Super-Hooper-Dyne Lizzies*, guided Curly through a faithful recreation of the routine in *Dizzy Detectives* (1943).* Lord continued to re-use elements of *Super-Hooper-Dyne Lizzies* in other Stooges comedies, including *Spook Louder* (1943), *Three Pests in a Mess* (1945) and *Shivering Sherlocks* (1948).

Lord bequeathed upon Curly every gag that had ever worked well for him in his career. For instance, the idea of using the sound of an adding machine to suggest Curly's mind at work was originated with Ben Blue in Lord's *Wreckety Wreck* (1933). The gag was further exaggerated with Curly by having him pull a strip of paper out of his mouth to read off the results of his calculations.

Another Sennett star, Harry Langdon, has a ghost scare in *His New Mamma* (1924) when a balloon decoration on a Christmas tree comes loose and floats up behind him. A menacing face painted on the balloon makes it seem that the balloon is chasing after Langdon with malicious intent. Writer Clyde Bruckman revived the routine to lesser effect for the Stooges' comedy *Spook Louder* (1943). In this manic two-reeler, the Stooges have taken jobs as caretakers in a creepy old mansion. Inexplicably, a balloon with a face drawn in ballpoint

---

*It is pointless for this routine to be staged without the hat, which occurs in *Raisin' Trouble* (1926) when Charles King is merely frightened by his own clearly recognizable big foot.

comes floating out of a chest. Curly panics and runs away, but the balloon has become latched onto his coat by a paper clip, and it seems to be chasing him through the hallways. This scene fails to capture the humor that the original scene had. First, the setup makes no sense. Why was the balloon in the chest? Why did it have a face? Why did it have a paper clip attached at the end of a string? Second, the balloon face was not funny. The original balloon had a vividly designed face that made it seem as if the balloon were a living character. The funny balloon, drifting weightlessly through Langdon's silent world, comes across as a magical, dreamlike creature. The new balloon is no more than an ink-stained plaything.

The routine actually turned up three years before *His New Momma* in a Harold Lloyd comedy called *I Do* (1921). Lloyd and his wife (Mildred Davis) are on edge when they read in the newspaper about a rash of burglaries in their community. That night, a strange light shining through their bedroom window prompts Lloyd to climb out of bed to investigate. Elsewhere in the house, the family cat is poking around a stack of gifts. Decorating the packages, along with festive ribbons and bows, is a balloon imprinted with an oddly grim face. The cat paws at the strings on the packages, causing the balloon to come loose and float away. Lloyd is making his way through a darkly lit room when the balloon face emerges out of the blackness. Lloyd, though frightened, musters the courage to leap at the apparent intruder, except the intruder's lack of a body causes him to tackle nothing but air and tumble down a staircase. In his fall, the balloon has somehow become latched onto the back of his collar. Lloyd advances through the house, unaware of the balloon trailing behind him. The drifting balloon bobs in the air and occasionally strikes him in the head, but Lloyd turns around and fails to see anything. Finally, the balloon bursts, which Lloyd assumes is the sound of the intruder firing his gun. Lloyd clutches his chest in the unquestioned belief that he has been shot. Lloyd's version of the routine is longer and more elaborately developed. Fear can incite the imagination and lead to confusion, which is the point emphasized by the scene, but this same point cannot be applied to Langdon. Langdon, a boy sneaking out of his bed at night to leave Santa a note, has no reason to be fearful, and his timidity and confusion is simply his natural state. As always, the stakes have been set higher for Lloyd, who plays a husband determined to protect his wife and his home from a violent burglar. He is willing to fight to the death, which he presumes has come when the balloon pops. It is this morbid terror that sends him into comic death throes. Langdon, upon hearing the balloon pop, is merely startled and scurries upstairs to his father (Andy Clyde). Still, a routine in which a comic character is frightened by a child's balloon seems more appropriate for Langdon. Also, the routine did not need all of the setup that Lloyd provided; it was, in fact, more effective in Langdon's slightly pared-down form. More important, Langdon's balloon still looks funnier, especially as the balloon has managed along the way to pick up a hat off a hatrack.

The balloon man, whose human likeness causes it to be mistaken for a man, functions in the same manner as the many comic mannequins that tricked and frightened comedians in the past. Langdon himself reworked this routine with a dummy in *Feet of Mud* (1924). He is seen creeping through an opium den when a broom latches onto a dummy. The audience sees the dummy suspended at the end of a broom, but Langdon comes to see this as a shady character looming over his shoulder. This time, Langdon reacts aggressively, pouncing on the dummy and attempting to wrestle it into submission.

A routine could fall flat if the people who appropriated it failed to understand why it had been funny in the first place. This is evident in *Raisin' Trouble* (1926). The scene starts out no differently than the *I Do* scene. Jack Cooper gets out of bed because he thinks he hears an intruder. But the nervous homeowner no sooner opens the bedroom door than the balloon comes floating in. He is momentarily frightened, but he can see clearly that it is only a balloon. He walks out of the door and the balloon hitches a ride with him. He is unaware as he walks through the house that he has the balloon trailing behind him, but the situation is without suspense as he has already has had his confrontation with the balloon and he cannot be expected to be surprised or confused if he turns and sees the balloon again. At one point, he is frightened by the *shadow* of the balloon, although it looks like nothing other than the shadow of a balloon. He continues to walk through the house and experiences other frights, including a marble making a noise as it rolls down a staircase, but none of this involves the pointlessly trailing balloon. Cooper is finally startled hearing the balloon pop. This is not the end of the routine as, elsewhere, Cooper's wife becomes terrified when spying a second balloon face stuck between the pillars of a balcony railing.

A bigger balloon was used when Langdon did the routine again in *The Big Kick* (1930). This time, he is working at a gas station and accidentally gets an air hose attached to the balloon. The balloon gradually inflates behind him until it is of an immense size. It is at this moment that Langdon turns around to look and is horrified at the sight of the monstrous giant. The balloon bursts with sufficient force to draw up a cloud of dust and knock Langdon off his feet.

Ideas can come from various sources. It is surprising to learn that *Survivor* inspired *Lost* and *Mad Max* (1979) inspired *Saw* (2004). Fans of Laurel and Hardy have long wondered if Alfred Hitchcock was inspired by *The Laurel-Hardy Murder Case* (1930). The chilling climax of Hitchcock's *Psycho* (1960) features Mother Bates, garbed in a granny-style dress, storming into a dark room with a large knife drawn. Hero John Gavin is struggling to get the knife out of her hand when Mother Bates's grey hair bun, which is no more than a wig, slips off her head. It has now been revealed that Mother Bates is, in fact, her son, Norman, in drag. This would have certainly been a familiar sight to a person who had seen *The Laurel-Hardy Murder Case*. In the closing moments of the film, Laurel and Hardy are sitting alone in a dark room when a grandmotherly housekeeper suddenly appears out of a secret doorway brandishing a large knife. Laurel pounces on the housekeeper to wrestle away the knife and, while they struggle, a wig slips off the housekeeper's head, exposing the housekeeper to be a man in drag.

The unwigging of Mother Bates was actually a scene invented for the source novel by author Robert Bloch. As a boy, Bloch found himself inspired by the fantastic nature of silent films. Years later, many surreal aspects of silent film migrated to the author's horror stories. He came to write about a number of subjects addressed in this book—a cursed painting, a supernatural mirror, and a demonic mannequin. Bloch's short story "The Chaney Legacy" is about a silent movie buff with a particular fondness for horror star Lon Chaney. The man purchases an antique mirror and finds that, whenever he looks into the mirror, Lon Chaney's most terrifying characters look back at him. These stories are characterized by a single common element—life being attained by human likeness. It could be that early film fans felt an anxiety about this magical new device that could capture the vivid images of men and women participating in various activities. Bloch could see the "thin line between horror and hilarity."[3] He said, "Both horror and humor require the same distorted conception of reality to be effective."[4]

Hitchcock was drawn to sensational stories, which is the reason that he became interested in Bloch's *Psycho*. It was also the reason he developed a fondness for silent film comedy. The point was made in the chapter on animal comedies that Hitchcock made use of sen-

Laurel (right) and Hardy spend the night in a spooky house in *The Laurel-Hardy Murder Case* (1930) (courtesy www.doctormacro.com).

sational thematic elements popularized by silent comedy films. He shared with the comedymakers a sense of cinematic flourish. The director, who saw drama as "life with the dull bits cut out,"[5] believed in making films that were thrilling and audacious. He provided audiences with surreal imagery, heightened danger, and perverse characters. His camera shots often conveyed the flamboyance typically reserved for uproarious comic action. A shot of Lupino Lane falling backwards down a staircase in *Summer Saps* (1929) somewhat resembles the shot of Martin Balsam falling backwards down a staircase in *Psycho*. Hitchcock was no different in his use of twists and decoys as plot devices. His protagonist, too, was often an ordinary person placed in extraordinary circumstances through mistaken identity or another odd turn of events.

It would be interesting to see a silent film comedian superimposed into a classic Hitchcock film. Let us imagine, for instance, *North by Northwest* (1959) altered so that it is Keaton fleeing the biplane and Lloyd hanging off the exterior of Mount Rushmore. Merrill Schleier, author of *Skyscraper Cinema: Architecture and Gender in American Film*, found *Safety Last!* (1923) to be a precursor to *Vertigo* (1958), which also featured a hero who must overcome his fear of heights to achieve his objectives. Certainly, Jimmy Stewart hanging off a building ledge is reminiscent of Lloyd hanging off the top of a building.

Hitchcock's ideas for *North by Northwest* were fleshed out by scriptwriter Ernest Lehman, who understood better than anyone the master filmmaker's sense of humor and his taste for bigger-than-life storytelling. Lehman further explored these ideas in *The Prize* (1963), a *North by Northwest*–inspired spy thriller that showcases a series of stock comedy routines. The lead character, played by Paul Newman, loses his clothes and walks through a hotel wearing only a towel. Desperate to escape gunmen, he acts wacky at a conference to prompt the conference organizers to call the police. He becomes uncomfortable when he falls into the clutches of a vamp (Micheline Presle). He avoids being caught on a freighter by climbing up the side of a wall and

Harry Langdon and Madeline Hurlock are surrounded by ghosts in this lobby card for *The First 100 Years* (1924).

hanging off the ceiling. He steals a uniform from a waiter, leaving the man in his underwear. He makes a getaway from gunmen by suddenly grabbing onto a passing truck, which is the same strategy that Keaton employed to escape a police squad in *Cops* (1922) and Harold Lloyd employed to escape a police officer in *Safety Last!* (1923).

Horror comedies remain popular today, as evidenced by the success of the *Scary Movie* franchise. Unfortunately, the current crop of horror comedies tend to be more gory than spooky and more shocking than funny. More recently, zombies have gotten people running and hiding in *Shaun of the Dead* (2004) and *Zombieland* (2009). *Zombieland* includes gags right out of a silent film comedy, including a piano getting dropped on top of a zombie. The heroes are, at one point, attacked by a zombie Chaplin. Zombies had long harkened back to early slapstick comedy. Zombies get pies in their faces in one of the seminal zombie films, *Dawn of the Dead* (1978). It is not surprising that *Zombieland*, with all its physical comedy, received a public endorsement from slapstick king Jerry Lewis.

8

Bombs and Burglars

Hooligan as a Safe Robber (1903), promoted by Biograph as a "comical and catchy subject,"[1] showed a safecracker caught up in an explosion and, according to Biograph, "going down in the debris."[2] This became a standard comedy premise. A Komic release called *Safety First* (1915) climaxed with two crooks (Chester Withey and Bobby Ray) being blown out of a window while trying to blast open a safe. Between May 6, 1915, and April 30, 1917, a period of less than two years, seven comedies were released with the title *Safety First*. The title was in no way to be taken literally, for safety was not at all what was presented in these comedies. Like the earlier Komic title, an L-KO comedy called *Safety First* (1916) centered on two bomb-toting burglars. The burglars are excited to have at last fulfilled their dream to commit a major robbery, but they are soon arguing about how the swag should be divided. The thieves try to outwit each other, but they end up blowing themselves up with one of their own bombs.

In *All Cooked Up* (1915), a member of the No Law and No Order League lights a bomb on a Fifth Avenue bus and tosses it at passengers. The passengers scramble out of the bus. The bomb flies out the window and lands besides a man on crutches, prompting the man to toss away the crutches and flee. The bomb then lands in a baby carriage, where it is fondled by the baby. The anarchist runs up and takes away the bomb, giving the baby a revolver to play with instead. Of course, the bomb finally rolls up to a group of anarchists and explodes just as expected. It is in keeping with this time-worn tradition that bumbling terrorist bombers accidentally blow themselves up in the recent *Four Lions* (2010).

It did not require much of an excuse for a comedy character to blow up something. *Another Name Was Maude* (1906), a comedy produced by American Mutoscope and Biograph, involves a farmer who becomes so frustrated with an uncooperative donkey that he ties the donkey to a tree and blows it up with a stick of dynamite. Random dynamite explosions were so popular that the 1913 Patheplay documentary *Dynamite, The New Farm Hand* simply showed dynamite being used to blast out tree stumps. Pathé Frères did not even bother to come up with a clever title when they marketed *A Bomb Explodes* (1910).

Bombs — whether in the hands of safecrackers, anarchists or frustrated farmers — played a large role in comedies from this period. Evidently, audiences laughed loudly whenever they saw someone being blown into the sky.

The makers of the L-KO series were determined to feature plenty of bomb explosions, even if it meant rehashing plots. In the L-KO comedy *Their Last Haul* (1915), Alice Howell works to reform Rudolph (Hank Mann) from his criminal ways. Mann is not willing to lead a lawful life unless he can commit one last big job. He sets out to blow up a safe, but he only manages to blow up himself instead.

The Keystone comedies had an even greater share of bombs. Charlie Murray hires a messenger to deliver a bomb to a rival in *Finnegan's Bomb* (1914). A chef plants a bomb in a turkey to get rid of romantic rivals in *A Lover's Might* (1916). Anarchists plant a bomb in a piano to kill the constable's wife in *The Fatal High C* (1914). Crooks gift-wrap a bomb and send it to the mayor's mansion in *Our Dare-Devil Chief* (1915). Chester Conklin is a spy well-stocked with bombs to blow up a factory in *An International Sneak* (1916). Roscoe Arbuckle is sleepwalking through a town holding a lit bomb in *Bombs and Bangs* (1914). A barrel of dynamite is at the center of *Love and Dynamite* (1914). A powder magazine brings about an explosive conclusion to *Zuzu, the Band Leader* (1913). Bombs were also prominent in *Dough and Dynamite* (1914), *The Noise of Bombs* (1914), *Do-Ri-Me-Boom* (1915) and *Bombs!* (1916).

The chemical reaction of explosive material can inflict grave injury and even death, but body displacement, clothing transference and skin-darkening are the strangely limited effects portrayed in film comedy.

Bombs fizzled out as a comic prop for a number of years. Then, in the 1960s, bombs enjoyed a resurgence due to two prominent comedy directors, Blake Edwards and Richard Lester. This was also the time that Stanley Kubrick created the ultimate bomb comedy, *Dr. Strangelove or: How I Learned to Stop Worrying and Love the Bomb* (1964).

One of the most unforgettable scenes in movie history is the scene in *Dr. Strangelove*

Charlie Murray (holding Jackie Lucas) foils a burglary by Jack Cooper in the Mack Sennett comedy *The Hollywood Kid* **(1924) (courtesy Cole Johnson Collection.)**

Stan Laurel (right) and Oliver Hardy are reluctant burglars in *Night Owls* (1930) (courtesy www. doctormacro.com).

where Slim Pickens rides a nuclear bomb through the cargo doors of a B-52. Pickens' bomb ride was the culmination of a comedy routine that had evolved in films for nearly half a century. The earliest version of the routine can likely be found in the 1915 Keystone comedy *A Submarine Pirate* (1915). The film climaxes with Sydney Chaplin falling into a torpedo tube and being launched with a torpedo. The routine was repeated by numerous comedians—Hughie Mack in *The Torpedo Pirates* (1918), Bobby Vernon in *Great Guns* (1925), Lloyd Hamilton in *Jolly Tars* (1926) and Billy Dooley in *The Dizzy Diver* (1928). It didn't take long for a comedian to take the routine airborne. In the Rolin comedy *Luke's Fireworks Fizzle* (1916), Harold Lloyd finishes his first day of work at a fireworks factory by "ascend[ing] to the clouds astride a giant skyrocket."[3] The routine persisted in multiple variations during World War II. The Three Stooges rode a cannon shell into the sky in *Boobs in Arms* (1940). Lou Costello rode a missile around an air base in *Keep 'Em Flying* (1941). Bud Duncan rode atop a moonshine-fueled rocket in *Hillbilly Blitzkrieg* (1942). The final appearance of the routine prior to Stanley Kubrick transforming slapstick silliness into political satire was the Three Stooges riding a rocket on the poster for *Have Rocket, Will Travel* (1959). Kubrick set the stakes higher, with Pickens' bomb possessing a bigger payload than all of the prior bombs put together, and Pickens, with his cowboy whooping and hat waving, was the first passenger to make the ride look fun.

The evolution of police techniques, including the procedure for handling bombs, can be seen in comedy films through the decades. In *His Silent Racket* (1933), the proprietor of a dry cleaning business (Jimmy Finlayson) is unable to pay off gangsters running a protection racket. Finlayson's new partner (Charley Chase) is driving the company delivery van, unaware that the package in the back contains one of the gangster's bombs. He has just picked up ballet costumes from a dance company when Finlayson catches up to him to alert him of the bomb. Chase rushes to the police station, where police officers surround the truck. When the chief of the bomb squad shows up to disarm the bomb, he is without a robot, a bomb suit, a digital X-ray system, or an armor-lined containment truck. He doesn't even have a wire-cutter. All he has is a bucket of water. He submerges the package into the water but, not surprising, the bomb blows up anyway. When the smoke clears, the police are dressed in the tutus from the delivery van.

Comedians usually did nothing more with a bomb than toss it out of a window, where it promptly exploded. A rare exception could be found in a 1955 episode of *Hey, Mulligan* titled "Seven Days to Doom," in which Mickey Rooney crudely attempts to defuse a bomb with a wrench, a sledgehammer and a hacksaw.

Disarming a bomb became a standard comedy routine in the nineties. Typically, the routine revolved around two partners arguing over whether they should cut the red wire or the blue wire. Variations of the routine can be found in a numerous films and television series, most notably *Naked Gun 2½* (1991), *Lethal Weapon 3* (1992) and *Rush Hour* (1998). The website tvtropes.org determined that the routine originated with *The Big Bus* (1976), which presumably presented the routine as a spoof of a bomb-defusing scene in the disaster movie *Juggernaut* (1974).

Burglars, whether armed with explosives or not, were a popular subject for early comedy films. A common plot of the early burglar comedies had a burglar breaking in on a couple and finding the wife to be much braver at defending the home than her husband. Typically, the craven husband can be found cowering under a bed or inside a closet, while the wife whacks the burglar repeatedly on the head with a broom. Examples of this subgenre are *Burglar in the Bed Chamber* (1898) and *The Burglar* (1903). Another recurring plot had a burglar being greeted warmly by a love-starved spinster. This turned up in *The Old Maid and the Burglar* (1898), *Burglar and Old Maid* (1903) and *The Old Maid and the Burglar* (1910). The plot never changed much so the title didn't need to change much either. According to the description for *Burglar and Old Maid* provided by the Lubin Catalog, The old maid "captures his pistol and forces him to get up, and after seeing that the door is securely locked, she pulls him down on her lap and almost devours him with her caresses."[4] The Edison company had a particular fondness for burglar comedies. The Edison film *Burglar's Escape* (1903) centered on a comic confrontation between a burglar and a patrol officer. The officer, hearing a disturbance in a home, pokes his head into a window, at which point the burglar slams the window down on him. The officer struggles futilely to free himself from this trap while the burglar makes a perfect getaway.

In the Biograph comedy *Jones' Burglar* (1909), Mr. Jones (John R. Cumpson) hires a man to pose as a burglar so that he can chase him off and look like a hero to his wife. The following year, Biograph reworked the premise on two occasions, first with *Too Many Burglars* (1911) and then with *A Convenient Burglar* (1911). The same year, the Lubin company borrowed this plot for *His Friend, the Burglar* (1911). Edison used the plot again in a 1913 comedy, *The Amateur Burglar*. Burglaries staged with the cooperation of the burglar are suggested by a number of other titles, including *The Burglar Helped* (1912), *Their Friend, the Burglar* (1915) and *Burglar by Request* (1917). The plot continued to turn up periodically in later years. Best known is the Laurel & Hardy comedy *Night Owls* (1930), in which a police officer persuades two tramps to break into the police chief's home so that he could show up, apprehend them, and look like a hero in front of his boss.

One way for a man to impress the ladies was to remain hidden behind a doorway curtain while pretending to be fighting a burglar. This ruse was employed by a number of comedians, including Max Linder (*Be My Wife*, 1921), Charley Chase (*Mighty Like a Moose*, 1926) and Bobby Ray (*My Baby*, 1926).

Burglars came and went so freely that people seemed to have little control over their own domiciles. This was made plain in *His Lucky Day* (1909). A young man hears a knock on the door and, worried that that his visitor is an irate creditor, he promptly hides himself inside a trunk. His visitor is, in fact, a burglar. The burglar lets himself into the room and begins his misdeed when a creditor arrives at the door. The burglar, to avert suspicion and get rid of the creditor, gives the man money to satisfy the debt. Other creditors follow and the burglar, as before, pays them to make them go away. In the end, the young man comes out of the trunk and surprises the burglar. He takes his goods back, gives the thief a good beating, and throws him out of the door.

Other burglar comedies came out at the same time. *Schneider's Anti-Noise Crusade* (1909) involves a man's frustration with modern devices, which make so much noise that he is unable to concentrate to write a speech. When burglars break into his house, he helps them to take away all of the noisy devices. The humor again comes from a burglary having an unexpected conclusion. *A Rude Hostess* (1909) was about a woman who catches a burglar in her home. The burglar tries to bluff the woman by telling her that he simply entered the wrong apartment. The woman, who knows he's lying, stalls him while her butler calls the police. *A Troublesome Satchel* (1909) involves a man who buys a used bag, unaware that it contains burglar tools. He tries to get rid of the bag but, instead, becomes involved with a band of thieves, who want his help to commit a robbery.

In the coming years, the stream of burglar comedies seemed to be endless. *What a Night!* (1924) depicts an inadvertent break-in. Lige Conley, coming home after a night of revelry, is too drunk to realize that he has come to the wrong house. The owner of the house, who is apprehensive about burglars, has set up booby traps for possible intruders. He has placed mousetraps beneath the windows. He has sprinkled roofing tacks in the halls. When Conley breaks in, the old man runs out of his bedroom with a rifle, but he is so excited that he forgets about the tacks and steps on them himself.

The trend, although it has abated, continued into modern day with the highly profitable *Home Alone* franchise, in which burglars are brutalized by assorted booby traps.

9

How to Disguise Yourself as Furniture and Fool Your Friends

This is an instance where two types of routines blended together to form a new type of routine. The first type of routine was derived from an inanimate object being propelled forward by a living creature hidden inside. The Lubin comedy *The Haunted Hat* (1909) involved a crowd of people breaking into a panic when they see a hat moving down the street, apparently under its own power. A city official is summoned immediately to address this crisis, but the official picks up the hat only to find a common house cat underneath. The second type of routine had to do with characters hiding inside of furniture or, even stranger, disguising themselves as furniture. The Commedia dell'Arte routine "Lazzo of Hiding" finds Arlecchino trapped in a woman's bedroom with the woman's lover at the door. Arlecchino, unable to find a place to hide, is persuaded by the woman to pose as a chair. Arlecchino extends his arms to form the arms of a chair and bends his knees to form a seat just before the woman throws a sheet over him. The lover enters and, unheeding of the woman's warning, sits down on Arlecchino. These routines eventually combined into a single routine where a person hiding inside of furniture makes it look as though the furniture has come to life.

In Georges Méliès's *The Tramp and the Mattress Makers* (1906), workers take a break from sewing together a mattress, at which time a drunken man crawls inside the mattress for a nap. The workers return, unaware of the tramp, and finish sewing the mattress together. The tramp awakens, finds himself trapped, and goes into a panic. The mattress suddenly sprouts legs and runs off, with the mattress makers in pursuit. A similar comedy produced by Essanay was *The Haunted Lounge* (1909), in which a tramp (Ben Turpin) escapes from a police officer by running into a secondhand shop and hiding inside a folding lounge. An old woman purchases the lounge and arranges for it to be delivered immediately to her home. The tramp has a bumpy ride inside the back of the express wagon. He gets banged up even more when the lounge falls out of the wagon. A car then slams into the lounge, which goes rolling down the street. Once the lounge is finally delivered, the old woman becomes frightened upon seeing the lounge move around and decides to get rid of the lounge by giving it to a neighbor. The neighbor has a similar experience with the lounge and brings it back to the secondhand dealer, who is able to sell the item to the police officer who chased the tramp into the shop earlier in the day. The police officer is resting on the

Duane Thompson hides in a cabinet in *Up and at 'em* (1921). The cheerful moving man is Vernon Dent (courtesy Cole Johnson Collection).

lounge when it starts to move. He rides the vigorous lounge around the room — sometimes on top, sometimes underneath. The lounge rolls down the stairs, crashes through the door, and ends up in the backyard. At this point, the police officer decides to burn the troublesome lounge. When the lounge finishes burning, the tramp emerges, unscathed, from the ashes.

In *How Cretinetti Paid His Debts* (1909), André Deed eludes creditors by climbing inside a carpet bag, which proceeds to glide away by means of stop-motion photography. Besides flying around in a carpetbag, Deed can make himself invisible and suspend people in time and space. A viewer who demands logic will have trouble accepting the idea that a man with all of these magical powers is unable to find the money to pay his grocery bill.

Larry Semon, although lacking Deed's magical powers, makes use of a similar ploy in *The Bell Hop* (1922). Semon, a bellhop being chased by a gang of criminals, sneaks into an empty room and hides under a bed. A guest (Frank Alexander) arrives at the room and Semon, afraid of being caught, looks for a way to leave without being noticed. He crawls up behind an easy chair and slips beneath the cover. At this point, the chair slides gradually towards the exit. Alexander tries to sit in the chair but it suddenly moves out of the way and he falls back, crashing to the floor. An irate Alexander chases the uncooperative chair around the room. He pulls out a revolver and shoots at the chair. Semon proves to be just as elusive moving around inside of the chair as Deed had been moving around inside of the carpetbag.*

A chair could also be a good hiding place for someone planning an ambush. In *The Haunted House* (1921), counterfeiters using an old house as a hideout look to scare away snoops by making it appear that the house is haunted. Buster Keaton, as an unwelcomed visitor, stumbles warily through the strange and spooky house. A gang member disguised as a chair waits until Keaton sits on him before he tightens his arms menacingly around Keaton's waist. Keaton, in a panic, wrests himself out of the chair's grip. The perfection of the gag is demonstrated by the fact that Max Linder reproduced it without variation in *Help!* (1924).

A rudimentary version of the original Commedia dell'Arte routine "Lazzo of Hiding" is worked into the Max Linder comedy *Love's Surprises* (1913). It is known from a review in *The Moving Picture World* that Walter Stull performed the routine in a lost 1916 Pokes and Jabbs comedy called *Reckless Romeos*. Laurel and Hardy can be seen in a recreation of the routine more faithful than the others in *Block-Heads* (1938). Hardy has to hide a woman when her husband arrives home unexpectedly. He quickly comes up with the idea to disguise the woman as a chair. He instructs her to crouch down and stick her arms out and then throws a cover over her. Laurel enters the room along with the wife and, unaware of Hardy's ruse, tries to sit on the woman, who responds by punching him in the arm. This action is repeated a number of times before the woman gets so fed up that she stands up and tears off the cover. Moe Howard uses the same trick to hide from an irate husband in *Don't Throw that Knife* (1951). Moe, not known to be a patient pantomimist, does not make an effort to develop a routine out this premise and merely employs it as a throwaway gag. Andy Clyde varied the routine in *His Tale Is Told* (1944). In an effort to hide from a woman's husband, Clyde throws a sheet over himself and pretends to be an ironing board, but an iron gets set down on his back and burns him.

Other variations of the same basic idea turned up over the years. In *The Flirts* (1919), a woman is afraid to let her husband know that a strange man has climbed into their bed and is hiding under the covers. She kneels down at the head of the bed, sets her head down on the mattress, and draws the sheets up to her chin to make it look like she is the person occupying the bed. The husband (Leo White) has the misfortune to cuddle up against the strange man, thinking that this person is his wife. A similar scene appeared in *Monsieur Beaucaire* (1946). The king is about to catch his mistress in the duke's bedroom until Bob Hope, as the duke's barber, comes up with a quick idea to hide her. He has the woman hunch down in his barber's chair and he covers her with a sheet. The duke then squats behind the chair and tucks the end of the sheet under his chin to make it look as if he is the person occupying the chair.

Other objects were also used as a form of cover for comedians. Max Linder remains concealed under a bathtub as he flees naked through Paris in *Max Takes a Bath* (1910). A

---

*A similar routine was devised by Georges Méliès for *The Bewitched Inn* (1897). A chair controlled by ghostly forces disappears just as a man is attempting to sit down. The chair reappears on the other side of the room and the man struggles to hold the chair in place long enough to allow himself to sit down. The idea was developed further in *Nerve Tonic* (1924), this time with Jimmie Adams as the victim. At first, a lively chair abruptly bends backwards, dumping the unfortunate man onto the floor. A table proves even more troublesome. Adams is seated at the table, prepared to eat a sandwich, when the table moves in one direction or another to keep the sandwich out of his reach. The same premise is behind Abbott & Costello's famous "moving candle" routine, which has Lou Costello frightened by a candle holder that mysteriously slides back and forth across a table.

pair of prowlers try to avoid capture by running off while hidden inside a hollow log in *A Walking Tree* (1908). In L-KO's *A Rural Romance* (1916), Billy Bevan falls into a hay baler and becomes trapped inside a bale of hay. In the next scene, this bale of hay with legs is shown running down the street. Bevan eventually falls into a feeding trough and a horse eats away the hay. In *Among Those Present* (1921), Harold Lloyd shields himself from a vicious dog by covering himself with a trash can. The trash can slides along the ground with the dog, bewildered but persistent, remaining in hot pursuit. In *The Daredevil* (1923), Ben Turpin hides under a barrel to sneak out of a building without attracting the notice of an agitated mob determined to pummel him. He blindly walks out into the middle of a busy street and cars have to swerve to avoid him. He has to dodge bullets along with cars when a member of the mob fires a gun at him. Turpin, still wearing the barrel, runs inside of a building, where he topples onto a moving platform and is carried quickly towards a buzz saw. The buzz saw cuts down the center of the barrel, which suggests that Turpin is being cut by half. It is not until the barrel finally comes through the buzz saw that Turpin is revealed to be tucked away safely in one half of the barrel (although the seat of his pants has been neatly sliced off). This gag was still used on rare occasions in the early sound era. Bob Hope and Bing Crosby are concealed beneath a tent as they sneak inside a desert encampment in *The Road to Morocco* (1942). Red Skelton attempts to escape enemy soldiers by stealing away beneath a dog house in *A Southern Yankee* (1948). A strange revival of the gag turned up in the low-budget horror film *The Killer Shrews* (1959). James Best, as a boat captain trapped on an island with giant mutant rodents, avoids getting chewed up by the ravenous creatures by cutting out eye holes in a chemical drum and wearing the drum while marching to his boat docked at the beach. The gag lives on today, as demonstrated when a group of animated toys scramble for cover underneath a recycle bin in *Toy Story 3* (2010).

Possibly the most outlandish variation of this routine formed the basis of the 1908 Pathé Frères comedy *Crocodile Turns Thief* (1908). A burglar who has broken into a taxidermist's laboratory is momentarily unnerved to find a crocodile skin rug lying on the floor. When he hears the taxidermist approaching, he moves quickly to take refuge underneath the scaly rug. The taxidermist, alarmed at the sight of the crocodile skin moving around the room, arms himself with a gun and opens fire on the beast. The burglar, crawling on all fours with the crocodile skin draped across his back, flees into the street, where he upsets a group of people. The burglar, still disguised in the rug, climbs up a drain pipe and enters an apartment. The occupants of the apartment are a quiet family at tea. The family, shocked to have their home invaded by this horrid human/crocodile hybrid, rush out of their home, fearing for their lives.

The climax of *The Adventurer* (1917) features Charlie Chaplin as an escaped convict in flight from prison guards at a fancy dinner party. The frantic chase sweeps the participants through a series of rooms. Chaplin hopes to escape detection by putting a beaded lampshade over his head and standing stock-still, as though he were nothing more than a lamp stand. This completely fools a police officer, who rushes past without incident. It is at this point that Chaplin's burly romantic rival, Eric Campbell, storms into the room and makes an unwanted advance on the lovely Edna Purviance. Chaplin removes the lampshade and drops it over Campbell's head, which obscures Campbell's view long enough for Chaplin to step up and punch Campbell in the stomach. Chaplin, preparing for a hasty exit, turns to bid farewell to Purviance. After the couple kiss, Chaplin extends his arm towards the door with melodramatic flourish, as if to suggest that "parting is such sweet sorrow." Then, just before he heads out, he plants the lampshade back on his head as if it is a sporty hat. Within a matter of moments, Chaplin was able to handle a prop as simple as a lampshade and alternately transform it into a disguise, a weapon and a fashion accessory.

Harold Lloyd was likely influenced by *The Adventurer* when he had a police squad chasing him around a gambling club in *Bumping into Broadway* (1919). In a variation of the lampshade routine, Lloyd looks to elude the police by hiding under a tablecloth and pretending to be a table. An officer sees the apparent table moving away and tears off the tablecloth to spoil Lloyd's ruse. Lloyd devised a more elaborate version of this routine for *A Sailor-Made Man* (1921). Lloyd is fleeing from a brutish, saber-rattling maharajah when he takes notice of a collection of striped floor pillows scattered around a palace chamber. Lloyd folds himself under a striped sheet to make himself look like one of the pillows, but the maharajah becomes suspicious and decides to run his saber through each and every one of the pillows. Lloyd flees just as the maharajah prepares to thrust his blade into him.

Comedians were not through using lampshades as disguises. In *Fresh Paint* (1920), Snub Pollard eludes a jealous husband (Noah Young) by putting a lampshade on his head. Compared to the original version this routine is rather spare. The gag took a surreal turn in the Three Stooges comedy *Dopey Dicks* (1950) when flaky Stooge Larry Fine ducks into a room to avoid a mad scientist's henchman. Larry puts a lampshade over his head and, as an additional enhancement, holds a light bulb in his hand. The henchman, falling for the ruse, tugs Larry's tie, at which point the bulb in Larry's hand miraculously lights up.

The Commedia dell'Arte routine "Lazzi of Arlecchino's Portrait," which was introduced in Paris in 1685, had a spy looking through a hole cut into a painting. This was another way in which comic characters used furnishings as a disguise.

Characters are invariably hidden inside of a painting in a haunted house comedy. The paintings usually have sliding peepholes which allow a person to put their eyes in place of the eyes in the portrait. This overused comic device has turned up in a variety of feature films, including *Murder by Death* (1976) and *The Haunted Mansion* (2003). The ruse has also been used extensively on television programs, including *Get Smart*, *The Monkees*, *The Andy Griffith Show* and *The Simpsons*. The Bowery Boys comedy *Smugglers' Cove* (1948) features an abundance of paintings with sliding peepholes. Huntz Hall finds a peephole built around the entire face in a portrait, which allows him to replace his homely face with the nobleman's face depicted in the portrait. This hoary gag has become subject to lampooning. A sketch in a 2010 episode of *Nick Swardson's Pretend Time* involves the owner of a spooky old mansion who becomes concerned when the eyes in his painting stop moving and takes the painting to a doctor to undergo laser surgery.

In *Uncle Sam* (1923), the title character has faked his death to see how his heirs will react in order that he may determine who is deserving of his fortune. The uncle stations himself in a false picture frame pretending to be his own portrait. Hank Mann, as a spoiled and prissy heir, grows impatient waiting for the will to be read and decides to take a lunch break. He slices an onion, which causes another potential heir (Lee Moran) to cry. Mann finishes his meal and daintily eats a breath mint. Meanwhile, the uncle sees Moran crying and thinks that he has found the one person grieved by his phony death. He secretly gestures for his lawyer to name Moran as his heir. Irate relatives take their anger out on the supposed portrait as they leave. A woman throws a clock at the painting, hitting Uncle Sam in the head. Mann delivers a hard uppercut to the painting, knocking the wind out of the old man. A dog, realizing that this is not a portrait, jumps through the frame and bites the man's foot. A black butler screams for help after he accidentally gets pushed into the painting. He soon returns with another black servant and they beat up the haunted painting with axes and clubs.

In *The Janitor* (1919), a government agent (Madge Kirby) has gotten a tip that an anarchist is sending a man to a café to blow it up. She suspects that Hank Mann is the bomber and approaches his table to investigate. Kirby, acting flirtatious, moves close to Mann and slips her arm around him, which allows her to reach under his jacket in search of the bomb. Meanwhile, a portrait behind their table rises up, opening up a panel in the wall and revealing a second agent. The agent, who looks exactly like the man in the portrait, expects to escape Mann's notice. He leans forward to slip his hand inside of Mann's jacket, but Mann clasps his hand and strokes it, thinking that it is Kirby's hand.

The false picture in the wall turned up later in spy-related comedies. *Yankee Doodle Andy* (1941), an Andy Clyde two-reeler, features a Nazi spy posing in a false picture frame. At one point, Clyde bumps into the wall and the frame tilts to one side. The spy, not wanting to be exposed, instantly changes his angle to match the angle of the frame. Later, Clyde chases after the Nazi spy and grabs him by the seat of his pants before he can climb back into the wall. He unintentionally yanks down the spy's pants, revealing long johns with a stylish swastika pattern and the words "HEIL HITLER" emblazoned across the seat.

Dudley Dickerson has a funny moment in *One Shivery Night* (1950) when he is poking around inside a dark, spooky mansion. Dickerson backs up towards a wall, where a hanging photograph of Gentleman Jim Corbett swings to one side. In a flash, a hand with a boxing glove shoots out of the wall and strikes Dickerson in the back of the head. The arm quickly disappears back inside the wall and the photograph moves back into place. Dickerson does a double-take when he see the photograph as he assumes that it was Gentleman Jim himself who punched him.

It was not as funny when Clyde Bruckman, the writer of *One Shivery Night*, used the gag again the following year on *The Buster Keaton Show*. Keaton is perusing the contents of a bookshelf. He peeks inside a book titled *The Art of Pugilism*, at which point a gloved fist shoots out of the book and strikes him squarely in the face. A viewer shown the image of a boxer with raised fists could quickly associate this with the gloved fist that comes out of the wall. On a subliminal level, it could appear to them, as it had appeared to Dickerson, that the painting had come to life. But the sight of a book cannot elicit the same association. Also, the original version of the gag, in which a thief just happens to use a sliding panel behind this particular painting to punch an intruder, was founded on coincidence and misunderstanding. Keaton went with a more surreal and direct version of the gag, and the results were far less interesting.

Paintings were used as camouflage by characters in other comedy films. In *WALL-E* (2008), a spaceship captain hides from a mutinous robot by standing in front of his own portrait. A hunter in a life-sized painting suddenly turns his rifle on Will Smith in *Wild Wild West* (1999). Less elaborate versions of this assassin-in-a-painting gag had been used previously in other campy action films, including *In Like Flint* (1967) and *Indiana Jones and the Temple of Doom* (1984).*

A separate category of living paintings also existed in silent film comedy. This is not in the category of furniture disguises, but it is, nonetheless, a fair opportunity to bring up the subject.

One of André Deed's more imaginative routines occurs in *The Inconsistencies of Boireau*

---

*By wearing an outfit with the same pattern as the wallpaper of the surrounding room, a shapely lady spy is able to go about her business unnoticed in *Yo Yo* (1965).

(1912), wherein Deed has to get dressed for a rabbit hunt. Deed approaches a full-length, life-size portrait of a man in a hunting outfit. He suddenly reaches inside of the portrait and snatches off the man's hunting cap. He proceeds to remove other articles of clothing until the man in the painting is left in his underwear. He then hurls the clothing against his body and, in the next instant, the clothing is perfectly fitted on his body and he is ready to go hunting. The scene is appropriately fantastic and funny.

Elements of the clothes-changing scene can be found in the Georges Méliès film *An Impossible Balancing Feat* (1902). Deed liked to build upon different Méliès concepts. In this case, he took an individual effect in which Méliès interacts with a living painting, and another effect wherein Méliès magically dons an outfit, and found a way to integrate both effects.

A popular variation of this routine, also devised by Méliès, had a man unable to get undressed; no sooner does he remove his outfit than another outfit magically appears on his body. Méliès originated the routine in *Going to Bed Under Difficulties* (1900). Rival film companies duplicated the routine (with little variation) in a string of films, including *Undressing Impossible* (1901), *Clothes Enchanted* (1901), *Undressing Extraordinary* (1901) and *The Inexhaustible Wardrobe* (1902).

Méliès is remembered for using a variety of camera tricks to create fantastic scenes. It is important to note, though, that the majority of Méliès's fantasies were comic fantasies, and they did much to define the Natural law to which comedians remained bound through much of the silent era. Méliès attributed the impossible actions in his films to mystical forces, sometimes a magician and more often malevolent creatures, such as imps, devils and witches. Later, these effects broke away from their evil supernatural origins and came instead to represent the natural phenomena belonging to this magical new world of cinema. Still, although the effects continued, it was necessary for films to become less surreal in order for audiences to fully relate to them. A car chase could get fairly outlandish, with a car crashing through a home and delivering the homeowner, asleep in bed, out into the road. But filmmakers no longer had a car riding in circles on the Rings of Saturn. The action, for the most part, came to be more earth-bound.

Comedy makers came up with a logical explanation when the clothes-changing effect was used in the future. In *Cold Hearts and Hot Flames* (1916), a blast of water from a fire hose transfers a dress from a clothesline onto an character's body. In *Hot Lightning* (1927), a man and woman have their outfits exchanged when they are struck by a bolt of lightning.

Buster Keaton performs a more literal interpretation of Deed's gag in *The Garage* (1920). The scene starts with a dog tearing off Keaton's pants. A woman becomes upset seeing Keaton indecently exposed in his underwear, and threatens to get a cop. Keaton sees a man pictured on a billboard and gets to work cutting off the man's outfit. By the time the woman returns with the cop, Keaton has attached the illustrated outfit to the front of his body. His ruse works until he turns around and the cop can see that Keaton remains uncovered in the back.

Other comic characters became entangled with paintings. In *The Animated Poster* (1903), a billposter working on the side of a building accidentally covers up a window with a poster of an actress in tights. An old woman, angered by this, throws open her window shutters and, in the process, cuts off the actress's head and puts her own head in its place. In *Wet and Warmer* (1920), a squirrel gets under a poster for a dancing girl and makes it look as if the dancing girl's posterior is moving. This gag continued to be recycled. In *Step*

This Way (1922), a man gets in the way while a poster of a woman is being pasted to a wall and his head wiggling around under the paper makes the figure of the woman move suggestively. In *The Big Squeal* (1933), Andy Clyde smashes his head through a painting of a woman, placing his bristly face atop the woman's voluptuous physique. In *It's a Bear* (1924), Joe Rock cannot let his landlord know that he has a dog living in his apartment. The dog knows that, at the first sign of the landlord, he is to fit himself inside of a dog-shaped cutout in an oil painting of a hunting party. Comedians are still becoming involved with posters and paintings today. More suggestive than the scene in *Step This Way* is a scene in *30 Rock* episode "Reaganing" (2010), in which Tina Fey is caught lying half naked beneath a poster of Tom Jones.

Films often featured books and paintings with images that magically came to life. Méliès likely introduced this concept in *The Magic Book* (1900), in which a variety of characters emerge from a storybook. Other film companies followed Méliès's example. Lubin's *The Living Posters* (1903) showed illustrated characters coming to life and stepping into the real world. Méliès colorfully expanded on this idea in *The Hilarious Posters* (1906). In the 1908 Lux comedy *Posthumous Jealousy*, a widow displays an enlarged photo of her late husband at a luncheon held in his honor. The image comes to life to play pranks on the widow and her suitor, both of whom finally flee in terror. The 1908 Pathé Frères comedy *Living Poster* introduces a series of drawings that adorn a fence. The first poster, which features cows grazing in a field, attracts the attention of a crowd when one of the cows pokes its head out of the paper. A second poster displays an advertisement for a brand of champagne. A boy who pokes the nozzle of a hose through a knot in the fence makes it look as if champagne is bursting out of the bottle. The third (and final) poster shows a troupe of ballet dancers who suddenly come to life to give the crowd a show.

In Méliès's *The Magic Lantern* (1903), two men operating a slide projector watch as images of various people are projected on a screen. The men open the slide projector and the living people emerge from the device. This would not be the last time that the people viewing a picture show would be able to interact with the characters onscreen. Buster Keaton, as a projectionist, steps inside of a detective movie in *Sherlock Jr.* (1924). In *The Purple Rose of Cairo* (1985), a handsome actor (Jeff Daniels) comes out of a movie into the real world, where he has a romance with a waitress (Mia Farrow) who is one of his most avid fans. The reverse could happen as well. In *Spiritualistic Photographer* (1903), Georges Méliès has a woman stand up in front of a blank canvas. Then, with a wave of the hand, he transforms her into an image on the canvas. This same trick was later used for a more horrific effect in the television movie *Night Gallery* (1969).

Surrealism exists in a realm that borders both comedy and horror. Terror can, without question, be found in the idea of a painting that can come to life. This was identified long ago by "Portrait," an 1834 short story by Russian author Nikolai Gogol. The story begins simply with a man purchasing a portrait in an art shop. Later, at home, the man dusts off the painting and finds himself disturbed by the subject's lifelike eyes, which he imagines were "cut from a living man and inserted." He comes to believe that the painting is demonic and it is using its evil powers to corrupt his soul. A 1915 film adaptation of "Portrait" climaxes with the painting's owner resting in bed while a menacing figure climbs down out of the painting. The sole existing print of the film ends abruptly with the figure looming over the man. Does this terrible apparition kill the man, or is the man able to execute a hair's-breadth escape?

The Edison comedy *Animated Painting* (1904) involves an artist busy at work painting a picture of a sunset. The sun in the painting miraculously ascends over the horizon and then leaves the painting altogether levitating above the easel. The artist, shocked by this sight, plunges the painting into a bucket of water, where it explodes. Should the viewer laugh at this or be frightened?

Charley Bowers sees a painting of Napoleon come to life in *Nothing Doing* (1927). Then, a milkman in a second painting throws a milk bottle at Bowers. These effects, the result of a special process developed by Bowers, are more advanced than the effects that Deed used when he interacted with the painting of the hunter.

Buster Keaton required no special process to bring a painting to life in *The Frozen North* (1922). Keaton came up with a gag inspired by Paul Émile Chabas' painting *September Morn*, which was scandalous in its day for depicting a nude woman holding her hands over her body as she wades into a lake. Keaton's gag was as risqué as the painting itself and it is no wonder it never made it into the finished film. At the task of robbing a saloon, the comedian shouts at the patrons to put up their hands, at which point the woman in the painting removes her hands from her body and sticks them straight into the air. Instead of relying on animation, Keaton had his prop master provide the bathing beauty with mobile arms that could be manipulated behind the scenes by a stagehand.

The Three Stooges have worse problems than Bowers when it comes to a lively painting of Napoleon that they encounter in *Loose Loot* (1953). Moe is tossing a satchel of loot to Shemp when Napoleon comes to life and snatches the satchel for himself. He tries to make a quick getaway, but Moe hurls a rock at him and Napoleon is knocked unconscious. The Stooges quickly climb into the painting to recover the satchel.

Comedian Mike Myers recalls *Sherlock Jr.* when he steps out of a movie screen in *Austin Powers in Goldmember* (2002). However, this is a throwaway gag that has no connection to character or story. It comes and goes, lacking the meaning or magic of the original scene.

The most eye-catching scene of *Night at the Museum: Battle of the Smithsonian* (2009) features Ben Stiller and Amy Adams jumping into Alfred Eisenstaedt's "The Kiss" photo. Suddenly, the actors are inhabiting a marvelous black & white CGI recreation of World War II–era Times Square.

Reality was indistinct in silent film comedy. In *Rolling Stone* (1919), Billy West is walking down a street wearing a sandwich board advertising Joe's Beans. A picture of beans painted on the board attracts a hungry dog, which sticks its snout up to the picture and licks desperately at the painted beans. Inhabitants of silent films, both dog and man, often managed to confuse the real with the unreal.

A recurring gag had a comedian mistaking an image painted on a backdrop for the real article. The earliest-known example of this occurs in the Sennett comedy *The Daredevil* (1923). Ben Turpin has raised the ire of a film crew for his constant mishaps as a stunt men. The crew is seen furiously chasing Turpin through the studio. Afraid of what the crew will do to him once they catch him, he is desperately looking for a way out. Turpin sees a doorway and runs for it, except it is really the image of doorway painted on a backdrop. He slams into the backdrop and gets knocked flat to the floor. In *Bromo and Juliet* (1926), Charley Chase has gotten drunk before having to go onstage in an amateur production of *Romeo and Juliet*. He staggers onstage and takes notice of a lake painted on the backdrop. Goaded by a spectator to "jump in the lake," Chase dives headfirst towards the "lake," only to bang his head and get tossed backwards onto the stage. In *Steamboat Bill, Jr.* (1928), Buster Keaton has just had a sandbag drop on his head before he dives toward a painted backdrop of an ocean, which he presumably confuses for an actual ocean. Turpin is in a tizzy. Chase is drunk. Keaton is disoriented.*

Keaton played with viewers' perception in *The Boat* (1921). A scene opens with Keaton decorating the cabin of his boat. He nails up a scenic seaside painting on the wall, but he drives the nail in too far and the boat springs a leak. The waves of this painted ocean become tumultuous as actual sea water comes spurting out of the painting. This is somewhat reminiscent of the gushing champagne bottle poster in *Living Poster*. A modern CGI–generated version of the same gag turns up in *The Chronicles of Narnia: The Voyage of the Dawn Treader* (2010). A painting of a ship out to sea manages, just as the painting in *The Boat*, to issue a forceful cascade of sea water.

Living paintings continued to stir the imagination of filmmakers. Pierre Étaix, who understood how important these funny paintings had been to silent film comedy, included four distinctly different gags of this type in his silent film comedy homage *Yo Yo* (1965). The film opens with the camera panning portraits of an illustrious family line. The man in the final portrait seems to come to life, except it is really the reflection of the present lord of the manor on display in an ornately framed mirror. In another scene, a servant reaches into a still life of a table setting to remove a liquor bottle camouflaged in an open slot among the various images of food, silverware and crystal. The Coen brothers provided their own variation of the living painting gag in *The Ladykillers* (2004), where a portrait of an old woman's deceased husband changes expressions in accordance to plot turns.

Director Terry Gilliam created the living embodiment of Botticelli's "Birth of Venus" painting in *The Adventures of Baron Munchausen* (1988). The inspiration of Georges Méliès is most evident today in the films of Terry Gilliam. Just compare Gilliam's *The Adventures of Baron Munchausen* or *The Imaginarium of Doctor Parnassus* (2009) to Méliès's *The Kingdom of Fairies* (1903), a hand-colored fairy tale with extravagant creatures, colorful costumes and eye-catching art direction. Méliès-style disembodied heads are on display in *The Adventures of Baron Munchausen*. The king and queen of the Moon have detachable heads. Later, a sultan chops off a man's head, which then flies through the air, lands in one of the harem baths, and winks at one of the sultan's wives. Méliès was a truly great surreal artist, and his lasting contributions to motion pictures can never be overstated.

---

*Keaton devised a less acrobatic variation of this gag for *Mixed Magic* (1936). The comic, dazed from a fall, turns to kiss a beautiful magician's assistant (Marlyn Stuart) and instead kisses a likeness of the woman displayed on a poster behind them.

10

The Amazing Trapdoor Chase

Lupino Lane excelled at tumbling and diving through trapdoors. In 1921, he made use of these skills in a production of "Aladdin" at the London Hippodrome. The story had Lane's character being chased by a demon and diving through dozens of stage traps as a means of escape. He also performed this routine as part of a ranch scene in *The Ziegfeld Follies of 1924*. As it was explained in press material for *Sword Points* (1928), "This act has been in the Lane family for more than three centuries, each succeeding member of the clan adding tricks and refinements to it, until today, it is recognized as one of the most difficult as well as the most unique acts onstage or screen."[1] George Lupino, Lane's uncle, was well known for his use of trapdoors in stage routines. It was a skill that actors had to learn if they were going to perform in British pantomime shows. The fantastic feats performed by fairy tale characters included a myriad of appearances, disappearances and transformations. The principal instrument used to accomplish these feats were hinged flaps in the stage called "star traps." The flaps were able to fall back as soon as the actor was ejected through the trap, leaving no visible opening and making it look as if the actor appeared out of nowhere. George had a routine he did in a graveyard, where the trapdoors were built into prop gravesites. He also did a routine with the trapdoors built into various parts of a castle set. He displayed great acrobatic skill in his surprising leaps from these traps. He was sprung through trapdoors as high as 15 feet.

Lupino Lane wrote, "Our family holds the record for hurtling through stage traps. My record of [jumping] 8 feet and 5 inches has never been beaten. My record of 83 traps in six minutes made at the London Hippodrome likewise has never been beaten."[2] Lane was certainly trying to outdo his Uncle George.

In *Sword Points* (1928), Lane finds the villainous duke and his henchmen have captured a messenger of the king, and they are demanding that he turn over secret orders he has in his possession. Lane grabs the papers before the duke can get them. A half-dozen swordsmen chase Lane up a staircase. Lane discovers the architectural plan for the inn and sees that it is filled with secret trapdoors and sliding panels. Built into the wall are two rows of panels, each panel possessing a swinging door. Lane cleverly uses the trapdoors and panels to evade the swordsmen. He crawls into one door and then jumps out of another. He climbs through another door and tumbles out of a different one. After a swordsman pursues him through a panel, he pops out of another panel and delivers a hard kick to the swordsman. Lane finally lays out the whole band of swordsmen and returns the papers to the king's messenger, only to find that he is holding decoy papers. Out of gratitude, a woman bends down to Lane, who is sitting on the floor, and plants a kiss on his cheek. Lane smiles broadly and leans back, dropping down into one last trapdoor hidden in the floor.

An actual study of *Sword Points* raises suspicions about Lane's claims. The set looked as if it has as many as six dozen trapdoors laid out across two floors, but Lane used only 25 of the trapdoors during the course of the scene. This was far less than Lane's alleged record of leaping through 83 traps in six minutes. Also, despite Lane's claim that the act was in his family for three centuries, the earliest record of a Lupino family member performing the routine is a newspaper review of the 1890 pantomime show *The Spider and the Fly*.

Nearly a quarter of a century before *Sword Points*, a similar act appeared in the 1904 Georges Méliès film *Sorcellerie culinaire* (known in America as *The Cook in Trouble*). The Méliès film starts out with a chef denying a meal to a beggar. The beggar, as it turns out, is really a sorcerer in disguise. The sorcerer, bent on revenge, conjures up three rodent-like imps to plague the chef's kitchen. The acrobatic imps leap through a window and tumbles out of an oven door. They dive into a big pot and come springing out of a drawer. They run out through a door and pop out of a window chest. The trapdoors are constructed into the kitchen set as George Lupino had once had trapdoors constructed into a castle set.

Similar routines suddenly turned up in a spate of films between 1918 and 1922. Harold Lloyd performed the earliest-known, bona-fide trapdoor chase in *Follow the Crowd* (1918). Still, other types of passageways could be used to the same ends. Trapdoors were scattered throughout the walls and floors of a criminal hideout or a sultan's lair, but a tramp character could find a substitute for a trapdoor on a city street. In *A Dog's Life* (1918), Charlie Chaplin eludes a police officer by rolling in and out of a hole beneath a fence. In *The Water Plug* (1920), Billy Franey outwits police by jumping in and out of manholes. An adequate replacement could just as easily be found in a simple rustic setting. In *Broken Bubbles* (1920), Hank Mann pops in and out of crevices in a hillside — much like a Whack-a-Mole. A comedian without the will or agility to leap in and out of trapdoors could serve the same purpose simply running in and out of revolving panels. This strategy is employed by Mann in *The Janitor* (1919) and *Herman Hero* (1919), and by Larry Semon in *The Sleuth* (1922).

A series of trapdoors was spectacularly incorporated into a chase scene in a Billy West comedy called *Ship Ahoy* (1919). The short, directed by Charley Chase, introduces West as a lodger at a seaside boardinghouse. A burly sea captain, who is involved in smuggling stolen jewels, arrives at the boarding house and makes aggressive advances on the landlady's daughter. The captain ends up taking the girl captive and bringing her to his ship. West comes aboard the ship to rescue the girl and ends up getting chased through the ship by the crew. The chase is strictly confined to four equal-sized cabins arranged two on the top and two on the bottom. A cutaway set was built so that the participants were visible in a wide-shot, traveling through doors, transoms and trapdoors. This intricately staged chase, which was both funny and exciting, turned out to be the highlight of the film.

Three months later, this setup showed up again in a Larry Semon prison comedy, *The Star Boarder* (1919). This time, the four rooms are four prison cells. At first, only two cells are visible onscreen. Semon is sitting in a cell at the bottom while another inmate, Chai Hong, is digging through the floor of a cell directly above him. Hong finally creates a hole large enough for him to fit through and climbs down into Semon's cell. He invites Semon to join him and his accomplices in a prison break. At this point, four cells become visible in the frame — two cells on top and two on the bottom. Semon and Hong are climbing up into Hong's cell while inmates in a cell in the top right corner are breaking a hole through

Sydney Chaplin attacks Edgar Kennedy as he comes up through a trapdoor in *No One to Guide Him* (1915). On the far left is Dixie Chene. Other extras are unidentified (courtesy Robert Arkus).

the outer wall. Holes broken through the floors and walls of the four cells allow the inmates to travel freely between cells and, in the end, gather together within the one cell to escape through the hole leading out of the prison. Unlike West, Semon does not exploit this setup for a chase scene.

Buster Keaton slips through a series of trapdoors to elude villains in *The High Sign* (1921). The set that Keaton had constructed for the scene consisted of a cross-section of a two-story home divided into four equal-sized rooms. This setup allowed the camera to capture Keaton in a long shot, traveling from room to room, floor to floor, in a single, stationary shot. It is no secret where Keaton is at any point in this scene. This is unlike Lane, who surprises the audience and the villains with where he is going to turn up next. The Keaton scene is more economical than the Lane scene: only six trapdoors are involved. There was a trapdoor in the wall that took Keaton from the first-floor living room into an adjacent bedroom; a trapdoor in the ceiling of the bedroom that took Keaton up to a second-floor bedroom; a trapdoor in the wall of the upstairs bedroom that brought Keaton into an adjacent room on the second floor; and a trapdoor in the floor of this last bedroom that brought Keaton back to the first floor. There was also a trapdoor under a bureau in a bedroom, which allowed Keaton to throw in one surprise, and a trapdoor from the living room to the basement, which is where Keaton sends the bad guys to dispose of them.* Keaton also included a stunt wherein, after diving out of a second-story window, he grabs hold of a drainpipe, which immediately bends in half and hurls him into a window on the floor below.

This shares many similarities with the chase scene in *Ship Ahoy*, including the four rooms, the cutaway set and the trapdoors. But significant differences are evident. First, Keaton's set is cleaner. The rooms do not have the clutter or cramped conditions found in the cabins of *Ship Ahoy*. Keaton's set also lacks the corridors that divide the cabins and create a thick distracting line down the center of the frame. Second, the action in Keaton's scene is not as busy and chaotic as the action in *Ship Ahoy*. Keaton is originally being chased by six gang members, but he is quickly able to dispose of the majority of his pursuers. He shoves a couple of them out of windows. He knocks a couple of them unconscious. For most of the chase, he has to contend with a single gang member. The scene was designed as a showcase for Keaton and no distractions were allowed to get into his way. West, by contrast, has to contend with five crooks at one time. While on the top floor running back and forth between cabins, West swings a lead pipe, battering the pursuing crew members. In one corner of the screen, two crooks struggle to climb up through a trapdoor. One climbs onto the shoulders of the other and is boosted up through the trapdoor. In another cabin, a crook has made it through the trapdoor and reaches down to pull up his companion. West is throwing furniture at the crooks to ward off their attack. At one point, he runs around, smashing vases over their heads. Something is happening in every room at every moment. In *The High Sign*, the viewer's eye is meant to stay trained on Keaton as he travels from room to room in a perfectly circular pattern. Keaton's scene has the orderliness and precision of a Swiss clock. Lane had a reputation for his precision when it came to arranging and timing routines, but Keaton manages to top Lane in this regard. All in all, Keaton's scene is undeniably more breathtaking than the West scene, but the West scene is funnier.

The question arises if Keaton had been influenced by either *Ship Ahoy* or *The Star Boarder*. The evidence is persuasive that either Keaton or his collaborator Eddie Cline was influenced by *The Star Boarder*, as other elements of the film also turn up in Keaton's *Convict 13* (1920): an escaped convict switches clothes with the hero, the hero is mistaken for the escaped convict by police and dragged off to prison for a pending execution, and the hero develops a romance with the warden's daughter.†

Lane, despite the long tradition that this routine had in his family, was a late comer in getting the trapdoor routine to the screen. Even someone of another species had performed the routine on film. In *Grief in Bagdad* (1925), a chimp eludes pursuers by using wall panels that revolve and flip. By flipping a panel, it hits one of the pursuers on the head. The chimp hangs on to the panel as it rotates around to avoid being caught by the man on the other side. He later utilizes a secret passageway in a staircase and plunges down an escape hatch built into a throne.

---

*Keaton originally used a trapdoor to dispose of bad guys in *Old West* (1918).

†Other comedians were forced to switch clothing with escaped convicts. This includes Harold Lloyd in *Take a Chance* (1918), Billy Bevan in *On Patrol* (1922), and Stan Laurel in *Detained* (1924). Laurel is marched off to the electric chair, but his execution does not go as planned. The man operating the electric chair is unable to get it to work and asks Laurel to step aside while he takes a look at it. Laurel plays with the levers on the machine, which unleashes a surge of electricity. The operator absorbs so much electricity that he shoots through the roof. An earlier version of the routine featured in the 1913 Éclair comedy *Gavroche, cambrioleur malgré lui* (*Gavroche, Burglar Despite Himself*) had a burglar evading police by switching clothes with an innocent passerby (Paul Bertho).

Buster Keaton, wrongfully imprisoned, kisses Sybil Seely farewell in *Convict 13* (1920) (courtesy www.doctormacro.com).

Michael Jackson used a star trap to make a splashy entrance during his "Dangerous World" Tour. Pyrotechnics were set off as Jackson was catapulted up through a trap door at the front of the stage. Audiences went wild over this stunt. Concert footage shows audience members gasping as though Jackson had just performed a miracle. Later in the show, Jackson appeared in an astronaut uniform complete with a rocket belt. At one point, Jackson appears to fly. This was, in fact, accomplished by having a stunt man dressed as Jackson shoot out of the same trapdoor in the stage.

Before his death, Jackson had planned to use star traps even more extensively in his "This is It" tour. A "Thriller" number, set in a cemetery, was to have dancers shoot out of graves. This is, in fact, similar to the routine that George Lupino had created for one of his pantomime shows.

Elaborate sets constructed in cross-section were later used for comic effect in *The Cameraman* (1928) (also a Keaton film), *The Ladies Man* (1961), *Tout va bien* (1972) and *The Life Aquatic with Steve Zissou* (2004).

11

Science and Magic

For centuries stage shows in England have featured comic protagonists with magical powers. The Harlequin wielded a magic bat with which he was able to transform settings and characters. "Alf's Button," a popular stage show, featured an ordinary man who discovers that a button on his jacket was fashioned from the metal of Aladdin's lamp, retaining all of the magical powers.

The extraordinary feats of fantasy and science fiction were present in early comedy films. In 1918, the Homeland Company produced a film series that also put a magical object into the hands of an ordinary man. That series, *The Blunders of Mr. Butterbun*, starred Lupino Lane as a man who discovers an ancient Babylonian ring that needs merely to be rubbed to alter reality. The supernatural effects of the ring were conveyed with a peculiar camera process that made use of distorting mirrors.[1]

An even stranger supernatural object turns up in the 1911 Éclair comedy *Tommy étrenne son cor de chasse* (known in America as *Tommy Gets a Trumpet*). Tommy Footit is looking to summon in the new year by blowing a horn, but he is unaware that the horn in his possession is bewitched. Whenever he blows into the horn, people are propelled into the air and houses collapse into rubble. The 1908 Pathé Frères comedy *Professor Bric-a-Brac's Inventions* involves an inventor who uses a high-powered magnet to turn people and objects upside-down. The professor is even able to use the magnet to propel two people into a violent mix.

The last big project for André Deed was a comic science-fiction adventure entitled *The Mechanical Man* (1921). A mysterious masked adventuress sends a lumbering, nine-foot-tall robot on a rampage. The storyline features grave schemes and tense turns, but then, according to blogger Kage Baker, there's "this little jumping guy stuck in here and there for comic relief."[2] A key action scene features the robot chasing Deed and his friends in an automobile. Deed used a variety of effects to visualize this scene, but none of the effects blended together well enough to make the scene convincing. Baker wrote, "First some speeded-up footage of the robot walking is superimposed behind the car; then, in a long shot, what appears to be a clumsy animation of the robot frantically waddling along; finally the robot is being towed behind the car on a trailer, only partially screened by smoke and firework effects."[3] The film climaxes at a costume party, where Deed shows up dressed as Lord Nelson. At first, the robot shows up pretending to be a guest. Casually, he sits down to join other guests for drinks. Paghat the Ratgirl, who maintains the "Weird Wild Realm" blog, writes, "The robot ... strives to be a real party dude."[4] It is a comical scene, although it is not clear if it was Deed's intention for the scene to be comical. But, then, the robot goes berserk and attacks the party guests. A second giant robot, built by the good guys, comes along to smash up the big bad robot at the Paris Opera House.

Harold Lloyd introduced gadgets and time-saving devices in *The City Slicker* (1918) and *On the Fire* (1919). In the latter film, Lloyd makes his job as a chef easy by creating an elaborate device operated by a line of ropes. He yanks one rope, which lowers a pan onto a burner. He yanks another rope and a rod tilts forward to pour a bowl of pancake mix into the pan.

In *It's a Gift* (1923), oil magnates express interest in Snub Pollard when they hear he has invented a gasoline substitute. At his introduction, the inventor is revealed to be living in a gadget-filled home. A metal rod attached to an alarm clock brushes a feather across the bottom of Pollard's feet to wake him. Pollard, as Lloyd does in *On the Fire*, pulls a series of ropes hanging over his bed to operate various devices to prepare his breakfast. A more elaborate breakfast-making machine was later introduced in *Pee Wee's Big Adventure* (1985). This multi-colored contraption was operated using toys, including pinwheels, water pistols, a ping-pong ball, patriotic flags and a Dippy Bird.

In *Skylarking* (1923), Harry Gribbon plays an inventor of the first air car — a Model T held aloft by a hot-air balloon. When a pelican pecks a hole in the balloon, the car drops into a lions' cage, where it is instantly set upon by a vicious pride of lions. Gribbon is able to launch his car into the air again without knowing that a lion has come along for the ride. A surreal image from the film, shown in a long shot, is Gribbon preparing to leap off the front-end of his flying car while the lion leans out from the driver's seat and swipes at him with its paw.

Lige Conley has come up with another imaginatively designed automobile in *Air Pockets* (1924). Conley, determined to eliminate the need for parking garages, has invented a car that can be folded up neatly to fit inside a portable wooden box. In the end, wind generated by the propeller of a biplane causes the wonder car to fall to pieces.

Wacky inventions were a specialty of Charley Bowers. Bowers, as a comedian and animator, produced 19 wildly imaginative two-reel live-action comedy films that used extensive camera effects. All but nine of those comedies are lost. The nine surviving comedies, collected in the two-disc set, *Charley Bowers: The Rediscovery of an American Comic Genius*, have received considerable attention from silent film comedy fans.

Bowers often played a socially awkward inventor who channeled his energies into constructing spectacularly immense and oddball machines. The machine that Bowers constructs in *Egged On* (1926) is so big that it takes up most of the loft in a barn. The odd purpose of the great machine is to produce a small and simple item: an unbreakable egg. Each of Bowers's machines is unique in its own way. The *Egged On* machine is dominated by wires, gauges, bicycle pedals, and a winding chute for the eggs. The *He Done His Best* machine is filled with buttons, dials, tubes and flashing lights. The *Wild Roomer* machine is a boxy device with pumps, levers, wheels, cranks, gears, pulleys, and automobile headlights. Bowers spectacularly rides this last machine through city streets on his way to conduct a demonstration. Mark Bourne, critic with the *DVD Journal*, writes, "We can only imagine what the local residents and shopkeepers thought about the goings-on filling their streets when Bowers brought his robotic behemoth chugging to town with a camera crew."[5] At the demonstration, a pair of mechanical arms, adorned in clean, white work gloves, extends from the front of the machine and latch around Bowers's grumpy uncle. The machine treats the man brutally as it lathers and shaves his face. Bowers's shaving machine in *A Wild*

Roomer (1927) anticipates the feeding machine in Chaplin's *Modern Times* (1936) by nearly a decade. Stills from the lost film *Gone Again* (1927) show a zany machine being employed by Bowers to improve the efficiency of a grocery store. Bowers is pictured pulling a lever to cause goods to slide down a chute and tumble down onto the checkout counter. Ben Turpin had relied on a similar machine to make his bakery more efficient in the Sennett comedy *Love and Doughnuts* (1921).

Bowers's big machines can do much to embellish a standard plot, making a story bigger and more exciting than it would otherwise be. In *He Done His Best* (1926), Bowers, eager to get the restaurant owner's blessing to marry his daughter, employs his mechanical wizardry to help the man when his staff goes on strike. The imaginative inventor constructs a machine that is able to do the work of multiple cooks and waiters. The machine has a long tube with a funnel at the end. The tube dispenses a tablecloth over a table and then it drops down menus attached by wires. A diner reaches up inside the tube and pulls out a phone, through which he is able to place his order. The machine proceeds to cook and serve food. At one point, a hose that extends from the tube dispenses soup into a bowl. In other instances, plates of piping-hot food are extruded out of the tube. A metal claw extends from the tube to clear off the dirty plates when the diners are finished eating. In the end, Bowers finds out that the restaurant owner's daughter is going to marry another man. Bowers, distraught, collapses onto his console. In the process, he lies across the controls and unintentionally presses various buttons. The lights flash wildly and an ample amount of food spews out of the tube onto the restaurant owner.

Even a comedian slipping on a banana peel is an elaborate and intriguing event in a Bowers comedy. In *Many a Slip* (1927), Bowers discovers through microscopic analysis that a banana peel is made slippery by a slimy little bug that lives on the peel. He creates a formula to kill the bug so that he can produce a non-slip banana peel. To test banana peels treated with his formula, he plants the peels on staircases around his home and waits to see if someone walking down the staircase will slip and fall. In one of his failed tests, a mailman goes sliding down an extravagantly long flight of steps outside of Bowers's eccentric home.

Bowers has often been compared to Buster Keaton. The comparisons come down to three similarities. First, both men were alike in size and build. Second, Bowers adopted Keaton mannerisms, including Keaton's deadpan expression and flat-footed walk. Third (and most important), Bowers shared Keaton's fascination with mechanical engineering. Keaton had preceded Bowers by several years with his own series of elaborate mechanical inventions. Keaton creates a saddle with a suspension system to absorb shocks in *The Blacksmith* (1922). Keaton stocked *The Electric House* (1922) with several practical gadgets, including an automated food server that uses miniature trains to deliver plates to the dining-room table. By the end of the film, the machines go awry, from the trains dumping plates into a woman's lap to a dishwasher flinging plates across the kitchen. Keaton's home in *The Scarecrow* (1920) is filled with dual-purpose devices—a phonograph player that converts into a stove, a bookcase that converts into an icebox, and a bathtub that converts into a sofa. The cleverly designed devices can simply be transformed by flipping and revolving a part or two. Keaton simply folds a Murphy bed into the wall to bring into view a piano which has been built into the bottom section of the bed. Keaton is about to settle down for dinner when he pulls a lever to lower a series of ropes with different condiments attached. The key difference between Keaton's and Bowers's inventions was that Keaton's inventions were workable machines that could be duplicated by a person with an understanding of mechanical engineering while Bowers's wildly absurd inventions were exercises of the imagination.

Bowers was at his weirdest and most fantastic with his creature animation. A highlight of *He Done His Best* (1926) is a scene wherein oyster soup is being prepared for a restaurant customer. A beady-eyed oyster crawls out of his shell, travels up a plank leading into a bowl of soup and swims around long enough to flavor the soup. Afterwards, the oyster crawls back down the plank and a mechanical hand locks him inside a miniature safe. In *Say Ah-h!* (1928), Bowers creates a strange feed for an ostrich by grounding up household items, including a broom, a hoe, a pillow, clothes, and a feather duster. The ostrich lays an egg, out of which emerges a strange type of ostrich made up of the household items. The bird has a feather duster for a tail, a pillow for a stomach, and broomsticks for legs. The surreal bird stalks around the barn and eats a number of items, including a metal stove. The bird later turns on a Victrola and performs a jerky dance. Willis O'Brien, the father of stop-motion animation, had included a scene in the comedy *Morpheus Mike* (1917) in which an ostrich hatched from an egg. But O'Brien's ostrich was the picture of normalcy compared to Bowers's daffy creation. One of Bowers's best special-effects scenes occur at the climax of *Egged On*, when eggs kept warm under a Model-T hood hatch dozens of adorably cute, fully functional baby Model T's. The baby Model T's come rolling down the fenders. Bourne wrote, "[The] gaggle of tiny Model T's ... unfold like origami and trundle around mama Ford until she snuggles them beneath her chassis."[6]

Bowers's special effects are done as an interlude. The actors are, in no way, incorporated into the scenes. The scenes do not even include reaction shots. Paul Brenner, in a review of the DVD collection, complained that, when Bowers introduces his effects, he "frequently stops his films cold."[7] That is not the case with *It's a Gift*, wherein Snub Pollard remains at the center of the action during the operation of his wacky inventions.

Bowers's most widely circulated comedy is *Now You Tell One* (1926), in which he discovers a magic process to graft any item that he chooses. He plants a graft at a farmer's feet and a tree proceeds to grow on the spot. The trunk extends up the farmer's pants leg, and leafy branches sprout out of his sleeves and out of the front of his shirt. The farmer ends up tangled up in a full-grown tree. Bowers next comes to a farm which, he finds, has been overrun by mice. An old man is in the fields smacking at mice with a broom. The old man has been wielding the broom with such force that most of the bristles have fallen out and the handle has snapped in half. However, he is able to walk over to a small boy carrying a golf bag filled with brooms, and get himself a fresh broom as a replacement. A pretty young woman is standing on top of a fence to keep away from the nasty rodents. Bowers escorts the woman inside her home, which is riddled with mouse holes. The mice have been gnawing away at everything, from banisters to picture frames. Bowers sees that the battle-weary cat is in bandages. A mouse comes out of a hole, draws a tiny revolver and fires at the cat, which scurries off to avoid further injury. Bowers decides to graft cats to get rid of the mice. The first cat grows without a tail, but Bowers grafts a tail separately and sticks it on the cat. Bowers soon produces an army of cats, which burst out of the room in pursuit of the mice. Bowers assumes that the pretty young lady is the old farmer's daughter and asks him for her hand in marriage, only to find out that the young woman is the farmer's wife. The farmer attacks Bowers with one of his brooms.

The mouse popping out of a hole to fire a gun at the cat is reminiscent of a scene in *Golf* (1922), wherein a squirrel pops out of a hole to fire a gun at Larry Semon. Before Bowers, Semon had periodically embellished his comedies with stop-motion creatures. This is also evident in *Dome Doctor* (1924), in which Semon shows an onion sprouting legs and scurrying away.

A plot similar to the plot of *Now You Tell One* can be found in the 1908 Gaumont comedy *A New Fruit* (1908), in which a man comes up with an ingenious way to grow pigs on trees.

Bowers's films, as suggested by *Now You Tell One*, never have a happy ending. Bowers's machine and his workshop are blown up at the end of *Egged On*. He finds out, after all his problems in *Many a Slip*, that the man who agreed to invest $50,000 in his no-slip banana is, in fact, an escaped lunatic. He is beaten up by his boss, the police chief, in the concluding moments of *Nothing Doing*. He ends up with his head stuck inside a loaded cannon in *Now You Tell One*.

Fatal Footsteps (1926), the most engaging of Bowers's surviving comedies, introduces the filmmaker practicing obsessively for a Charleston contest. White chalk outlines of feet, laid out to indicate dance steps, are spread out across the floor, walls and furniture of his bedroom. He dances so hard that he knocks plaster loose from the ceiling. The family, who is eating in the dining room below him, becomes angry when chunks of plaster drop into their food. The same premise can be found in the 1915 Cines comedy *Kri Kri balla* (known in America as *Kri Kri Dances*). Kri Kri (Raymond Frau) becomes a nuisance while practicing dance steps at home. This short relies largely on slapstick violence, which is evident in a scene where the aspiring dancer becomes a whirling dervish and accidentally punches a maid in the face. Another comparable routine, this one replacing a quick step with a backswing, can be found in *Golf* (1922). This time, Larry Semon obsessively practices his golf swing at home, oblivious to the irritation he is causing the other people who have to live with him.

Making use of his engineering skills, Bowers's dancing fool installs springs and wheels in his shoes to create automatic dancing shoes. The shoes, however, assume a life of their own and walk down the stairs to the living room. Father, who is getting ready for a meeting with his anti-dance civic group, grabs the shoes by mistake and puts them on. The members of the group are gathering around the table as the shoes become active. The father leaps onto the table and dances wildly. In the end, everyone is the family is overtaken by dance fever. Even the goldfish, which leaps out of its bowl and dances across the table.

A lively pair of shoes is a trademark of a surreal artist. Georges Méliès created an effect in *The Inn Where No Man Rests* (1903) wherein a possessed pair of boots walk around a hotel room. In *Le Roman de Max* (1912), Max Linder finds his vacation disrupted when his shoes fall in love with a pair of high-top high heels belonging to a pretty young woman. Linder must chase his smitten shoes across town as they rush off to rendezvous with the fair booties. Michel Gondry, a current director whose work relies on in-camera tricks to create eccentric and surreal comic scenes, has been compared to Méliès and Keaton. Gondry devised a scene in a 2008 music video for "Deadweight" wherein songwriter Beck is led down the street by his own shoes. The effect is simple. Gondry had the shoes tied to Beck's feet with fishing wire and then had him walk backwards. All that was necessary to complete the effect was to reverse the footage. Gondry also demonstrated his fascination with living shoes in the feature film *The Science of Sleep* (2006), in which the stop-motion creatures that populate a young man's dreams include a pair of shoes that are able to tie their own laces. The film also includes a stop-motion rag-doll bird that resembles one of Bowers's strange creatures.

Bowers's films are packed with crazy images. In *There It Is* (1928), Bowers plays a Scotland Yard detective who carries a matchbox containing a kilt-wearing cockroach assistant called MacGregor. The pair is out to capture an ingenious villain responsible for a number of strange disturbances. William Morrow, an IMDb reviewer, wrote, "The cook cracks open an egg from which a fully grown chicken emerges; the butler sees a pair of trousers dancing atop his dresser; and strangest of all, the Fuzz-Faced Phantom makes frequent, inexplicable appearances — sometimes on wheels — carrying such items as a hatrack, a broom, a rifle, boxing gloves, or a chunk of ice. The objects aren't especially strange, but the phantom himself is an alarming piece of work.... Paintings come alive within their frames, a child's wagon vanishes through the wall, the cuckoo clock is invaded by a cat (who takes over the cuckoo's job).... Charley goes to bed and wakes up dangling over the bathtub.... At the finale, an 'explanation' is offered for some of these phenomena but it doesn't explain a thing, and we don't care: this freaky experience has been entirely too much fun for explanations."[8]

Bowers's missing comedies have not received the attention they deserve. The New York Public Library for the Performing Arts is in possession of press sheets for a number of these lost films. Included in this material are story details for four of Bowers's shorts: *Hop Off*, *Goofy Birds*, *Whoozit* and *You'll Be Sorry* (all 1928).

In *Hop Off*, Bowers makes his living as the proprietor of a flea circus. The fleas perform a variety of acts, including juggling, balancing and tumbling. At one point, they use a bald man's head as a skating rink. A separate episode of the film involves Bowers stumbling upon a fluid that is able to transform items back to their natural state. He uses the fluid on a cigar, a plate of hash, a couple of sausages and, finally, on himself. The press sheet articles fail to note the outcome of the transformations, but it is imaginable that the cigar grew out into a tobacco plant, and the sausages expanded into a full-sized pig. Bowers, himself, presumably shrunk down to a baby. This astoundingly potent fluid was not unlike the miraculous grafting mixture that Bowers utilizes in *Now You Tell One*.

In *Goofy Birds*, Bowers is a hunter who travels to Africa to capture the rare Umbrella Bird, whose unique umbrella-like tail can be used as propeller, a sunshade, or as means of defense. The bird is more intelligent than Bowers's inept character, and he is able to resist the hunter's efforts to capture him. According to the press sheet, a highlight of the film is a scene in which the Umbrella Bird pursues an animated worm. Bowers, no doubt, had an obsession with birds. Other freakishly constructed birds turn up in *Say Ah-h!* (1928)and *It's a Bird* (1930). Bird eggs are used to elaborate ends in *Egged On* (1926), *There It Is* (1928) and *Believe It or Don't* (1935).

Whoozit involves Bowers's experiences as a janitor in an apartment house. He gets into a battle with cockroaches that have grown large enough to throw dishes at him and shoot off guns. Later, a group of oysters, about to be fried in a tenant's kitchen, flee their shells and take refuge in the basement with the kindly janitor.

You'll Be Sorry features police officer Bowers aided in his work by a uniquely designed crime dog, whose unusual features include suction feet, a prehensile tail, and a pair of ears that enable it to fly.

No one exploited the surreal nature of silent film comedy more fully than Bowers, and it is for this reason that he deserves to be commemorated.

Science-fiction comedies remained rare for decades. The 1950s science-fiction craze, which brought to the cinema space travel, gigantism and alien invasions, produced only three significant contemporary spoofs: *Abbott and Costello Go to Mars* (1953), *The 30-Foot Bride of Candy Rock* (1959) and *Visit to a Small Planet* (1960). With the 1970s came arguably the funniest of all sci-fi comedies, *Sleeper* (1973). Later advancements in special effects inspired more outrageous alien invasion comedies, including *Little Shop of Horrors* (1986), *Mars Attacks!* (1996) and *Men in Black* (1997). Eccentric inventors have been at the forefront of many science-fiction comedies, including *Monkey Business* (1952), *The Absent-Minded Professor* (1961), *Chitty Chitty Bang Bang* (1968) and *Honey, I Shrunk the Kids* (1989). In recent years, time travel has proven to be a fertile source of humor as in *Back to the Future* (1985), *Bill and Ted's Excellent Adventure* (1989), *Click* (2006) and *Hot Tub Time Machine* (2010). Comedy makers have looked to spoof the *Star Trek* and *Star Wars* franchises with other science-fiction comedies, including *Spaceballs* (1987) and *Galaxy Quest* (1999).

12

Tooth Extraction and Laughing Gas

A Commedia dell'Arte routine that displayed dentistry to comic effect was called "Lazzi of Tooth Extraction," which originated in Rome in 1560. Arlecchino disguises as a dentist to fool his ill-tempered master, Pantalone, into thinking that a rotten tooth is causing him to have bad breath. Arlecchino proceeds to use ridiculously oversized forceps to extract a tooth from Pantalone's mouth.

Dental issues continued as a subject of film comedy. The toothache was a staple of early comedies. This is suggested merely by the film titles, which include *Oh, That Toothache!* (1906), *An Awful Toothache* (1909), *A Lucky Toothache* (1910), *Grandma's Toothache* (1911), *Bedelia Has a Toothache* (1912), *Father's Toothache* (1912), *Hubby's Toothache* (1913), *Toothache* (1913), *Andy Has a Toothache* (1914), *Bloomer's Toothache* (1914), *Charlie's Toothache* (1914), *Whiffles Has a Toothache* (1914), *Jeff's Toothache* (1916), and *Toothaches and Heartaches* (1917). Additional dentistry comedies included *An Old Fashioned Way of Pulling a Tooth* (1902), *He Pulled the Wrong Tooth* (1903), *An Obstinate Tooth* (1908) and *As the Tooth Came Out* (1913).

The Edison comedy *Laughing Gas* (1907) shows a female patient at a dentist's office reacting strongly to a dose of laughing gas. The patient leaves the dentist's office, laughing hysterically. She manages to spread her merriment to others, who find it impossible to resist laughing along with her. The message, simply, is that laughter is contagious.

Laughing gas turns up as a comic device in a Keystone comedy also titled *Laughing Gas* (1914). Charlie Chaplin, who is pretending to be a dentist, subjects a patient to a heavy dose of laughing gas. The patient becomes overwhelmed with laughter and no amount of pleading from Chaplin can get him to calm down. The man, out of sheer ebullience, throws his arms out to his sides, which results in Chaplin getting socked in the jaw. This is more than Chaplin can take. Chaplin laughs along with the man as he picks up a large mallet and knocks him unconscious.

Snub Pollard performs essentially the same routine in *The Dippy Dentist* (1920), except that animated stars appear around the patient's head once the man is struck with the mallet. Pollard gets his pliers latched onto a tooth and drags his diminutive patient around the office. At one point, he pulls too hard and swings the patient out of a window. Next, Pollard attends to a pretty young lady with a toothache. He manages to knock her out with gas and takes this as an opportunity to assail her with kisses.

A lost Vitagraph comedy, *Dames and Dentists* (1920), included a scene wherein a dental assistant (Jimmy Aubrey) attended to a pretty young woman with a toothache. The scene was censored by the Kansas State Board of Review, which found the activity of Aubrey and the woman to be sexually suggestive. Other patients did not fare well under Aubrey's care, either. Aubrey used a mallet, hammer and chisel to extract a tooth from one patient. Another patient had so much laughing gas pumped into him that he floated to the ceiling.

In *Leave 'Em Laughing* (1928), Laurel and Hardy leave a dentist's office under the influence of laughing gas. They cause a huge traffic jam and arouse the attention of an ill-tempered traffic cop (Edgar Kennedy), but their only reaction to the situation is to laugh uncontrollably. The humor comes from the comedians laughing despite being in jeopardy. *Boobs in Arms* (1940) has the Three Stooges as soldiers on a mission to invade enemy headquarters. The Stooges fire a missile straight up into the air, but it falls back down on them. The explosion of the shell releases a great amount of laughing gas. The Stooges continue to battle enemy soldiers while laughing uncontrollably. A second missile comes soaring through the building and takes the Stooges on board as it comes past. The Stooges, still laughing, ride the missile out of the building and across the limitless sky.

Writer/director Blake Edwards, a self-avowed fan of Laurel & Hardy, designed a laughing-gas scene as the climax of *The Pink Panther Strikes Again* (1976). Today, the closest that we have to a laughing-gas routine is YouTube's popular "David After Dentist" video.

Dental instruments, including drills, forceps, chisels and scalers, were not safe in the hands of Billie Ritchie, who was known in promotional literature as "Dangerous Billie." In

Laurel (left) and Hardy are driving under the influence (of laughing gas) in *Leave 'Em Laughing* (1928) The unlaughing policeman is Edgar Kennedy (courtesy Bruce Lawton Collection).

The Avenging Dentist (1915), Ritchie gets into a fight with his girlfriend's father and punches him in the mouth. The father, who is obviously in great pain, is urged by his daughter to visit a dentist. Father visits a dentist, who just happens to be Ritchie. Universal Weekly reported, "Billie gets his forceps on the largest molar left in papa's jaw and jerks his fat and ferocious-looking enemy out of the chair. Wild with pain, papa threshes right and left."[1] Ritchie punches the man so hard that he has to be taken home on a window shutter.

It was mainly the character of Dangerous Billie who propelled the comic action towards violence. Henry Lehrman, the producer of *The Avenging Dentist*, had previously directed a gentler version of this story at Keystone. *Cupid in a Dental Parlor* (1913) does not have the suitor yanking out the father's teeth. Instead, the suitor (Fred Mace), simply gasses the father to have him unconscious while he elopes with his daughter. Nonetheless, the brutality of the dental torture, undoubtedly more *Saw* than slapstick, did have a precedent. A 1910 Gaumont comedy called *Avenging Dentist* (1910) related the story of a pair of thieves who break into a dentist's home and rob his safe. Hal Erickson, in describing the comedy for the All Movie Guide, wrote, "Tricking the thieves into his dentist's chair, the tooth-tugging hero subjects them to all sorts of hideous oral tortures. By film's end, the toothless miscreants are begging to be taken off to jail."[2]

The idea of a dentist making use of his dental pliers on a foe may seem tasteless but an even more gruesome variation of this plot could be found in the L-KO comedy *A Surgeon's Revenge* (1916). The plot is set in motion when a tramp named Dinty saves a doctor's life and is invited to stay at the doctor's home for dinner. During the meal, Dinty engages in flirtations with the doctor's wife, which includes slipping the woman notes under the table. After dinner, the tramp becomes more familiar with the hostess, inciting the doctor to eject him from his home. Dinty remains undeterred. Disguising his identity, he phones the doctor to tell him that he needs to leave his home immediately to attend to an emergency. Dinty then steals a car and takes the doctor's wife for a joy ride. After crashing the car, Dinty is transported to the hospital for surgery. The doctor to perform the surgery is the same doctor whose wife Dinty has taken on the romantic outing. The doctor cannot wait to work his knife on Dinty, but Dinty escapes and leads the doctor on a chase through the hospital corridors.

A vengeful dentist is pivotal to the plotline of the Oscar-nominated *Reuben, Reuben* (1983). The dentist, enraged that his wife slept with a lecherous poet, tears out the last tooth that the poet has to support a permanent bridge, which serves to destroy the poet's smile.

No comedy team utilized dentistry more hilariously than the Three Stooges. In *All The World's a Stooge* (1941), the Stooges are working as janitors in a dentist's office when a desperate patient rushes into the office. The patient, who assumes that the janitors are dentists, demands that they take care of his bad tooth. Curly obligingly knocks out the man with a mallet, at which point Moe eagerly jams forceps into the man's mouth. The Stooges, with their incompetent use of dental instruments, follow in the tradition of Ritchie and Aubrey.

An old premise, discussed in the opening chapter, was revived for the Century comedy *Painless Pain* (1926). Wanda Wiley is anxious to improve business for her dentist boyfriend so that he will have the money to marry her. She hires a thug to walk the street, punching passersby in the mouth. While they are attending to their aching jaws, she walks up and hands out business cards for her boyfriend's practice.

Harry Gribbon stars as a loony dentist in *The Halfback of Notre Dame* (1924). In one scene, Gribbon wrestles frenziedly to extract a patient's tooth. The patient wraps his legs around Gribbon's waist as the force of the dentist's grip lifts him out of the chair and drags him across the floor. This is an even more muscular version of the *Dippy Dentist* routine. W. C. Fields performs the same routine in *The Dentist* (1932), only his patient is a shapely young woman and Fields, by grappling with her, turns the scene into something risqué. (It was even cut out of television prints of the fifties and sixties.) This could be similar to the censored scene in the lost *Dames and Dentists*. Fields creates some extra funny business with the woman, getting her foot stuck in the pocket of his jacket, which is an annoyance to him. Unlike the deranged Gribbon, Fields is not happy to be having so much difficulty pulling this tooth. Fields, still holding a firm grip on the tooth, sits back for a breather while his nurse uses a hand fan to cool him down.

Gribbon relies on automation when a second patient, Jack Cooper, arrives to have a tooth extracted. He attaches one end of a rope to a chandelier and the other end of the rope to Cooper's tooth. He then releases an appropriately labeled "500-pound weight" which forces the chandelier to lift up sufficiently to draw on the rope and yank out the tooth.

Gribbon was not the first or last comedian to rig up a rope to pull a tooth. In *The Scarecrow* (1920), Buster Keaton seeks to rid himself of a painful tooth by hooking up a string between his tooth and a doorknob. Without warning, his roommate (Joe Roberts) comes through the door and slams it shut, which jerks out the tooth sooner than planned. In *The Cockeyed Family* (1928), Ben Turpin tries to uproot a bad tooth by attaching a rope from the tooth to a chandelier and then jumping off a chair. Predictably, he only succeeds in tearing the chandelier out of the ceiling and having it crash down, crystal, bulbs and all, upon his head. Similar routines were later performed by the Three Stooges in *I Can Hardly Wait* (1943) and *Pardon My Clutch* (1948). An engine was literally strapped onto the routine in an episode of *The Abbott & Costello Show* ("The Dentist Office," 1952). In that scene, a rope is tied to the bumper of an automobile that — as it just so happens — is being used by bank robbers to make a getaway. Costello gets dragged down the street, but his tooth holds fast and stops the car in its tracks. This allows police the opportunity to arrest the robbers, which makes Costello a hero.*

A chandelier enters into Fields's routine too, but in a much different manner. A young woman stomping around on the floor above causes pieces of the chandelier to break off and fall into a patient's gaping mouth. In a later scene, Fields borrows a bit of business from a 1919 Sennett comedy, also titled *The Dentist*. In that film, a heavily bearded patient sits down in the dentist chair to be treated. The dentist (Charlie Murray) has to rummage around in his beard to find his mouth. Fields expanded the gag by having a bird suddenly fly out the beard. Fields then pulls out a hunting rifle to shoot it down.

The insanity of dentistry lived on in *Little Shop of Horrors* (1986), which features Bill Murray as a masochistic patient who thrives on dental pain. Steve Martin plays a sadistic dentist who liked to get high on his own nitrous oxide.

---

*This is not the only problem that Costello has to endure before resolving his toothache. He also has an appointment with a nearsighted dentist, who cannot tell the difference between a patient's nose and a "protruding tonsil."

13

Into the Looking Glass

Alice Guy-Blaché, a pioneer French filmmaker, revealed the comic potential of a man being duped into believing a lookalike is his mirror reflection in a 1912 Solax film called *His Double*. A father stubbornly rejects a man that his daughter loves because the man does not have, in his estimation, an appealing face. Ignoring his daughter's wishes, the father arranges for his daughter to marry a vain count, whose greatest obsession is his own lavishly stylish moustache. The woman's true love disguises as the count, complete with moustache, to take his place at the wedding ceremony. Meanwhile, a cracked mirror is removed from its frame by repairmen. The count believes that he is admiring himself in the mirror when he is, in fact, looking at his double on the opposite side of the empty frame. The story comes across as a fable, the moral of which is that a vain man never truly sees himself when he looks into a mirror. The scene, though, is fleeting and never has a chance to develop. It took others less interested in a moral to extend the idea.

In 1913, the Schwartz Brothers introduced a comedy routine called "The Broken Mirror" in a Broadway show called *A Glimpse of the Great White Way*. Broadway historian Gerald Martin Bordman described the act as "a mirror dance in which one brother seemed to be miming into an invisible mirror while the other brother became his reflection."[1]

In *The Floorwalker* (1916), Charlie Chaplin's resemblance to a store's floorwalker (Lloyd Bacon) leads to mistaken-identity complications. At one point, Chaplin and Bacon enter an office through opposite doors and meet in the middle of the room. They stare at each other, astounded by the likeness. The two men look each other up and down in the same manner. They scratch their heads at exactly the same time, in exactly the same way. Their every movement, by sheer coincidence, matches perfectly. They both reach out to see if they can feel a mirror in their way, but their hands meet and they realize to their amazement that they are lookalikes. Chaplin imitator Billy West, who mirrored so much of Chaplin's work, duplicated this routine in *Rolling Stone* (1919). West pulls out a pin and sticks himself to make sure he is not a reflection.

In *The Marathon* (1919), Harold Lloyd is in a situation in which he has to trick Eddie Borden into thinking that he is Borden's reflection. At one point, Borden turns away and pulls out a handkerchief. Not having a handkerchief, Lloyd must act quickly to tear off a piece of his shirt tail.

Max Linder developed the mirror routine even further in *Seven Years Bad Luck* (1921). A valet and maid who are part of Linder's servant staff are embroiled in a passionate embrace when they bump a mirror, which topples backwards and breaks. The valet immediately

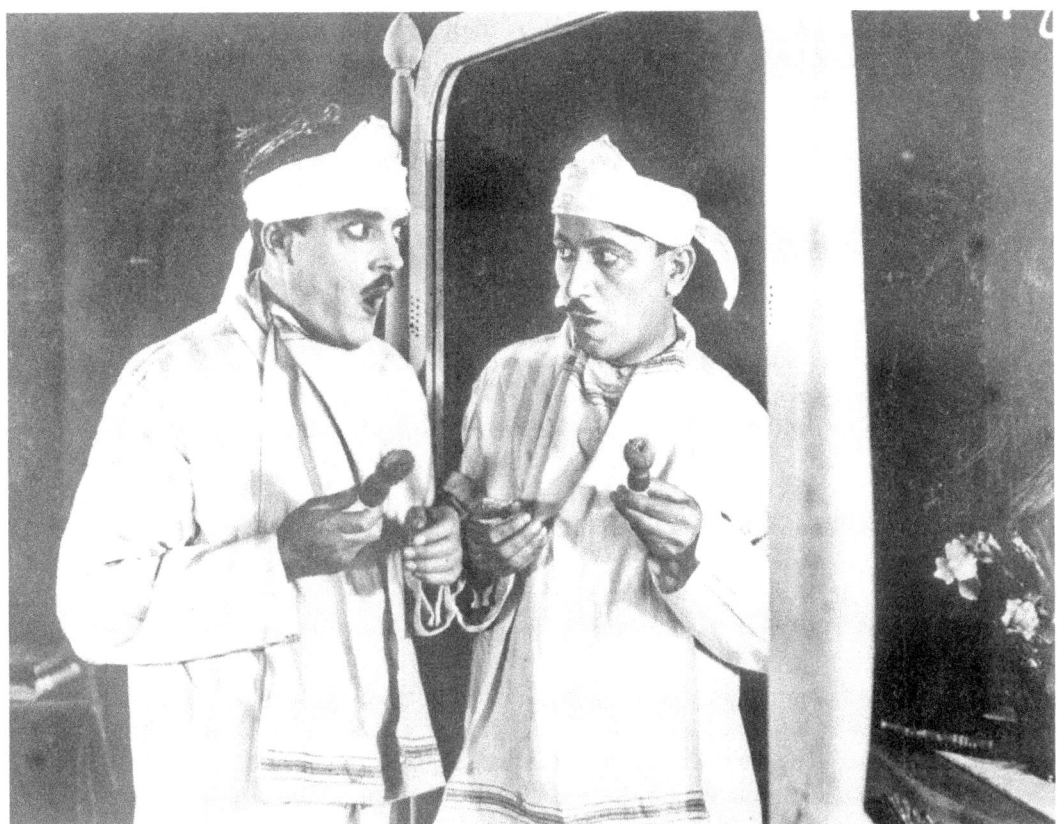

Max Linder (left) is puzzled by his strange reflection (actually, Harry Mann) in *Seven Years Bad Luck* (1921) (courtesy Robert Arkus).

phones a furniture store to have a replacement mirror rushed to the house. In the meantime, he must conceal the mishap from Linder. The ruse is carefully planned by the servants. A servant, dressed in pajamas identical to those worn by Linder, takes his places on the opposite side of the empty mirror frame. Linder, who had been drinking heavily the night before, staggers out of his bedroom suffering the ills of a hangover. His valet tells him that he looks under the weather from his late night. Linder stares into the mirror looking bewildered. "I wouldn't have recognized myself," he exclaims. Linder does not make quick or surprising movements, which makes it credible for the servant to be able to mimic his actions. A large segment of the routine has Linder simply shaving in front of the mirror. Linder drops his razor and bends over to find it. The servant also bends over. Linder turns suddenly towards the mirror and now finds himself staring at his servant's backside. As appalling as this sight is, Linder sighs in relief: he has now exposed the ruse and knows that he is not going crazy. Linder has to step away to answer the phone in the other room. While he is gone, the new mirror arrives and is set up. Linder returns to the room brandishing a shoe as if prepared to strike his servant, but he now steps up to the new mirror and his own actual likeness. He should be able to recognize himself, but he now overestimates the mimicry of his false reflection. He hurls the shoe at the reflection, shattering the mirror into pieces. The routine follows a logical progression and maintains a strong narrative structure. Viewers can easily identify a beginning, a middle and an end.

Charley Chase, who directed Billy West through his version of the mirror routine, went before the cameras to perform the scene himself in *Sitting Pretty* (1924). Chase becomes barricaded in a home with a heavily bearded homicidal lunatic known as "Loco" Larry (played by Chase's brother, James Parrott). Chase catches Larry talking to himself in the mirror and gets the idea to make a beard out of a fur carpet and substitute himself for the man's reflection. The criminal is suspicious, sensing that something is slightly askew, and he makes a series of sudden, random movements to challenge the reflection. Chase is able to mimic the actions as if he knows exactly what movements Larry will make before he makes them. Larry still isn't convinced. He sees a bunch of hats sitting on a table and decides to outsmart the clever reflection by donning a series of hats in quick succession. Chase, not to be thrown, not only anticipates each hat switch but is able, in every instance, to produce an identical hat. Chase, by impossibly anticipating the maniac's movements and producing the matching hats, pushes the routine towards the surreal. This recalls tricky double-exposure routines that predated the Schwartz Brothers routine. One example is Ernest Bourbon having to contend with an evil doppelgänger in the Gaumont comedy *Onésime contre Onésime* (1912). Bourbon finally rids himself of the doppelgänger by tearing him into pieces and eating him. In the Cines comedy *Kri Kri Smokes Opium* (1913), Raymond Frau is under the influence when he imagines that he is being taunted by his own mirror image. The image eventually emerges from the mirror to attack Frau. Frau struggles desperately with the image until it suddenly disappears.[2] Yet, Chase uses no camera tricks to make the scene fantastic. The action is not necessarily explainable, but it never becomes impossible. The routine ends with both men laughing and nudging each other. This has turned into a fun game and, at least for the moment, these men no longer care about their original interests. Film historian David Kalat found this version of the routine, as directed by Leo McCarey, to be superior to Linder's version. He pointed out that the stakes are higher — Chase is fearful of exposing himself to a homicidal maniac — and the pacing of the routine is much faster.[3]

Lloyd Hamilton and Lige Conley performed the mirror routine in *Hello, Hollywood* (1925). In that two-reeler, Conley has sneaked onto a studio lot and is trying to evade a security guard determined to toss him out. He hides out in a dressing room belonging to comedy star Lloyd Hamilton. When Hamilton enters the dressing room, Conley pretends to be his mirror reflection to avoid being exposed. Unfortunately, this is the one version of the routine that has been lost.

Sherlock Sleuth (1925), a Roach two-reeler, features Arthur Stone getting dressed in a lion costume and then coming upon actual lion, which he assumes is his own mirror reflection.

McCarey revived the routine with the Marx Brothers in *Duck Soup* (1933). The story centers around Groucho being appointed the leader of a small, bankrupt country called Freedonia. Harpo, sent out to spy on Freedonia's new president, infiltrates the presidential palace disguised as none other than Groucho. Harpo is running through the palace when he slams into a mirror, which bursts into pieces. It is at this moment that Groucho comes along and Harpo, fearful of being caught, pretends to be Groucho's reflection. Groucho is immediately suspicious. He challenges his dubious likeness by suddenly wiggling his backside and performing the Charleston. Harpo mirrors these actions precisely. Groucho then finds a Panama hat and holds it behind his back. Harpo grabs something and puts it behind his back. Has he been able to produce a matching hat? Groucho is curious to know and tries to sneak a peek behind Harpo's back. But Harpo leans away from Groucho to prevent him from getting a look. Groucho persists in trying to get a look behind Harpo's back. He follows Harpo around in a circle until the men have completely traded places. If Groucho was willing to accept that Harpo was his reflection, then he now has to accept that he has, in fact, become the reflection. Visible now behind Harpo's back, in Groucho's view, is a top hat. Groucho decides that it is finally time to bring out his hat. He brings out his Panama hat at the same moment that Harpo brings out his hat, which is now, miraculously, a Panama hat. (Harpo has not only produced a matching hat but he has bested Chase by transforming a black top hat into a white Panama hat.) But the top hat is still visible in Harpo's other hand, which remains hidden behind his back. Harpo, in fact, had two hats. Harpo accidentally drops the Panama hat. Groucho does not act at all excited that this blunder has exposed Harpo. Instead, he reaches for the hat and respectfully hands it back to Harpo. Marx Brothers biographer Joe Adamson wrote, "[Groucho] is having far more fun with this game of determination than he could ever have by cornering an old spy."[4] Chico, also dressed like Groucho, suddenly appears — a second reflection to further complicate matters. This is finally too much for Groucho to take. Harpo tries to push Chico out of the way, but Groucho is able to grab Chico by the tail of his nightshirt before he can get away.

Other renditions of the routine turned up on occasion. Andy Clyde performed a version of the routine in *Lodge Night* (1937). In the Disney cartoon *Lonesome Ghosts* (1937), a ghost inhabits a mirror to confuse and frighten Goofy. This mirror imp is easily able to befuddle Goofy. "For a moment," says Goofy, "I thought it wasn't me." Curly Howard essays a brief, uneventful mirror routine with a wolfman in the Three Stooges comedy *Idle Roomers* (1944).*
Bugs Bunny and Elmer Fudd go through the routine in *Hare Tonic* (1945).

Lou Costello performed the mirror routine opposite Joe Sawyer in *The Naughty Nineties* (1945). Costello, hanging outside of a window to eavesdrop on Sawyer and his criminal confederates, removes a shaving mirror in front of the window to get a view of what's going on inside the room. This leaves Costello visible within the window frame when Sawyer turns towards the mirror to shave. Sawyer, who expected to see his reflection, is bewildered to come face-to-face with Costello. Previous versions of the routine had been done with lookalikes, which included three sets of brothers (Schwartz, Chase and Marx) who shared a strong family resemblance. But Costello and Sawyer look nothing alike. Even their outfits are different. It turns this scene into pure nonsense for Sawyer to accept the possibility that Costello is his reflection when, clearly, he is a pudgy little Peeping Tom at the window. Nonetheless, Costello, fearful of being exposed, does his best to pretend that he is Sawyer's reflection. Costello grabs a spare straight razor and smears shaving cream on his face. The scene is left without hats and without dancing. By replacing a full-length mirror with a much smaller shaving mirror, the creators of the scene have restricted the routine to head movements and hand gestures. The only activity that Costello has to mimic is the standardized movements of Sawyer shaving. The scene owes nothing to McCarey's work. It is Linder's version of the scene, if not the original Schwartz Brothers' version, that is the model. This is evident from the shaving business, Sawyer bringing up a hangover to justify his confusion, and the off-colored gag that closes the scene. The final gag required slightly more setup. While Sawyer is turned away from the mirror, Costello sees this as an opportunity to beat a hasty retreat. He signals Abbott, who grabs the rope onto which Costello is hanging and works to pull up his friend as fast as possible. Costello twists around on the rope so

---

*This was not the first furry reflection. In *A Sailer-Made Man* (1921), a monkey dislodges a shaving mirror from its frame and is standing on the opposite side of the empty frame by the time that apish Noah Young comes to use the mirror.

that his back turns towards the window just as Sawyer turns back around. Sawyer sees that his "reflection" now resembles a backside, does a double-take to the camera, and the scene ends. Costello performed a brief version of the routine with his brother Pat in a 1953 episode of *The Colgate Comedy Hour*. This continued the tradition of brothers performing the mirror routine.

The routine was adopted by clowns Pipo Sosman and Enrico Sprocani, who introduced it to their circus show in 1950. This was most unusual as clowns rarely obtain routine from the movies.

Harpo Marx became so identified with the mirror routine that similar bits became part of his repertoire. In *The Big Store* (1941), Harpo engages in an impromptu musical number while receiving accompaniment from mirror reflections of himself. He also returned to the original mirror routine as a guest star in a 1955 episode of *I Love Lucy*. Harpo finds his movements aped by Lucy, who is dressed in Harpo's trademark outfit. Harpo reaches out his hand and makes a circular motion as if to clean the imaginary mirror, which is something that Linder did in his 1921 version of the routine. Harpo turns his back to the mirror. He is deep in thought, trying to come up with a plan to outsmart this pretender. Finally, he has an idea. He puffs out his cheeks and bulges out his eyes in his trademark "Gookie" face. He turns back to the mirror and is startled to find Lucy awaiting him with the same exact expression. Lucy claps when Harpo claps, except that Harpo purposely has his hands miss on one clap, which Lucy fails to do. This exposes Lucy's fraud, but the two keep up the game anyway. Harpo removes his top hat. Lucy removes *her* top hat. Harpo drops the hat, a move that Lucy imitates, except that Harpo's hat, which is attached to his hand by a rubber band, bounces back, while Lucy's hat remains unattended on the floor.

In the sixties, other films and sitcoms tried to do something new with the routine. A 1963 episode of *The Patty Duke Show* features a unique version of the mirror routine with Patty Duke performing opposite a double-exposure version of herself. Most versions of the routine after this were accomplished using double-exposure, which removed the most thrilling aspect of the routine — two performers acting in perfect synchronization. A scene in *The Pink Panther* (1964) has David Niven and Robert Wagner performing the mirror routine dressed in identical gorilla costumes. A 1966 episode of *Gilligan's Island* features a version of the mirror routine with one modern story element — plastic surgery. The Soviets have become aware of the castaways' settlement on the island and assume they are scientists conducting experiments for the United States government. A Soviet spy is surgically altered to look like Gilligan, and he is then dropped off on the island to see what he can find out. The concept of a spy disguised as the person upon whom he is spying fits the same logic that had Harpo dress up as Groucho as he prowled around the Freedonia presidential palace. However, the match-up of the Gilligans turns into a pale imitation of the *Duck Soup* routine. The scene, after a short time, is resolved with a simple involuntary reflex. Gilligan feels a sneeze coming on. He is able to hold in the sneeze while the spy, wrongly anticipating Gilligan's actions, follows through with the sneeze. The spy, exposed, runs off.

In Woody Allen's *Sleeper* (1973), it is a glitch in a futuristic high-tech mirror that is responsible for the disparity between Allen and his reflection. Allen, by fiddling with the dials, manages to change channels and tune in to a reflection of a frumpy housewife.

Benny Hill lent a lewd aspect to the routine in a 1980 television sketch. Hill, also a spy, has to dress in drag to pretend to be the reflection of a woman. The ruse is exposed when the woman, played by voluptuous Pat Ashton, removes her dress, thereby forcing Hill to reveal his decidedly unfeminine physique.

In *Big Business* (1988), Bette Midler is a public bathroom when she has an unexpected encounter with a heretofore-unknown twin. This scene is unique in that the bathroom has mirrored walls that surround Midler with reflections. When Midler first sees her twin in a passageway, she simply assumes that she is looking at another reflection on another mirrored wall. During the course of the scene, Midler moves back and forth from the passageway and the wall, which leads her to alternately interact with both her twin and an actual reflection. This makes the situation especially disorienting. Midler, one of the few females to perform this routine, manages to assert her gender into the routine. Instead of wiggling her backside like Groucho, the brassy actress thrusts out her breasts and shakes them. This scene is also unique in that the twin is not trying to deceive Midler. She just happens to be making the same movements at the same time as her lookalike. The premise is that the twins are having the same experience on either side of the "mirror" and their identical responses can be explained by a genetic predisposition that both twins share. Midler concludes the matter by reaching out and grabbing her reflection by the nose. Isn't it about time that someone did this? Midler now knows, without a doubt, that her supposed reflection is a flesh-and-blood lookalike. She screams at the top of her lungs. She accuses the lookalike of being a pod person out to snatch her body. Midler makes a good point. The impossible phenomena posed by either an uncooperative mirror reflection or an unexplainable lookalike can only be described as otherworldly. This is the reason that the mirror routine was later co-opted by supernatural movies such as *1408* (2007) and *Mirrors* (2008) and television programs such as *The X-Files* and *Heroes*. Goofy's mirror imp had now taken charge. Not that the comic origins of the routine could ever be totally forgotten. David Duchovny makes a point in the *X-Files* version to incorporate Groucho's classic butt-wiggle into his performance.

The routine has become such a part of pop culture that it was recently spoofed in a *Family Guy* episode wherein Stewie travels back in time and has a sudden confrontation with Adolf Hitler in his Berlin headquarters. In the classic tradition of Linder, Chase and Marx, Stewie tries to fool the Führer into thinking that he is simply his mirror reflection. And yes, the butt-wiggle is repeated here yet again.

14

Sleepless Nights

It is difficult to get a night of undisturbed sleep in a slapstick comedy. The most common problem had to do with the beds, whether bunk beds, train berths, hammocks or Murphy beds.

The first film known to feature a Murphy bed was a Biograph short called *A Bulletproof Bed* (1900). This film no longer exists, but Edison remade the film three years later as *Subub Surprises the Burglar* (1903), which has survived and has become available on YouTube. The Edison film shows Subub awakening to find a burglar rummaging through his belongings. He pulls a lever, which causes his bed to fold up into the wall. The bottom of the bed is fully armor-plated and has rows of gun slots, through which the homeowner shoots a variety of firearms at the intruder. The burglar suffers under a hail of fire and explodes in a cloud of smoke.

The comedians at the Keystone company exploited the comic possibilities of the Murphy bed. Charlie Murray had an early encounter with a Murphy bed in *Cursed by His Beauty* (1914). Fatty Arbuckle has a misadventure with a Murphy bed in *Fatty's Reckless Fling* (1915). The bed, which rolls in and out of a closet on casters, becomes useful to Arbuckle, who rides the bed into the closet to hide from a jealous husband (Edgar Kennedy). Unfortunately, the bed proceeds with such force that it crashes through the wall and comes out into the next room. Kennedy pounces into the bed with Arbuckle, and the two of them are wrestling when the bed rolls back into the wall.

He Wouldn't Stay Down (1915) makes much greater use of a Murphy bed. The film opens with Ford Sterling getting into an argument with his wife (Minta Durfee). Sterling waves his arms around flamboyantly as he shouts at Durfee, then storms out of the door. Sterling got laughs with exaggerated gestures and facial expressions. In the film he makes use of this when he gets a fishing hook stuck in his backside. As the story proceeds, Sterling becomes despondent about the argument. Charley Chase, billed as "False Friend," encourages Sterling to commit suicide so that he can marry Sterling's widow and collect on his friend's life insurance policy.

The Murphy bed finally enters the story in the second reel. Chase becomes frustrated that no one is cooperating with his plan. First, Durfee shuns his advances and, left with no choice, he tries to force himself upon the lady. Durfee manages to break free from his clutches and hides inside the wall in the Murphy bed. Later, Sterling shows up very much alive. This is more than Chase is willing to tolerate, so he pulls out a gun and charges after Sterling. Sterling also gets the idea to hide in the wall with the Murphy bed, but he does

14. Sleepless Nights 169

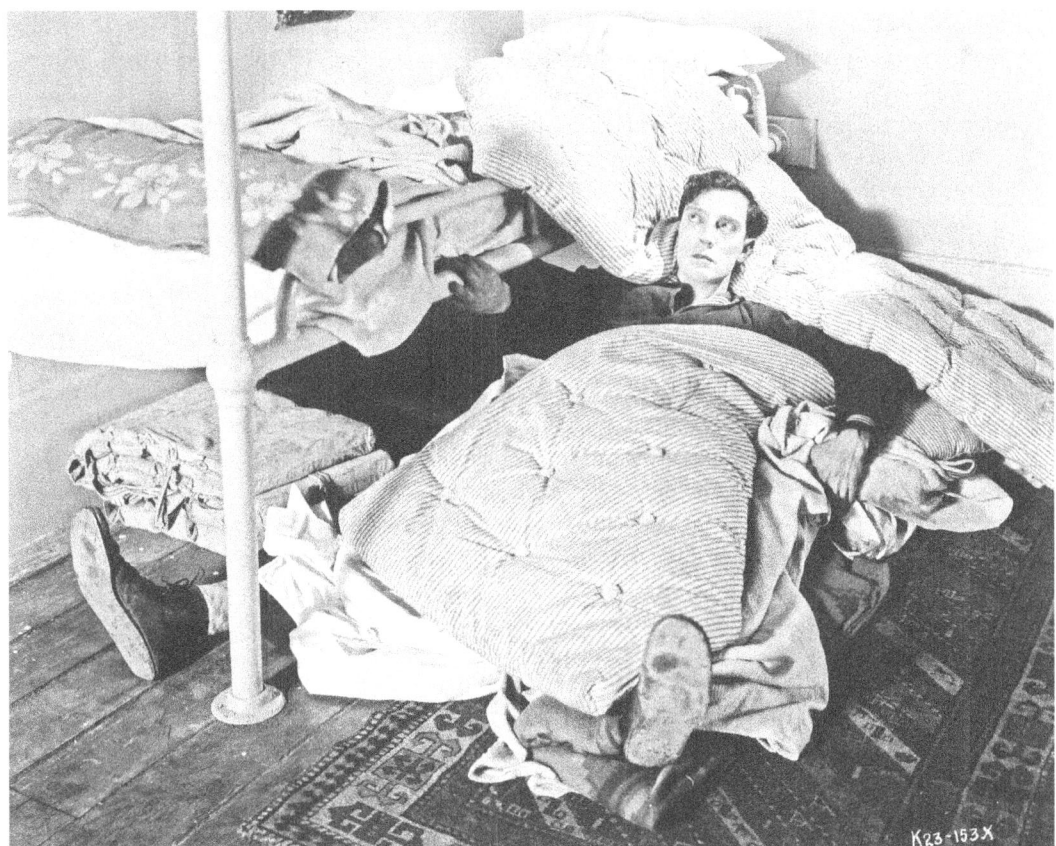

Buster Keaton is having trouble sleeping in *The Navigator* (1924) (courtesy www.doctormacro.com).

not move fast enough and his head gets trapped in the passageway between the bed and the wall. The camera comes in for a close-up on Sterling, whose head is sticking out of the wall. Sterling is able to provide a great deal of his trademark mugging before the film fades out.

The Murphy bed continued to show up in Keystone comedies. In *Bath Tub Perils* (1916), hotel manager Fred Mace upsets his wife (Dale Fuller) by flirting with a pretty guest (Anna Luther). That night, Fuller confiscates Mace's clothes so that he will be unable to stray from the marital bed. Mace, undeterred, sneaks to Luther's room in his pajamas. Luther's husband (Hugh Fay) arrives unexpectedly. Mace, afraid to be caught in a married woman's room in his pajamas, quickly hides inside a Murphy bed.

Chaplin had his own problems with a Murphy bed in *One A.M.* (1916). Chaplin, who has come home drunk, is confused at first that his bedroom is lacking a bed. It takes a moment for him to remember he has a Murphy bed. He then presses a button on the wall to release it. The bed, mounted on a swing arm, is able to pivot between the bedroom and a closet. Chaplin gets snatched up by the pivoting bed as it spins around inside the closet. The bed then comes crashing down on him. After climbing out from under it, Chaplin sits on the edge of the bed to have a smoke. The cigarette falls out of his hand. He stands up to retrieve the cigarette, at which point the bed springs up behind him. Chaplin, unaware that the bed has moved, goes to sit back down and tumbles to the floor. He struggles to get the bed back down. The bed jumps up suddenly, hitting him in the mouth. Then, the bed bucks up and down with Chaplin riding on top. At one point, Chaplin gets closed inside the wall with the bed. The bed seems to have a mind of its own. The scene goes on for more than six minutes, ending with Chaplin giving up and going to sleep in the bathtub.

In *Vivacious Lady* (1938), James Stewart and Ginger Rogers have a similar scene wrestling with an uncooperative Murphy bed, which they eventually name "Walter." Their frustration is even greater because, more than trying to get to sleep, they are trying to consummate their marriage.

Mel Brooks recreated Chaplin's *One A.M.* routine for *Silent Movie* (1976). Brooks, his character having drunk himself into a stupor, is having difficulty managing the Murphy bed in his hotel room. He is in the process of sitting down on the bed when it suddenly folds up into the wall. He falls flat on his backside, much like Chaplin had done more than sixty years earlier. On *Laverne and Shirley*, Penny Marshall and Cindy Williams copied a number of gags from the Chaplin routine. The woman cling to a Murphy bed as it bucks up and down, after which the bed closes them into the wall.

Spies and Guys (1953) includes the least appealing recreation of the Chaplin routine. This is Chaplin's Murphy bed routine absent all traces of subtly, nuance or intelligence. Joe Besser, playing a prisoner of war, discovers a retractable bunk bed in his prison cell. Joe has

Harry McCoy (left) and Sid Smith catch up on lost sleep in *False Roomers* (1921) (courtesy Cole Johnson Collection).

no doubt that this bed is purposely working against him and trying to harm him. He shakes his fist at it, he smacks it, he punches it, and he sticks his tongue at it. He cries, "No bunk's gonna make a monk out of me!" He becomes so flustered that, in the end, he throws himself on the floor and thrashes around uncontrollably.

The same type of gags was used with a retractable ironing board in the Three Stooges short *Sing a Song of Six Pants* (1947). Shemp has trouble making the ironing board stay down. He eventually climbs on top of the ironing board, which promptly springs up and traps him inside the storage closet. A Murphy bed collapses on top of Larry Fine in *Corny Casanovas* (1952). The strident sound effects could just as easily have been used for a bear trap or a medieval torture rack. No other Murphy bed scene had these sounds—not the clanging, not the wonky spring noises, not the crunching (presumably, the sound of Larry's spine shattering). The sound effects turn the Murphy bed into a clanking iron beast and manage, in the process, to give the scene a distinctive Stooges flavor. No film offered worse bodily harm from a bed until *Freddy vs. Jason* (2003), in which homicidal bogeyman Jason Voorhees folded up a young man backwards in a rollaway bed.

In *PHFFFT* (1954), Judy Holliday has Jack Lemmon over to her studio apartment to help her with her taxes. When Lemmon asks her where her bed is, Holliday presses a button and a bed comes sliding out of the wall. Holliday presses the button again to make the bed retract but Lemmon, in an amorous mood, playfully presses the button to make it pop out again. The couple continues to press the button, making the bed come in and out. The couple ends up marrying. In the closing moments of the film, the couple kisses, the bed spontaneously slides out of the wall, and they fall into it.

An innocent husband could use a Murphy bed to avoid misunderstandings with his wife. In *Nothing But Pleasure* (1940), a drunken woman wanders into Buster Keaton's motel room. Keaton has to get rid of the woman before his suspicious wife returns. He picks up the woman to put her into bed when the bed suddenly folds up into the wall. This routine had originally been performed by Keaton without the Murphy bed in *Spite Marriage* (1929). The Murphy bed was added as a way to further complicate matters.

Bob Hope revived this routine 26 years later for a pivotal scene in *Boy, Did I Get a Wrong Number!* (1966). Hope tries to do a good deed by letting a movie starlet (Elke Sommer) spend the night in his cabin. When he learns that his wife is on her way to the cabin, he goes to ask Sommer to leave but finds out she has taken sleeping pills and cannot be awakened. He decides to use a Murphy bed as a hiding place. Hope has to grapple with this unconscious woman and battle with a bed that is unwilling to cooperate. The routine, as scripted, is essentially the same as Keaton's version, except for a few 1960s-style embellishments. A woman who has drunk too much has now been replaced with a buxom, pill-popping actress. The fact that the curvy Sommer is scantily clad makes the scene more sexual than it was originally intended. The overall routine, as executed by Hope, is torpid and dull.

A flurry of Murphy bed gags have shown up in films and television for more than one-hundred years. In *Be Big!* (1930), a Murphy bed closes into the wall with Laurel and Hardy stuck inside it. *The Panic Is On* (1931) has a scene wherein Charley Chase, excited by a self-improvement book he is reading, slams his fist into the wall. In the next apartment, a Murphy bed is jarred loose from the wall and collapses onto his neighbor's head. Chase later closes a gangster inside a Murphy bed in *Time Out for Trouble* (1938). *Annie Oakely* (1935) features a comic scene in which Sitting Bull, fresh off the reservation, becomes confused by a Murphy bed. In *Hit the Ice* (1943), Bud Abbott shoves Lou Costello into a Murphy bed, which promptly closes up into the wall. Costello bursts through the wall and ends up in bed with a couple next door. The same basic gag was staged on a larger scale in *Buck Privates Come Home* (1947), when Costello comes flying through a window and lands on a Murphy bed. He no sooner lands on it than it closes up. The *Buck Privates Come Home* sequence was closely duplicated in *It's a Mad, Mad, Mad, Mad World* (1963). In *A Maid Made Mad* (1943), Andy Clyde closes an irate husband inside a Murphy bed. The Three Stooges ride in and out of the wall on a Murphy bed during a chase in *Hot Scots* (1948). Firemen have to extract Henry Kulky from a Murphy bed in *Fireman Save My Child* (1954). An episode of *The Beverly Hillbillies* features Granny being trapped inside a hideaway bed by one of Elly Mae's monkeys. In *Foul Play* (1978), Dudley Moore's swinging bachelor pad has a red, heart-shaped Murphy bed. In *Spy Hard* (1996), a female assassin is lying in bed, about to shoot Leslie Nielsen, when the bed flips into the wall. Ted Danson gets trapped in a Murphy bed in an episode of *Cheers*.

The most involved Murphy bed routine occurred on a 1971 segment of *Love American Style*, which featured retractable bed expert Joe Besser. The segment, entitled "Love and Murphy's Bed," fully exploited the idea of an adulterer using the Murphy bed to hide a lover from their spouse. Sarah (Jo Ann Pflug), a married woman, returns from a trip a day early and brings home a man she met during her travels. Complicating matters, Sarah's husband John (Jim Hutton), who doesn't expect anyone to be home, arrives unexpectedly with his buxom girlfriend, Irene (Carol Wayne). The wife, having heard her husband come in the door, hurriedly hides her boyfriend in their Murphy bed. Sarah calls out to John, who panics upon finding out that his wife is home. John immediately shoves Irene into a hallway closet, although he later needs to transfer her to the Murphy bed. The couple, each of whom want to get the other out of the place, agree to go out to dinner together. Before they can get dressed and leave, a number of visitors arrive at their home. First, Irene's irate husband comes looking for his wife. John intercepts the man before his wife sees him and throws him into the Murphy bed. Then, an irate woman, who followed her husband and Sarah home from the bus station, storms through the door. Sarah promptly disposes of her in the Murphy bed. Besser, a neighbor who is hearing people shouting inside the walls, assumes that his neighbors are having a party next door and he comes over to complain.

In the World War II comedy *Soft Beds, Hard Battles* (1974), the working girls at a Paris brothel have rigged a folding bed to dispose of German officers. As soon as the officer lays down, the bed can be activated to spring up into the wall, launching the officer on a fatal head-first dive down a long and precipitous chute. This bed, with its grinding pulleys and coiled heavyweight springs, is more lethal than the Three Stooges' bed ever hoped to be. Peter Sellers is ensnared by this murder contraption, but he avoids the chute by becoming wedged between the bed and the wall trim (not unlike Ford Sterling's fate nearly sixty years earlier).

These Murphy bed parodies were not good for retailers, however. A Vancouver store owner who sold Murphy beds included the following text in an ad: "Now is an excellent time to address your space needs with a Murphy Bed. Yes, we said 'Murphy Bed.' They're back and more popular than ever. Gone are the days of Laurel and Hardy where the beds were portrayed as a fold away trap for your worst enemies. These days the beds are sleek, reliable and built for comfort."[1]

Hammock Over Water (1903), an early one-gag comedy produced by American Mutoscope and Biograph comedy, opens with a fashionably dressed young couple walking through a tree-shaded area beside a lake. The couple climbs into a hammock, stretched out over an inlet of the lake. The two are engaging in a romantic embrace when the hammock breaks and they tumble together into the water. This was the start of many hammock routines. Margarita Fisher tangled with a hammock in the 1916 Mutual comedy *Miss Jackie of the Navy*. Lloyd Hamilton had a hard time trying to settle into a hammock in *Jolly Tars* (1926). Billy Dooley twirls around in a hammock at a rapid speed in *Shore Shy* (1926). Lou Costello takes several hard falls out of a hammock in *In the Navy* (1941). Shemp Howard finally gets settled in a hammock when the hammock catches fire in the Three Stooges comedy *Dunked in the Deep* (1949). Andy Clyde takes a spin in a backyard hammock in *Heather and Yon* (1944).

In *Quiet Please!* (1933), Edgar Kennedy has problems on a train trip with his brother-in-law. At the peak of frustration, he sets out to throw water into his brother-in-law's sleeping berth, but he misguidedly throws the water into a berth belonging to a man he had angered earlier in the day. The man leaps out of his berth and furiously attacks Edgar.

Berth gags were introduced onscreen in *The Deadwood Sleeper* (1905), a comedy produced by American Mutoscope and Biograph. Comical misadventures associated with berth travel remained the primary focus in *Pullman Bride* (1917) and *A Pullman Blunder* (1918). The berth offered filmmakers ample comic possibilities. Social awkwardness inevitably dominates when a large group of people, most of whom are strangers, are forced to sleep together in close quarters separated only by peek-a-boo privacy curtains. The rocking of the Pullman car makes it easy for a passenger to get tossed into another passenger's berth, which happens

Lige Conley isn't sure he will be able to get Peggy O'Neil in her berth in *Casey Jones, Jr.* (1923). The passenger on the left is Claude Gillingwater (courtesy Robert Arkus).

to Buster Keaton repeatedly in *Pardon My Berth Marks* (1940). Climbing into an upper berth puts a passenger at risk of stepping on another passenger's face, which is something that Harry Langdon learns in *Luck o' the Foolish* (1924). The situation gets downright risqué when Lee Moran mistakenly places a drunken man in a berth with a strange woman in *Upper And Lower* (1922). It isn't difficult for one passenger's problem to become another passenger's problem. In *Rattling By* (1921), a passenger spills a bottle of water in an upper berth, causing the water to drip down on a passenger (Bud Duncan) in the lower berth. It is travel at its most disturbingly claustrophobic. A routine performed by Eddie Lyons in *All Aboard* (1915) and Lloyd Hamilton in *Going East* (1924) had a man unpleasantly squeezed in a sleeper overnight with the rambunctious children of a traveling companion.

The inadequacy of the privacy curtain was the subject of a number of gags. The shadow of a woman undressing is visible on a privacy curtain in *The Gumps* (1925). Scandal arises from a shapely mannequin leg sticking through the curtains of a man's berth in *Call the Cops* (1919). The flimsy protection provided by the privacy curtain was also demonstrated by W. C. Fields, who beans a man with a mallet through a privacy curtain in *Never Give a Sucker an Even Break* (1941).

Harold Lloyd starred in an exceptionally elaborate train travel/berth comedy called *Now or Never* (1921). This film was likely an inspiration for Langdon's *Luck o' the Foolish*. Lloyd, too, steps on the face of a man while climbing into a berth. Lloyd, too, has problems shaving in a washroom compartment crowded with other passengers. However, feet slipping through privacy curtains of the berths form the basis of the funniest sequences. Lloyd is looking to clasp his girlfriend's hand when an old woman's foot slips out of a berth and ends up resting in his hands instead. Later, Lloyd is set with the task of delivering a cup of water to a little girl attempting to sleep in one of the berths. He fills a cup at a water cooler and proceeds up the aisle towards the girl's berth. Suddenly, a foot springs out of a berth and knocks the cup out of his hand. Lloyd retrieves another cup of water and makes his way up the aisle again. He is cautious to switch the cup to his other hand before the lurking foot can make another surprise attack, but he no sooner makes the switch than a different foot pops out on the other side and whacks the cup from his hand. Refusing to give up, Lloyd takes military-style evasive action against protruding feet by carrying a cup of water down the aisle while crawling on his belly.

The best-known example of train-travel humor can be found in *Berth Marks* (1929), which features Laurel and Hardy struggling to change clothes in the cramped confines of a berth.

Berth humor was sustained throughout the years by Our Gang (*Choo-Choo!*, 1932), the Three Stooges (*A Pain in the Pullman*, 1936) and Leon Errol (*Berth Quakes*, 1938), among others. Even more sophisticated comedies made use of these type of gags. In *The Palm Beach Story* (1942), Claudette Colbert is struggling to get up into a berth when she steps on Rudy Valee's face and breaks his eyeglasses. This turns into an ideal "meet-cute" situation.

Beds continued to be a problem in the coming decades. O. J. Simpson is folded in half when his electric hospital bed raises up at both ends in *The Naked Gun* (1988). The inability of a bunk bed to support the weight of Chris Farley causes the entire top half of the bed to come crashing down on David Spade in *Black Sheep* (1996). The same routine was used, unchanged, in *Step Brothers* (2008).*

---

*The same routine was performed by the Three Stooges using a triple-decker bunk bed in *In the Sweet Pie and Pie* (1941).

Sleepwalking was a critical problem in old comedies. Characters removed of conscious thought lack the inhibitions necessary to assure appropriate behavior. Roscoe Arbuckle sleepwalks through a town holding a lit bomb in *Bombs and Bangs* (1914). Charley Chase takes to stealing while sleepwalking in *The Nightshirt Bandit* (1938).

Harold Lloyd presented a couple of unique sleepwalking routines. In *High and Dizzy* (1920), Lloyd develops an attraction for a young woman with a sleepwalking disorder. Lloyd has to rush to the woman's rescue when her latest sleepwalking episode takes her out onto a building ledge. In *Hot Water* (1924), Lloyd chloroforms his mother-in-law to assure that he has a quiet evening, but it appears that he has used too much chloroform and has murdered the woman. Later, when he sees his mother-in-law sleepwalking, Lloyd believes that she has risen from the dead to haunt him.

Always a Gentleman (1928) opens with Lloyd Hamilton sleeping in bed with his boxer roommate. The boxer, dreaming of a bout, is throwing punches in his sleep. One punch lands hard on Hamilton's nose. The roommate then leaps on top of Hamilton and throttles him. Hamilton wrestles to get the roommate off of him, and the two roll onto the floor. The roommate wakes up and climbs off Hamilton. Hamilton sits up with a look of pure disgust.

The same premise was used to more elaborate ends in the Clyde Cook comedy *Should Sailors Marry?* (1925). Cook finds himself having to share a bed with an unfriendly wrestler, played convincingly by former weightlifter Noah Young. Young dreams that he is in a

Harold Lloyd is about to be frightened by his sleepwalking mother-in-law (Josephine Crowell) in *Hot Water* **(1924).**

wrestling match against Cook (the viewer knows this because they are briefly taken inside Young's dream). The wrestler remains unconscious as he rises up and reaches out to grab Cook. The shadowy lightning makes Young looks as menacing as the homicidal somnambulist in *The Cabinet of Dr. Caligari* (1919). Young picks up Cook and spins him over his head. He throws him on the floor and gets him in a headlock. He jams his foot down on Cook's throat. Cook's long rubbery legs and long rubbery neck are so loose and slippery that Young is unable to get a secure grip. Cook, a noodle-necked, limber-limbed comedian, seems not so much human as a character out of a cartoon.

The routine was staged in diminished form in the Columbia short *In the Doghouse* (1935). Andy Clyde gets into bed with his rambunctious little grandson, who has fallen asleep wearing boxing gloves. The boy, dreaming that he is boxing with Max Baer, throws a punch and socks Clyde in the nose. That is the extent of it. Clyde is not strangled or knocked out of bed or kicked in the throat. The one punch is treated as a sufficient gag, and the scene is over. It often happened that a routine became so familiar to audiences that filmmakers were able to present a shorthand version and still get laughs. In these cases, the audience's laughter most likely came out of remembering an earlier rendition of the routine and had nothing at all to do with the rendition at hand.

A funny variation of this routine appears in the Abbott & Costello comedy *The Naughty Nineties* (1945). Tough guy Joe Sawyer is dreaming that he is a soldier fighting Indians when

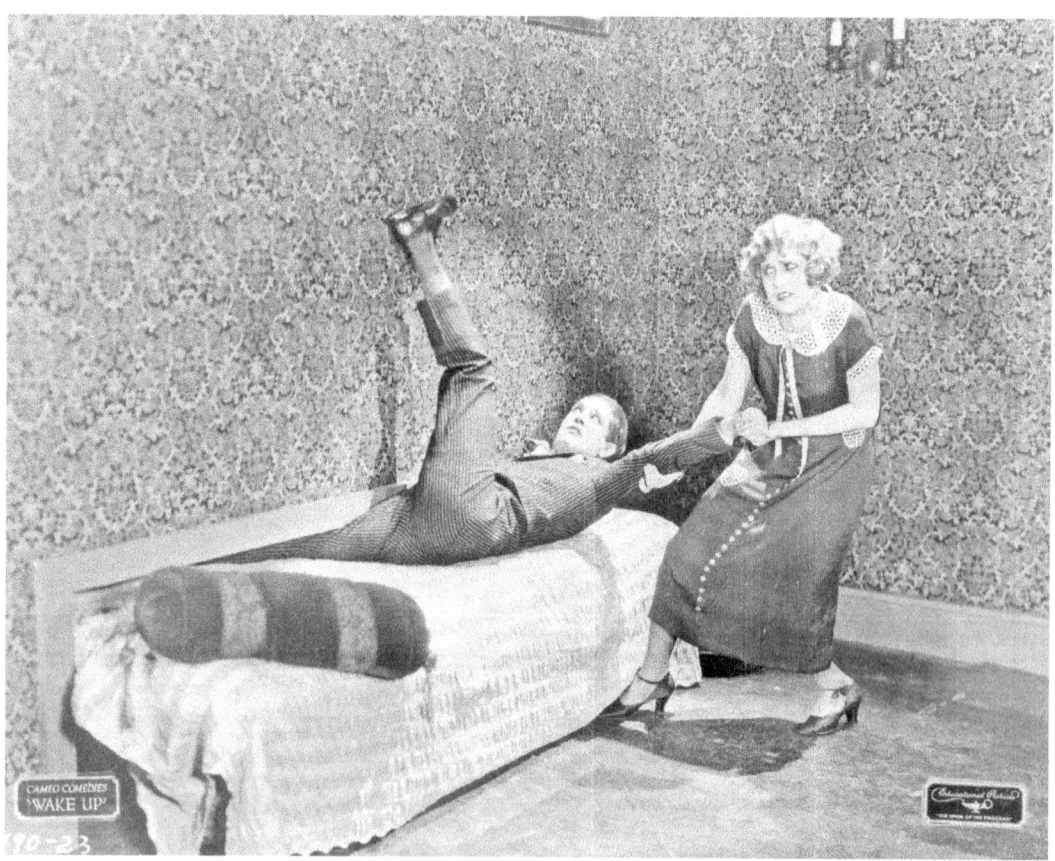

Cliff Bowes is dragged out of bed by Virginia Vance in *Wake Up* (1925) (courtesy Robert Arkus).

he repeatedly sleepwalks across the room and slaps and chokes Costello, whom he imagines to be a "little Indian."

One thing more dangerous than a sleepwalker is two sleepwalkers. Will Ferrell and John C. Reilly are sleepwalking in tandem when they tear apart their parents' home in *Step Brothers* (2008). When their father tries to wake them, the pair pummels him into submission and throws him down a flight of stairs.

The simple fact is that, in the world of cinema history, no rest exists for the weary slapstick comedian.

15

Fathers to *Sons of the Desert*

Laurel & Hardy's *Sons of the Desert* (1933), possibly the most perfect comedy ever made, relied on an intricate storyline that had been refined through repeated use over a period of two decades. Hardy wants to get out of a vacation to the mountains with his wife so that he and Laurel can attend the annual convention for their fraternal lodge, the Sons of the Desert. Hardy gets the idea to feign illness. Meaning to put on a good show, he wraps a wet towel around his forehead, plunges his feet into a basin of steaming hot water, and moans incessantly. Dr. Meddick, a veterinarian hired by Laurel, shows up at his house to perform a phony examination. Before he leaves, Meddick tells Hardy's wife that the only thing that would do her husband any good is an ocean voyage to Honolulu. The plan works perfectly and the duo is able to sneak off to Chicago for the convention. The day that Laurel and Hardy are due to return home, news arrives that the ship arriving from Honolulu sank in a typhoon. The wives are in a panic. While waiting to hear news about the ship's survivors, they decide to go to the movies to take their minds off their troubles. The women no sooner sit down in the theatre than they see a newsreel showing a parade held by the Sons of the Desert in honor of their annual convention. Laurel and Hardy suddenly appear onscreen, all smiles and merriment, as they march in the parade and play up to the newsreel camera. The boys return from their trip, surprised that their wives are not home to greet them. They take notice of a newspaper with a headline about the ship disaster and realize that they have put themselves into a dire predicament. They need to stay out of sight until the rescue ship with the survivors arrives the next day, and they are on the way out the door when they see their wives coming up the walkway. They scramble with their suitcases to hide in the attic. A series of mishaps later force the men into a confrontation with their wives. The pair tries their feeble best to lie their way out of this dilemma. They say that they didn't need to bother waiting for the rescue ship because they "ship-hiked" their way home. The story only enrages the wives more. Hardy ends up getting clobbered by his wife with a seemingly endless supply of pots, pans and plates. Laurel, who confesses everything to his wife, is treated like a King.

The Biograph comedy *A Wreath in Time* (1909) has a plot similar to that of *Sons of the Desert*. A married man (Mack Sennett) agrees to join his friends at a burlesque show but he tells his wife that he needs to take a train out of town to attend a fraternal conclave. The train is wrecked and the man's wife, left to assume that her husband died in the accident, buys a wreath in his memory. The wife realizes, when her husband suddenly arrives home unharmed, that his story about taking the train out of town had been nothing more than a ruse.

Laurel (left) and Hardy attend a lodge meeting in *Sons of the Desert* (1933) (courtesy Bruce Lawton Collection).

One key difference between *Sons of the Desert* and *A Wreath in Time* is that Sennett claims as his alibi that he needs to attend a fraternal conclave, while Hardy has to come up with an alibi so that he *can* attend a fraternal conclave. These gatherings, where men established and maintained important business contacts, were socially acceptable venues for businessmen. Hardy's wife, however, is fed up with her husband spending so much of time with the "sacred order" of the Sons of the Desert, which she believes is causing him to neglect his marriage.

In the Keystone comedy *The Tale of a Black Eye* (1913), Fred Mace receives a shiner for flirting with a woman, but he tells his wife that he got the black eye while saving a baby from being hit by a car. The actual eye-bruising event, captured by a newsreel cameraman, is later exhibited in a theatre in plain view of his wife. Sennett remade this film a number of times. The basic plot remained the same: a husband lies to his wife about where he spent the day, and his wife later sees newsreel footage exposing his true activities. Roscoe Arbuckle turns up onscreen, marching in a parade in *Fatty at San Diego* (1913); Arbuckle has been captured in amusement-park footage flirting with a young woman in *A Reckless Romeo* (1917); Billy Bevan is caught on film during a Purity League raid in *Giddap!* (1925); and Franklin Pangborn is exposed in scenic beach shots, frolicking with bathing beauties, in *The Candid Camera* (1932). The lie is now exposed by newsreel footage instead of a news story. In each case, a public event intrudes on a private lie.

Edison borrowed elements of *The Tale of a Black Eye* and *A Wreath in Time* for a film called *Black Eyes* (1915). The film provides a more even-handed depiction of marriage. This time, both the husband *and* wife lie to each other about their respective outings, and *both* the husband and wife end up with a black eye. The wife seeks treatment to get rid of the black eye before her husband arrives home on the noon express from Trenton. She is waiting in a medical office when she picks up a newspaper and reads the headline, "Noon Express from Trenton Wrecked, Nearly All Passengers Believed to Have Been Killed." The woman barely has time to absorb the bad news when she finds her husband in the next room having his own black eye treated.

A similar plot was written by Marshall Neilan for the Kalem comedy *A Peach at the Beach* (1914). The film opens with Lloyd Hamilton stealing his wife's purse to finance a secret outing to the beach, but he becomes so preoccupied with the flirtatious Mrs. Hothead (Ruth Roland) that he fails to notice when a pickpocket makes off with the purse. Hamilton's wife, played by Lucille Kellar, later sees footage of Hamilton's dalliance at the beach. Kellar stands up in the middle of the movie theatre to thrash her husband. The same day, the pickpocket, who has reformed, returns the stolen purse to Hamilton's wife. He manages, in the course of his apology, to describe the circumstances of the theft, mainly that he stole the purse from her husband at the beach. The newsreel exposed her husband's cheating and

(Left to right) **Stan Laurel, Oliver Hardy and Charley Chase celebrate at a lodge convention in *Sons of the Desert* (1933) (courtesy www.doctormacro.com).**

now the pickpocket has exposed her husband's thievery. Kellar responds by beating her husband doubly hard.

The purse, or variations of the purse, play into future versions of this story. In *Ambrose's First Falsehood* (1914), Mack Swain tells his wife he took a train to visit a friend, unaware that the train had crashed. Making it worse, a dancer shows up at his home looking for her

Laurel (right) and Hardy need to practice hand signs to keep official lodge business from their wives in *Sons of the Desert* (1933) (courtesy Bruce Lawton Collection).

purse. In *By Golly!* (1920), Bevan is exposed by a watch, which was stolen by a waiter while he celebrated at a stag party. *Ambrose's First Falsehood* was a direct remake of *A Wreath in Time,* while *By Golly!,* like *Black Eyes,* combined the train wreck from *A Wreath in Time* with the incriminating newsreel from *The Tale of a Black Eye.*

Laurel and Hardy first made use of this premise in *We Faw Down* (1928). The boys tell their wives that they are going to spend the day at the Orpheum Theatre when they are really going to play poker. On their way to the game, they meet a couple of attractive young women who invite them back to their apartment. Meanwhile, their wives become distressed upon receiving news that the Orpheum Theatre has burned down. The wives are on the way to the theatre when they see their husbands climbing out of an apartment window to avoid a boyfriend who showed up unexpectedly. Later, when the husbands arrive home, they are still unaware that the theatre had burned down. Hardy's wife (Vivien Oakland) sits in a chair scowling at her husband. Hardy asks her if she doesn't believe him that he was at the theatre. He proceeds to describe the show in great detail, going so far as to wear a lamp shade around his waist to recreate the performance of the hula dancers. His dance is interrupted when one of the girls arrives at his house to return his vest, which serves the same function as the purse and watch in the previous versions.

Additional story elements and gags originated with *Be Big* (1931), in which Hardy's desire to attend a stag party instead of going on vacation with his wife and the Laurels motivates him to fake an illness. Just like *Sons of the Desert,* this film starts with Hardy moaning woefully as he presses a wet towel to his forehead and climaxes with the wives coming after the duo with hunting rifles. But it is mainly the story points of *We Faw Down* that were carried forward in *Sons of the Desert.*

The duo is exposed in *We Faw Down* three times: by the news report, by their appearance escaping from the girls' apartment, and finally by the return of the vest. Each revelation further tightens the nooses around their necks. In *Sons of the Desert,* Hardy had, in the same way, mounted one lie on top of another, and this flimsy construct of lies was bound to come crashing down on his head (along with the pots, pans and plates). The film manages to humorously expose the eternal foolishness of lying, which remains just as relevant today.

16

The Big Jangly Box, the Sliding Ladder and Other Comic Props

Props have always been important in comedy. The success of a routine could depend on a change of an object. This is apparent in the case of the Sennett two-reeler *His Marriage Wow* (1925). Harry Langdon, on the way to his wedding, drops his wedding ring in the street. A car runs over the ring, which becomes embedded in the tire treads. Harry climbs onto the car hood and, while the car continues down the road, he stabs at the tire with a penknife to remove the ring. By the time he retrieves the ring, the tire treads are in shreds and the inner tube has gone flat. Harry hands the driver a jack before he departs. In *His Bridal Fright* (1940), Charley Chase performs the same routine with a single variation: the wedding ring has been replaced with a rare postage stamp. The postage stamp is simply not as interesting as the wedding ring and Chase's version of the routine, along with the tire, falls flat.

Monty Python's John Cleese was unsatisfied with a routine he wrote about a man returning a broken-down used car to the dealer. Cleese couldn't get the routine to work until he replaced the broken down car with a dead parrot. The rest is comedy history.

A ladder was a favorite prop in the Commedia dell'Arte. A popular ladder routine had a comedian trying to set a ladder against a wall, but the ladder slips down at the end of every attempt. Slipping ladders, in different variations, showed up in films on many occasions. The slipping-ladder routine in its most basic form was performed by Lou Costello in *It Ain't Hay* (1943). Most of the time, though, filmmakers were able to introduce into this old stage routine both natural real-world elements and modern mechanical devices. In *Be Reasonable* (1921), Billy Bevan is looking for a way to escape some policemen who are pursuing him. He sees a ladder lying in front of a store, and gets the idea to use the ladder to climb into a window. However, he sets up a ladder atop a sidewalk elevator. As he is trying to reach the top of the ladder, the elevator descends and delivers him back to the sidewalk into the waiting arms of the police.

A ladder sometimes slipped if it was bearing too much weight. In *Jonah Jones* (1924), Lloyd Hamilton has taken pity on a young woman being forced into a marriage by her father. He dutifully sets up a ladder under her bedroom window. However, sprinklers are making the lawn soggy at the same time that Hamilton's rotund girlfriend boards the ladder to drag her boyfriend away from this other woman. It does not take long for the ladder to sink into the mud. In *A Lady Lion* (1928), Fred Spencer is at a snowy mountain lodge trying to set

Brooms were another useful prop for the slapstick comedian, as demonstrated by Dave Morris (left), Billy Bevan (middle) and an unidentified associate (courtesy Robert Arkus).

up a ladder outside of a cabin. The heavyset comedian is making his way up the ladder as it slowly descends into a snow bank.

Other ladder routines were developed by the Commedia dell'Arte. In one routine, the comedian no sooner climbs to the top of the ladder than he slips down the rungs. Another routine had the comedian standing on top of a ladder to pick apples out of a tree. He has just finished filling a basket with apples when a rival appears and tries to shake him off the ladder. The upper half of the ladder bends back and forth as the comedian panics and struggles to hold on.

Elements of these routines turned up in silent films. A burglar slipping down a ladder was a featured routine in the 1903 Edison comedy *The Irrepressible Burglars*. Later films showcased more elaborate ladder stunts. In *Drama Deluxe* (1927), Lupino Lane has to climb a ladder to hang a poster on a signboard, but the poster is blocking his view and he fails to see that he has set up the ladder on the edge of a cliff. Lane, who has problems holding steady on a ladder, looks as if any moment he will fall to his death. In *Out Bound* (1924), Sid Smith is backing up his truck when a ladder comes loose in the back and slides through a bedroom window. The ladder slips under a bed where Cliff Bowes is sleeping. When Smith drives forward, the bed *and* Bowes are carried along with it. Smith manages a wild ride through busy streets. Soon, the back of the truck, along with the bed, is hanging over the side of a cliff. Smith climbs the ladder to rescue Bowes, but his weight causes the ladder to tilt further over the cliff. The ladder swings back and forth as the men struggle desperately to climb to safety.

This is not to say that a good comedian still did not see the merit in a simple, old-fashioned ladder routine. In *Smithy* (1924), Stan Laurel has difficulty carrying a roll of tar paper up a ladder and soon becomes tangled up in the rungs. In *The E-Flat Man* (1935), Buster Keaton sets up a ladder under his girlfriend's bedroom window for a planned elopement, but he is soon battered by luggage being tossed out of the window by his girlfriend. He eventually loses his grip and slips down the rungs.

A ladder routine familiar to fans of classic comedy is presented as the climax of Laurel & Hardy's *Hog Wild* (1930). Hardy has to prop up a ladder on the floorboard of Laurel's Model T to be able to reach his roof. Hardy has reached the top of the ladder when Laurel accidentally steps on the starter pedal. The car speeds off down the driveway taking Hardy and the ladder along with it. Hardy struggles desperately to hang onto the ladder as the car runs out of control through heavy traffic. The ladder is swaying a lot more wildly than the ladder ever did in the Commedia dell'Arte routine. This scene refurbishes a long-established routine by installing wheels and attaching a four-cylinder engine. It also throws in a variety of hazardous obstacles, including a low-set bridge and a double-decker bus.

The Roach company tried to expand on this routine. In *Air-Tight* (1931), the scene starts out with Mickey Daniels hanging from a ladder propped up in back seat of a speeding car. The ladder gets latched onto a low-swooping plane and Daniels and the ladder are carried off into the sky. The next step in the evolution of this routine can be found in *What Price Taxi* (1932), in which the legs of a ladder are straddled between two speeding cars. Billy Gilbert is climbing up one side of the ladder in an effort to attack Clyde Cook on the other side. These expanded versions of the routine, as big and busy as they were, were no longer about the characters and their reactions as those found in *Hog Wild*. It is inevitable that, when the comedian gets lost in the action, the comedy will get lost as well.

A discussion of ladder routines would be incomplete without the mention of a ladder *tour de force* performed by Woody Allen in *Sleeper* (1973). Allen, pursued by police, struggles futilely to climb out of a second-story window using the shortest of ladders.

Popular clown props included brooms, buckets, chairs, ladders and crates. In 1910, a French clown named Pierre Leandre debuted a popular routine wherein he is exhausted by having to repeatedly load and unload the same crates on and off a wagon for an indecisive boss. The routine, called "Load! Unload!," was later turned into the Abbott & Costello rou-

Laurel (right) and Hardy take a wild ride in *Hog Wild* (1930). The actress who is seeing them off is Fay Holderness (courtesy Bruce Lawton Collection).

tine "Pack/Unpack," which was featured in *Hit the Ice* (1943). The physical aspect of the routine was removed as the crates were replaced by suitcases, which Costello was required to pack and unpack as Abbott kept changing his mind as to whether or not they should leave town.

The ultimate crate routine, which retains the physical exertion of Leandre's routine, was performed by Laurel & Hardy in their Academy Award–winning short, *The Music Box* (1932). The film's title is appropriate. The action surrounds a big crate which periodically emits musical notes, including chimes clanging and keys jingling, as movers Laurel and Hardy strain to carry it up a long flight of stairs.

Undeniably, a significant influence on *The Music Box* was the Keystone comedy *His Musical Career* (1914). Charlie Chaplin and Mack Swain are disparately sized piano movers who are having a hard time accomplishing their duties. Their first delivery has them struggling to carry a piano up a flight of stairs. Swain, the much larger mover, gets tired at one point and has Chaplin lift the piano on his back and carry it on his own.* In another scene, Chaplin and Swain transport the piano up a sharply inclining sidewalk that functions in much the same way as the lofty staircase in *The Music Box*. Chaplin and Swain are straining to advance the piano up this slope when they meet up with a rotund, ill-tempered man dressed in a top hat and tails. The man becomes angry at the way the movers are handling his piano. He shouts. He rattles his cane. Swain does not like this behavior and gives the man a hard slap. The man responds by kicking Swain in the backside. The piano, jarred into motion, goes sliding down the incline along with Chaplin and Swain. The piano ends up crashing into a lake. The piano is sinking into the water as Chaplin merrily pounds the keys and launches into song.

A second influence was a Sennett comedy called *Ice Cold Cocos* (1926), in which Billy Bevan is an ice man who has to carry an icebox down an enormous flight of stairs. *Ice Cold Cocos*, under the direction of Del Lord, was a cartoonish escapade. Bevan is able to effortlessly carry the icebox on his back, even though the box is obviously bigger than he is. Bevan's problem isn't so much bearing the weight as it is keeping the cabinets shut to stop fruit and vegetables from tumbling out. Stop-motion effects are used to show Bevan and the icebox taking a sudden tumble down the stairs.

The third and last predecessor of *The Music Box* was another Laurel and Hardy comedy, *Hats Off* (1927). In this outing, Laurel and Hardy have to carry a washing machine up a long flight of stairs. This was the same staircase used in *Ice Cold Cocos* and the same staircase later used in *The Music Box*. Laurel, on his own, had once exhausted himself climbing these steps in *The Pest* (1922).

Five years later, when Laurel and Hardy first set out to rework this routine, the biggest change that they made was to replace the washing machine with a piano crate. The crate — large, noisy and unmanageable — was a funnier prop than the washing machine. The increased size of the prop proved particularly crucial to the plot. The crate is so big that people coming down the stairs cannot get past, which becomes a great source of conflict between the movers and passersby. The most troublesome passerby is a rotund, ill-tempered man dressed in a top hat and tails (expertly played by Billy Gilbert). This character is similar to the one who fought with Chaplin and Swain in *His Musical Career*. On three separate occasions, a mishap or skirmish occurs to cause the movers to lose their grip on the crate,

---

*Ham the Piano Mover, which came out less than a week later, placed Ham and Bud in the same situation. Ham, like Swain, had his smaller partner, Bud, lift a heavy piano on his back and carry it by himself.

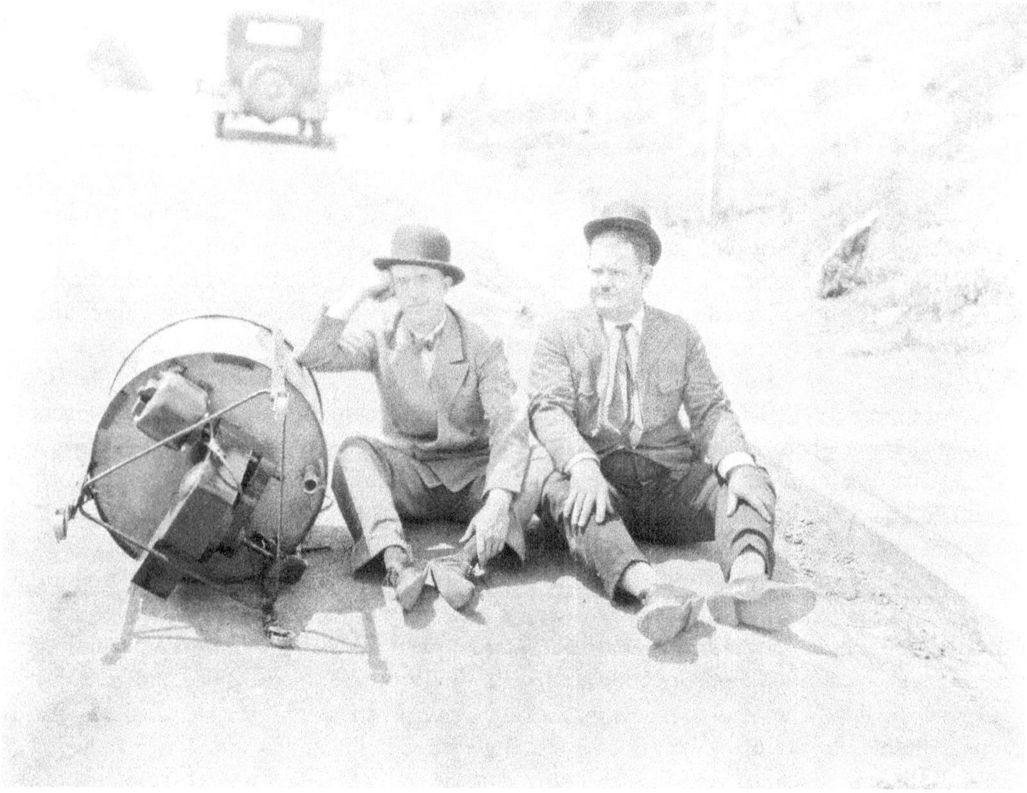

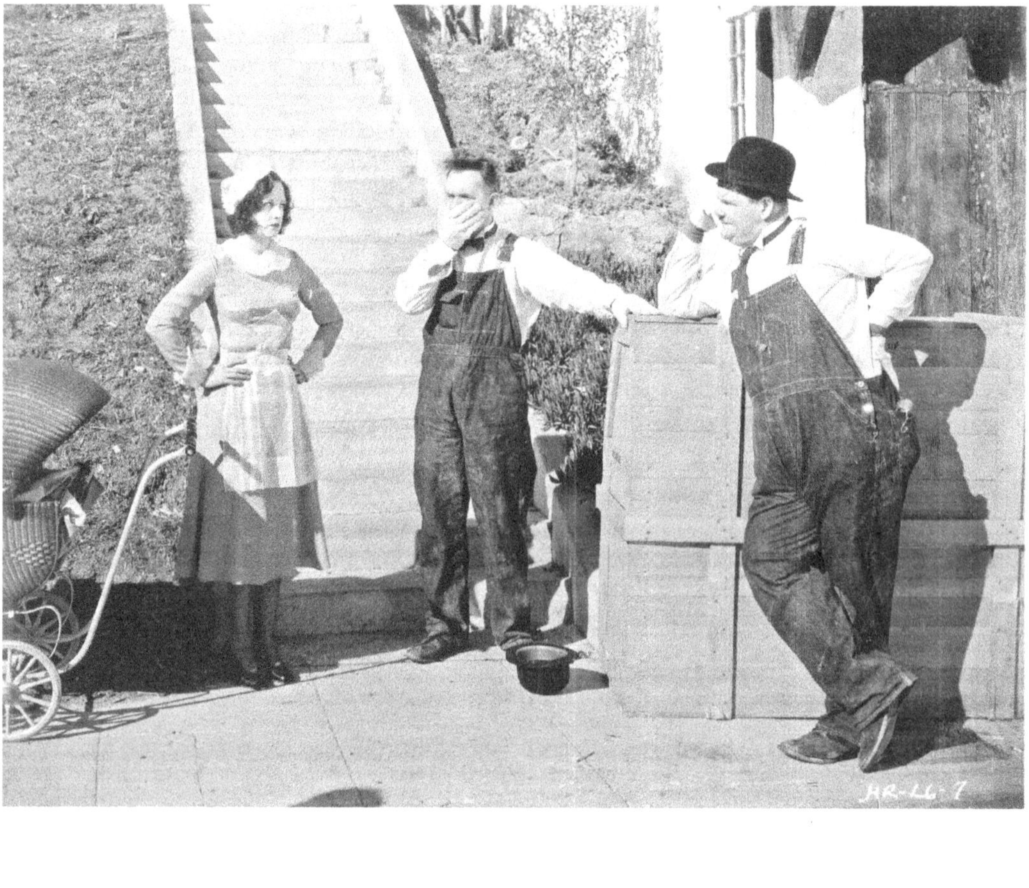
HR-LL-7

which then goes sliding back down to the bottom of the steps. Each time, the movers need to start anew to carry the crate to the top of the steps. One time, Hardy latches onto the crate as it starts to tumble, only to get dragged down the steps behind it. This would not be so different from the *Ice Cold Cocos* scene wherein Bevan tumbles down the staircase with the icebox except that we can now hear each heavy thud that the crate makes as it strikes the steps and we can hear the pained cries that Hardy makes as he receives each new bruise. *Ice Cold Cocos* is a surreal, effects-driven comedy, unlike the painfully realistic, character-driven *Music Box*.

The movers strain to get the piano up the steps, the whole time calling out, "Heave-ho!" This phrase is a manly term originated by sailors who had to hoist multi-ton anchors, and the efforts of the movers certainly recall such exertion. Laurel and Hardy express a great deal of exertion the entire time that they are hauling the crate up the stairs. At times, as they slump over the crate, breathing heavily and perspiring profusely, it seems that they are exhausted and will not be able to go on. Nonetheless, they have a job to do and they are determined to get it done. "Service with a smile," says Hardy. The film derives its tension from the difficulty of this undertaking and the mounting fatigue of these determined laborers. The repetitive action of moving a crate up and down a flight of stairs proves far more exhausting than the repetitive action of moving a crate up and down off a wagon.

While transporting the piano into the home itself, Laurel and Hardy blow up a radio, tear a chandelier from the ceiling, short-circuit the electricity, smash vases, and flood the living room. This scene has a precedent in *No Loafing* (1923), in which Gentle Furniture Movers employees Poodles Hanneford and Joe Roberts also manage to demolish a home while delivering a piano.

Lord remade *Ice Cold Cocos* as *An Ache in Every Stake* (1941), which introduces the Three Stooges as clumsy team of ice men. The Stooges have to haul an icebox to a home at the top of a long flight of stairs. The Stooges, if they had taken a cue from Hitchcock's *The 39 Steps* (1935), could have called this film *The 147 Steps*, which is the total length of the staircase (as counted by Stooge fans visiting the site). The staircase, although similar to the staircase used previously by Bevan and Laurel & Hardy, was, in fact, a new location.

An Ache in Every Stake lacks the surreal gags of *Ice Cold Cocos*. The sultry stare of a vamp-like housewife caused Bevan's block of ice to rapidly melt down to the size of an ice cube (a funny image achieved through stop-motion animation). Nothing is sultry about the housewife who wants ice from the Stooges. Curly's block of ice melts simply due to the severely hot weather.

The Stooges are soon overheated and exhausted by their labors. As they take a breather, the icebox gets away from them. A man (Vernon Dent) carrying a birthday cake home is knocked down by the runaway icebox as it rockets down the stairs. The main difference between *The Music Box* and *Ache in Every Stake*, and a great difference in general between the teams, is that Laurel & Hardy are made victims in their encounters while the Stooges succeed in making *others* into victims.

Hal Yates, the director and writer of *Hats Off*, later reclaimed his old routine for an Edgar Kennedy short, *It's Your Move* (1945). Yates returned to using a washing machine for the scene. It is less likely that he maintained a stubborn attachment to the washing machine

Opposite, top: **Laurel (left) and Hardy have difficulty carrying a washing machine and keeping their hats straight in *Hats Off* (1927) (courtesy Bruce Lawton Collection).** *Opposite bottom:* **A monumental staircase awaits deliverymen Laurel (center) and Hardy, but they must first deal with a sassy nursemaid (Lilyan Irene). The film is the Academy Award–winning *The Music Box* (1932).**

Stan Laurel (right) and Oliver Hardy (center) deliver a piano to Billy Gilbert in *The Music Box* (1932).

and more likely that he recognized that the piano crate had become so closely identified with Laurel & Hardy that it would forever belong to the team.

Closer to the traditional "Load! Unload!" routine was "Return the Christmas Gifts," a routine that Abbott and Costello performed on a 1952 episode of *The Colgate Comedy Hour*. Abbott and Costello arrive at a home to deliver a number of items, including a grandfather's clock, a television, a stove, and a Christmas tree. The delivery men find themselves caught in the middle of an argument between a husband and wife. The wife has ordered the items as Christmas gifts, but her husband, who believes that Christmas is a waste of money, demands that the men take the items back to the store. The argument, as expected, takes twists and turns. Costello is gathering up and the items and moving them out the door when the husband has a change of heart and asks the delivery men to bring the items back into his home. For a second time, Costello sets up the Christmas tree, he stands the grandfather's clock against the wall, he pushes the television into the living room, and he carries the weighty stove back through the door. By then, the couple is quarreling again and the husband demands that the items be removed immediately from his home. This goes on a number of times, leaving Costello fatigued and frustrated. The sublime Sid Fields, who plays the husband, is as blustery and hostile as Billy Gilbert was in *The Music Box*. Gilbert did not want to accept delivery of the piano as he hated music and Fields does not want to accept delivery of the Christmas presents as he hates Christmas.

Blake Edwards filmed an updated version of Laurel & Hardy's piano-moving routine with Ted Danson and Howie Mandel for *A Fine Mess* (1986), but the scene was excised prior to the film's release.

The two staircases — the one used in *The Music Box* and one used in *An Ache in Every Stake* — remain intact to this day. The staircases, which are located near each other in the Silver Lake district of Los Angeles, have become popular tourist attractions for fans of classic comedy.

17

The Buster Keaton Variations

The Méliès Influence

Many examples of Georges Méliès's influence on comedians can be found. Still, no other comedian was more influenced by Méliès than Buster Keaton. Take for example *The One Man Band* (1900), in which Méliès relies on multiple-exposures to show himself as seven musicians playing together in a band. More than two decades later, Keaton revived this routine for a scene in *The Playhouse* (1921), wherein he played seven members of an orchestra. In *The Haunted House* (1921), Keaton gets caught in a spooky house with thieves dressed up as skeletons and devils. Two skeletons walk past Keaton holding body parts. They assemble the parts by methodically stacking one on top of the other. As the head is secured, the man comes to life. Méliès often assembled and disassembled bodies in his films. This scene from *The Haunted House* has more than a passing resemblance to Méliès's *Extraordinary Illusions* (1903). The Méliès comedy *Terrible Turkish Executioner* (1904) features a sword-wielding executioner lining up four men for beheading and slicing off their heads with one clean sweep of his blade. This type of gruesome gag was no longer acceptable in Keaton's time, yet Keaton flirted with decapitation gags when he first started in films. He attempts to take off a villain's head with an axe in *Back Stage* (1919) and he nearly loses his own head in *The Cook* (1918). The latter film includes the more elaborate of the routines. Roscoe Arbuckle is in a restaurant kitchen cutting up meat when an exasperated restaurant manager thrusts his blundering waiter, Keaton, through the kitchen door. Keaton falls across the chopping block just as Arbuckle is bringing down his meat cleaver. His knife's edge comes so close to Keaton's neck that Arbuckle is astonished to see Keaton rise up fully intact. Just to make sure, he grabs hold of Keaton to conduct a critical examination of his neck.

No comedian would be losing his head for the time being. Stan Laurel, who had a notoriously "black" sense of humor, was able to get a number of gruesome gags into his films, but he failed in his efforts to conclude *Block-Heads* (1938) with his and Hardy's heads mounted on the wall of a big game hunter. Decapitation gags would not become acceptable again until a killer rabbit chewed off Terry Gilliam's head in *Monty Python and the Holy Grail* (1975).

In features, Keaton had to become more literal to develop the believability and logic required to sustain longer stories. When surreal scenes cropped up in *Sherlock Jr.* (1924) and *The Navigator* (1924), he made a strict point to impose limits on them. The scene in

Sherlock Jr. is, from the start, established to be a dream. *The Navigator* had its most farfetched material ultimately excised by Keaton. The scene in question occurs towards the end of the film. Keaton, submerged underwater in a diving suit, patches a leak in a ship using a lobster and swordfish as tools. A swordfish attacks him, to which he responds by raising up his swordfish and dueling bill-to-bill. Additional footage was shot of Keaton assuming the role of traffic cop to direct schools of fish coming from different directions, but this gag, as funny as Keaton thought it was, never made it into the finished film. Preview audiences found the underwater sequence to be a distraction from the story, especially as Buster still needed to rescue the heroine from savage natives. He therefore eliminated the

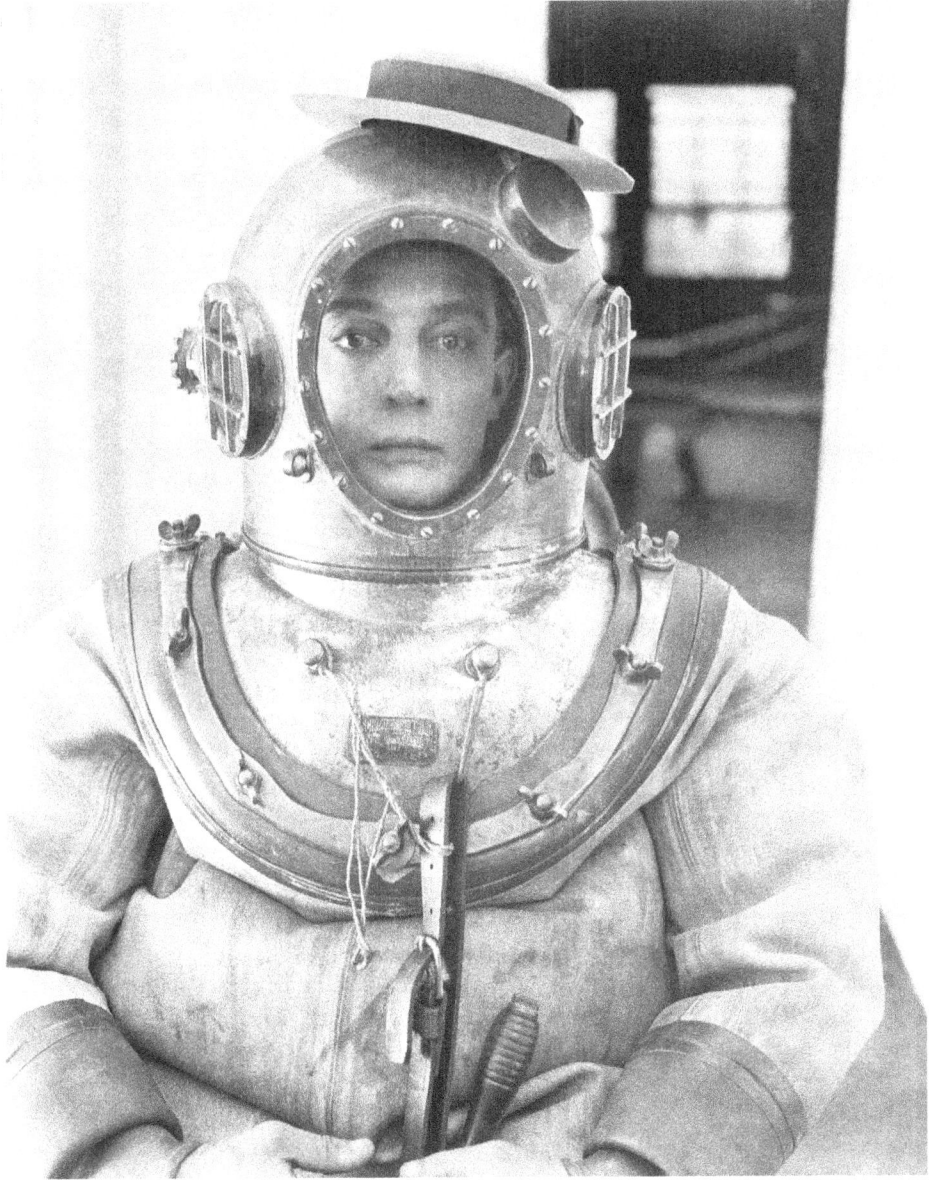

Buster Keaton in a diving suit in *The Navigator* (1924) (courtesy www.doctormacro.com).

traffic cop business to get him back to the surface more quickly.* Still, another otherworldly scene remained. Keaton, still encased in his diving suit, emerges from the ocean onto a beach landing on a tropical island. Film historian Jim Kline noted that "the sight of this sea god" causes the savages to "run screaming into the jungle."[1] It was possible that, in this instance, Keaton was influenced by André Deed, a Méliès disciple who created a kindred scene for his 1912 Pathé Frères comedy *Boireau en mission scientifique*. When Deed's film was exhibited at the 2010 Pordenone Silent Film Festival, observers could not help but make comparisons.†

Keaton was likely a fan of these forgotten old comedies. Other outstanding gags from classic Keaton comedies can be traced back to older films. Take, for example, a key routine in *Neighbors* (1920). Keaton, who is carrying on a romance with the girl next door, finds the girl's burly father less than pleased to catch the couple in a warm embrace. Rather than wait for the father to throttle him, Keaton executes a hasty retreat by grabbing hold of a clothesline and riding it across the courtyard. Frank Darien used this same gag for the same basic purpose in a 1915 Komic comedy called *Over and Back*. No print is known to exist of *Over and Back*, but it is hard to imagine that Darien delivered something as breathtaking or amusing as Keaton's clothesline ride. At one point, Keaton is propelled by the clothesline through a window, slides down a banister, sails through a doorway, and ends up back on the clothesline for an unfortunate return trip to the girlfriend's menacing father.

"Eight Bells," an acrobatic comedy extravaganza performed by the Byrne Brothers from 1890 to 1914, also concerned a romance developing between young neighbors in a courtyard and an elopement scheme that involved a three-man pyramid to help the bride escape through her bedroom window. An "Eight Bells" routine that featured the brothers performing acrobatics with a ladder balanced on a fence was later used by Keaton in *Cops* (1922). The Byrnes adapted "Eight Bells" into a film in 1916, but no print of this film is known to exist.

The shot of Keaton sliding down the banister was later copied by Jackie Chan in *Project A* (1983). More recently, the shot received the CGI treatment in the computer-animated comedy *Rio* (2011). Keaton's slide down the banister was funny as part of a long ride from building to building and then back again, but it is not as funny as a single isolated feat. It is barely funny at all performed by *Rio*'s cartoon macaw.

Later, when he returned to making short films, Keaton again indulged in surreal gags. Making use of double-exposures, he staged an enchanting encounter with spirits in *The Gold Ghost* (1934). Keaton's television series, produced from 1950 to 1951, featured such Méliès standards as disembodied heads and magical paintings. A 1951 episode called "The Detective Story" depicts a nightmare in which Keaton lifts the lid off a serving tray and finds his own decapitated head alive and breathing. On another episode called "The Haunted House," a painting of a knight comes to life and swings a sword at Keaton. Other examples appeared throughout the series. Keaton, as the manager of a struggling community theatre, cannot afford to pay a billposter and sets out with his assistant (Hank Mann) to post a bill to a billboard. Their efforts do not go well. The billboard stand collapses on top of a gardener (Heinie Conklin) and, when Keaton goes to drag the gardener out of the rubble, he finds

---

*The undersea traffic cop routine did not go to waste. Keaton included the routine in the film's trailer, where it received big laughs, and Billy Bevan found himself unencumbered by plot concerns when he performed the routine in *A Sea Dog's Tale* (1926).

†Keaton was not the first comedian to make use of this routine. In *Ham the Diver* (1916), beachgoers are panicked by the monstrous sight of Lloyd Hamilton angrily stalking out of the ocean wearing a bulky diving suit.

The Byrne Brothers' "Eight Bells" was an inspiration for Buster Keaton.

that the man now resembles a flat cut-out picture of himself. In the same episode, Keaton steps up to a painting of an apple tree and plucks off a real apple.

More on The Playhouse (1921)

Keaton far surpassed Méliès with *The Playhouse*, using novel multiple-exposure techniques to portray more than two dozen characters. Keaton's main role is that of a harried stagehand. His other roles include a bratty boy in a Little Lord Fauntleroy outfit, and the boy's grouchy old mother. They create problems for an old couple in a theatre box beneath them when the boy drops a sticky lollipop in the woman's lap and the mother spills soda on the man's head.

The Playhouse had a second likely influence in "Mumming Birds," a popular sketch that had been part of Fred Karno's music hall revue. The sketch involved a series of vaudeville acts being disrupted by rowdy patrons, including a drunk and a bratty boy. Charlie Chaplin, who rose to stardom playing the drunk from 1908 to 1913, worked out a film version of "Mumming Birds" entitled *A Night in the Show* (1915). Chaplin chose to play two troublesome patrons, appropriately named Mr. Rowdy and Mr. Pest. The low-class Mr. Rowdy spills beer on other patrons and throws cream puffs at the acts. Mr. Pest, better dressed but not better behaved, punches the conductor and shoves a fat lady into a fountain. Dee Lampton plays a bratty fat boy who provokes a pie fight.

Larry Semon later assembled the essential elements of *A Night in the Show* for a two-reeler titled, simply, *The Show* (1922). Again, the patrons are not well-mannered. A family

Charley Chase provides his version of the one-man band routine in *Four Parts* (1934) (courtesy Robert Arkus).

prepares sandwiches in a theatre box and, in the process, spills a gargantuan jar of jam on the patrons sitting below them. Again, performances are ruined. A magician has trouble with a chicken that gets loose onstage, a singing quartet has their clothing torn off by a wind machine, and a barrel of lamp black gets dumped on the audience. Again, the star comedian appears in multiple roles. Semon first appears as an ill-tempered old man sitting in the audience. The old man heckles a magician onstage, fights with the escaped chicken, and breaks a bottle over the head of a woman sitting in front of him. Otherwise, Semon plays a property man suffering through a series of backstage misadventures. This role is no different than the accident-prone character that Semon usually played. Unlike Chaplin and Keaton, Semon failed to rise to the challenge of playing multiple roles. He showed no interest in creating distinct, believable characters. In the last six minutes of the film, Semon deviates from this premise entirely so that he can stage one of his standard chase scenes.

Lupino Lane produced an adaptation of "Mumming Birds" for a short entitled *Only Me* (1929). A series of absurdly bad acts perform and audience members react with derision. Lane tried to rival Keaton by playing every one of the film's 24 roles. He plays a drunk and a bratty boy in the audience, and he also plays all of the performers onstage. The fact that the story was presented from the impaired perspective of a drunken man was meant to justify all of the characters looking alike. Unfortunately, this does not prove to be Lane's best film. His 24 roles are nothing more than 24 funny costumes. Also, the film's effects compare poorly to the technical wizardry of *The Playhouse*. Split-screen effects are used sparingly and, even then, no more than two of Lane's characters appear onscreen at the same time. Keaton populated his theatre with multiple-exposure versions of himself. Much of the action in *Only Me* is carried by doubles disguised in Lane's various wigs and beards. Lane's brat is exceptionally active, throwing prodigious amount of food at people. A tomato splatters against the drunk. Soda is spilled on a flamenco dancer. A cream pie is slammed into the face of a flute player. The liveliest part of the film occurs when the drunk turns a fire extinguisher on a juggler performing a fire act, which is much like Chaplin's Mr. Rowdy blasting a hose at a fire-eater. Lane seems to the most enthusiastic playing the bad entertainers in the show. The worst performer is a ballerina who loses her wooden leg at the climax of her dance.

The Playhouse stands as one of Keaton's greatest achievements. He was able to provide the most impressive and exciting visit to the theatre without resorting to cream pies, chickens or fire hoses. He relied, instead, on developing a series of astonishing and ingenious sequences. The film's influence has carried on over the years. In *Kind Hearts and Coronets* (1949), Alec Guinness plays six relatives in a single shot using the same trickery developed by Keaton and cameraman Elgin Lessley for *The Playhouse*.

Comedy Teams Take on Keaton

A scene in the Three Stooges short *Three Dumb Clucks* (1937) finds Moe trying to pick out a hat for Curly to wear at their father's wedding. Curly takes a liking to a checkered cap, but Moe does not approve of this as proper formal wear for a wedding. Curly is too stubborn to accept this. Whenever Moe turns away, he sneaks the cap back onto his head. Moe, exasperated, snatches off the cap and tosses it across the room. The cap, like a boomerang, comes flying back towards them and settles perfectly on Curly's head. Scriptwriter Clyde Bruckman recycled this routine from Keaton's *Steamboat Bill, Jr.* (1928). The final twist, though, did not appear in *Steamboat Bill, Jr.* The boomerang hat gag, along with the entire hat-changing routine, in fact originated in a Lloyd Hamilton comedy called *New Wrinkles* (1927).[2,*]

The original scene in *Steamboat Bill, Jr.* provides significantly more nuance and variety than the Stooges' scene. Ernest Torrence, as Keaton's father, demands that Keaton buy a new hat to replace his effeminate beret. The scene does much to establish the relationship between a shy son and his gruff father. The payoff gag is more realistic and more touching. Keaton steps out of the shop and has a stiff breeze carry away his new hat (a foreshadowing of the film's windy climax). This, however, is not a criticism of the Stooges. Their style of comedy simply could not accommodate poignancy, nuance or reality in the way that Keaton's style could.

Those routines in which Keaton's stoically determined and resourceful screen persona coped with predicaments did not seem generally suited to the broader comedy styles adopted by comedy duos or suited to the functions that multiple protagonists had within the context of a team. Keaton's character was a loner, and his efforts were as intricate as they were introverted. Still, other teams came to remake Keaton routines. A routine from *The Cameraman* (1928) was adapted by two very different but equally popular teams. The routine had a

---

*For years, a juggler named Harry Barrett had performed a standalone boomerang hat routine in vaudeville. Larry Semon performed a more fantastic version of Barrett's routine (no doubt using wires) in *Horseshoes* (1923). The gag was employed again onscreen during the classic nightclub scene in *Airplane!* (1980).

Buster Keaton (right) is looking for a new hat under the watchful eye of Ernest Torrence in *Steamboat Bill, Jr.* (1928) (courtesy www.doctormacro.com).

simple setup: Keaton learns upon his visit to a bath house that he must share a dressing room with a stocky, ill-tempered stranger (Ed Brophy). The men soon find that they lack sufficient space to change into their swimming trunks at the same time. Keaton is the victim of most of the bedlam that ensues. He is nearly choked to death when Brophy's suspenders become wrapped around his neck. His head gets stuck inside Brophy's undershirt and is yanked in several directions before it finally comes free. Keaton looks especially pained when Brophy's elbow cracks him in the nose. The silliest gag in the scene occurs when Brophy bends to pull off his pants and then manages as he comes upright again, to lift Keaton on his back.

The routine was reworked by Laurel and Hardy for a train-travel short titled *Berth Marks* (1929). This time, the action was moved from a dressing room to a sleeping berth. The scene, tiresome in its execution, is uncomfortable to watch. It is understandable that Laurel and Hardy authority William K. Everson called *Berth Marks* "one of the few really poor comedies that the team made."[3] Keaton gave viewers a reason to root for him. He not only has to change his clothes in this restricted space but he also has to stand up to Brophy's bullying. Though the two men ended up in the same dressing room by mistake, Keaton entered the dressing room first, and it is only because Brophy refused to leave that they are in this predicament. In this way, the comedian's effort to change his clothing turns into a battle with a tangible foe. But the *Berth Marks* version of this routine is not a battle. The scene has lots of kicking, smacking and shoving, but the comedians do not mean to be causing injury to each other. The action is no more than a pair of fools fumbling around. Hardy bangs his head into the ceiling and gets Laurel's foot jammed into his face. Laurel gets Hardy's suspenders wrapped around his throat. Incredibly, this fumbling goes on for ten minutes, which is half the running time of the film.

The team performed an even more tedious version of the routine in *The Big Noise* (1944). The veteran comedians, now 15 years older, are noticeably sluggish in their movements. Their waistlines had by now expanded considerably and this left them with little room to maneuver for comic effect. In addition, new elements were added to the routine. Further getting in their way were a noisy accordion that Laurel pointlessly removes from his luggage, and a drunk (Jack Norton) who climbs into the berth by mistake. The part of the scene with the least amount of artistic merit occurs when "The Boys" turn away to take down their pants and manage, in the process, to crowd the frame with their abundant backsides. This image, sufficiently intrusive to achieve the illusion of 3-D, can make the audience suddenly feel short of space.

The classic stateroom scene in the Marx Brothers feature *A Night at the Opera* (1935) started out as a variation of the Keaton routine. The fact that Keaton worked on the film as a gag man suggests that he may have introduced the routine to the team himself. The premise, as scripted, is that Groucho has to dress in a cramped stateroom. Frustrating his efforts are a persistent stream of visitors to the room. The room is eventually crowded by

The classic stateroom scene from the Marx Brothers' *A Night at the Opera* (1935) The men are (left to right) Jack "Tiny" Lipson, Groucho Marx, Chico Marx, Harpo Marx, Allan Jones, and Frank Yaconelli. The ladies are unidentified (courtesy www.doctormacro.com).

the visitors, which include stowaways, chambermaids, an engineer, a manicurist, a cleaning woman and stewards. Groucho finally has to go out in the hall to put on his clothes. The problem was that the Marx Brothers previewed the scene in front of a live audience and the audience responded without much enthusiasm. The brothers deviated from the script in a bid for laughs and managed in their improvisation, to create the anarchic routine that finally made it into the film. Groucho is no longer struggling to get dressed as Keaton had been in *The Cameraman*. Keaton was a victim of the uproar and confusion, but Groucho is the architect of the uproar and confusion. Groucho is ecstatic to invite the visitors into the stateroom. As the scene draws to a conclusion, he is clearly entertained to see this collection of people climbing on top of one another. Audiences did not expect the Marx Brothers to suffer indignities like the rest of us. "[Pathos] had nothing to do with them," said Keaton. "They never got into a situation where you felt sorry for somebody."[4] It was simply the job of the brothers to create anarchy and make trouble for other people.

The stateroom scene may have also had its origins in a stage sketch introduced by the Hanlon-Lees pantomime troupe in 1879. The sketch, titled "A Trip to Switzerland," involved an evil guardian's efforts to coerce his lovely young ward into accepting his marriage proposal while the pair shared a compartment on a train. The ward's true love enlists various friends to assume disguises (including train conductors, custom inspectors and other railway personnel) to invade the cramped compartment and create a sufficient nuisance to disrupt the proposal. In 1914, the Byrne Brothers, a popular troupe heavily influenced by Hanlon-Lees, reworked this routine into a sketch entitled "An Aerial Honeymoon." This time, a newlywed couple finds it impossible to get privacy in a sleeping car aboard a crowded airship. The

The vaudeville show "An Aerial Honeymoon" was a likely inspiration for the stateroom scene in *A Night at the Opera* (1935).

Marx Brothers had no marriage proposal to disrupt, no marriage to consummate, and not even a need to get dressed or undressed. Their antics, as always, were nothing more than sheer nonsense. Keaton was correct when he said of the Marx Brothers, "There was no sense to anything they did."[5]

Watch the Birdie, a 1950 remake of *The Cameraman*, had Red Skelton applying his skills to the dressing room routine. Cast opposite Skelton was Dick Wessel, a stocky, bulldog-faced character actor who somewhat resembled Brophy. Keaton served on the film as an advisor, but this failed to make this reenactment stand up well to the original. A routine that was pantomime in origin is now updated with pointless dialogue and annoying sound effects. Sound effects emphasizing the tearing of clothing and the snapping of suspenders has more intensity than the hopelessly contrived performances on display.

An underlying conflict existed between Keaton and Brophy, but Skelton and Wessel leave no doubt about their conflict as they smack and shove one another. Sympathy shifts from Skelton to Wessel as Wessel falls victim to Skelton's relentless bungling. Being trapped in a cramped space with a fool is a true ordeal. Wessel gets his clothing torn (first his vest and then his pants) and finds himself defenseless as Skelton has a sneezing fit and repeatedly splatters him with mucous.

The clownish acrobatic stunt of Keaton being lifted on Brophy's back was reworked by Keaton as a stand-alone gag for a 1953 episode of *The Ken Murray Show*. This time, the action was moved into a phone booth. Keaton disappears from view in the phone booth when he bends down to pick up a coin that he has dropped. A woman (Keaton's wife, Eleanor) assumes that the phone booth is empty and walks in to make a call. Keaton manages as he comes upright to lift the woman on his back and send her bursting through the roof of the phone booth. Keaton reprised this gag on other programs, including the 1965 special *Salute to Stan Laurel*.

Synchronized Walking

A well-timed routine, wherein a comic follows a man step-for-step without the man knowing it, is a traditional routine that clowns have performed in the circus. Clown historian Pat Cashin wrote, "The red clown following the white clown back across the ring goes back to 19th century circus clowning and probably has roots that go back through the harlequinade to Commedia Dell Arte."[6]

In *Seven Years Bad Luck* (1921), Max Linder navigates in front of and behind a much larger passenger at a train station to avoid being seen by a ticket agent. At all times, he manages to walk perfectly in tandem with the man.

Keaton performs a more straightforward version of this routine in *Sherlock Jr.* (1924). Keaton, an amateur detective attempting to shadow a criminal suspect, walks directly behind the man, effectively mirroring his every step. The man stops short. Keaton stops short. The man stumbles. Keaton stumbles. The man takes a drag on a cigarette before tossing it over his shoulder. Keaton catches the cigarette, takes a drag himself, and tosses it over his shoulder.

In *Who's Afraid?* (1927), Lupino Lane is being chased by a police officer. He ducks behind a post and, when the officer comes past, he slips out behind him. He remains close behind the officer, copying his movements exactly as they make their way down the street. The officer looks right. Lane looks right. The officer looks left. Lane looks left. Finally, the officer turns around and sees Lane, who responds by sliding between the officer's legs, springing to his feet behind the officer, and sprinting away as fast as he can. Lane has, in effect, turned the routine into a backwards chase.

The most durable comedy routines can accommodate a variety of twists. In *Twenty Legs Under the Sea* (1927), a pair of detectives takes to shadowing a suspected jewel thief (Richard Walling). Walling becomes wary to see these strange men sticking to his trail — he takes a step forward and they take a step forward, he makes a turn and they make a turn. Walling performs an impromptu jig and the detectives, committed to following every move that he makes, duplicate the jig with perfect accuracy.

In *Help Wanted* (1928), Poodles Hanneford needs to retrieve a phone number that he has written on the back of a man's collar. He follows the man down the street, trying to get a look at the number. He gets as close to the man as he can without bumping into him. The fact that the man is much larger than Hanneford requires that the comedian repeatedly jump up to get a clear view of the number. Eventually, he stops jumping and merely walks in synchronization with the man. The man stops suddenly, which causes Hanneford to slam into him. This scene — with Hanneford jumping in the air and ultimately colliding with the man — lacks the orderliness exhibited by Linder, Keaton or Lane. This is a crucial flaw. It is the comedian precisely synchronizing his movements with the movements of the man that he is following that makes the scene both captivating and funny. It is the same sort of mimicry that has made the mirror routine popular for so long.

It stands that the most captivating and funny version of this routine was performed by Keaton. It is a scene that has deservedly turned up in many film retrospectives.

The Great Expanding Routine

Keaton was in the habit of expanding the scope of his gags by increasing the participants, enlarging the props, and heightening the danger. An obvious example of Keaton's specific predilection for enlarging props can be found in his upgrade of a simple fishing boat in *The Boat* (1921) to an immense passenger liner in *The Navigator* (1924).

Another prop used in *The Navigator* came to receive Keaton's Supersize treatment in a later film. In *The Navigator*, Keaton has to fend off cannibals attacking his steamship. He drags a miniature cannon on deck, loads it with gun powder, and lights the fuse. But then, suddenly, he gets his foot tangled in a rope attached to the cannon. The cannon is about to fire in Keaton's direction and no matter how hard he tries to get away, he cannot help but drag the cannon after him. He stumbles and falls, at which time the cannon fires over him and kills a cannibal boarding the ship. Keaton used essentially the same gag in his Civil War feature *The General* (1927). This time, Keaton is operating a locomotive in pursuit of enemy spies who have hijacked his locomotive, the *General*. He has brought along a heavy mortar cannon, which is coupled to the locomotive on a flat car. The hook that connects the tender comes loose and latches itself around Keaton's foot, which leaves him caught in the line of fire. At the last possible moment, the locomotive goes around a bend, which changes the position of the cannon in relation to Keaton and causes the cannon to change its target from Keaton to the *General*. Keaton made this gag grander and funnier mostly by making a little cannon into a big cannon.*

---

*The routine was reduced again for the small screen when Mickey Rooney tangled his foot in a rope attached to a bomb in a 1955 episode of *Hey, Mulligan* titled "Seven Days to Doom."

Buster Keaton readies a cannon in *The General* (1927) (courtesy Bruce Lawton Collection).

One of Keaton's most famous scenes occurs in *Cops* (1922) when an anarchist tosses a bomb off a roof and the bomb is caught by Keaton, who quickly tosses it into a police parade. The explosion of the bomb breaks up the parade and sends hundreds of policemen chasing after Keaton. Since the early days of film comedy, comedians were always being chased by cops. At times, the comedian looked to be hopelessly outnumbered by the police. It appears in *Seven Years Bad Luck* (1921) that Max Linder has every cop in town chasing after him. But, if the frames are examined more closely, it becomes apparent that at no point does the comedian have more than seven men in blue on his tail. *Cops*, in its own unique way, far surpassed previous cop chases, both in terms of numbers and ingenuity.

Only four earlier comedies could be found with notable similarities to *Cops*. In *Bumping into Broadway* (1919), Harold Lloyd is about to take home substantial winnings from a gambling club when he gets caught up in a police raid. The scene expands on the climactic chase scene of *The Adventurer* (1917), in which prison guards pursue Chaplin through a high-society home. The gambling club is considerably more spacious than the cozy estate and, instead of simply fleeing from four police officers, Lloyd has to flee from roughly two dozen police officers. Lloyd, in the manner of Chaplin, still relies on agility and resourcefulness to outwit, outplay and outlast the lawmen.* In *From Hand to Mouth* (1919), Lloyd

---

*Much of this chase scene, including pursuit on a dual staircase and a coat rack gag, was duplicated by Bobby Vernon in *Reno or Bust* (1924).

Buster Keaton creates comedy on a large scale in *The General* (1927) (courtesy Bruce Lawton Collection).

runs around assaulting police officers to get them to chase him to a criminal hideout, where a beautiful heiress is being held captive. Soon, he has an army of cops chasing him down the street. This scene, by comparison to the *Cops* scene, demonstrates major differences between Keaton and Lloyd. Lloyd acted willfully to have the cops chase after him, and he was, at all times, in control of the situation. Keaton, no matter how inventive he is able to be, is never in control in *Cops* and, unlike the purposeful effort by Lloyd, it is an unwitting action on Keaton's part that has brought the full weight of the law to bear down on him. It takes Keaton awhile to even realize that the cops are chasing after him. *Be Reasonable* (1921), which was released two months before *Cops*, features Billy Bevan being pursued by a multitude of police officers. The scene does have a distinct resemblance to the *Cops* scene, even including action where Bevan climbs a fence to escape the cops much like Keaton would later do. The fourth and final precursor to *Cops* was another Keaton film, *Convict 13* (1920), in which a crack unit of police officers comes marching after Keaton in lockstep. The sequence in *Cops* starts off similarly but then expands considerably on this initial idea, having a growing number of police officers converge for the sole purpose of catching Keaton. The scene builds up to a massive scale unprecedented in the prior films.

Keaton staged a comparable chase scene only a few months later in *Daydreams* (1922). He bulked up the scene by replacing a car with a trolley for a key gag. The scene, though, pales in comparison to the cleverly designed and fast-moving *Cops* scene.

Prior to *The General* (1926), Lige Conley manned a locomotive for laughs and thrills in *Casey Jones, Jr.* (1923) (courtesy Robert Arkus).

The Comic Cyclone and the Falling Building

Keaton climaxed *Steamboat Bill, Jr.* (1928) with a famous cyclone scene. The scene had limited (but notable) precedent.

Georges Méliès included a hurricane in his comedy *Robert Macaire and Bertrand* (1907). Robert Macaire, a noted criminal and assassin in France, is not a particularly funny subject and, yet, Méliès chose to create a slapstick version of the manhunt and capture of Macaire by French police. In this short film, police officers chase after a criminal after he and his henchman have robbed a bank. At first, they chase the fugitives through a busy train station. A commuter is knocked down, which triggers a chain of pratfalls. The police continue to chase the criminals through the city. A storm breaks out. Rain falls. Wind blows. The artificial buildings included among the scenery shake forcefully. People flee through the village square in a panic. Debris falls from the buildings and crashes into the street. A tower is torn off a building and flies through the air. Finally, the winds lift the criminals into the air and transport them across the sky.

Eddie Cline found when he directed the Fox Sunshine comedy *A Schoolhouse Scandal* (1919) that a tornado could be useful in stirring up a rapid-fire succession of extravagantly absurd gags. A cyclone tears through a home, causing the building to spin around at a high rate of speed. A bed, with a person sleeping under the covers, lifts off the floor and floats in mid-air. Other furniture is blown through the rooms. At one point, a car comes flying through the air. Cline later reprised the house-spinning gag in a storm scene featured in Keaton's *One Week* (1920).

Snub Pollard loses his home to a cyclone in the Roach two-reeler *California or Bust* (1923). The cyclone snatches the home off its foundation, leaving nothing behind except Pollard, blissfully sleeping in a hammock on the front porch. The effects of the cyclone are so silly that the audience cannot possibly perceive the cyclone as a serious threat. This is especially true when a woman climbing into a storm cellar has her wig blown off.

When he adapted *The Wizard of Oz* into a film in 1925, Larry Semon had to recreate the crucial cyclone which serves to deliver Dorothy to Oz. Semon did not think to make much of the cyclone's heavy winds, focusing instead on using animated lightning bolts as the basis for gags. The scene, in general, is unremarkable.

The climax of *Tramp, Tramp, Tramp* (1926) tosses Harry Langdon into the middle of a cyclone that has descended upon a small rural town. The town has been deserted by the time that Langdon shows up. The eternally naive Langdon is bewildered by both the absence of people and the extreme vigor of the wind. The storm proceeds to give the Little Elf an exceptionally hard time. Langdon dodges debris as he runs across town. He takes refuge in a barber shop, but the storm is soon rocking the building wildly from side to side. He has no choice but to flee before the shop collapses. He is startled when the front of a building tears loose and collapses into the street. Another building front begins to come loose and slumps forward in his direction. He escapes through a doorway just before the building crumbles into pieces. Langdon angrily throws bricks at the cyclone and, when it suddenly turns around, he assumes that he has scared it off.

Keaton is caught alone in a small town, River Junction, under the onslaught of a cyclone. He happens to have been lying unconscious in a hospital while the other residents took refuge in storm cellars. The storm tears across River Junction with a fearsome power, and the gags — in keeping pace with the storm — are delivered with equal ferocity. Keaton did not rely on Méliès's fake buildings or Semon's animated lightning bolts. Six powerful airplane engines were used as wind machines to tear apart a breakaway town at the same time that Keaton was being hurled through the air, attached to a 120-foot crane. The scene, with its dynamic energy, daring stunts and spectacular gags, unquestionably surpasses the cyclone scene in *Tramp, Tramp, Tramp*. *This* is a storm to fear.

Though unequal in scale, the two cyclone scenes share a number of similarities. Langdon runs inside a building only to have the shelter yanked away from him. Keaton is introduced in the scene when the winds yank up an entire building and reveal him lying in a hospital bed. Langdon is carried through the air trapped in a phone booth. Keaton is blown through the air hanging onto an uprooted tree. Langdon exits a building just before it collapses. Keaton exits a building just before it collapses. Langdon survives a collapsing wall by passing through an opening in the wall. Keaton, too, survives a collapsing wall by passing through an opening in the wall.

That last similarity brings us to a major difference in the nature of the scenes and brings us to the single-most famous gag of silent films. In the case of *Tramp, Tramp, Tramp*, the building does not collapse suddenly and Langdon has enough time to make a decision to escape through a doorway. But this is not how it works with the collapsing wall in *Steamboat Bill, Jr.* Keaton, in a daze from being buffeted around town, is standing before the building, unaware that the front of the building has come loose and is in the process of falling down on top of him. He only avoids being crushed because he is standing in the

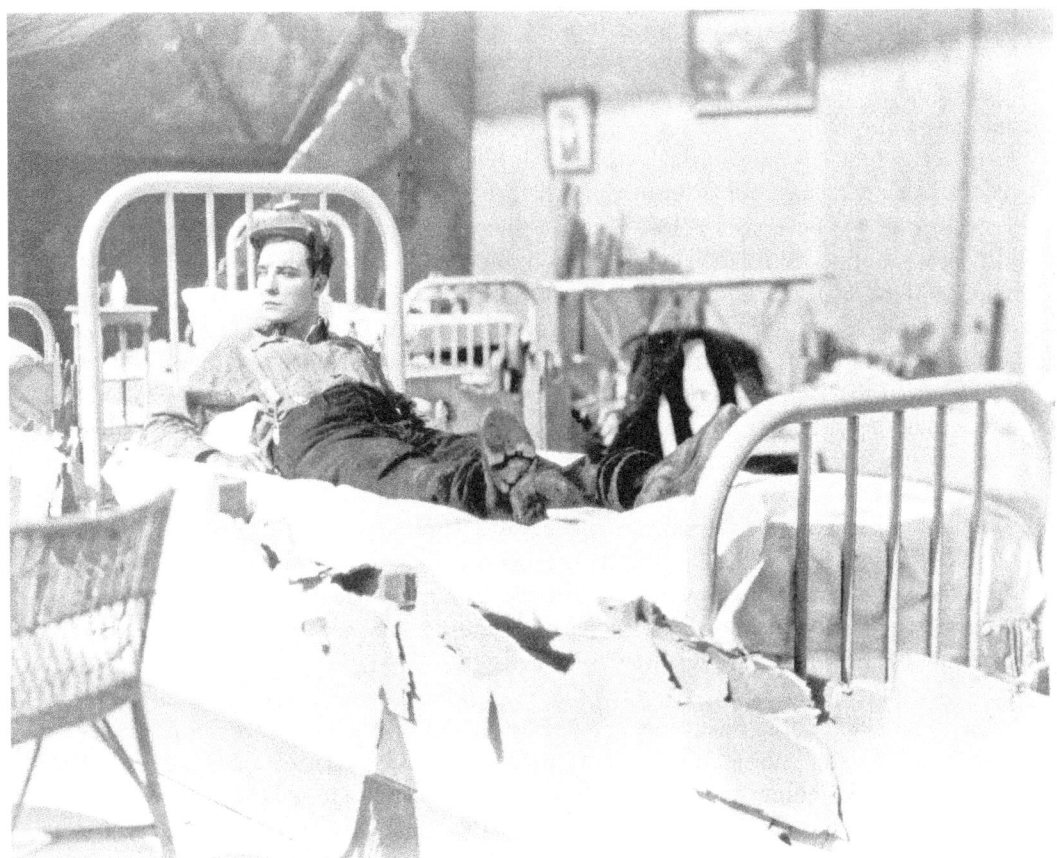

Stoically observing the carnage as it begins: Buster Keaton as *Steamboat Bill, Jr.* (1928) (courtesy Bruce Lawton Collection).

path of an open window. Keaton is standing in exactly the right place at exactly the right moment to pass through the window. It is an astonishing act of fate that is at once breathtaking and funny.

This was a gag that Keaton had devised twice before on a smaller scale. In *Back Stage* (1919), Roscoe Arbuckle is performing in a theatre show. He is standing beside a thin flat painted to look like a building façade and playing a ukulele for a young woman sitting in an open window. Keaton is bumbling around backstage and accidentally knocks out a brace that is holding up the flat. The flat topples down towards Arbuckle, but Arbuckle passes through the open window. In *One Week* (1920), Keaton plays a newlywed working hard to assemble a build-it-yourself house. The front wall, which he has not yet finished securing, suddenly falls forwards towards him, but he passes harmlessly through a window opening, just as Arbuckle had done. These scenes show that Keaton never let go of a good gag and that he was always looking for a way to make gags bigger and better.

Keaton could never surpass the collapsing building scene in *Steamboat Bill, Jr.*, and he knew better than to even try. Keaton comes upon another deserted town in *The Gold Ghost* (1934). The town was long ago abandoned by residents after the resources of the local gold mine were depleted. The buildings are falling apart due to the ravages of time. Keaton stands in front of a building much like he stood in front of the building in *Steamboat Bill, Jr.* The door suddenly tears off its hinges and topples forward, just barely missing him. Keaton fearfully glances up at the building as if afraid that the rest of the structure will come down next. Keaton, as implied by his worried look, was now committed to keeping out of the way of falling buildings. He returned the routine to its safe and rudimentary *Back Stage* origins in a 1950 episode of his television series, where a flat gets loose during a performance of the balcony scene from "Romeo and Juliet."

Keaton was never again able to stage a film on the scale of *Steamboat Bill, Jr.*, but he did have the opportunity to entertain more ambitious ideas working as a gagwriter at MGM from 1938 to 1951. It was through these efforts that he revived the collapsing building gag in large and distinct form for the Marx Brothers' *Go West* (1940). The star of *The General* had been consulted to come up with gags for a train chase planned as the film's climax. He in effect put two of his most iconic gags in a blender and pushed the purée button. A runaway train that has come off its tracks drives straight into a house, but, instead of smashing the house to pieces, the locomotive becomes lodged inside the structure and carries it along in its advance. The house-on-wheels is unstoppable as it steams towards Harpo. Just when it looks as if Harpo will be struck down, the front door of the house swings open and Harpo is able to pass through it safely and emerge again out a back door. The scene at first brings to mind the *One Week* scene where a train crashes into a house, but then it winds up as a wacky, high-speed version of the collapsing building routine. Of course, the collapsing building has now become a hurtling building.

Good luck was not always on the side of the comic hero. At the climax of *The Fuller Brush Man* (1948), Red Skelton is pursued by a gang of criminals through a war surplus warehouse. Skelton climbs atop a row of prefabricated house façades. He pushes forward one façade after another in the expectation that at least one of the heavy slabs will fall on top of the criminals. Each time, though, the criminals safely pass through the doorway and window cut-outs. Skelton jumps down to make a getaway. A façade topples over and the comedian, not as fortunate as the criminals, soon finds himself crushed beneath a solid wall of plywood and plaster.

Others have tried to duplicate the collapsing building stunt over the years. The Goodies, a British comedy team, staged the stunt on their television series in 1975. Jackie Chan, who acknowledges Keaton as his biggest influence, mounted a personal homage to the stunt in *Project A II* (1987). Chan wrote, "I saw Buster Keaton do this in *Steamboat Bill, Jr.*, so of course I had to do it too."[7] The stunt was revived yet again for a 1991 episode of *MacGyver* called "Deadly Silents." MacGyver and silent film star Pinky Burnette (Henry Gibson) are being pursued on a studio lot by armed criminals. MacGyver rigs a building façade to fall. The façade crushes the criminals while MacGyver and Pinky pass safely through a pair of windows. The routine, which is no longer about the force of nature or the mystery of fate, is reduced to nothing more than a MacGyver rope trick. These recreations, in general, lack the formidability of the original. To begin with, the façades are made from more lightweight materials. Even a greater problem, though, is the way in which these scenes are staged. Keaton was careful to build suspense before the wall was dropped. He had audiences expecting the building to crush him and then, through a silly and miraculous twist, he was able to emerge unscathed. But the recreations move at a much faster pace, which diminishes the possibility for suspense or surprise. Also, the human element is missing from the later versions. Keaton not only performed this daring stunt, he stayed in character the entire time, reacting in a way that made him both comical and sympathetic.

In 2006, Johnny Knoxville was injured while trying to accomplish the stunt for *Jackass*

In this gag photograph for *Sherlock Jr.* (1924), Buster Keaton poses as a child to get into a movie theatre at a reduced price. The ticket seller is Ruth Holly (who actually plays a candy store clerk in the film). Other comic characters have posed as children to get into ballparks, amusement parks and movie theatres, to save money. Charley Chase attempted the ruse in *Movie Night* (1929). The plot of Billy Wilder's classic *The Major and the Minor* (1942) is set in motion when Ginger Rogers disguises herself as a 12-year-old girl to pay a reduced price for a train ticket (courtesy Bruce Lawton Collection).

Number 2 (2006). "My head went through the window but my body got smashed," said Knoxville. "If my head had been smashed, it would have killed me."[8] The actor took the blame for the mishap, admitting that he had moved out of place. Review of the film's outtakes shows Knoxville struck by a thin flat painted to look like a saloon front. It was not even close to being as thick and heavy as the actual building front that had come down on Keaton. The "Jackass" team specializes in performing ridiculously dangerous stunts, and yet not even *they* would perform this epic stunt in the same bold way that Keaton had performed it. It is abundantly clear to anyone who reviews the conditions of the original stunt that Keaton had risked his life before the cameras that day. Still, Knoxville's finished take of the gag is well-staged by director Spike Jonze; it even includes a twist ending that would have likely pleased Keaton. Knoxville survives the building collapse only to have a wrecking ball swing into the frame and knock him flat.

Star Wars: The Clone Wars (2008) includes a version of the gag similar to the "MacGyver" version. Ahsoka Tano, a Jedi apprentice, needs to take action when Anakin Skywalker is surrounded by droids. A massive stone wall with a large hole in the middle is behind

Skywalker. Tano uses the Force to cause the wall to topple forward. Skywalker conveniently passes through the hole while the droids around him are crushed.

It is comforting to know that, in a galaxy far, far away, Keaton remains an important inspiration.

Additional notes are in order for the other sensational building gag that served to get the scene started. The effect of the building being torn off its foundation was achieved by attaching a lightweight building front to a cantilever. The same effect was later used for a cyclone scene in the Wheeler and Woosley feature *The Rainmakers* (1935). This time, the effect was staged from the interior of the building. The camera follows Robert Woolsey as he escapes indoors. A surreal spectacle ensues as the structure breaks loose from its foundation and the walls soundlessly disappear around the unsuspecting refugee.

This jettisoned-covering gag also appeared in lesser form, minus cantilever and wind, in an indeterminable number of films that preceded *Steamboat Bill, Jr.* One example is featured during a camping scene in the Snub Pollard comedy *California or Bust* (1923). Pollard accidentally gets his car hitched to a tent and, when he drives off, he yanks up the tent and exposes Jimmy Finlayson bathing in a wash tub.

No Spilling

In *When Spirits Move* (1920), Hank Mann is so amused by chorus girls performing high kicks that he bursts out in applause. But then a dancer, preoccupied by her routine, abruptly kicks a teacup out of Mann's hand. The good-natured comedian is not at all bothered. He playfully holds out a plate to see if the dancer will kick it out of his hand, but she instead kicks him squarely in the face. Slapstick comedy, after all, is largely about mayhem and injury.

Lloyd Hamilton has a different experience with high-kicking chorus girls and dishware while working as a waiter in *Waiting* (1925). Hamilton, on his way to deliver a plate of food, has to cross the dance floor upon which chorus girls are performing high kicks. Hamilton's tray is repeatedly kicked by dancers. Each time, the plates on the tray leap into the air and then fall back down, perfectly in place. It is as if the plates are being protected by a divine force willing to intervene on Hamilton's behalf. In place of mayhem and injury is order and security.

Restaurant comedies are distinguished by broken plates, scorched hands and food stains. Order is not usually to be found. Comedians realize, though, that getting an audience to laugh often involves playing against their expectations and finding various ways to trick them. A slapstick waiter may be expected to be surrounded by broken plates, but it is possible to give an audience something unexpected.

Keaton, working as a waiter in *College* (1927), gets slammed by a swinging door while on his way to deliver a cup of coffee. Amazingly, he does a complete backward somersault without spilling the coffee. This stunt was derived from a Commedia dell'Arte routine called "Lazzi of Spilling No Wine," which originated in Paris in 1717.

Earlier, Keaton had provided a more fanciful version of this routine while playing a waiter in *The Cook* (1918). Roscoe Arbuckle, a short-order cook, expresses delight in tossing around plates and knives while preparing meals. Arbuckle, told by Keaton that a customer wants coffee, tosses a steaming cup of coffee across the room. Keaton, miraculously, catches the cup on a saucer without spilling a drop. He even flips the cup in the air and catches it again without losing coffee. It is an impossible action achieved by clever camera effects that were not at the disposal of Commedia dell'Arte performers. Harold Lloyd created a similar special effect gag in *On the Fire*— he flips a number of pancakes across the room and each one lands perfectly on the waiter's plate. The gag was stretched to more absurd lengths in a low-budget clone of *The Cook* called *The Chef* (1921). When the customer complains that his pancakes are undercooked, the waiter flips the pancakes over his shoulder with sufficient force and accuracy to cause the pancakes to shoot across the restaurant, pass through the doorway of the kitchen, and land directly into a frying pan. After letting the pancakes sit in the pan for a few moments, the chef (Billy Franey) tosses them out of the kitchen and the pancakes land back on their original plate, at which point they are proudly served to the customer.

In the Three Stooges comedy *Yes, We Have No Bonanza* (1939), Curly hurls mugs filled with beer across the barroom to Larry. In the end, he fails dismally in the "no spilling" aspect of the routine.

CGI allowed a man to effortlessly juggle mugs of beer in a recent Heineken television commercial ("Men with Talent," 2010).

The Track Switch Gag

Harold Lloyd is determined to kill himself in *Haunted Spooks* (1920). He steps in front of an oncoming trolley car but, at the last possible moment, the trolley car switches tracks and avoids him entirely.

This scene was played out before by André Deed in *Le Suicide de Boireau* (1909) and Marcel Perez in *Bungles Lands a Job* (1916), but it was the popularity of Lloyd's rendition that led to a spate of like routines. Keaton took this gag, enlarged it, and added a second twist for the purposes of *One Week* (1920), which was released little more than five months after *Haunted Spooks*. Keaton, a newlywed, finds that building a do-it-yourself home is an ordeal. When he finally gets the house built, he learns that he has set it up on the wrong lot and has to move it. Keaton is hauling the house across railroad tracks when it becomes stuck in the path of an oncoming train. Keaton and his wife stand out of the way, fully braced for the collision, but the train switches tracks and misses the home. The couple is expressing their relief when another train comes from the opposite direction and smashes through the home. Keaton later explained, "I always wanted an audience to out-guess me and then I double-cross them."[9]

Larry Semon indulged in a number of gags having to do with near-misses. In *The Bakery* (1921), Semon and a villain are sitting at the opposite ends of a ladder teetering on a fence. At one point, Semon is lowered directly onto the path of a speeding truck. Just as the truck is about to strike, the ladder rises up and delivers Semon out of harm's way. But this reprieve from danger is brief. Later in the film, Semon gets cake frosting in his eyes, which prevents him from seeing he is walking towards an open shaft of a sidewalk elevator. He is just about to take a tumble into the shaft when the elevator rises up and allows him to safely walk across. Under the circumstances, the track-switch gag was the type of nifty near-miss trick that Semon could not resist trying himself.

Semon liked to do everything big. This is evident in the details of a simple clerk-in-a-dress-shop comedy entitled *The Gown Shop* (1923). Semon is unable to do ladder stunts unless he uses a 20-foot ladder. He cannot have Oliver Hardy sit on an iron and burn his backside without the iron blasting enough steam to fill the room. And, yet, his adaptation of track-switch gag from *One Week* was not big at all. Semon chose to reduce the gag in scale by substituting the home (as the central prop) with a two-foot-tall Grecian statue. The scene, from *The Suitor* (1920), starts out in a mansion. Semon bumps into the statue, which causes it to wobble on its pedestal as if it is about to fall. Semon runs around to catch it, but the statue suddenly changes direction, and Semon has to rush to the other side to catch it. Semon is cradling the statue in his arms when he gets bumped out of the door. He stumbles down a flight of stairs and winds up in the street directly in front of an oncoming trolley car. The trolley car switches tracks and misses him. He rests the statue down at his side, at which time a car abruptly speeds into the frame from the opposite direction and smashes the statue to pieces. This scene comes across as a trifle compared to the *One Week* scene.

The following month, Keaton revived the gag in its original form for *Hard Luck* (1921). It is nearly identical to the scene in *Haunted Spooks*, complete with the suicide attempt, the trolley car and the abrupt track switch. Semon, who was not through with this gag either, provided different versions of the routine in *The Bakery* (1921), *The Bell Hop* (1921) and *The Show* (1922). In *The Bell Hop*, Semon rushes to rescue a little girl sitting in a baby carriage on a trolley car track. He is too busy checking to see if the girl is all right to notice that a trolley car is rushing towards them. The endangerment of the child makes this scene more cliffhanger than comedy.

Semon devised a separate scene in *The Show* wherein he introduces a house in transit much like the house in transit featured in *One Week*. The house is being hauled across railroad tracks when the trailer becomes unhitched from the tow truck. A train comes barreling down the track and bursts through the home, shattering it to pieces. This scene, compared to the *One Week* scene, is vacuous — and not only because it lacks a funny twist; it also lacks the misfortune and poignancy. The *One Week* house had been put together with great care and effort by hopeful newlyweds. The house in *The Show* was simply a big prop that Semon randomly introduced into the action for the sole purpose of smashing it to pieces.

Roscoe Arbuckle recycled the routine yet again when he wrote and directed the Lupino Lane comedy *Fool's Luck* (1926). Arbuckle succeeds in effectively staging the crash, but the scene lacks the right twist to make the revival of the well-worn routine worthwhile. That same year, the routine was also performed by Raymond McKee in *Love's Last Laugh* (1926).

The following decade, Keaton scaled down his props for his sound features at MGM. The track-switch gag was remade with an automobile in place of a house in *Parlor, Bedroom and Bath* (1932). The eight-foot boulders that pursued Keaton down a hill in *Seven Chances* (1925) were replaced with ordinary barrels in *What! No Beer?* (1933). The new routine resembled a scene in the 1907 Gaumont comedy *La Course aux potirons* (released in America as *The Pumpkin Race*), wherein enormous pumpkins fall out of the back of a cart and roll down the street. The amok pumpkins travel far and wide, causing a variety of disturbances. Anything that could roll down a hill could be used in place of boulders. Keaton was working as a gag writer on *A Southern Yankee* (1948) when he came up with the idea of having the film's star, Red Skelton, chased down a hill by a big spiked wheel presumably used to harvest cotton.

Bridezillas

In *Seven Chances* (1925), Keaton stands to inherit $7 million from his grandfather's will if he marries by 7:00 P.M. on his 27th birthday. He has just a matter of hours because it so happens, *today* is his 27th birthday. The plot was hardly unique.

The plot turned up at first in *Personal* (1904), a comedy produced by American Mutoscope & Biograph. A man places a personal ad to express his interest in meeting a prospective wife. He designates a place and time for those women willing to meet with him. The man is overwhelmed when he finds himself mobbed by women who have arrived in response to the ad. He sees no choice but to flee. The man is pursued aggressively by his suitors, who overcome a series of obstacles in their effort to catch him. This film proved to be so popular that Biograph's rivals got to work immediately to duplicate the film. Lubin remade the film as *Meet Me at the Fountain* (1904). Pathé remade the film in 1905 as *Dix Femmes pour un mari* (released in the United States as *Ten Women for a Husband*). The Spanish company Luis Macaya y Alberto Marro remade the film, also in 1905, as *Los guapos del parque*, or *The Ladies' Man in the Park*.

The producers of *Personal* were the most upset that a remake was made by the Edison Company, which had become aggressive in their habit of replicating American Mutoscope & Biograph's successes. Edison did not wait long to produce a scene-by-scene recreation of *Personal*, entitled *How a French Nobleman Got a Wife Through the New York Herald Personals Column* (1905). Biograph sued Edison the following year, but it was difficult at the time to establish authorship and proprietorship in reference to a motion picture. The lack of complexity in the storytelling made it difficult to justify copyright protection for early films. As far as a judge was concerned, *Personal* was a simple chase film, a genre which was hardly in short supply. It would take several years and several lawsuits to clearly define the law when it came to protecting motion picture copyrights and judges were, in the interim, lenient in the defendant's favor when it came to determining if their actions went far enough to infringe a copyright.

A subplot concerning a will was added to the plot with *He Must Have a Wife* (1912), a Biograph comedy directed by Mack Sennett. Gus Pixley is informed that, as the condition of his uncle's will, he has a scant few hours to find a wife to gain his uncle's fortune.

Lloyd Hamilton attracted a bunch of women after taking a love potion in *Ham and the Experiment* (1915). Other "love potion" comedies during this era included *Love Drops* (1910), *The Love Potion* (1911), *Liquid Love* (1913) and *The Love Dope* (1917). Hamilton was chased by even more women after taking possession of a love magnet in a comedy appropriately titled *The Love Magnet* (1916).* A shot in which the women are shown climbing over a fence is directly copied from *Personals*. Love potions were a comic staple, but nothing was a greater love potion than money. This was to become a major point of *Seven Chances*.

Seven Chances, a play written by Roi Cooper Megrue, opened on Broadway at the George M. Cohan Theatre on August 8, 1916, and ran for 151 performances. The plot centered on a confirmed bachelor named Jimmie Shannon (Frank Craven) who is forced to marry in haste by an unorthodox stipulation in his grandfather's will.

The *New York Times* called the play "a severe disappointment."[10] Critics, in general, found this farce to be unoriginal and obvious. Drama critic George Jean Nathan complained that he was bored of short stories and plays that centered on a marital stipulation in a will. He surmised that the trend started with an 1896 play by Charles Hale Hoyt called *A Black Sheep*.

The play was, no doubt, the inspiration for the two-reel comedy *What! No Spinach?* (1920). A self-avowed woman-hater (played by Harry Sweet) is distressed when his lawyer arrives at his flat to tell him that he needs to marry immediately in order that he may obtain

---

*L. Frank Baum introduced a "Love Magnet" in his 1909 book *The Road to Oz*.

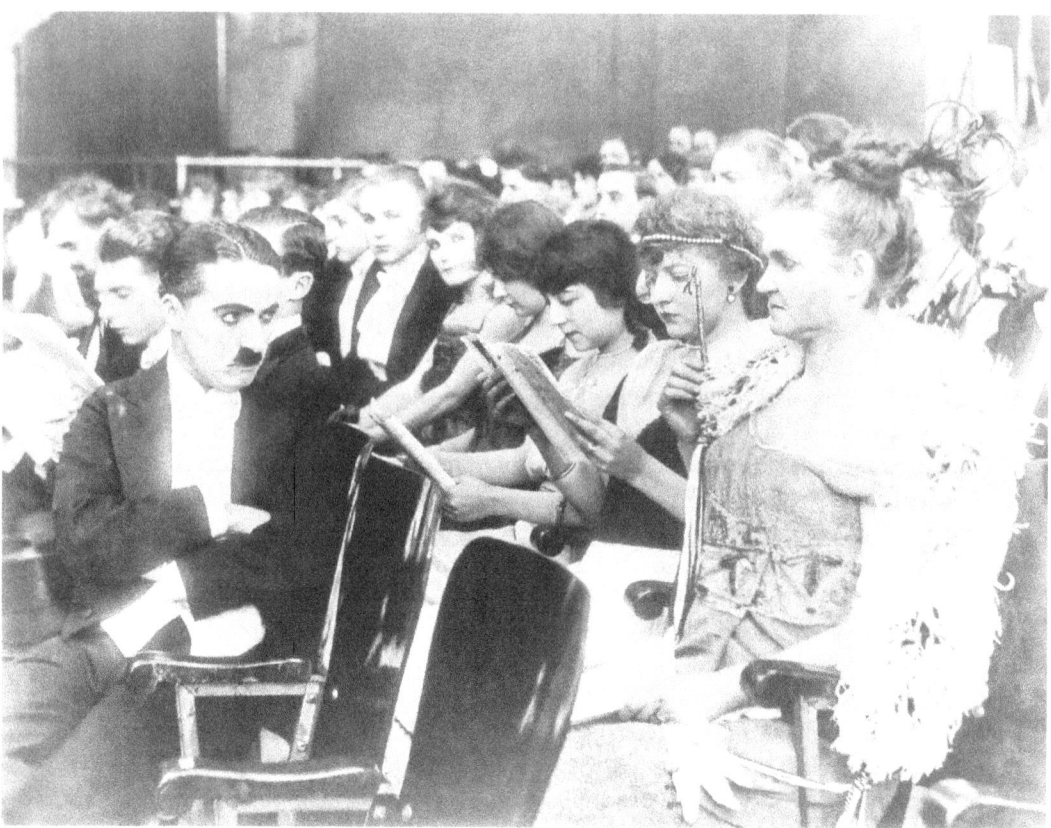

Charlie Chaplin plays Mr. Pest in *A Night in the Show* (1915) Audience members are unidentified (courtesy www.doctormacro.com).

his uncle's inheritance. His landlady (Gale Henry) overhears the conversation and becomes determined to use her broom to stave off any other woman who tries to get near Sweet. Henry's efforts fail, though, which leaves Sweet fleeing from a mob of brides.

Seven Chances had the same format as the ABC television series *The Bachelor*. In the play, Shannon's friends round up seven eligible brides at the country club. Shannon arrives to introduce himself to the ladies, make acquaintances, and offer proposals of marriage. The seven ladies are his "seven chances." Keaton did without most of the country club farce in favor of gag sequences and an epic *Personal*-inspired closing chase.

Three obvious changes in the play were made for the film: the lead character's age was changed from 30 to 27; the amount of the inheritance was changed from $12 million to $7 million; and the deadline was changed from midnight to 7:00 P.M. These changes, though they may seem to relate to numerological superstitions, were more likely put into effect as simple plot devices. In the play, Shannon manages through sheer personal will to reach the age of 30 without marrying. At this point in history, a strong social stigma was attached to someone being unmarried by that age. Keaton's Shannon is not at all a confirmed bachelor. He is in love with a woman who has repeatedly put him off about getting married. It is not a case of him being unmarried because he is noncommittal and unromantic. Quite the opposite: he is not married because he is devoted to this woman and holds an undying affection for her. The inheritance sways him from his affections only because he desperately needs money to save his brokerage firm, which is on the brink of bankruptcy. The time change was obviously designed to avoid staging the climactic chase in the dark. Making the time specifically 7:00 P.M., along with making the inheritance $7 million dollars, was, in all probability, meant to make the number seven prominent in a movie called *Seven Chances*.

Just as Keaton had once expanded a small group of cops to hundreds, he now expanded a small group of women to hundreds. Minor obstacles, including climbing over a low fence, now became major obstacles. The potential brides hijack a trolley, ford a stream, get attacked by bees after disturbing a beekeeper's hives, and get caught in an avalanche of boulders.

The premise was later minimized with the Three Stooges comedy *Brideless Groom* (1947), which was written by former Keaton writer Clyde Bruckman. Shemp is in line to inherit a half-million dollars, which was a considerable drop from the $12 million inheritance from the 1916 stage play. It could be that the Stooges' cut-rate producers felt obligated to cut the rates noted in their scripts. As the story progresses, the local newspaper publishes a story about the inheritance, and all of the women who rejected his earlier proposals have come looking for him. Shemp prepares to marry a homely woman who had a crush on him before he became eligible for the inheritance. This low-budget film has no chase scene. The

Buster Keaton (center) seated with his team of writers: (from left to right) Joe Mitchell, Clyde Bruckman, Jean Havez and Eddie Cline (courtesy www.doctormacro.com).

Justice of the Peace (Emil "Hold Hands, You Lovebirds" Sitka) is prepared to conduct the marriage ceremony when his home is besieged by six women, each one demanding that Shemp marry her. The women get progressively more violent. They kick, batter, and pull hair. One woman smashes a birdcage over the head of the Justice of the Peace. Another woman squeezes Shemp's head under a press. The Stooges were, after all, about close physical comedy and had no need for a big chase. Their style of comedy was Intimate Partner Slapstick. This climax bears a strong resemblance to the climax of another Buster Keaton comedy, *Three on a Limb* (1936).

In *Le Soupirant* (1962), Pierre Étaix is under pressure from his mother to marry. The first half of the film is essentially a reprise of Keaton's mishap-filled bride search from *Seven Chances*, but, while Étaix retains the premise of the Keaton routine (and even adheres to Keaton's style and manner), the gags are designed in a fresh way and the misunderstandings are entirely Étaix's own. In *Seven Chances*, Keaton has trouble finding the right woman, or at least a *real* woman. This becomes apparent when he mistakes a mannequin for a woman in a barber shop. Other misunderstandings follow in rapid succession. Keaton strikes up a lively conversation with a woman only to find out that she doesn't speak English. He draws near a shapely woman walking ahead of him and, when the woman stops and turns around, he is startled to see that she is black. He meets an elegantly attired young woman at a country club and is escorting her to his automobile, when an older woman rushes up to them in alarm. She yanks off the younger woman's coat and hat, revealing her in her true underage trappings — pigtails, Mary Jane shoes, and a frilly party dress. The girl stamps her feet in bratty protest before being dragged away. Étaix, too, has misunderstandings. He sees a long-tressed blonde sitting with her back to him in a parked car. When he attempts to greet her, he finds that the "blonde" is actually an Irish setter. Étaix sees how easily a man is able to start a conversation with a woman by offering her a compliment about her dog. Étaix is walking through a park when he looks beyond a row of bushes and sees a pretty woman walking past with a leash in hand. He rushes over to the woman, ready to feed a biscuit to her dog, but, when he gets to the other side of the bushes, he finds attached to the other end of the leash a blankly staring toddler. His presumed miss is, in fact, a missus.

Seven Chances was remade as *The Bachelor* (1999). Chris O'Donnell stars as a confirmed bachelor much like the character from the original stage play. He describes himself as a wild mustang, free to run the open plains. *The Bachelor*, a bland romantic comedy, did not try to recreate Keaton's epic rock slide or much else that made the film version special. Lisa Schwarzbaum, *Entertainment Weekly* film critic, called the film "a strained remake of Buster Keaton's effortlessly delightful ... comedy...."[11]

Adam Rifkin was under the inspiration of *Seven Chances* when he had a tribe of cavewomen chase him across dusty plains in *National Lampoon's Stoned Age* (2008). "To me," said Rifkin, "Keaton is the pioneer of the action comedy.... Keaton movies are really exciting, really innovative and really funny.... *Seven Chances*, with the rocks and the hundreds of brides chasing him — it's unbelievable, that stuff, it's huge."[12]

A risqué variation on this scene appeared in *Monty Python's The Meaning of Life* (1983), showing Graham Chapman being chased off a cliff by a horde of topless women wearing crash helmets and G-strings. A commercial produced for a British eyewear company, Spec-Savers, surpassed prior versions with the number of bikini-clad beauties in pursuit ("The Specs Effect," 2010). The commercial was a cheat, though, as most of the women were created by CGI.

Helping an Unconscious Woman Get Home

In *The Strong Man* (1926), Harry Langdon finds himself in the awkward situation of having to carry a seemingly unconscious woman (Gertrude Astor) up a long flight of stairs. Astor is pretending to have fainted so that Langdon will be forced to take her to her apartment, where she intends to retrieve a roll of money hidden in his jacket. Harry is overwhelmed by the weight of the woman, who is larger than he is, and is unable to see where he is going. Harry props the woman up against a banister so that he can remove a bucket that has gotten stuck on his foot, but the woman goes sliding down the banister at a rapid speed and ends up sprawled out at the bottom of the staircase. Harry, not seeing her right away, is bewildered as he tries to figure out how he could have lost the woman. He finally sees her and scrambles down the steps after her. His legs tired, he sits down on the stairs, rests the woman in his lap, and ascends the stairs by raising his backside up from one step to the next. He is unaware that he has reached the landing and continues to scoot backwards up a ladder. He comes to the top of the ladder, falls back, and topples headfirst to the floor.

Frank Capra, the director of *The Strong Man*, went on to stage a truncated version of this routine with Frank Sinatra and Carolyn Jones for *A Hole in the Head* (1959). The new scene is absent the tension that made the original scene engrossing. The staircase, at a significantly shortened length, poses no overwhelming challenge to Sinatra. Sinatra, by having this shapely young lady harmlessly cozied up in his lap, looks to be in a position that is nothing short of enviable. Capra even went as far as to replace the ladder with a step stool, which entirely eliminates the threat of the scene's climactic gag.

Keaton found himself in much the same predicament as Langdon in *Spite Marriage* (1929). Keaton expects to have a fun night out at a nightclub with his new wife (Dorothy Sebastian), but Sebastian gets wildly drunk and makes a spectacle of herself. The doting husband struggles to get his bride under control as he gets her into her coat and escorts her out of the club. He is dragging her up a staircase when she falls backward and causes the two of them to tumble together down the steps. Sebastian has passed out by the time that Keaton has gotten her back to their hotel room. Keaton is not having trouble with the woman's weight, which was Langdon's problem; it is the ungainliness of this limp lady that is causing him problems. No matter how hard he tries, he cannot keep a firm grip on her, and she keeps slipping out of his arms. At one point, Keaton has her standing up and goes to shut the door, but she collapses at his feet and he ends up tripping over her. His next task is to lift her off the floor to get her into bed. Keaton, more resourceful than Langdon, uses a chair as a dolly to hoist her off the floor. It isn't long, however, before she spills out of the chair and is back in a heap on the floor. Keaton finally hauls her up onto the bed. She momentarily rouses from her slumber and grabs onto him before she topples over the side of the bed, taking him along with her.

Lupino Lane affected a role-reversal when he reworked the routine for *Naughty Boy* (1927). It is Lane who is unconscious, and it is a *woman*, an Amazon-sized stepmother played by Blanche Payson, who carries him up the flight of stairs. Payson finds Lane to be heavier than she expected, and she stops at the top of the stairs to catch her breath. She props up Lane in a chair, but he slumps forward and tumbles down the staircase. The routine works well for Lane, who proves he can be funnier unconscious than most comedians can be wide awake. He performs the scene in much the same way that Terry Kiser did when he played a dead man being carted through the Hamptons in *Weekend at Bernie's* (1989).

In *Love 'Em and Weep* (1927), Jimmy Finlayson is in a fix when an old flame (Mae

Busch) shows up at his home threatening to tell his wife about their torrid relationship. Finlayson demands that Busch leave, but she is hysterical and refuses to cooperate. Finlayson, hoping to scare her away, pulls out a gun and threatens to kill himself. The sight of the gun terrifies the woman, who instantly faints. Finlayson, in a panic, calls upon a faithful employee (Stan Laurel) to help him to sneak the unconscious woman past dinner guests and take her home. The two men repeatedly slip and fall as they try to carry her out into the hallway. Laurel fails, in repeated attempts, to prop Busch up against a wall. No matter how many times he tries, she keeps falling forward, and he has to catch her before she falls flat on her face. Laurel has even greater problems when he tries to get Busch into her mink coat. He starts out mistakenly putting the coat on Finlayson and then he gets his own arm stuck in a sleeve. It is at this point that Finlayson initiates a desperate plan to get the woman out of the house without arousing attention. The men proceed down the hall, with Finlayson hidden under the coat, supporting Busch on his back, and Laurel, walking alongside them, holding the limp woman upright and steady as though she is nothing more than a guest, casually departing the premises with her escort.

The scene expresses an easily recognizable comic tension as the duo has to carry off their unconscious woman without anyone — especially Finlayson's wife — figuring out what they're doing. The scenes with Keaton and Langdon are darker and have a tension which is harder to identify. The humor of the *Spite Marriage* routine is, in fact, better realized when the scene is released from its moorings, as melancholic as they are, and presented in excerpt form. After all, no humor can be found in a newlywed groom having to act as a caretaker to his loveless bride because she feels too disgusted with the marriage to stay sober on their honeymoon. It is disturbing, too, for Langdon to be in the clutches of a cruel criminal, willing to stab him to death to recover her money.

Langdon's childish befuddlement and Keaton's dogged methodicalness may be more intriguing than Laurel's absolute panic. But panic has its place in comedy and this is something that Laurel knew how to play well. The other actors in the scene are in top form as well. The normally fiery Busch is game about being thrown against the wall and dropped on the floor. Seeing the outraged, squinty-eyed Finlayson bent up under Busch's coat brings to mind a crab tucked away in its shell. The scene also provides a rich assortment of gags. This action, when all is said and done, is just plain funny. Streamlined versions of the routine that focused solely on the outrageous disguise turned up in two Laurel & Hardy comedies: *Sugar Daddies* (1927) and *Chickens Come Home* (1931). *Sugar Daddies* featured Laurel fully conscious and in drag carried atop Finlayson's shoulders.

The *Spite Marriage* routine was recreated by Red Skelton and Eleanor Powell for a 1943 remake of *Spite Marriage* called *I Dood It*. The scene closely follows the choreography of the original scene with one small exception. For Keaton, the awkwardness of the scene came from the fact that he was handling a living, breathing woman, his beloved bride no less, and he couldn't bang her around like a sack of potatoes he was carrying into the pantry. Keaton made a point throughout the scene's boisterous action to treat Sebastian in a sensitive manner even though he had no real way to avoid dropping her, dragging her and tossing her around. Skelton understood this point well and he emphasized it by taking a moment to plant a small kiss on Powell's forehead.

Pierre Étaix has his own problems with an unconscious woman in *Le Soupirant* (1962). Étaix masterfully combines key elements of both the Langdon and Keaton routines. The Keaton elements are more obvious. Étaix, bringing a drunken woman home from a nightclub, struggles to control her gangly limbs and cope with her unwieldy dead weight. In a gag directly out of *Spite Marriage*, the woman drops to the floor and Étaix trips over her. But Étaix is not trying to put this woman to bed. Like Langdon, he has the chore of trying to get a woman much larger than himself upstairs to her apartment. Étaix has an advantage that he has access to an elevator, and yet this provides surprisingly little help. He props up the woman in the elevator so that his hands are free to unlock the door to her apartment. He is unaware that, while he is finally getting the door open, the elevator has been summoned to the floor below: it descends without warning with the woman still inside. Just like Langdon, Étaix has lost the woman and has to scramble down the stairs to retrieve her.

Other leading men were able to carry off an unconscious women with little exertion. William Powell simply has Carole Lombard slung over his shoulder as he makes his way up a staircase in *My Man Godfrey* (1936). This became a stock routine in romantic comedies — the woman gets drunk and passes out and her he-man of a lover carries her home in unmitigated caveman style. A passel of examples can be provided. Take, for a start, George Peppard carrying Audrey Hepburn in *Breakfast at Tiffany's* (1961), or Rock Hudson carrying Leslie Caron in *A Very Special Favor* (1965), or Peter Sellers carrying Goldie Hawn in *There's a Girl in My Soup* (1970), or Harrison Ford carrying Melanie Griffith in *Working Girl* (1988). Gregory Peck shows how smoothly the job could be done when — using nothing more than a guiding hand, a commanding voice and an arch smile — he gets a drunken Audrey Hepburn home and safely into bed in *Roman Holiday* (1953). Poor Harry Langdon. The fact that he lacked the brute force of Hudson or the command of Peck meant that he was bound to have problems in this situation.

The routine is last known to have been performed by Lucille Ball and Gale Gordon on *The Lucy Show* ("Lucy and the Ring-a-Ding Ring," 1966). Ball becomes unconscious through newer means — Valium (introduced in 1963). The unconscious woman was mostly used as a prop by Langdon and Keaton, but Ball shifts the attention to herself by making goofy faces to the camera and working her spindly legs to alternately wobble, drag and crumble. Kiser later employed essentially the same strategy in *Weekend at Bernie's*, but he played the part more loosely and never forced his actions in the way that Ball does. Ball came from a school of comedy that promoted split-a-seam pratfalls and head-banging missteps. She possesses too much of a make-'em-laugh ethos to keep herself limp. Kiser's laid-back charm proved in the end to be more effective than Ball's overactive monkeyshines.

Unveiling a Statue

In *The Goat* (1921), the mayor unveils a statue of champion thoroughbred Man O' War and discovers Buster Keaton sitting atop the statue, posing as a proud rider. Spectators accept Keaton as a clay jockey until the clay horse buckles under his weight. The unveiling of a statue in *City Lights* (1931) reveals Charlie Chaplin cradled like a child in the ample lap of a giant stone woman. Chaplin is climbing down from the statue when a sword upraised by a warrior figure slips up the back of his jacket. Chaplin struggles to free himself, but he remains caught on the sword. These routines include all of the same elements — a man is exposed atop a statue during an unveiling; the man has humorously incorporated himself into the statue's design; and the man is ultimately thwarted by the statue itself. Chaplin, who comes across as a peculiar baby, provides the more elaborate and funnier version of the routine.

The One-Man Baseball Game

Frank "Slivers" Oakley, the star clown of the Barnum & Bailey circus from 1899 to 1907, was excellent at both acrobatics and pantomime. One moment, he could be thrilling an audience by jumping on a springboard and vaulting over four elephants. The next moment, he could be making an audience laugh by performing a one-man baseball game. The clown was able to apply his exceptional pantomime skills to act out every position on both teams. Keaton, who was a great admirer of Oakley, staged a memorable recreation of Oakley's baseball routine at Yankee Stadium for *The Cameraman* (1928). Unfortunately, a comparison of Keaton and Oakley's efforts are not possible as Oakley was never recorded on film performing the baseball routine.

Gone Fishing

No comedian devised more fishing routines than Buster Keaton. He fishes off the side of a floating naval target in *The Love Nest* (1923). He feeds jumping beans to fish in *The Timid Young Man* (1935). He battles a fish that has swallowed his golf ball in *Convict 13* (1920). But his most memorable fishing routine occurs in *Hard Luck* (1921). This is where he catches progressively bigger fish by using each one he catches as bait for the next. It is

Buster Keaton extended his fondness for trick photography to the design of publicity stills (courtesy Bruce Lawton Collection).

while struggling to haul in a particularly hefty fish that Keaton gets dragged into the river himself. This routine was so perfectly designed that it was reworked (with little variation) by Lou Costello in *The Naughty Nineties* (1945).

Buster Keaton was indeed an innovator and a remarkable physical comedian. These are but two of the reasons that The Great Stoneface has left a century of viewers laughing.

18

The Harold Lloyd Variations

In his essay "Lloyd vs. Keaton," film historian David B. Pearson cited 19 instances when a routine was used at one time or another by both Buster Keaton and Harold Lloyd. Pearson wrote, "Back in *Girl Shy*, the brakes on a Model-T Harold Lloyd is cranking slip, and the car goes crashing into a gully, totally destroyed. Harold looks at the crank still in his hands, shrugs, and tosses it away. A similar thing happens to Keaton while racing along in *The General*. Early in the picture, Buster's hand car derails and crashes into a gully, totally wrecked. Buster gets up, looks at the ruined car, then at the handcart handle still in his hands, shrugs, and tosses it away."[1] In *High and Dizzy* (1920), Harold Lloyd throws a horseshoe over his shoulder for good luck but manages in the process to hit a police officer in the face. Keaton does the same gag without variation in *The Goat* (1921). Pearson wrote, "In *The Three Ages*, Buster finds that the girl he loves is about to marry a bigamist, so goes to the wedding and steals the bride. Lloyd's *Girl Shy*, made a few months later, has an identical climactic plot."[2] Others commonalities could be added to Pearson's list. For instance, Lloyd hides inside a doghouse only to be bitten and chased off by a dog inside in *Among Those Present* (1921). Keaton, tossed around by a cyclone, is swept into a doghouse and comes out grabbing the seat of his pants in *Steamboat Bill, Jr.* (1928). Lloyd uses his tie as a fake moustache in *Hey There!* (1918). Keaton does the same in *Cops* (1922). In most of these instances, it was Lloyd who preceded Keaton with gag ideas.

Many original ideas can be found in Lloyd's work. He is known to have inspired more than his share of big trends, including thrill comedies and sports comedies, but he probably deserves credit for even more than that. This is evident just from looking at one of his lesser-known films, *From Hand to Mouth* (1919). In this two-reeler, Lloyd plays a kindhearted tramp who adopts a poor little waif (Peggy Cartwright). The two of them scheme together to get food to eat. This film was released more than a year before Chaplin's tramp character appeared on theatre screens caring for his own adopted waif in *The Kid* (1921). At the climax of *From Hand to Mouth*, a gang of criminals kidnap a young woman and drive off with her in a speeding car. Lloyd, against all odds, initiates pursuit on a bicycle. This situation recurred many times with other comic heroes, including Larry Semon and Lupino Lane. Many of Lloyd's films can be combed for novel ideas, both big and small.

Lloyd's go-getter character had things to do, places to be, and people to impress. This gave a tension and excitement to his films that made the gags and routines even funnier and more engaging. In *Number, Please?* (1920), Lloyd is competing with a rival (Roy Brooks) to take Mildred Davis for a ride in a hot-air balloon. Davis explains that she cannot go without her mother's permission. She then states that whichever boy gets her mother's permission first will be the one who can take her on the ride. Brooks immediately speeds off in his car. Lloyd does not have a car, but he figures he can make contact with the mother sooner by calling her on the phone. He rushes inside a hotel lobby and finds that all their phone booths are occupied. One person no sooner leaves a booth than someone else slips past Lloyd to take their place. Billy West replicated the routine in *Line's Busy* (1924), except he neglected to give his character an urgent need to make his call, and the lack of tension in the scene rendered the character's frantic efforts meaningless and unfunny.

The urgency was even greater when Chaplin performed an earlier version of the routine in *A Dog's Life* (1918). Chaplin, a starving tramp, is desperate to claim a job at an unemployment office. He sits at the edge of his seat and, every time a job is announced, he leaps up and rushes to the clerk's window. But, no matter how fast he moves, another job seeker manages to slip ahead of him just in time to claim the job for himself.

Chaplin was meticulous in working out the timing and choreography of this comic dance. Enjoyment of the scene can come out of pure appreciation of the skill used to coordinate the action. But the emotional content of the scene is important, too. The audience has to be rooting for Chaplin to eventually get a job, even if the pattern of events has come to diminish their hopes. The scene has the sort of suspense that gets a baby giggling in a game of peek-a-boo. The repetitiveness of the action creates a predictability, and yet the actors' sharply timed actions still manage to elicit laughs out of viewers.

Lloyd makes the fancy footwork merely the starting point for his routine in *Number, Please?*. He goes on to introduce a variety of gags, situations and characters before the routine is through. Chaplin only had to contend with fellow job applicants, but Lloyd has to contend with a number of different characters, including a testy midget, a crying baby, a sassy telephone operator, and a distractingly beautiful woman carrying a tall stack of parcels.

Lloyd was a classic go-getter who refused to give up and his fans *knew* that he was bound to find a way to make his phone call. The fun comes from watching him work his way through the obstacles. This is in stark contrast to Chaplin's tragic character, who is unlikely to succeed. His experience in the unemployment office does, in fact, not end well. The other job applicants have taken jobs and made their way out of the office. A clerk notifies Chaplin that the office is closing for the day. Chaplin stands alone in the office looking forlorn.

The one flaw in this analysis is that, despite Lloyd's persistence and resourcefulness, his ultimate fate in *Number, Please?* is less a reflection of Lloyd's characteristic optimism and more a reflection of Chaplin's tragic sense. Lloyd does finally get to make his call, but he has failed to reach the girl's mother in time to beat out his rival. His cause is surely lost by now, but Lloyd still refuses to give up. He rushes off to meet up with the girl, desperately hoping to win this date with her after all. On the way, he becomes mixed up with a pickpocket fleeing from the police. The pickpocket slips a stolen purse into Lloyd's pocket, which soon gets Lloyd in trouble. (Proving how often these comedians traded routines back and forth, Chaplin came to reuse this routine in his 1928 feature *The Circus*.) Lloyd, having been plagued by problems, has to concede defeat in the end. The final fade-out is preceded by a title card that reads, "A lone wanderer roams the world facing the drab dawn of a dead tomorrow." Chaplin's films may have traded in pathos, but they never ended with a message as hopeless as this one.

Also in *Number, Please?*, Lloyd is distressed to see his body distorted in a funhouse mirror. With every move, the entire shape of his body changes. First, his forehead is stretched

Harold Lloyd and Ann Christy look at themselves in a funhouse mirror in *Speedy* (1928) (courtesy Robert Arkus).

to inhuman proportions, then his neck raises up high above his shoulders, then his body is squashed into a dwarf-like build and, finally, his legs grow as tall as stilts. Lloyd is relieved to step away from the mirror and see that his body has, in fact, retained its normal shape. Lloyd, who is often preoccupied with self-image, glances around as if he is worried that people spied him in his distorted states. In *Moony Mariner* (1927), Billy Dooley giggles like a small boy when he faces himself in a funhouse mirror and sees his normally tall and lanky legs stretched to an even more exaggerated length. The fact that he has nothing at stake makes this a hollow experience. He looks into a funhouse mirror, sees funny images, and he laughs. That is exactly what is supposed to happen when a person looks into a funhouse mirror. Lloyd, through the strength of his "Glass Character," gave this simple experience depth and substance.

Number, Please? provides a steady succession of strong routines. Others may have been able to forage the film for ideas, but it was hardly guaranteed that they could make this material as funny as Lloyd had. In the film's climax, Lloyd needs to get past police officers without being recognized. He hides inside a roomy overcoat while a small boy (Ernie "Sunshine Sammy" Morrison) sits on his shoulders and sticks his head out through the top of the coat. The wily lad acts confidently while posing as an adult to the police. His confidence makes him convincing even though something about him is highly suspicious. Stan Laurel copied this routine in *White Wings* (1923), except that he used an infant in place of a small boy. The uncomprehending infant cannot provide a convincing performance for the police, and his blankly staring face on top of this great big body is not so much funny as it is oddly disturbing. As the scene ends in *Number, Please?*, Lloyd and Morrison have their ruse exposed when they run into a store awning and Morrison is left behind, hanging perilously off the awning. Lloyd briefly presses on, unaware that he has lost his "head."

This became a stock routine for the film's director and producer, Hal Roach. In Roach's *Love 'Em and Weep* (1927), Jimmy Finlayson is hosting a dinner party when an old flame (Mae Busch) shows up looking to make trouble. Finlayson argues with Busch in his study and, when he produces a gun, the woman faints. Finlayson now has an unconscious woman on his hands, and he summons a trusted employee, Stan Laurel, to help him get rid of her. Finlayson crouches underneath Busch's mink coat and has Laurel set the woman on his back. Then, acting as a human-lift dolly, he bears Busch's weight while Laurel walks alongside holding Busch steady and upright. Finlayson expects his wife (Charlotte Mineau) and the guests to assume that Busch is casually departing the premises with her date, but it isn't long before Finlayson's hairy, bowed legs give away the deception.

Another Roach series, Our Gang, made use of the routine in *Teacher's Beau* (1935). Spanky seeks to get rid of his teacher's fiancé by posing as an angry old boyfriend. He pastes on a fake moustache, pulls on a man's overcoat, and arranges for Alfalfa to slip under the coat to boost him up on his shoulders. This time, the child's disguise is challenged. The fiancé, never for a moment fooled, presses Spanky to partake of a cigar. Spanky drops the cigar down inside of the coat, which smokes Alfalfa out of his hiding place.

Later versions of this human pyramid were further exaggerated by adding a third participant. Examples can be found in *Malice in the Palace* (1949) and *Silent Movie* (1976). Humor in these cases was derived from the wobbly manner in which the disjointed trio plodded toward their inevitable downfall. The group typically fell to pieces when the person at the top of the mount bumped his head into the overhead arch of a doorway. An exception occurs in *The Court Jester* (1955), when a pair of midget acrobats use the trick to free Danny Kaye from the king's soldiers.

It was a common joke among the many incarnations of the routine for a head or arm to suddenly poke through the front flaps of the coat. In *Rolling Stones* (1922), Lloyd Hamilton has a plan to get a free meal for himself and his little brother (Bobby DeVilbiss) at a cafeteria. He uses a belt to suspend DeVilbiss from his waist, and then hides the boy beneath his spacious overcoat. Hamilton pretends to be eyeing the fare while, occasionally, DeVilbiss's arm slips out to steal a dish.

In God We Tru$t (1980) introduced yet another variation of the routine. Marty Feldman, as a guileless monk visiting Los Angeles, has a stroll down Hollywood Boulevard interrupted by a frantic hooker (Louise Lasser). Lasser pleads with the monk for "sanctuary" as she needs to get away from her pimp. Feldman hides Lasser by letting her slip inside the back of his robe. The pair then casually walk away on their combined four legs, looking like a malformed centaur.

In *Austin Powers in Goldmember* (2002), Mike Myers bizarrely overturns Harold Lloyd's original arrangement — he sits on top while a small cohort (this time, midget Verne Troyer) is supporting him on the bottom. A guard is startled to see a silhouette of Troyer's arm extending out of Myers's coat. At first, it resembles an impossibly long sexual appendage, but then it takes hold of an apple and the guard has no idea what to think.

The routine has developed over the years into a clear authoritative form, as ideally demonstrated by the British stop-motion animated series *Shaun the Sheep* ("Take-Away,"

2007). Three sheep looking to travel to town to buy a pizza pretend to be a farmer by stacking one on top of the other and concealing their peculiar arrangement beneath a scarecrow's coat. A woman at a bus stop screams when she sees a sheep peeking out of the coat. The woolly column is tottering into the pizza shop when the top sheep bumps its head into an overhead sign. All of the established elements are present.

The business has remained popular largely as a stock routine in animated films, including *All Dogs Go to Heaven* (1989), *Babar: The Movie* (1989), *A Close Shave* (1995), *Casper* (1995), *Space Jam* (1996), *The Hunchback of Notre Dame* (1996), *Muppets from Space* (1999), *Chicken Run* (2000) and *Madagascar* (2005).

This praise for Lloyd's pioneering efforts is not to say that Lloyd himself did not look elsewhere for inspiration. His most critically acclaimed film, *The Kid Brother* (1927), borrowed much of its story from *Tol'able David* (1921) and *The White Sheep* (1924). As stated before, sharing ideas was simply part of being a silent film comedian.

Lloyd finds himself in yet another embarrassing situation in *Grandma's Boy* (1922). The young man is getting dressed for a party when his grandmother steps in to help by shining up his shoes with goose grease. Lloyd no sooner arrives at the party than a number of kittens come over to him to lick the grease off his shoes. Charley Chase was similarly plagued by cats in *Girl Grief* (1932). Chase has just started a job as a teacher at a girl's school when his students decide it would be a great prank to sprinkle cat nip in his bed. Chase is soon startled to find dozens of cats climbing around in his bed. In *Hotsy Totsy* (1925), Alice Day gets food stuck in her shoe, which causes cats to follow her down the street.

Lloyd Hamilton performed an extended version of this routine in *Careful Please* (1926). Hamilton was able to create his best routines out of embarrassing situations. A guest at the home of a young society woman, he is sitting on a couch when a maid approaches him with a serving tray. Hamilton removes a small sardine sandwich off the tray. As he goes to take a bite, the sardine slips out and falls down his shirt. He picks up another small sandwich and, this time, the sardine falls into the cuff of his pants leg. The sardines make Hamilton of interest to a litter of kittens. Kittens are climbing up his legs and back. At one point, he reaches up and finds a kitten perched atop his arm. He goes to cross his legs and a kitten on his foot goes flying into the air and lands on top of his head. Hamilton is unaware that he has a kitten on his head. Seeing the kitten makes the girl laugh. Thinking that she's being friendly, Hamilton laughs, too.

Harold Lloyd is best known for climbing up to a clock tower in *Safety Last!* (1923). The comedian did not have to look hard to find his inspiration. This was an era in which the American public celebrated "the human fly," a type of stunt entertainer who attracted crowds by scaling the exteriors of skyscrapers. For years, footage of these stunts had been the highlight of newsreels. It was by showcasing his climbing skills in a Pathé newsreel that Frederick Rodman Law was able to find stardom in serials. In his autobiography, Lloyd claimed that his climbing stunts were specifically inspired by Bill Strother, who climbed up the 12-story Brockman Building in Los Angeles. However, he may have also been inspired by George Gibson Polley, a more comically oriented human fly who acted clumsy and feigned slipping as a way to increase the suspense of his climbs.

Other comedians had preceded Lloyd up to lofty heights. Hank Mann teetered on a rooftop ledge in *A Tale of Twenty Stories* (1915). Billie Ritchie hung by a ladder off a highrise balcony in *The House of Terrible Scandals* (1917). Larry Semon managed to perform both of these feats in *Dunces and Dangers* (1918), which involved the comedian being chased across the roof of an apartment building by an angry mob of bill collectors. The most clever

The iconic image of Harold Lloyd hanging off a skyscraper clock in *Safety Last!* (1923) (courtesy Bruce Lawton Collection).

premise for this aerial business can be found in *He Comes Up Smiling* (1918). Douglas Fairbanks plays a bank teller entrusted by his boss to care for a beloved parakeet. The boss makes it clear that, if anything happens to the bird, the teller will lose his job. The bird escapes to take flight across rooftops and Fairbanks, desperate to recapture the bird, takes to scaling the sides of buildings, leaping from rooftop to rooftop, and walking along power wires.

Still, despite the amusing antics of Mann, Ritchie, Semon, Fairbanks and others, no other comedian took greater dares or developed the high-and-dizzy concept more fully than Lloyd. Lloyd scaled a building for the first time on film in *Ask Father* (1919). This is a brief sequence wherein Lloyd merely climbs the wall to get into an office. He does not bother to enact a single gag during the climb; the sole purpose of his action is to show off his character's daring and determination. It was in later comedies, including *Look Out Below* (1919), *High and Dizzy* (1920) and *Never Weaken* (1921), that Lloyd combined gags with his increasingly daring climbs to create film comedy's most thrilling routines. Lloyd's character is able to assume death-defying heights even when a tall building is nowhere in sight. This is demonstrated when he hangs over the side of a train speeding across a bridge in *Now or Never* (1921). By the time of *Safety Last!*, Lloyd had made the climb pivotal to the plotline and character development. The comedian's character is unable to achieve his goals until he first

Al St. John (right) was a rival to Lloyd when it came to "high and dizzy" comedy (courtesy Robert Arkus).

overcomes his fear of heights. Other comedians took to climbing buildings. Lige Conley went as far as borrowing specific gags from *Safety Last!* when he climbed a building in *Neck and Neck* (1924). Al St. John, one of silent film comedy's foremost acrobats, performed a *Safety Last!*–inspired routine in *High Spots* (1927).

The iconic image of Lloyd hanging from a clock tower in *Safety Last!* has come to be overshadowed by the image of Christopher Lloyd (no relation) hanging from a clock tower in *Back to the Future* (1985). Director Robert Zemeckis wrote this scene as a homage to *Safety Last!* (a Harold Lloyd clock appears in the opening sequence), but he dishes out to his hero even more intense problems. As wind, rain and lightning rage around him, Christopher Lloyd's character, Doc Brown, must channel electricity from a lightning bolt into the power supply of a time-traveling DeLorean. Off screen, the actor was in much less peril than his predecessor. He did reach an elevated height, clinging to a clock tower on the Universal lot, but he was not kept at this height for long. Zemeckis believed that the audience only needed to see him on the clock tower for a couple of shots to accept that he was in danger. The majority of the close shots display the actor on a fake exterior of the clock tower. The more dangerous outdoor shots feature stunt man Bob Yerkes, who hangs on while an airplane engine mounted on a cherry picker batters him with heavy winds.

19

Hysterical History

For many years, in England, comedian Fred Evans specialized in costume parodies. These included *Pimple's The Battle of Waterloo* (1913), *Pimple's Ivanhoe* (1913), *Pimple's Charge of the Light Brigade* (1914), *Pimple's Lady Godiva* (1917) and *Pimple's Three Musketeers* (1922). Evans did not make fun of historical events but, rather, made fun of the genre conventions of lavish historical dramas. He made his lack of production values part of the joke. In *Pimple's Battle of Waterloo*, Evans used pantomime horses in place of real horses. It was similar to Monty Python banging cocoanut shells together to make it sound as if their knights were riding horses in *Monty Python and the Holy Grail* (1975). Scenes in *Pimple's Battle of Waterloo* include Pimple, as Napoleon, crossing the Alps on a pantomime horse. Pimple's army ends up being defeated by a Boy Scout troop. Evans set up these scenes in a serious manner, only to suddenly perform a pratfall or nick his finger on a sword.

Costume comedies appeared in America not long after the Pimple's historical forays began. Vitagraph produced *The Misadventures of a Mighty Monarch* (1914), which starred John Bunny and Flora Finch as a king and queen in old England. In the Keystone comedy *Hogan's Aristocratic Dream* (1915), a tramp (Charlie Murray) dreams that he is a nobleman in pre-revolutionary France. King Fizzle (Fred Mace) cheats on the queen (Laura Oakley) in *Those Good Old Days* (1913). Mack Swain appears as King Ambrose in a Keystone variation on the Robin Hood legend entitled *Ambrose's Lofty Perch* (1915). Harold Lloyd starred in a burlesque of Roman dramas called *Luke, the Gladiator* (1916).

The early 1920s saw a spate of costume comedies. The trend started with *A Connecticut Yankee in King Arthur's Court* (1921), which transported a modern man (Harry C. Myers) to the sixth-century England of King Arthur. According to IMDb critic F. Gwynplaine MacIntyre, "[Myers] soon sets about remaking sixth-century England to resemble jazz-age California."[1] Variations of this plot were later employed for *Vamping Venus* (1928), *Roman Scandals* (1933) and *Du Barry Was a Lady* (1943).

The Courtship of Miles Sandwich (1923) gave Snub Pollard an opportunity to spoof the Charles Ray film *The Courtship of Myles Standish* (1923). The film is full of deliberate anachronisms. The pilgrims are greeted on the beach by Indian bathing beauties. An Indian with full headdress is waiting in a wagon to provide the visitors with shuttle service to their lodgings.

Anachronisms became a big part of costume comedies as comedy makers insisted on imposing modern ways on ancient civilizations. Their goal, as was the goal of Harry C. Myers in *A Connecticut Yankee in King Arthur's Court*, was to remake the past to make it

Heinie Conklin (left), Charlie Murray (center) and Phyllis Haver in *Salome vs. Shenandoah* (1919) (courtesy Robert Arkus).

feel like the present, thereby making it more comfortable for a modern audience. In *Monsieur Beaucaire*, Bob Hope is trying to make a hasty exit when trouble arises. "I have a horse outside," he quickly explains. "I'm double-parked." In *The Three Musketeers* spoof *The Three Must-Get-Theres* (1922), Max Linder suddenly pulls out a telephone. In *Robin Hood: Men in Tights* (1993), a black swordsman (Dave Chappelle) takes a break from battle to pump up his sneakers. *Love and Death* (1975), which is set in the Napoleonic Era, shows Woody Allen wearing his modern trademark eyeglasses. The film also includes a black drill instructor training Russian troops and a vendor hawking hot dogs on a battlefield. In *The Frozen North* (1922), Buster Keaton emerges from a subway exit in the middle of the Yukon wilderness. In a later scene, he rides a sled with an automobile design.

Keaton included a number of anachronisms in *Three Ages* (1923). In the Stone Age, Keaton defeats a rival caveman in battle. Fellow cavemen gather around him and drape animal furs around his shoulders just like the corner men would put a robe on a boxer who has just won a match. In ancient Rome, Keaton's chariot has a license plate. Keaton is supposed to be preparing for a chariot race, but he looks like he's preparing for a race across the frozen tundra — he attaches sled runners to the chariot in place of wheels and ties dogs to his chariot in place of horses. On the track, he repeatedly lashes his sled dogs to get them to run faster. When a dog hurts his paw, he goes to a rear trunk and pulls out a spare dog.

Three Ages also had Keaton lapsing into parodies of Bible stories, enacting his own variations on Samson pulling down the temple and Daniel becoming trapped in the lion's den. Keaton looks heroic while pushing down pillars, but then chunks of loose brick and mortar conk him in the head and he stumbles around in a daze. The film is, in this way, a forerunner of *Life of Brian* (1979) and *Year One* (2009).

Keaton sought with *The Frozen North* to spoof the ultra seriousness of William S. Hart, known as the "good badman." In *Hell's Hinges* (1916), *The Narrow Trail* (1917) and other films, Hart tended to go through a melodramatic transformation from bad guy to good guy. Ron Schuler wrote, "Hart's photoplays were usually about the moral awakening of his protagonists—the hard-bitten lone wolf, whose ethical sense blooms in the aftermath of an impromptu good deed or upon meeting a chaste heroine."[2] By 1922, the formula had grown tired and only had value as parody. Harold Lloyd had already spoofed Hart's melodramatic westerns in *Billy Blazes, Esq.* (1919). The ending of *The Frozen North* reveals that Keaton's character has dreamed the silly story while sleeping in a movie theatre. Hart was said to have been offended by the film.

Jim Kline detected a "Griffith influence"[3] in Keaton's two best period films, *Our Hospitality* (1923) and *The General* (1927). Kline wrote that *The General*, which was based an actual incident from the Civil War, has "painstakingly accurate historical detail"[4] and "faith-

Sid Smith is emboldened by his extravagant costume in this unidentified pirate comedy. The ladies are unidentified (courtesy Robert Arkus).

fully capture[s] the time period."⁵ This historical film does look authentic. This is unique in that the general rule of costume comedies was that historical accuracy be damned.

Valentino's overheated performance as an amorous Arab chief in *The Sheik* (1921) was ripe for spoof. Neal Burns was quick to poke fun at Valentino's sheik with *That Son of a Sheik* (1922). James Parrott declared war on the sheik with *Soak the Sheik* (1922). A distaff comedy version starring Bebe Daniels was titled *She's a Sheik* (1927). Baby Peggy did her own unique take on the sheik in *Peg o' the Movies* (1923). Ben Turpin offered the most ridiculous and most memorable send-up of the great screen lover with *The Shriek of Araby* (1923).

Other costume comedies include a Larry Semon spoof of *The Prisoner of Zenda* called *A Pair of Kings* (1922). *A Backyard Cavalier* (1922) featured Bobby Vernon as a Fairbanks-type swashbuckler. Bull Montana and Dot Farley starred in a Robin Hood spoof titled *Rob 'Em Good* (1922). Stan Laurel starred in a series of costume spoofs from 1922 to 1924. These spoofs included *Frozen Hearts* (1923), a parody of Russian melodramas; *Mud and Sand* (1922), a lampoon of Valentino's *Blood and Sand* (1922); and *Monsieur Don't Care* (1924), a slapstick version of *Monsieur Beaucaire* (1924). Laurel, in satirizing Fairbanks in *When Knights Were Cold* (1923), performs a number of acrobatic stunts, including scaling a rose trestle to get inside a castle.

The Three Must-Get-Theres (1922), a goofy parody of Douglas Fairbanks's *The Three Musketeers* (1921), features Max Linder as a highly practiced swordsman who bids farewell to the family farm with the hope of becoming a king's musketeer. However, being good with a sword does not mean that he will not have problems along the way. His problems start even before he leaves the farm. His horse, who is smitten with a cow, remains steadfastly opposed to leaving for Paris until the swordsman promises to introduce the horse to a "chic little mule" in the French capital. It is at this point that the horse leaps to its feet and prances down the road with Linder secure in the saddle.

Linder moves around quickly during a swordfight against four members of the Cardinal's Guard. He gets them to chase him single-file around a large oak tree so that he is able to pick them off one by one. Linder is dismayed to see that the fight has dulled his blade. He strolls over to one of his prostrate victims and stamps down on the man's stomach, at which point the man's legs shoot straight into the air, and Linder is able to sharpen his sword on the leather soles of the man's boots. Moments later, Linder runs a man through with his sword, but courteously holds the man up while he clears a rock out of the ground where he is about to fall. In the end, the swordsman lassoes a half dozen of the Cardinal's Guard and then ties the rope to his horse so they can be dragged off.

Linder gets into another swordfight in a tavern. He is able to show off some fancy footwork until he gets stabbed in the foot and has to hop around on one foot while continuing the battle. When he loses his sword, he jumps over the bar for cover. He pops up and down behind the bar to avoid getting stabbed. He finally disposes of his opponent by coming up with a liquor bottle and smashing it over the man's head.

In yet another swordfight, Linder chases an opponent up a trellis. The two men cross swords on a balcony and move the fight into a bedroom. Linder jumps on a bed, awakening a black man occupying the bed. The black man, frightened by the swords, rolls from side to side in the bed to avoid the cutting blades. The bed eventually collapses.

The musketeers, summoned on a mission for the queen, slide down a fire pole beside their bed. A horse waiting below catches the first musketeer and gallops off in haste. Another horse moves in position, in time to catch the next musketeer, and then leaves just in time for a third horse to snare the final musketeer.

Frank Alexander (second from left) look on in disapproval as Joe Rock (seated) woos Billie Rhodes in the costume comedy *Aladdin* (1922). Identity of the man on the left is unknown. Rock recycled the costumes and sets from an earlier comedy, *Ali Baba* (1922) (courtesy Cole Johnson Collection).

Lupino Lane is equally energetic as a swordsman in *Sword Points* (1928). Lane embellishes his swordfights with a steady stream of gags. He gets the opposing swordsmen to take a break as he feels a sneeze coming on. He finally sneezes, the force of which sends him somersaulting over his opponents. Lane is soon back to crossing swords with the villains. Lane's opponent clumsily snaps off a part of his sword. To make things even, Lane snaps off a piece of *his* sword. Another piece breaks off from the opponent's sword, which inspires Lane to snap off an even larger segment of his sword. This goes on until neither swordsman has any blade left, and the other swordsmen — with no other way to continue the battle — simply punches Lane in the face.

Costume comedies experienced a resurgence in the early 1930s. In *Roman Scandals* (1933), Eddie Cantor dreams that he is a slave in Ancient Rome. He experiences a series of adventures: he works as the emperor's food-taster; he woos a captured princess; he has a stint in a torture chamber; and he flees Roman soldiers in a chariot. Laurel & Hardy are bandits in 18th-century Italy in *Fra Diavolo* (*The Devil's Brother*) (1933). *Cockeyed Cavaliers* (1934) ushered Wheeler & Woolsey back to the 15th-century England, where the duo is able to ride in a horse-drawn coach, sleep at a rustic inn, and get drunk in an old tavern. It was Wheeler & Woolsey as usual, except they were in a fresh setting, they got to fool around with strange new props, and were able to wear silly-looking hats. For years, costume

Bert Wheeler enjoys wine, women (Dorothy Lee) and funny costumes in *Cockeyed Cavaliers* (1934).

comedies were mostly an excuse to use antiquated objects as funny props. In *Roaming Romeo*, Roman soldiers chase Lupino Lane onto a banquet table. His brother, Wallace Lupino, tilts the table to make the soldiers roll off into a bath. Wallace catches Lane just before he tumbles into the bath himself. This is the usual Lupino Lane chase except that Lane has use of Roman baths and marble columns. Helmets and shields, too, were nothing more than a new set of props to the comedian. At one point, Lane uses the plumes of his helmet crest to brush out the dirt beneath his fingernails. He then checks his reflection in his shiny shield. The comedy provides no social commentary on ancient Rome. Woody Allen got fifteen minutes' worth of gags from a chastity belt in *Everything You Always Wanted to Know About Sex * But Were Afraid to Ask* (1972). Peter Sellers accidentally smashes a piano with a mace in *The Pink Panther Strikes Again* (1976).

A full harness of plate armor, designed to deflect the onslaught of crossbows, sabers, lances and arquebuses, looks ridiculous from a modern perspective. A soldier donning armor is, to all intents and purposes, a man closing himself inside a big tin can. Just the sight of man in armor has been funny enough to get an audience to laugh. An absurd moment occurs in *Max and the Statue* (1912) when Max Linder, dressed in a suit of armor for a costume party, comes lumbering into the frame, strumming on a guitar. Linder soon learns that nothing comes easy to a man wearing a suit of armor. The worst part of this experience comes when the debonair gentlemen goes to kiss his date and finds the helmet getting in

Charles King is startled to see Spencer Bell in a suit of armor in *That's No Excuse* (1927) (courtesy Cole Johnson Collection).

the way. *A Bad (K)Night* (1902), a comedy produced by American Mutoscope and Biograph, shows a man coming home drunk and engaging in a friendly conversation with a suit of armor. The man's wife storms down the staircase in her nightgown, grabs a cudgel out of the gloved hand of the armored suit, and relentlessly thrashes her drunken husband. In *Happy Jack, a Hero* (1910), a man hiding in a suit of armor kicks and smacks two men who have their backs turned to him. The men, each blaming the other for the blows, get into a fistfight. Stan Laurel got laughs as a knight in full armor in the Metro comedy *When Knights Were Cold* (1922). In *A Connecticut Yankee in King Arthur's Court,* Harry Myers creates an automated walk-thru wash for knights in armor. In *The Court Jester* (1955), a lightning bolt magnetizes Danny Kaye's suit of armor, which exerts such a strong pull on his opposing knight's mace that it causes the knight to be yanked out of his saddle.* Peter Sellers becomes more clumsy than usual when maneuvering around in a suit of armor in *The Pink Panther* (1964). In *Silent Movie* (1976), Mel Brooks, Marty Feldman and Dom DeLuise find their armor to be so stiff and heavy that they repeatedly topple to the floor. Monty Python sometimes simply ended a sketch with a man in a suit of armor smacking a person with a rubber chicken.

*A similar situation befell a man in the 1908 Pathé Frères comedy *The Magnetized Man*.

Harold Lloyd finds that a suit of armor can be helpful in modern times in *Ask Father* (1919). Lloyd is seated with Bebe Daniels. The four men standing directly behind them are (left to right) Bud Jamison, Noah Young, Snub Pollard and Sammy Brooks. Others are extras.

Armor could be useful in dealing with modern hazards. A police officer wears a suit of armor as protection when he enters a lion's cage at a zoo in *Seven Years Bad Luck* (1921). Jack Cooper shows up to a fencing match well protected inside a suit of armor in *Scarem Much* (1924). In *Ask Father* (1919), Harold Lloyd needs to visit a business executive at his office to obtain the man's consent to marry his daughter. The man, however, is too busy to see Lloyd and keeps having him thrown out. Lloyd, whose backside has gotten sore from the hard landings, finally returns to the man's office in a full set of armor.

In *Crazy House* (1928), Our Gang visits a friend at a lavish mansion without knowing that the friend's dad has set up tricks to scare guests as part of an April Fool's Day celebration. The father's tricks include wires that have been rigged to make a suit of armor move. A haunted suit of armor turned up in a lot of Columbia "scare" comedies in the 1930s and 1940s. The Three Stooges centered an entire story around a haunted suit of armor in *The Ghost Talks* (1949). The Andy Clyde comedy *Spook to Me* (1945) provides a twist on the old gag. Clyde sees a suit of armor raise its arm. Typically, the comedian raises the visor, sees no one is inside and runs off in fright. In this version, Clyde raises the visor and inexplicably finds a beautiful woman inside. He goes to kiss the woman and the visor slams shut on his lips. This entire concept goes back to the earliest days of film, beginning with a ghost materializing in a suit of armor in Georges Méliès's *The Haunted Castle* (1897).

Comedy writers, whose minds were more on present-day life than life in the past, were focused on transplanting contemporary thinking and sensibilities to historical settings. Their characters were no more than modern-era people in ancient-era costumes. In the process, the filmmakers conveyed arrogance and self-congratulation. It was modern people, saying that they were smarter and lived better, mocking people of the past.

Bob Hope's most memorable films include three costume comedies: *The Princess and the Pirate* (1944), *Monsieur Beaucaire* (1946) and *Casanova's Big Night* (1954). At first, all the court intrigue in *Monsieur Beaucaire* seems nothing more than an excuse for Hope to get his hands on a new set of props. Within moments after making his first appearance, Hope accidentally smacks King Louis XV in the face with a wig powderer. He gets to make wisecracks about the duke getting a run in his stocking. He makes quips about the funny hats.

Hope, who is the funniest when at his most cowardly, makes it a point to run away from sword fights. A nobleman is appalled by Hope's cowardice. "You're a man," he insists. "You got blood in your veins!" Hope replies, "Yeah, and I want to keep it in there. It's the squirty kind." He even gets frightened when he falls into a stream and gets a trout stuck on the end of his sword. "Shark!" he shrieks. No one played cowardly better than Hope. It is because of this that he is incapable of providing a thrilling swordfight in *Monsieur Beaucaire*. His biggest problem in the duel is not that his heart is nearly pierced by a blade, but that his notoriously pronounced nose gets entangled in the strings of a harp. This would not have been an acceptable climax in the silent era. Max Linder and Lupino Lane had obviously learned how to fence, but their successors did not particularly care to develop these skills for their comic swashbuckling. Shemp Howard takes a sword in hand for the Three Stooges comedy *Musty Musketeers* (1954), but he cannot find anything better to do with the sword than to use it to fling apples at his opponents. Diminishing returns are evident in Mel Brooks's *Robin Hood: Men in Tights* (1993), which ends with perhaps the dullest swordfight in film history.

Monsieur Beaucaire spoofs foreign alliances, class issues, and adultery in the French court. The writers, Melvin Frank and Norman Panama, were knowledgeable of historical

It remains to be seen if a suit of armor can protect a man from a bullet. The star of this 1919 Sennett comedy, *Reilly's Wash Day,* is Charlie Murray (on the far left). Others are (left to right) Baldy Belmont, Bob Finlay, Eddie Gribbon, Marie Prevost and Russell Powell (courtesy Robert Arkus).

facts and historical people even though they were willing to alter those facts and people whenever it suited the story. Frank and Panama came to specialize in historical costume comedies. Their credits include *A Southern Yankee* (1948), a Civil War comedy starring Red Skelton, and *The Court Jester* (1956), a comedy that transplanted Danny Kaye to medieval England. *The Court Jester* has a serious plot. Lord Ravenhurst (Basil Rathbone) has massacred the king and his family to place the tyrannical Roderick on the throne, but the Black Fox has found an infant who survived the massacre and is determined to put forth this infant as rightful heir to the throne.

Most costume comedies were no more than spoofs of Errol Flynn and Douglas Fairbanks, Sr., costume adventures. The same idea is behind *Start the Revolution Without Me* (1970), which is set during the French Revolution. Two peasants are mistaken for the Corsican Brothers, who are famed throughout the country for their great swordsmanship. The film is not a satirical look at the French Revolution but a parody of novels about the period, including *A Tale of Two Cities* and *The Corsican Brothers. Love and Death* (1975), which involves an effort by Woody Allen and Diane Keaton to assassinate Napoleon, is filled with commentary on war and politics, but Allen is not focused on historical circumstances. The film is largely a satirical take on Russian epic novels, such as those by Dostoyevsky and Tol-

Hollywood's most recent *great* comic swordfight was staged for *The Court Jester* (1955). The swordsmen are Basil Rathbone (left) and Danny Kaye (courtesy www.doctormacro.com).

stoy. A subplot involving Allen having an affair with a countess and having to duel her jealous lover is a spoof of Ingmar Bergman's *Smiles of a Summer Night* (1955). Most of all, the film stands as an homage to Hope's classic *Monsieur Beaucaire*.

The historical dramas tend to stress high principles and goals to create battles between good and evil. It is all very idealistic. Also, studio executives figure that, as long as they are spending lots of money to recreate historical scenes, the scenes might as well look good. These films, therefore, showcase extravagant sets and elaborate costumes. The satirist is often better at getting to the truth of matters. For years, films about medieval times led people to believe that the poor farmers, who lived off their own labors and enjoyed the great abundance yielded by the earth, had nothing less than an idyllic existence. At times, these films conveyed pastoral scenes in which peasants dance around Maypoles and sweethearts lay together in soft green meadows. It took *Monty Python and the Holy Grail* (1975) to let us know that the peasants in medieval times did backbreaking work in the fields and were usually covered in manure. A film about medieval times that does not have peasants scratching at the lice and fleas on their body is not at all authentic. Victor Mature looks regal wearing his centurion helmet in *Demetrius and the Gladiators* (1954), but maybe it was not all pride and splendor wearing those bulky headpieces. Buster Keaton, in his awkwardly fitted Roman helmet, may have been more authentic as an ancient soldier than Mature. In fact, helmets were seen as comical years before Keaton came along. Gaumont Film Company produced an early comedy that addressed the helmet issue directly. *A Heavy Headpiece* (1909) was devoted entirely to a soldier's experiences managing his weighty headgear.

The members of Monty Python heavily researched the King Arthur legend before writing *Monty Python and the Holy Grail*. Michael Palin said, "We were all sort of library nerds, really, all of us brought up to respect reference books and all that."[6] Terry Gilliam said that, by the time they started production, they were "immersed in time and place."[7] This is the reason that anachronisms are kept to at a minimum in *Grail* as well as Python's *Life of Brian* (1979). John Cleese said that, originally, the script to *Life of Brian* included scenes with Jesus reserving the table for the Last Supper and Jesus consulting with his writing staff after the Sermon on the Mount to get their notes. These scenes, though, fell by the wayside as the Python crew focused on history, faith, religious dogma and Biblical text. Still, *Life of Brian* turned out, to a lesser degree, to be a spoof of Hollywood Biblical epics. Eric Idle said, "There were all these awful Hollywood films and we realized that that's the target, really ... the portrayal."[8]

It stands that the greatest value can be found in letting a satirist examine history.

20

Bugs

It has been established by now that Commedia dell'Arte routines turned up in many early comedy films. In *No Loafing* (1923), Poodles Hanneford gets a job as a mover with Gentle Furniture Movers. He uses a pulley to lift a piano up the side of a building. He finds that he cannot fit the piano through the window, so he breaks a huge hole in the wall. Hanneford is moving the piano into place when a butterfly flutters through the hole. The mover grabs a wrench and breaks a table trying to squash the butterfly. He continues to demolish furniture and walls with his wrench, managing to ruin the home by the time that the police arrive to arrest him. This expands on the Commedia dell'Arte routine "Lazzo of the Fly," wherein the comic servant Arlecchino knocks over furniture, breaks items and even injures himself while trying to swat an annoying fly. Hanneford, who remains straight-faced throughout the entire reel, goes through his routines with a craftman's precision. The film is self-mocking in its excess. It is the same sort of wanton destruction that later became the forte of the Three Stooges.

"Lazzo of the Fly" later became incorporated into a clown routine called "The Waiter." In this classic bit, a clown waiter chases a fly around a restaurant with an oversized broom. The fly retreats out of the waiter's reach by landing on the ceiling. The waiter is climbing a ladder to reach the fly when he suddenly trips and falls. He lands on a table, which collapses under his weight. This routine found itself an unlikely home when it was used as the basis of a 2010 episode of *Breaking Bad* called "Fly."

In *Cold Hearts and Hot Flames* (1916), a giant bug flies into a window and lands on Billie Ritchie's head. Ritchie, unaware of the bug, puts his top hat on over it. Then, suddenly, he winces, which suggests that the bug has bitten him. He whips off the hat and the bug flies down onto a table. It is resting on the table with its wings flapping. Large flies often show up in silent film comedies, but this fly — as horrifically large and grotesque as it is — is exceptional. It looks like a bug out of *The Mist*. Ritchie gets a bat and swings at it. The bug flies off and lands on Joe Murphy's bald head. Ritchie goes to squash the bug with the bat. The bug flies away just as Ritchie comes down with the bat and slams Murphy instead.

This monstrous bug is a throwback to an earlier time when films were inundated with surreal imagery. In *A Terrible Night* (1896), a man is awakened in the middle of the night by an oversized bedbug crawling into his bed. The irate man chases the bug around the room with a broom. *A Jersey Skeeter* (1900) features a huge mosquito attacking a farmer and carrying the man off by the seat of his pants.

Lloyd Hamilton is pestered by a fly in *The Educator* (1922). The young girl is Josephine Adair (courtesy Robert Arkus).

Max Linder becomes cross-eyed looking at a fly resting on the tip of his nose in *Une nuit agitée* (1912). This was already a stock gag by the 1920s, when it showed up in program-filler like the FBO "Telephone Girls" comedy *For the Love of Mike* (1924). Yet, the gag became a key plot point in the First National feature *Ella Cinders* (1926). Ella (Colleen Moore) is having her picture taken for a beauty contest when a fly lands on her nose. She looks cross-eyed in the picture, but the judges are so amused that they declare her the winner.

This simple gag has many varieties. A man pretending to be dead or unconscious has to deal with an annoying fly landing on his nose. When no one else is looking, he desperately blows on the stubborn pest to get it to go away. In *Crushed* (1924), Lloyd Hamilton has a fly land on his nose while he is in the middle of exchanging wedding vows. He shakes his head to get the bug to fly away, but the minister and the bride assume that he is shaking his head to decline the vows. The exchange of wedding vows is even more terribly disrupted in the 1913 Eclipse comedy *Monsieur Papillon prend la mouche* (known in America as *Mr. Butterfly Takes the Fly*), in which the groom's effort to remove a fly from the bride's cheek leads the groom to slap the bride across the face.

Swatting a fly was always a problem. The 1908 Rossi comedy *The Troublesome Fly* finds an artist distracted by a fly that has gotten loose in his studio. The artist goes wild, repeatedly trying to strike the fly with his paint brush, but he only succeeds in ruining his painting and covering a porter with paint. In *Never Give a Sucker an Even Break* (1941), W. C. Fields is taking a swig out of a liquor bottle when a fly lands on his forehead. He unthinkingly raises his hand to swat the fly and smashes the bottle against his head. In the Our Gang comedy *Night 'n' Gales* (1937), Alfalfa is unable to fall asleep as he is being pestered by a moth. He picks up a shoe looking to crush the moth, but he has a hard time getting a good shot at it until it lands on his friend's sleeping father (Johnny Arthur). Alfalfa slams down the shoe and ends up cracking Arthur in the nose.

Bugs—pests that they are—create chaos, frustration and distraction, which are elements conducive to comedy.

The comedy trope of the comedian plucking petals off a daisy while reciting the phrase "She loves me, she loves me not" was derived from a game created in France in the 1800s. *He Loves Me, He Loves Me Not* (1903), an early Edison, film, was a straightforward minute-long film showing a pretty young lady playing the romantic game. It was used to greater effect onscreen in later years. *The Covered Schooner* (1923) opens with Monty Banks blissfully plucking a petal from a daisy. As he tosses away the petal, the camera pulls back to reveal thousands of petals piled up alongside him. Buster Keaton, although not the most romantic figure in film history, relented to play this whimsical game in *Three Ages* (1923). When a bee hidden in the flower stings him, it quickly sours Keaton's mood and gets him to give up on the game.

In nature films, bees are shown collecting nectar from flowers, aiding in pollination, and producing honey. In slapstick comedy, they are largely known for stinging people. This idea goes back centuries. A 19th-century illustration of the Commedia dell'Arte shows a character fighting off a swarm of bees.[1]

In the Grease (1925) includes a scene wherein a mischievous boy puts a beehive down Jimmy Finlayson's pants. Finlayson reacts by springing up and down and leaping out of a window. In *He Comes Up Smiling* (1918), the acrobatic Douglas Fairbanks responds to a bee attack by scaling a tree. In *The Bees' Buzz* (1929), a golf ball knocks a beehive off of a tree and down Harry Gribbon's pants. Gribbon leaps around the golf course frantically trying to rid himself of the bees. *Cheap Skates* (1925) is a lost film, but reviews of the period suggest that a key scene featured Lige Conley panicking when bees fly down his pants.

A beehive down the pants was just something that happened to silent film comedians. How a comedian responded to the bees distinguished the ingenious comedian from the standard comedian. A mischievous boy drops a beehive down Harry Langdon's pants in *Smile, Please* (1924). At this time, Langdon was new to films and had yet to fully develop his slow-witted character. His frantic reactions are, in every way, standard. However, significant changes are evident in Langdon by the time he has his next encounter with bees. In *Remember When?* (1925), Langdon is a tramp who carries his meager belongings wrapped up in a bundle at the end of a stick. Unbeknownst to Langdon, the bundle strikes a beehive, drops off, and the similarly shaped beehive gets latched onto the stick in its place. Langdon goes to remove an item from the bundle and is slow to recognize that he has gotten hold of a beehive. Bees are pouring out of the hive, yet Langdon acts as if he has no idea what a bee is. He reaches inside the hive, agitating the bees, which attack him. Langdon tosses off the hive, which lands on the chair of a man who is about to sit down with his family for a picnic. The man leaps up after getting stung in the backside and overturns the picnic table. His entire family flees from the scene. Meanwhile, a circus owner, seeing Langdon tumble around to rid himself of the bees, assumes that he is a comic acrobat and hires him to perform in his show.*

Langdon continued to use bee attacks in films. In *Skirt Shy* (1929), he is trapped inside an all-glass greenhouse when a beehive drops off a tree and crashes through the roof. The camera, positioned outside of the greenhouse, reveals the greenhouse becoming filled with bees and Harry being stung repeatedly.

Another original comedian was Larry Semon, who is attacked by bees in *The Wizard of Oz* (1925). A close-up on Semon shows a bee crawling into one of Semon's ears and almost immediately coming out of his other ear. It is as if Semon, this impossible creature, is functioning without a brain inside his head. Langdon, for all of his improbable ignorance, is at least human. Who or what is this strange creature known as Larry Semon?

---

*Chaplin may have recalled this scene when he was working on *The Circus* (1928). In that feature, a ringmaster witnesses Chaplin running away from a police officer. He finds Chaplin so amusing that he offers him a job as a circus performer.

21

Scared Black Servants, Dice-Playing African Cannibals, and the Most Racist Comedy in Silent Cinema History

Off to Bloomingdale Asylum (1901), a film by Georges Méliès, features four black men in a slapstick brawl. Every kick or punch has the effect of transforming the men's skin color — black to white, white to black. In the end, the men merge into one big black man. The meaning of this film could be debated to exhaustion. The purpose of black characters was made more obvious in later American films.

The idea that black people are superstitious is behind a large-scale gag in *For Heaven's Sake* (1926). A carton of Black Cat Coffee, adorned with a life-sized silhouette of a cat, falls out of the back of a delivery truck. Harold Lloyd's black chauffeur (Oscar Smith) is driving directly towards the box when he spots the logo and mistakes it for an actual black cat crossing the road. The chauffeur flies into a full-blown panic, swerves the car to get away from this source of bad luck, and has a head-on collision with a truck in the next lane.

Black people were portrayed unflatteringly for years before *For Heaven's Sake*. *The Watermelon Patch* (1905), an early short produced by Edison, features a farmer dressing up as a skeleton to frighten away a group of black men who are stealing watermelons off his land. These black men, who demonstrate dance skills in a later scene, were likely to have been vaudeville entertainers.

It was due to the influence of the 19th century minstrel shows that early comedies portrayed black men sneaking onto farms to steal watermelons or chickens. But the harsher elements of the minstrel show stereotypes were in time rejected by filmmakers. These routines broke away from their roots and became absorbed into the repertoire of white mainstream performers. Harry Langdon steals a chicken in *Remember When?* (1925). Dorothy Devore steals a watermelon in *The Little Rube* (1927). But another aspect of the minstrel show stereotype, also showcased in the Edison film, remained well intact for the duration of the silent film era. The premise that blacks were overwhelmed with superstition allowed for scenes where black characters easily became terrified by a man in a skeleton costume. The idea likely survived the longest because it was bolstered by its tie-in with an even stronger Commedia dell'Arte tradition — the scared servant. The Zanni servants, too, could be readily frightened by a man in a skeleton costume, and the fact that black characters were usually the servants in silent films (as a reflection of a role they played in the real world) left it to them to carry on this longstanding tradition.

The scared black servant remained a stock character that an inventive comedian could, according to his own style and preference, fit into numerous contexts and shape into a variety of forms. It must be said, though, that these characters, in all their forms, rarely seemed designed to convey hostile attitudes or create political repression. First and foremost, this material, regardless of its controversial nature, deserves a thorough examination as opposed to a bitter denunciation.

In early films, black characters were more often portrayed by white actors in blackface. Billy Quirk appeared in blackface in *How Rastus Gets His Turkey* (1910). Quirk, as the highly stereotypical Rastus, sneaks into a farmhouse to steal his Thanksgiving bird. Less is known about the 1913 Lubin comedy *Rastus Among the Zulus*. Biograph's *A Close Call* (1912) finds Fred Mace in a serious predicament. Mace, made up in blackface for a minstrel show, is nearly lynched by a mob that has mistaken him for a black man who is wanted for kidnapping. In *Father's Choice* (1913), Mabel Normand and Fred Mace start a fire to distract Mabel's father while they flee the house to elope. The couple ends up having to hide in the chimney and, just as the father is about to catch them, they rub ashes on their faces to make themselves look black. The father fails to recognize the couple. His simple thought, as expressed by an intertitle, is, "Only a pair of coons." *Those College Girls* (1915), a Keystone free-for-all, involves a group of college girls wreaking havoc at a hotel. As a prank, the girls blacken the face of a snoozing bellhop. Nick Cogley, a Keystone director, had a fondness for blackface comedy. He directed several, including *A Colored Girl's Love* (1914) and *Colored Villainy* (1915). Other blackface comedies produced during the early film era include *Chicken Thief* (1903), *Wooing and Wedding of a Coon* (1905), *His Wife's Sweethearts* (1910), *The Pickaninnies and the Watermelon* (1912), *The Elite Ball* (1913), *That Dark Town Belle* (1913), *Coon Town Suffragettes* (1914) and *A Dark Lover's Play* (1915).

A premise introduced in 1908 was popular enough to be used by multiple film companies, including Pathé Frères (as *Husband Wanted*) and Urban-Eclipse (as *Sammy's Idea*). A rich man advertises to find a husband for his daughter, who has been unable to attract a man due to a large birth mark on the side of her face. A number of men who answer the ad beat a hasty retreat once they see this disfigurement, but a young black suitor is not at all deterred. The suitor applies a lotion to the woman's face that not only darkens the woman's skin to match his own but also succeeds in concealing the birth mark.

Even odder films centered on black characters. *Burlesque Lions and Their Tamer, Hagenbeck's Circus* (1903) featured four black men acting like lions in a lion tamer's act. The men snap and growl as they walk around in a cage on all fours. The lion tamer manages to subdue them by poking them with a pointed rod.

The fear of a black man raping a white woman is behind a disturbing sequence in a 1916 "Pokes and Jabbs" comedy called *Reckless Romeos* (1916). The film finds Pokes (Walter Stull) and Jabbs (Bobby Burns) in a heated rivalry for the affections of Edna (Edna Reynolds). Jabbs is escorting Edna on a date when a burly black man appears and steals away Edna. The black man tries to force himself on Edna by threatening her with a straight razor. When the woman begs for mercy, the black man grabs a towel and wipes paint off his face to reveal himself to be Pokes.

In 1916, Biograph hired famous black stage comedian Bert Williams to write, produce, direct and star in two comedies, *A Natural Born Gambler* and *Fish*. This was the one occasion in early films when a black comedian appeared in a starring role. Still, elements of the minstrel show stereotypes persisted in his characterization.

In *Out West* (1918), Roscoe Arbuckle and Buster Keaton join a group of cowboys harassing a black man (Ernie Morrison, Sr.) by firing their guns at his feet. The scene is disturbing mainly because Morrison looks genuinely distressed. He has tears streaming down his face by the time a Salvation Army worker (Alice Lake) comes to his aide and rebukes the rowdy cowboys. Although the scene had a compassionate ending, it is hard to forget the cruelty that preceded it. The next year, Harold Lloyd included a similar scene in *Billy Blazes, Esq.* (1919), except that it is a Chinese man who has gunfighters shooting at his feet, and it is the tavern keeper's daughter (Bebe Daniels) who comes to his aid. Ethnic stereotypes, as victims of bigotry, were at times interchangeable.

Black menials played a significant role in lions-on-the-loose comedies. *Roars and Uproars* (1922) includes an extended sequence in which a lion attacks two black porters. The encounter is introduced with the intertitle "When Africa Meets Africa." A black porter is shocked to glimpse a roaring lion through a keyhole. When he tells his friend, he is told, "Calm yo'self, my friend, the D.T.'s hab overtaken yo.'" The first porter trapped in bed with the lion reemerges as an angel. The second porter figures to hide from the lion by climbing into a bathtub and submerging himself under water. However, the water quickly drains out of the tub and the porter, having presumably drunk all of the water, is next seen with his stomach impossibly bloated.

A *Moving Picture World* critic noted in a review of *Drink Hearty* (1920) that Snub Pollard was "assisted by the clever colored lad, Sambo."[1] This was a reference to child actor Ernest Morrison, who played Pollard's resourceful young sidekick in Roach comedies. Morrison inspired the nickname "Sambo" because his character resembled the lead character in the 1898 children's book *The Story of Little Black Sambo*. The small black boy of the storybook finds himself surrounded by four hungry tigers, and it looks like he has no chance for survival. But the boy remains eager and optimistic. He quickly comes up with a plan to outwit the tigers. In much the same way, Morrison was often able to get the bumbling Pollard out of trouble. The term "Sambo" is now regarded as a racial slur, but the Sambo character contradicts the image of the black man as lazy and ignorant.

Morrison, in his resemblance to Sambo, also ran very much counter to the stereotype. He had an effervescent personality that made him seem fearless, energetic and full of ideas. The actor soon abandoned the "Sambo" name and was billed as "Sunshine Sammy" for the next 20 years. His great success at Roach made him the first black comedy star in motion pictures.

A familiar comedy scene opens on a well-dressed, attractively shaped woman with her back to the camera. The woman draws the attention of the comedian, who promptly approaches the woman to flirt with her. The woman turns around and reveals her face, which is shockingly ugly. The man recoils and runs off. A variation of this routine can be found in *The Masher* (1907), a Selig comedy about an obnoxious man who repeatedly forces his attention on women. The man finally garners the interest of a woman wearing a veil. The woman raises her veil to introduce herself and reveals that she is black. The man, without a moment of hesitation, rushes off. Larry Semon performed the same scene in *Frauds and Frenzies* (1918); Buster Keaton did it in *Seven Chances* (1925); and Lloyd Hamilton did it in *Waiting* (1925). It was a simple, straightforward, one-size-fits-all gag executed without variation. The reaction to the homely lady is shock and revulsion, but the reaction to the black woman is dominated by fear. The scene, in this context, suggests the taboo against interracial coupling. Semon provided the strongest reaction. He grimaces painfully, then skips off as if he has just lost his mind.

Bobby Ray presented a slight deviation from the usual routine in *Service a la Bunk* (est. 1926). Ray is admiring a woman's legs when a car engine backs up in his face and leaves him with a blackened complexion. Before Ray has a chance to clean his face, the woman drops her purse and Ray rushes forward to provide assistance. Ray is startled to discover that the woman is black, but the woman shows an interest in the dark-skinned man and reacts with disappointment when he turns on his heels and runs away. In this instance, the focus of the big laugh has shifted from the comedian's response to the woman's response.

A variation on this routine replaced the black woman with a black baby. In *The New Baby* (1912), an expectant father is shocked when he goes to greet his new arrival and finds himself gazing upon the cook's black baby. Similar confusion occurs when Mack Swain's newborn accidentally gets switched with a black baby in *By Stork Delivery* (1916). *I'm a Father* (1935) focuses on Andy Clyde's misadventures as a nervous expectant father. Clyde gets the news that his wife has gone into labor. He rushes into the hospital and sees a nurse holding a baby. "Is that mine?" he asks. The nurse opens the blanket to let him take a look. "Is it?" she replies. Clyde, seeing that the baby is black, becomes upset. "No," he snaps. The scene was reworked nine years later with Hugh Herbert for *Oh, Baby!* (1944). Herbert is amused when he sees that the baby is black. Unlike Clyde's angry rejection of the baby, Herbert smiles pleasantly, tickles the baby's nose, and tells the nurse that the baby is cute. The differences in these responses may have reflected changing mores, or it could have simply reflected the contrast between Clyde's cantankerous character and Herbert's mirthful imp.

Clyde showed a kinder disposition to a black baby in *A Bundle of Bliss* (1940). At the close of the film, Clyde adopts a number of babies. He is questioned if he wants a baby who happens to be black. Clyde, after a slight hesitation, agrees to take the black baby, too. The baby smiles as if thankful. Post-production dubbing and the superimposition of an animated mouth allows the baby to add an enthusiastic "Yeah, man!" The jiving, proto-E*Trade baby is a shock to Clyde, who responds with a double-take.

The routine continues to be used to this day. It turned up recently in the Robert Downey, Jr., feature *Due Date* (2010) as well as an episode of *Children's Hospital* ("Nip/Tug," 2011).

Even repetitive material can be elevated by a talented performer. An unidentified black actor provides an exceptionally funny performance in *That's the Spirit* (1924). The film opens with Alice Howell reading a book on the spirit world. Her husband, Billy Bletcher, doesn't believe in spirits and tries to discourage his wife from taking the book seriously. Howell, undeterred, arranges a séance. It is a spooky night to be summoning spirits. Lightning is visible outside the window. A coyote is shown howling at the moon. Nonetheless, Howell begins her summoning. The curtains rattle abruptly, but Bletcher remains skeptical. "Either the spirits are working," he says, "or the curtain needs fixing." Howell asks the spirits to knock. Just then, an intruder makes noises while breaking through the door. It is a black man hiding out from police, who are out to arrest him for stealing chickens. His bag breaks open and the chickens get loose, running amok through the house. One of the chickens flies around the room trapped inside a human skull. The black man, in a clear imitation of *Ziegfelds' Follies* star Bert Williams, is wearing a long black coat, a top hat, slapshoes, and spats.

Howell, equipped with a camera, is looking to get a picture of the spirits. The camera goes off and the resulting flash burns the black man's backside. Startled, the black man jumps up onto a chandelier. Bletcher hears so many people running around his house that he starts to believe the house really is haunted. The black man is hiding in the closet when a skeleton's hand comes down on his shoulder. He pulls out a straight razor. "I'll carve your ectoplasm with this African javelin," he says. He swings to cut the flying skull but, instead, slices the crown of his top hat. His ruined hat flops down, hanging dismally in front of his eyes.

Spencer Bell, who developed his skills performing in vaudeville and minstrel shows, worked more prolifically in silent film comedy than any other adult black actor. Larry Semon gave Bell his start in movies and featured him prominently in many of his films. Bell was the Cowardly Lion in Semon's feature-length version of *The Wizard of Oz* (1925). Semon does not introduce the Cowardly Lion, Scarecrow and Tin Man as actual characters but as disguises adopted by farmhands from Dorothy's farm. While Dorothy and the other two farmhands are swept into Oz by a tornado, Bell is launched to Oz by a lightning bolt. Although Bell is made to stick to the racial stereotype (he gets caught in the field eating watermelon when he's supposed to be working*), he also gets to be heroic in the climax when he pilots a biplane to rescue Semon.

Bell received a great deal of screen time in other Semon comedies, including *Lightning Love* (1923), *Trouble Brewing* (1924), *Kid Speed* (1924) and *The Perfect Clown* (1925). In general, Semon acts respectful and friendly to Bell onscreen. The two men, by all indication, relate to each other on equal terms. When they are dropped into a lion's den in *Oh, What a Man!* (1927), neither of them is able to get their legs moving and their scared reactions in general do not make one man superior to the other. However, Bell is never allowed to escape racial stereotyping. *Kid Speed* features Semon as a race-car driver preparing for a big race. Bell, as Semon's mechanic, performs a couple of gags while tuning up the car at the garage. Later, he plays a central role riding alongside Semon in the race. Bell shouts at the other drivers while shaking his fist in the air defiantly. He cheers uninhibitedly when their car finally gets ahead in the race. He dominates this scene until Semon gets a sheet stuck on his head while driving through a clothesline and Bell, thinking Semon is a ghost, takes a desperate leap out of the car. He is not seen again for the remainder of the film.

Bell was too often restricted to running away from imagined ghosts. This is evident in *The Counter Jumper* (1922), *Her Boyfriend* (1924) and *The Cloudhopper* (1925). In *The Counter Jumper*, a story is published in the newspaper about the Famous Cottage Ghost. Oliver Hardy wipes his face with a sheet, leaving grease smudges on the sheet that look like a face. He discards the sheet on the handle of a dolly. Bell becomes afraid of the sheet, which he assumes to be the ghost. As Semon pushes the dolly in his direction, it looks to Bell as if the sheet is pursuing him. The dolly rolls off an incline of a loading dock and barrels after Bell, who is running as fast as he can to get away.

Oliver Hardy is introduced in *Her Boyfriend* as Killer, the leader of a gang of rum runners. Killer and his men gather at the dock to load trucks with crates of bootleg liquor. He approaches Bell, a dock worker who is aiding the bootleggers. Killer shoves a gun into Bell's hand and instructs him to use it if a lawman should come snooping around. Bell looks nervous handling the gun. As soon as Killer is out of sight, he tosses away the gun and pulls out a straight razor instead. He grins gleefully before licking the edge of the blade. This, clearly, is the man's weapon of choice. Crates behind Bell are suddenly moving. Emerging

---

*Semon, who the farmer catches sleeping in the hayloft, is no less lazy.

from the stack of crates are two robot-like creatures composed entirely of crates. This is Semon and his partner, undercover detectives who have camouflaged themselves to spy on the rum runners. It panics Bell to see these creatures. First, his cap pops off his head and twirls around in the air. Then, his clothes tear off his body and fly up into the air. Then, Bell leaps out of his shoes. Finally, he dives off the dock and swims frantically for distant shores.

In *The Cloudhopper*, Frank Alexander falls into a barrel of white wash. Bell sees him, assumes that he is a ghost, and runs out of the building. Buster Keaton was also frightened by a man covered in whitewash in *The Goat* (1921). Keaton believed that, according to theatre traditions, a comedian acting foolishly was funny — regardless of the comedian's race.[2] A celebrated Commedia dell'Arte routine called "Lazzi of Fear" had an old man and his servants express extreme fear at characters who appear to be ghosts. The man and his servants are in hysterics, running around and knocking into one another.

Bell later worked extensively for producer Jack White, who saw black comedians as funny actors who worked cheap. White said, "They didn't know they were funny, but I knew it. I paid them $75 a week to be a janitor and an actor."[3]

White teamed Bell with Lige Conley in a series of comedies. These are unique in that they did not require Bell to perform what Steve Massa has termed as "crazy fright gags."[4] A rare exception occurred in a scene in *Wild Game* (1924). Conley and Bell take refuge inside a storeroom to hide from an evil sheik. The two men quickly barricade the door with crates and barrels. The sheik smiles wickedly as he pulls a rope hanging outside the room. Immediately, a panel behind Conley and Bell raises up and releases a lion into the room. Bell turns and sees the lion. His socks roll down, then roll up again. He tries to run but is unable to move. "Oh, Lawdy," he cries, "lubricate my ankles!" The sheik, though, is even more frightened to see the lion. His eyebrows pop off his head and twirl around like pinwheels. The sheik promptly jumps into a pool.

Bell had a substantial role in the Jack White comedy *Creeps* (1926). Bell is funnier in the film than either of the leads (Lou Archer and Phil Dunham), and manages to dominate the action in the second reel. At one point, Bell tries to run away but he discovers that his feet are sticking to the ground. His legs shake vigorously. He has to finally jump out of his shoes to escape. It was a restrictive role, as all of these scared black servant roles were, but he was funny nonetheless, which is a testament to his talent.

Bell turned up in a number of places during the 1920s. Monty Banks favored using the actor, who took center stage in a picnic scene in Banks's *The Golf Bug* (1924). Also, Bell starred with an all-black cast in *Tenderfeet* (1928). This comedy, produced by Midnight Productions, was likely a pilot film that was made to secure financing for an ongoing series. Unfortunately, no series followed. Bell died in 1935, at the age of 47.

The successor to Spencer Bell was Oklahoma-born black comedian Dudley Dickerson, whose comic expressions of fright enlivened many "scare" comedies of the 1930s, 1940s and 1950s. Dickerson's first "scare" comedy was Our Gang's *Spooky Hooky* (1936), in which the actor plays a janitor frightened by strange noises in a schoolhouse during a stormy night. The noises are coming from students Spanky, Alfalfa, Buckwheat and Porky, who have broken into the school to retrieve a note. Mayhem begins when a schoolroom skeleton becomes latched onto Buckwheat's shirt. Buckwheat tries to flee, but the skeleton maintains a firm grip on him. The janitor, to whom it appears that the skeleton is chasing Buckwheat down the hall, shrieks in terror.

In 1940, Dickerson went to work at the Columbia short-subject department, where he remained as a popular stock player for the next ten years. The comedian obtained his most substantial roles accompanying either Andy Clyde or Hugh Herbert into a haunted house.

The first of Dickerson's "scare" comedies at Columbia was *Host to a Ghost* (1941). The comedy has a strong Stooges' influence, with Dickerson occupying the bumbling and silly "Curly" role, and Clyde assuming the bossy and scornful "Moe" role. The pair has been hired to do construction work on an old home reportedly haunted by a pair of warring Civil War generals. The house is not really haunted until Dickerson gets killed in an explosion and returns as a ghost.

Dickerson is at his best in the fast and funny *Get Along Little Zombie* (1946), wherein he plays his scared black servant role in a more subdued and natural manner, managing to keep his frightened reactions to a minimum. An innocent "race" gag occurs in a scene when Dickerson helps Herbert hide in a closet to get away from tough guy Dick Curtis. Curtis sees Dickerson poking his head out of the closet and asks him if he saw where Herbert went. Herbert, cowering behind Dickerson, puts forward his hand, meaning for it to be taken for Dickerson's, and points toward the opposite end of the hall. "He went that way," pipes Herbert. Herbert's white hand obviously does not belong to Dickerson, but it takes Curtis a while to catch on.

In sharp contrast to Dickerson's subdued performance in *Get Along Little Zombie* is his loud and obnoxious performance in *Tall, Dark and Gruesome* (1948). For most of the film, Dickerson flees desperately from scary creatures, including a gorilla and a devil (actually, a man in costume for a masquerade party). He has nothing more to do than scream incessantly, run through rooms, and make frantic gestures. At one point, he runs so fast that he is able to outrun a speeding car.

Special-effect enhancements were important to Dickerson's comedy. In *Nervous Shakedown* (1947), a skeleton rises out of a window chest next to Dickerson, who is so frightened that his body disintegrates to dust. The effect of Dickerson disintegrating inside his clothing and the empty clothing collapsing to the floor is a truly impressive sight. The effect had been greatly improved since it had been originally used in the 1925 Sennett two-reeler *Super-Hooper-Dyne-Lizzies* and by Larry Semon in *The Stunt Man* (1927).

Another impressive effect was used in *One Shivery Night* (1950) when Dickerson is so frightened that he is able to dive underneath a door. Absent cleverly executed special effects or performers as talented as Bell or Dickerson, the "scared-black-man" routine would have otherwise grown tiresome.

Of all the films reviewed for this book, none offered a more negative portrayal of blacks than Larry Semon's 1927 feature *Spuds*. Semon, an army private, gets covered by a sheet while walking back to his barracks in the middle of the night. He goes past a barracks in which an all-black regiment resides. One of the soldiers sees Semon outside the window and assumes that he is a ghost. Through stop-motion animation, the soldier is shown gliding impossibly across the floor, as if he is so frightened that he has risen off the ground. The other soldiers become frightened, too. Crude animation is used to show their eyes getting big and bright. The soldiers then leap into the air so high that they disappear out of frame. The only thing that comes back down is their pajamas. Another soldier stands straight up and twirls around in circles. Yet another is stuck in place and is unable to run away. His body is leaning forward but he cannot lift his feet. He flaps his arms, which seems futile at first, but then he suddenly flies off. Other soldiers slide out of the room. This unfunny scene goes on for a long time with a series of stop-motion effects and animation. After years of filmmakers portraying black servants as cowardly, it takes the concept to a new low to portray an entire regiment of black soldiers as cowardly.

Actors in blackface were less common in the 1920s, but they still turned up every so often. In *Seven Years Bad Luck* (1921), Max Linder manages to disguise as a black porter without the use of burnt cork, greasepaint or shoe polish. Instead, Linder pulls a black stocking over his head, which proves a sufficient disguise as long as he averts his face from the direct gaze of the train passengers. Baby Peggy appears in blackface surrounded by black children in *Nobody's Darling* (1923). Billy Armstrong can be seen in blackface in *One Spooky Night* (1924). A white actor appears in blackface to play a scared black servant in *What a Night* (1924). "Something tells me, boss," he says, "that I'll be scared white before morning." Lloyd Hamilton wears blackface to infiltrate a gang of black bootleggers in *His Darker Self* (1924). Buster Keaton wears blackface to get a waiter job in *College* (1927).* Keaton makes himself look foolish with his unrealistic interpretation of a black man. He is working alongside several black cooks and waiters, none of whom are shuffling along or otherwise acting in this absurd manner, and his actions draw bewildered looks from his co-workers. Keaton, who was accustomed to putting himself in demeaning situations, did not care to make himself look superior. In *Convict 13* (1920) his inept golfing technique causes his black caddy to chuckle behind his back.

Keaton rarely resorted to conventional racial stereotypes. A close inspection of his films reveals only three glaring examples. A group of black men is presented playing craps in *Three Ages* (1923); a black hired hand, portrayed by a white actor in blackface (Jules Cowles), is conspicuously slow-witted in *Seven Chances* (1925); and a scene in *Neighbors* (1920) shows Keaton hiding himself under a sheet and frightening a black family who mistake him for a ghost.

Another scene in *Neighbors* is far more intriguing. A belligerent neighbor, played by Joe Roberts, causes Keaton to fall headfirst into the muddy ground. Keaton, his face blackened from the mud, picks up a broom and goes after Roberts, but he ends up striking a police officer by mistake. The officer chases after this dark-skinned individual, but Keaton has washed the mud off his face by the time that the officer catches up to him and is now utterly unrecognizable to the lawman. The officer no sooner bypasses this light-skinned fellow than he arrests a black man who happens to come along at the same moment. But this is not the end of the routine. The black man manages to escape custody while, elsewhere, a painter on a scaffold spills a bucket of black paint on Keaton's head. Keaton has only managed to wash the black paint off one side of his face when the officer meets up with him again. The officer becomes confused: Keaton looks like a black man when he is turned in one direction, but he looks like a white man when he is turned in the other direction. It is as if he is magically switching from color to color, much like the characters of *Off to Bloomingdale Asylum*. This is the only known two-tone blackface comedy routine. The routine is not so much about race as it is about illusion. That is the reason that Keaton was later able to successfully rework the routine without reference to race. The new version was devised to help Red Skelton avoid getting shot on a battlefield in the Civil War comedy *A Southern Yankee* (1948). This time, it is the comedian's uniform that is a different color on either side. The soldiers hold fire while Skelton walks down the middle of the battle line because the Northern army only sees the half of the uniform that is Union blue, and the Southern army only sees the half of the uniform that is Confederate gray.

---

*The Edison comedy *Getting Evidence* (1906) featured a bumbling detective blackening his face to go undercover as a waiter. The practicality of Keaton blackening his face to get a job is more questionable. This is reminiscent of *A Chocolate Cowboy* (1925), a strange comedy involving a white man who pretends to be black to get a job shining shoes.

Buster Keaton (left) is joined in a hiding place by Jules Cowles, a white actor who specialized in blackface roles, in *Seven Chances* (1925) (courtesy Bruce Lawton Collection).

The blackface tradition continued into the sound era. This make-up was used for comic effect in the occasional low-budget feature, including *Daring Young Man* (1942), *Redhead from Manhattan* (1943), *Zombies on Broadway* (1945) and *Crazy Over Horses* (1951), but it mostly turned up in short comedies. Mack Sennett featured blackface comedians Moran & Mack and Bert Swor in a series of short comedies in the early thirties. Vernon Dent poses as a black porter in *Tied for Life* (1933). Patsy Kelly provides an over-the-top impersonation of a mammy in *Done in Oil* (1934). (A modern audience would no doubt be uncomfortable watching Kelly's performance.) Edgar Kennedy, working as a private detective, disguises as a mammy maid in *Cooks and Crooks* (1942). Kennedy, whose character is afraid of giving away his identity, says and does little in the mammy role. This big, barrel-chested Irishman skulking around as a mammy looks downright creepy. *Tall, Dark and Gruesome* (1948) finds a more creative way to get its star, Hugh Herbert, into blackface. Herbert, trying to recover pages sucked up by his vacuum cleaner, reverses the suction and gets dirt spewed into his face. He sees himself in a mirror with his face blackened and mistakes himself for his black servant (Dudley Dickerson).

Blackface recently returned to the big screen with *Tropic Thunder* (2008), in which Robert Downey, Jr., plays a serious method actor who has his pigmentation surgically altered so that he can authentically portray a black man in his new movie. Other characters mock Downey's character for being wildly insensitive and inappropriate.

The minstrel stereotype of the lazy black man was something that rarely turned up in the films reviewed for the book. The truth is that only one obvious example turned up during research. In *His Silent Racket* (1933), Charley Chase offers a black man a job in his dry-cleaning store. The notion of work panics the black man, who wastes no time in bolting out of the door.

Blacks were not the only ethnic groups subjected to derogatory racial stereotyping. Other groups singled out were Germans, Jews, Dutch, Irish, Swedes, Mexicans, Spaniards and Italians.

In 1920, Universal produced the "Charlie of the Orient" comedy series starring Asian actor Chai Hong. Originally, the gimmick of the series was to have an Asian comedian made up and costumed to look like Charlie Chaplin. Later series entries, which included the titles *Charlie, the Hero*, *Charlie Gets a Job*, *Charlie in Turkey* and *Charlie, the Little Daredevil*, were focused on exploiting Asian stereotypes.

The most common stereotype for an Italian man was that of a fruit seller with a dozen small children. *Oh, Baby!* (1920), a Hall Room Boys comedy, features a Italian fruit seller whose wife has just given birth to her 13th child and, rather than take responsibility for this addition to her family, she dumps the baby on the doorstep of a pair of inept bachelors (Neely Edwards and Hugh Fay). Italians were also depicted as detestable anarchists hidden

Lloyd Hamilton, disguised in blackface to infiltrate a bootlegger ring, has attracted the attention of "Darktown's Cleopatra" (Irma Harrison) in *His Darker Self* (1924) (courtesy Steve Rydzewski).

behind dark, drooping moustaches. They were made to look grotesque, sucking down heaps of spaghetti and guzzling down bottles of wine. The make-up and costuming is not as offensive as the attitude of the characters and the reaction that the other characters demonstrate towards them.

Silent film comedy was, in many instances, xenophobic. "South of the border" comedies, including *Are Married Policemen Safe?* (1918) and *Hot Tamale* (1920), depict Mexico as an unfriendly and unstable place. Snub Pollard experiences repeated earthquake tremors while visiting Mexico in *Shake 'Em Up* (1921). The camera jiggles, bricks drop off buildings, and actors fall down.

Beans and Bullets (1916), a Joker one-reeler, exploits many stereotypes associated with Mexico, including revolutions, duels and lazy peasants. A general (Jack Francis) and a major (Milburn Morante) fight over the affections of the president's daughter (Lillian Peacock). The officers decide to settle their differences with a duel. The major hires Pedro (Billy Franey) to throw pepper in the general's eyes to spoil his aim. The general, unaware of the major's arrangement with Pedro, hires Pedro to throw pepper in the major's eyes. The duel ends with both men getting pepper in their eyes and neither of them feeling happy about it. The men, according to *Moving Picture World*, take "shots at Pedro to soothe their feelings."[5] The military men decide to stage a revolution to take the president's daughter by

The most frightened reactions in lion comedies usually came from black actors. A "fright" take is provided by an unidentified black actor in this still from *Fares, Please!* (1925) (courtesy Robert Arkus).

force. Pedro volunteers to lead an army in support of the president (Charles Conklin). The two armies, not more than a few men between them, meet up on the battlefield. Pedro proves cowardly when the battle gets underway. Then, Pedro's wife (Gale Henry) shows up. The wife, who has been looking for Pedro to do his chores, hurls a stick of dynamite at him. He ducks in time to avoid the dynamite, but the dynamite then lands in the middle of the battlefield and blows up the revolutionary army. The president forgives the revolutionists and allows them to attend a party in his garden. The wife, upset at seeing Pedro enjoying the party, routes the members of *both* armies to lead Pedro to the washing.

No Soup (1916), another Joker short, starred Ernie Shields as an American consul stationed among the savage Igorrotes. The minister's daughter is in tears when her small dog goes missing. Ernie is worried because he is aware of the Igorrotes' dog-eating habits. The consul searches butcher shops and soup pots to find the dog. At one point, he sees what he assumes to be the young woman's dog, but he realizes after an exhausting chase that he has gotten hold of the wrong dog. He finally rescues the dog from natives who are preparing to chop up the pet for dinner.

The stereotypes of silent film comedy do not convey the ill intent that is manifest in current stereotypes. *Everyone* was fair game as long as a stereotype served the plot or made people laugh. Today, stereotypes are often calculated to conform with a political agenda. Propagandists are determined to manipulate the media in ways that demonize the people outside their political and ideological base. The pervasiveness of mass media and the growing involvement of government agencies in our lives makes stereotyping a much greater problem today than it was 90 years ago. With government controls regulating rights and benefits, the perception of a group has never been more important to their status and treatment in society.

Cannibals

Winsor McCay's early cartoons included a black cannibal boy named Imp. Imp, a mischievous child who was often the catalyst for his friends' misadventures, did not behave in accordance to racial stereotypes. But his physical characteristics, which included a grass skirt, kinky hair and oversized lips, may have been the inspiration for the more derogatory African cannibals who appeared in later live-action films and cartoons.

Cartoons introduced the most outrageous types of cannibals. Felix the Cat encounters the Boola Boola cannibals in *Felix Dopes It Out* (1925). These cannibals, with their white gloves and spats, display a strong minstrel-show influence. The Disney cartoon *Alice Cans the Cannibals* (1925) features young Alice and her cat driving along the coast when they accidentally ride off a cliff and plunge into the ocean. A fish tows them to a tropical island, where they are assaulted by hyperactive cannibals. The cannibals in *Bosko Shipwrecked!* (1931) are largely distinguished by the big bones knotted up in their hair. In *Plane Dumb* (1932), two pilots who have crashed their plane off the coast of Africa adopt blackface to go unnoticed among the natives. The pilots' shuckin' and jivin' are not accepted by the natives. *Jungle Jitters* (1938), directed by Friz Freleng, has drawn controversy in recent years for its negative portrayal of blacks. In that Looney Tunes cartoon, a salesman travels through Africa offering big-lipped, spear-carrying natives vacuum cleaners, batteries and light bulbs. The natives respond by throwing the salesman into a cooking pot and ransacking his goods. More than one gag has to do with the natives' nose rings. One native wears a nose-ring so large that it hangs to the ground. He lightheartedly swings the nose ring around so he can hop in and out of it like a little girl playing jump rope. A jungle native named King Saucer Lips is part of a circus freak show in the Warner Bros. cartoon *Buddy's Circus* (1934). The native manages to entertain crowds by spinning records inside his distended lips. *Chew Chew Baby* (1958) has become a cult favorite. A tourist driving through the jungle encounters a cute, childlike pygmy with exceptionally pointy teeth. After taking a picture of the pygmy, the tourist jokingly tells the little fellow to look him up if he ever gets to Cincinnati. The pygmy does, in fact, show up at the man's home and eats a number of people before the man realizes that he is a cannibal. His coloring is indistinct, which makes it hard to identify if he is meant to be black or Asian. The film was banned from television not for its racial stereotyping but for its carnivorous violence.

Dusky cannibals were featured in early live-action comedies, including the Universal Joker short *Mike and Jack Among the Cannibals* (1913) and the Broncho Film Company's *Shorty Among the Cannibals* (1915). Oliver Hardy played an actor made up to look like a cannibal in Lubin's *The Cannibal King* (1915). Snub Pollard experienced difficulties with cannibals in *Red Hot Hottentots* (1920). Billy Bevan battled cannibals led by King Gumbo (Andy Clyde) in *A Sea Dog's Tale* (1926). In *Save Me, Sadie* (1920), a young man is upset because his girlfriend (Helen Darling) is more interested in becoming a missionary than in becoming his wife. He thinks that he can bring Sadie to her senses by having a friend show

A cannibal boy (right) sees if Mickey Daniels (left) is tender enough to eat in *Wild Babies* (1932). Daniels's companion in the pot is Grady Sutton (courtesy Cole Johnson Collection).

up at her house pretending to be a bloodthirsty cannibal. The phony cannibal gets carried away and creates a greater uproar in the household than planned.

Cannibal comedies continued into the early sound era. In the Roach two-reeler *Wild Babies* (1932), Mickey Daniels and Grady Sutton have a nightmare about African cannibals. The duo spends much of the film simmering in a cooking pot. At one point, a hungry little boy comes along and bites down on Sutton's arm. This dismays the chef, who shoos away the boy for "nibbling before dinner." *Kid 'in' Africa* (1933) featured Shirley Temple as a missionary visiting Africa to convert the natives to Christianity. The missionary, oddly named Madam Cradlebait, is instantaneously thrown into a cooking pot by native savages.

The Our Gang classic *The Kid from Borneo* (1933) managed, even more than *The Cannibal King* and *Save Me, Sadie*, to make fun of prejudice and stereotypes. The story was simple: at a carnival show, the gang comes face-to-face with Bumbo, billed as "The Wild Man from Borneo." Bumbo, a hulking, childlike black man dressed up in horns and other stereotypical African native regalia, is affected by an overpowering passion for candy. Seeing Stymie with a bag of candy incites him. He bolts towards the children roaring, "Yum, yum! Eat 'em up!" The gang, assuming that Bumbo is a cannibal looking to eat them, flees from the carnival in terror. The wild man, determined to get his hands on the candy, pursues the panicked children to their home.

The cannibals disappeared from films for several years, but then inexplicably showed up again in Abbott & Costello's *Africa Screams* (1949). These cannibals had not been tempered by time. They were outrageous stereotypes with every possible flourish, including big bones in their noses.

Dark-skinned cannibals returned yet again in *Pirates of the Caribbean 2: Dead Man's Chest* (2006). These were old exaggerated stock characters who could be trusted to get laughs and the filmmakers did not expect anyone to be offended. However, the unflattering caricatures drew heated protests from the National Garifuna Council of Belize, and Charles Williams, chief of the Dominica Carib Territory. Blogger Marc Singer wrote of the film, "It uncritically recycles racist propaganda and it's part of a larger pattern of insulting portrayals of nonwhite characters."[6] However, most movie fans did not agree. An online petition to "Stop Racist 'Pirates'" received only 25 signatures.

22

Other Variations

The Lamppost

A popular music hall routine involving a drunken man's misadventure with a lamppost was introduced onscreen by Max Linder in *Max and the Quinquina* (1911). The routine begins with Linder exiting a bar. He drunkenly struggles to put on his coat, not realizing that his coat has become wrapped around a lamppost. He no sooner buttons up his coat than he realizes that he has attached himself to the lamppost. A police officer comes along and helps Linder to get loose.

Buster Keaton later reworked this gag in *The Goat* (1921). This time, though, the police officer is not friendly. When the grim-faced officer comes up behind him, Keaton assumes he cannot move forward because the cop has taken hold of him. He argues with the officer, who assumes that Keaton is crazy and walks away.

The routine became more aggressive when revived by Stan Laurel in *Pie-Eyed* (1925). Laurel, too, leaves a bar, drunk. After bounding himself to the pole, he takes a grand step forward only to be yanked backwards into the pole. As he struggles harder to get loose, he is pulled backwards and goes spinning. A police officer frees him by giving him a strenuous tug, which splits the back of his coat.

Harold Lloyd included the routine in *High and Dizzy* (1920), but he is not the one who gets entangled with the pole. Lloyd is clumsily helping his drinking buddy on with his coat when he wraps the coat around a pole. Lloyd gradually becomes aware of the situation and, as drunk as he is, he is determined to come up with a solution. It says much about Lloyd's character that he has faith in his own problem-solving abilities even when intoxicated. His questionable solution, executed with great self-assurance, is to neatly tear the coat in half.

Chaplin devised loose variations of this routine wherein he became tangled up with other objects. One example can be found in *One A.M.* (1916) when, after a night of merrymaking, he drunkenly staggers out of a cab that has delivered him home. He slips his hand into his pants pocket, unknowingly looping his arm through an open window of the cab door. He is trying to step forward onto the curb when he discovers that his arm is interlocked with the door and he cannot pull himself free. In *Pay Day* (1922), Chaplin's drunken efforts to put on his coat gets him trapped inside the coat with a hefty, equally inebriated buddy (Henry Bergman), who ends up staggering down the street with Chaplin dragging helplessly behind him. Bergman is as bulky as a lamppost and, being stupefied from drink, he is initially as stiff as a lamppost. But he is able to walk away, which is something that a lamppost could never do, and it is by replacing a fixture with a breathing, active man that Chaplin was able to further enliven this stock routine.

Tickling

Tickling, like drunkenness, was about a pleasurable loss of control. This is evident when Roscoe Arbuckle and Buster Keaton tickle gunman Al St. John into submission in *Out West* (1918).

Tickling could also have a sexual component. Ethel Teare plays an amusingly flirtatious woman in the Ham and Bud comedy *A Flyer in Flapjacks* (1917). Teare flirts with Ham. She flirts with Bud. She flirts with a cook. She flirts with a policeman. However, these flirtations go no further than Ethel tickling Ham. This playfulness may seem innocuous but it had implications all its own.

The sexual nature of tickling is more glaring in *Max and the Lady Doctor* (1909). Max Linder proves to be highly ticklish while being examined by a lady doctor. He finds the experience so enjoyable that he immediately asks the lady doctor to marry him. The next scene shows Max staying home to care for the couple's baby while his wife runs her medical practice. One day, Max comes to visit his wife at her office and finds a bunch of leering men waiting eagerly to be examined by the pretty doctor. Max barges into the examining room and finds a man giggling as his wife examines him. Max is furious. He kicks the man out of the room and clears the other men out as well. The closing scene reveals Max sitting back in his easy chair joyfully puffing on cigar as his wife, now retired from her medical practice, bounces their bawling baby on her knee.

Tickling could get a man in trouble. In *Fluttering Hearts* (1927), Charley Chase agrees to help his girlfriend get through a crowd at a sheet sale. He tickles a number of matronly women to get through, but one of these women assumes that Chase is flirting with her. Leering, she turns around and tickles Chase. Chase is laughing so hard that he steps out of line, allowing a bunch of women to stampede ahead of him. He ends up exhausted from the experience and is left farther back in line than he was originally. Still, it could have been worse. When the routine was reused by James P. Burtis in *The Bargain of the Century* (1933), Burtis's efforts to tickle women ended up getting him smacked in the face.

It was not even necessary for the people engaged in the tickling to be of opposite sexes. *Red Noses* (1932) involves ZaSu Pitts going to a Turkish bath to get rid of a cold. A lady masseuse no sooner applies an electric hand-massager to Pitts's back than she is writhing uncontrollably and giggling in delight. The scene cannot help but convey a sense of homoerotism.

The full comic potential of tickling was achieved in *Way Out West* (1937). Lola Marcel (Sharon Lynn), a sultry saloon singer, pounces on Stan Laurel to take a valuable deed from him. The dancer, dressed in a clingy satin nightgown, wrestles with Laurel on her bed. She tears open his jacket and shoves her hand down his shirt. Laurel bursts into fits of laughter. The scantily clad woman rolling around on a bed with Laurel, who is laughing hysterically, has a great deal of sexual implication.

Shaving Nicks

Shaving, which can be a hazardous activity if not done carefully, was seen as an appropriate subject for a slapstick comedy. In *A Dull Razor* (1900), an embryonic Edison comedy, a man sloppily lathers up his face, scrapes a straight razor across his neck and jowls, and contorts his features into a pained expression. Audiences found this activity entertaining enough that rival companies, including Lubin and Selig Polyscope, turned out counterfeit versions of the film to market to exhibitors. The Edison Company itself produced a race-oriented revamp titled *A Dutchman Shaving* (1902). Another Edison comedy, *A Bowery Five Cent Shave* (1902), featured a barber who inexplicably gases his customers before he shaves them. *A Close Shave* (1901), produced by American Mutoscope & Biograph, involved two mischievous boys who tie a bearded gentleman to a barber's chair and proceed to shave his face bare. Other early shaving films meant to amuse included George Albert Smith's *Comic Shaving* (1897) and Pathé Frères' *A Funny Shave* (1905).

Shaving routines were to become more elaborate in the coming years. *The Bell Boy* (1918) shows Roscoe Arbuckle at work shaving a heavily bearded Rasputin-like customer. He manages with a few swipes of his razor to transform this man into an exact likeness of General Ulysses S. Grant. Then, he does some more trimming and the man comes out looking like Abraham Lincoln. Finally, he makes the man into Kaiser Wilhelm and becomes so incensed by the evil visage that he cannot resist smacking the fellow in the face with shaving cream.

In *Luck o' the Foolish* (1924), Harry Langdon is traveling by train to a new city where a job awaits him. Langdon wakes the next morning after spending the night in a berth and

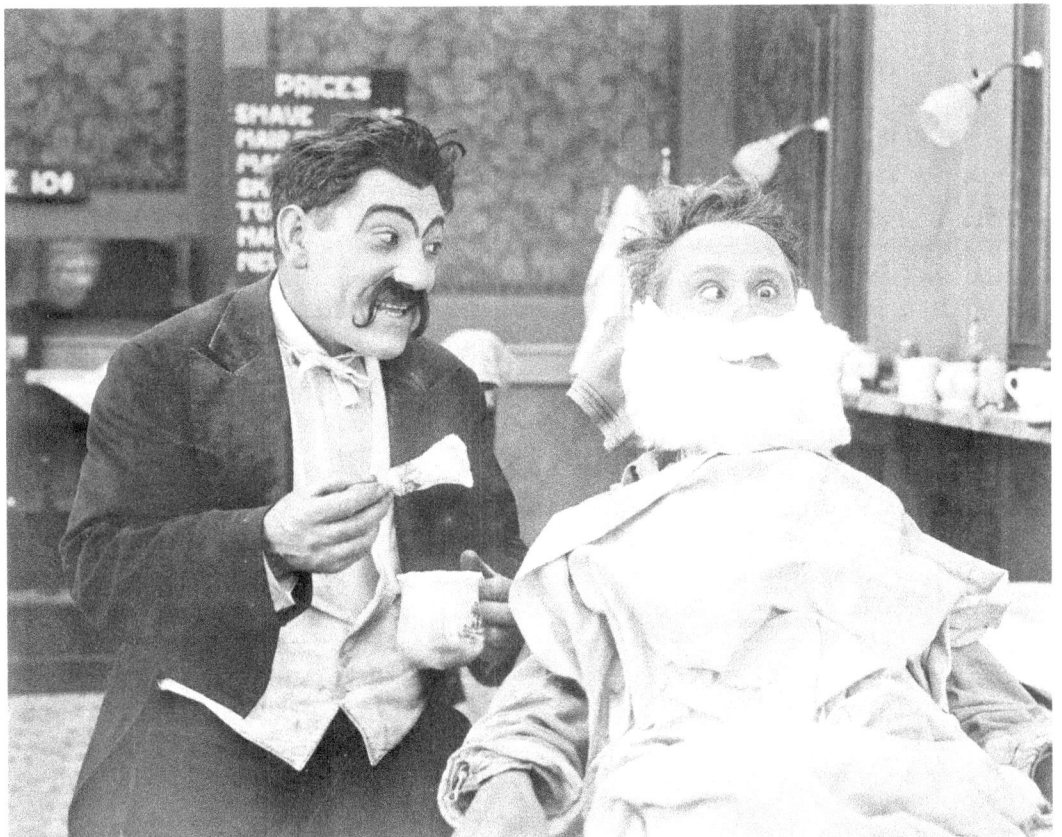

Ben Turpin (right) doesn't look happy to be getting a shave from Heinie Conklin in an unidentified Sennett comedy (courtesy Steve Rydzewski).

enters a washroom on the train to shave. He has to share a mirror with another man who is shaving (Yorke Sherwood). Sherwood becomes unnerved by Langdon's recklessness with a straight razor in a moving train. At one point, the rocking of the train causes Langdon to jerk forward and nick Sherwood in the back of the neck. Throughout this process, Langdon remains nonchalant and, at one point, sticks the razor inside his ear to remove stray shaving cream. Sherwood is appalled, then suddenly remembers something that he read. He snatches up a newspaper and stares at an article about the police pursuing a mad serial killer man who slaughters his victims with a straight razor. The idea of the innocent and boobish Langdon as a serial killer is absurd, but Sherwood believes this to be true and is terrified by the razor-wielding eccentric.

Lloyd Hamilton performs a novel shaving routine in *Always a Gentleman* (1928). Hamilton has a razor at the ready as he approaches a mirror on his bedroom wall. No sooner does he lift the razor to his face than he is interrupted by a neighbor practicing a dance number in the next apartment. The dancer's stomping on the floorboards succeeds in shaking the walls and causing Hamilton's mirror to swing back and forth. Hamilton struggles to stay with his reflection while shaving, swaying back and forth to catch a glimpse of himself before he taking the next blunt swipe with the razor. The dancing no sooner stops than the maintenance man starts to work on the fuses, which causes the lights to flicker on and off. Hamilton positions the razor while the lights are on but he can never finish before the lights go out again. In utter frustration, Hamilton collapses against the wall. He asks his roommate to hold up a candle while he shaves. The roommate falls asleep while trying to help, and his snoring blows out the candle. When the light comes back on, it is revealed that Hamilton, instead of shaving his face, shaved all of the hair off his roommate's head.

A well-known shaving routine was performed by W. C. Fields in *It's a Gift* (1934). In that classic scene, Fields takes a break from shaving to make room for his teenage daughter, Mildred (Jean Rouverol), in front of a bathroom mirror. Mildred, who is applying lipstick, gargling and brushing her hair, increasingly takes up space until she pushes Fields aside entirely. Fields gives up trying to find space for himself after he chokes on one of Mildred's stray hairs. Fields hangs a shaving mirror off a ceiling hook in order to finish shaving. However, the mirror will not stay in place and Fields has to follow the mirror around as it twirls in a circle. Fields steals swipes whenever the mirror twirls past him. In the end, he turns the mirror upside down and reclines on a stool to shave.

In *Smoked Hams* (1934), Shemp Howard handles a straight razor with ferocity. He could be the razor-wielding serial killer from the Langdon film. He accidentally pokes himself in the eye, blinding himself. He takes out tweezers to pluck a few chin hairs that he missed. The sound of the whiskers being plucked is represented by the plucking of violin strings. The comedian yelps with each and every hair that is removed. Shemp asks his wife (Daphne Pollard) to shave the back of his neck. Pollard gets a wooden block to stand on while she shaves Shemp's neck. She drops the razor down the back of his shirt and tears his shirt as she attempts to extract the razor.

Shemp performs another shaving routine in the Three Stooges comedy *Brideless Groom* (1947). In that two-reeler, he gets extremely messy with the shaving cream. The stuff gets into his eye at one point and he becomes distressed, screaming at the top of his lungs that he has been blinded. Fields had his teenage daughter interfering with his efforts to shave by monopolizing the mirror. Interfering with Shemp's efforts is his brother Moe, who is sewing up the cuffs on his pants and repeatedly poking him in the leg with a needle. Shemp, like Fields, has a problem with the mirror twirling around uncontrollably. At one point, the mirror turns backwards and Shemp, unable to see his reflection, goes into a panic thinking that he has cut off his own head.

The Fields scene is tender and touching as Fields, a loving father, is willing to sacrifice his own convenience for his daughter's sake. The daughter's high-pitched gargling and Fields's choking on a hair does not make this a completely subdued routine, but it is considerably more subdued than Shemp's scene. The decapitation scare, the blinding by shaving cream, the bloodcurdling screams and the needles driven into Shemp's leg creates a more raucous type of comedy.

Chester Conklin employs elements of both the Hamilton routine and the Fields routine in *Keystone Hotel* (1935). In this celebrated short, Conklin's wife (Vivien Oakland) gets the room shaking when she turns on her reducing machine. Conklin, unable to hold his razor steady, hangs up a shaving mirror on the fire escape, where he then has a problem keeping track of his reflection while the mirror twirls in circles.

In *Never Give a Sucker an Even Break* (1941), W. C. Fields performs a shaving scene that combines elements of the Langdon and Hamilton routines. Fields and another man are shaving side by side on a moving plane. The lights go out briefly and, when they come back on, Fields and the other man are tangled up and shaving each other. Scriptwriters continued to find the shaving-in-the-dark idea viable. Ben Blue has just this problem during the Great Northeast Blackout of 1965 in *Where Were You When the Lights Went Out?* (1968).

An Ache in Every Stake (1941) has the all-time silliest shaving routine. The premise has The Stooges being hired to prepare the meal for a dinner party. Moe asks Curly to "shave the ice." Curly sets up a block of ice in a chair, ties a towel around the middle, and spreads shaving cream on the ice. He then engages in small talk (such as, "Are you married or happy?") as he scrapes the ice with a straight razor.

The Cabin Boy and the Mean Captain

Comedians turned up occasionally playing cabin boys opposite mean, burly captains. This included Lloyd Hamilton in *April Fool* (1920), Buster Keaton in *The Love Nest* (1923), Harry Langdon in *Shanghaied Lovers* (1924), and Lupino Lane in *Be My King* (1928). But, in one instance, it was the mean, burly captain who took center stage and got most of the laughs. The film, produced by Fox, was *A Deep Sea Panic* (1924).

Paul Parrott is shanghaied to perform duties on a ship. Parrott is incompetent as a galley cook, which he demonstrates by accidentally serving the captain (Kalla Pasha) a rubber mat instead of a steak. Pasha gets mad and bites Parrott's ear. Ear-biting was, in fact, a Pasha trademark. Pasha becomes so sick from Parrott's food that his stomach swells up and visibly pulsates. Pasha, furious, tosses Parrott around the cabin. For the purposes of this absurdly violent scene, it is an obvious dummy that Pasha actually thrashes.

Pasha later decides that he wants a haircut. He drops his rugged façade to admit that he wants to look nice. "Make me dainty," he tells Parrott. He looks into a mirror and the mirror cracks. Seconds later, tar spills onto Pasha's face. A monkey jumps on Pasha's face and gets stuck to the tar. Pasha runs through the cabin struggling to tear the monkey off his face.

Pasha, driven mad by Parrott's incompetence, is truly the star of this very funny short. *A Deep Sea Panic* is equivalent to Chaplin's *Easy Street* presented from the perspective of heavy Eric Campbell. Pasha, a beefy one-time professional wrestler, is most familiar for his

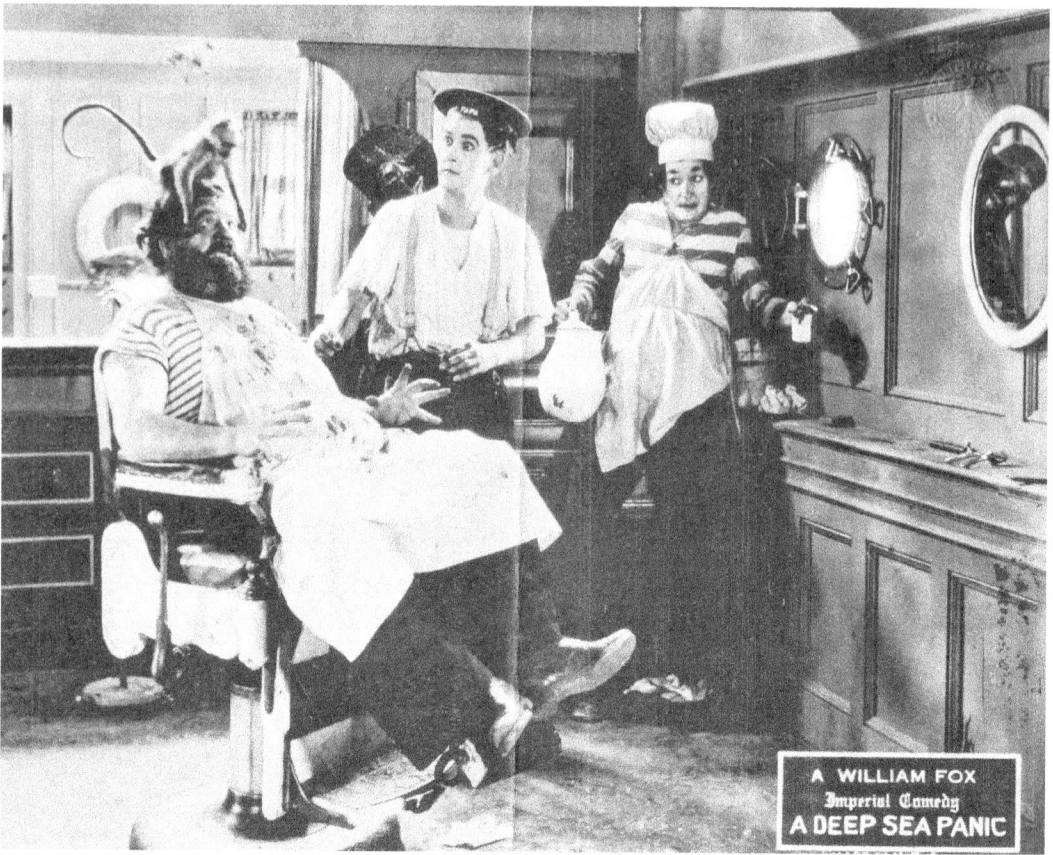

Kalla Pasha (seated) is alarmed to have a monkey stuck to his face in *Deep Sea Panic* (1924). The onlookers are James Parrott (center) and Bobby Burns (courtesy Cole Johnson Collection).

numerous appearances in Sennett comedies during the early 1920s. He can be found at his best playing the title role in the Ben Turpin comedy *Yukon Jake*. It is unfortunate that Pasha did not receive more roles that put his comic talents in the forefront.

In real life, the actor came to a tragic end. The facts of his final days were brought to light by film historian Steve Massa. Massa wrote, "After sound arrived his roles were reduced to bit parts, and he soon began acting out some of his screen antics in real life. In a 1932 altercation with a streetcar conductor he broke an ink bottle over the man's head, but was found not guilty by reason of insanity and committed to the Mendocino State Hospital. He died there a year later in 1933."[1]

Sticky Situations

Glue was a popular comic staple. Glue pranks abound in the 1909 German comedy *Klebolin Sticks Everything*, which proves that a bratty boy can create a great deal of mischief with a glue pot. The same premise was used in Lubin's *Father's Glue* (1909) and Pathé Frères' *A Sticky Stepmother* (1910). Adhesive mischief was still in effect by 1913, when Pathé Comica released *Glue of Titi*.

Glue accidents had to be more inventively constructed than glue pranks. In a 1913 Éclair comedy, *The Ruse of Willy*, a homeowner is determined to identify the person who has been stealing food out of his pantry. He spreads flour on the floor of the pantry expecting to get the impression of the thief's shoes. He has no idea that the thief is his young son Willy, who catches on to his father's trap and wears his father's shoes for his next raid on the pantry. Undeterred, the father makes a point on the following night to fill his shoes with glue. Willy repeats his trick but is unable to remove the shoes.

A glue routine builds into a comic calamity in a 1908 Pathé Frères short *It Sticks Everything—Even Iron*. A homeowner is assisted by his maid as he tries to glue a stovepipe that has blown down on his roof. However, the maid gets the pipe stuck to her hand and, as the man is trying to pull it loose, he kicks over his glue pot and the contents drip down onto the sidewalk. A policeman steps into the glue and gets his foot stuck to the ground. Others come to help but they are soon stuck together in a human chain. This chaos was surpassed by *The Leaking Glue Pot* (1908), in which passersby become glued to the ground in several different locations.

American comedians, too, refused to become unglued. In *Creeps* (1926), Lou Archer reaches for hair gel but sticks his hand in a jar of glue instead. Soon after, he tries to tip his hat to a woman, but he cannot remove his hat.* In *The Haunted House* (1921), Buster Keaton does not prove to be the most competent bank teller, as he spills glue in his cash drawer. This proves a problem for robbers when they force Keaton to hand over the sticky loot. A comedy reminiscent of *It Sticks Everything—Even Iron* was Laurel & Hardy's *The Finishing Touch* (1928). The duo is putting a roof on a new home when a police officer (Edgar Kennedy) comes to address a noise complaint from a neighbor. A bucket of glue tumbles off the roof and drenches Kennedy with its contents. Shingles, which also roll off the roof, rain down on Kennedy and become stuck across every part of his body.

Max Linder devised the most clever glue routines. In *Max Will Not Marry* (1910), the dapper star is on his way to have dinner with his girlfriend and her parents. He is excited because he plans to ask the parents for their consent for him to marry their daughter. While at a bakery to buy a cake, Max comes in contact with a sheet of fly paper lying on the counter. Now, as a result, he sticks to everything that he touches. Embarrassed, he struggles to hide this from his girlfriend's parents during his visit. He gets stuck to a letter, a wine glass, a napkin, and a fork. He tries to pass a plate to his girlfriend's father, but the plate becomes locked in his grip. The father gets enraged because he thinks that Max is refusing to let go of the plate and forcibly ejects Max from his home.

Linder elaborated on the glue routine for a segment of *Seven Years Bad Luck* (1921). Linder, posing as a station agent at a train depot, gets glue on his hands while affixing a label to a mail package. He soon gets his hand stuck to his hat. He fails to remember that he has glue on his hand when he affectionately places his hand on the shoulder of the station agent's daughter. He hears her father in the other room and is unable to remove his hand from her shoulder. His efforts to pull himself loose only manage to cause the seams in the girl's dress to split. Linder comes halfway out of the room to greet the father. The whole time, he continues tugging to get his hand free. Inside of the other room, the girl's dress is slipping down off her shoulders to the girl's outward embarrassment. The old man, who does not know Linder, becomes suspicious, pulls out a gun, and demands that Linder raise his hands. Linder, desperate to cooperate, yanks hard to raise his hands and the entire dress

---

*In much the same way, molasses stuck a hat to Buster Keaton's head in *The Butcher Boy* (1917).

Buster Keaton cannot give away money (it's glued to his hands and face) in *The Haunted House* (1921).

comes off in his hand. The father becomes even more suspicious and tries to see what it is that Linder is hiding behind his back. Linder moves in a circle away from the father, frantically stuffing the entire dress into the back of his pants. Soon, the station agent discovers his daughter dressed in nothing but her slip, and chases after Linder with his gun. This routine must have been effective with audiences as Jimmie Adams reprised the routine only a few months later in *Sunless Sunday* (1921).

In the Three Stooges' *Healthy, Wealthy and Dumb* (1938), Curly grabs a container of glue thinking it is a container of maple syrup, and pours it freely over his pancakes. Curly isn't bothered by the taste of the glue, but he has a problem when he cannot remove his fork from his mouth. The scene becomes gruesome when Moe's efforts to remedy the problem nearly extract Curly's tongue along with the fork. The situation is even worse in *A Snitch in Time* (1950) when glue seals Moe's eyelids shut. Shemp and Larry employ a series of heavy tools — including a chisel, screwdriver and pliers — to get Moe's eye open. Moe then gets his hands stuck to a board, prompting Shemp to use a hacksaw to cut him loose.

Linder constructed his glue routine within the context of the story and relationships while the Stooges focused on bodily injury and heavy work tools. Others, though, were content to simply return to the original glue pranks, as Harpo Marx demonstrates by applying glue to the seat of a foreign ambassador's pants in the political farce *Duck Soup* (1933).

Glue and glue-like substances *did* have their benefits. In *The Daredevil* (1923), Ben Turpin gets stuck to a saddle by hot tar and, when the horse is unable to throw him, the crowd assumes that Turpin is an expert rider. In *Gum Riot* (1920), Hank Mann is mixing up a batch of Fixo Gum with his hot-headed boss, Vernon Dent. Mann recognizes a tempting opportunity when Dent gets his hands covered in the gum mixture and become stuck to a table. Mann, after smiling at the camera, proceeds to kick Dent, tweak his nose, and give him a hard smack across the face. This is similar to a routine later performed by the Three Stooges in *Calling All Curs* (1938). Moe breaks through an intercom to punch Curly in the face, but he finds that he has become stuck in the wall. Curly proceeds to recite, "She loves me, she loves me not" as he plucks out hairs from Moe's eyebrows. The Stooges recycled this basic situation in a number of films, including *Nutty but Nice* (1940), *Loose Loot* (1953) and *Fling in the Ring* (1955).

As these scenes suggest, the Stooges did not need glue to get themselves stuck. Moe gets his head stuck in a pipe in *Higher Than a Kite* (1943). Shemp gets *his* head stuck inside a fishbowl in *Hold That Lion!* (1947).

Glue gags are rare today. The last major motion picture to feature a glue gag was *American Pie 2* (1999), in which Jason Biggs glued his hand to his penis. Of course, this was the same series in which pie-in-the-face comedy was set aside for penis-in-a-pie comedy.

John Hughes, one of the last of the comedy traditionalists, scripted a penis-free glue routine for Chevy Chase to perform in *National Lampoon's Christmas Vacation* (1989). After getting sap on his hands from setting up a Christmas tree, Chase has trouble using his sticky fingers to turn the pages of a magazine. His foolish efforts to get his fingers loose cause him to pull the magazine to pieces. Chase is effective in the scene through his use of spastic gestures and a hopelessly dim expression. Still, these adhesive mixtures have so securely bonded themselves to film comedy that it doubtful glue gags will ever entirely disappear.

Mass Transit, Mass Chaos

The difficulties of mass transit were explored in three different comedy films of 1924, *Feet of Mud*, *Crushed* and *Hot Water*.

In *Hot Water*, Harold Lloyd has difficulty paying a trolley conductor while his arms are filled with groceries, which include two bags stuffed with boxes and vegetable stalks, a stack of parcels and a very live turkey. Lloyd manages to hold onto most of his items except for the turkey, which gets away from him and settles under the skirt of an old woman. Lloyd has to find a way to get the bird back without disturbing the woman. This turns out badly for him. The turkey pecks the woman's foot, the woman leaps up in fright, and Lloyd and the bird are tossed out into the street by the conductor.

In *Feet of Mud*, Harry Langdon is shocked and dismayed to be shoved along, knocked down and finally trampled by a relentless stream of subway riders. Langdon, a street cleaner who got caught up in the crowd, is not even supposed to be on the train. The passengers manage, while stepping on Langdon, to drive the handle of the street cleaner's broom into his neck. He is relieved when passengers clear out at the next station and he holds the door shut to prevent a new crowd from boarding. Unfortunately, this plan is thwarted by a conductor, who roughly pushes the harried passenger aside to open the door. Langdon, though, remains undeterred. He displays a knowing grin as he opens a door on the opposite side. By the time the conductor has pried open his door, so much pressure has built up that the crowd bursts straight through the car and flies out the door Langdon has opened.

Harold Lloyd and Ann Christy are part of the commuter crush in *Speedy* (1928). Other passengers are extras (courtesy www.doctormacro.com).

Harold Lloyd is ejected from a trolley in *Hot Water* (1924). Conductor and passengers are unidentified (courtesy www.doctormacro.com).

Lloyd Hamilton finds himself in both situations at the same time in *Crushed* (1924). In this two-reeler, he has his arms filled with groceries as he tries to contend with a rampant mob in a subway station. Harold Lloyd had bags that were nicely packed and parcels that were neatly bundled. Hamilton is in a less favorable situation. He is burdened with considerably more groceries, including bags and baskets overflowing with boxes, cans and extravagantly leafy vegetables. Like Lloyd, he also has live poultry, but, in place of a turkey Hamilton has a stout and testy duck. He is not as successful as Lloyd in holding onto his groceries, which are repeatedly scattered across the floor. His celery stalks hardly look appetizing after people have trampled them.

Hamilton reacts to the mindless shoving of the subway riders not so much with dismay as with grief and disdain. He is eventually brought to a state of total frustration, becoming so upset at being knocked to the floor that he kicks his legs and breaks down in tears. And the crush of the crowd is not his only problem. The subway car itself seems to be out to get him. Various parts of his anatomy, including his head and his backside, get seized at various times by the automatic sliding doors.

Once settled on board, Hamilton manages to perch the duck on his shoulder before joining the other straphangers, but he is soon in trouble again when his duck nips at another passenger. The duck, much like Lloyd's turkey, eventually gets away and hides underneath a woman's skirt. Hamilton is trying to coax the duck to come back to him when the woman stands up to leave, unaware that she has taken on a duck as a stowaway.

Hamilton provides a fully developed and funny depiction of the mass transit system. Lloyd's trolley ride is dull and restrained by comparison. Langdon's forced subway ride has considerably less variety and characterization.

A Wooden Leg

In the Commedia dell'Arte, comic characters displayed a myriad of disabilities and deformities. One of the Commedia dell'Arte's most prominent character was a hunchback named Pulcinella.

A Cork Leg Legacy (1909) was discussed in the book *The Cinema of Isolation: A History of Physical Disability in the Movies*. The film opens with a widower discovering that his wealthy one-legged wife left him nothing except her fake leg. The husband throws the leg away in disgust, but later learns that it contains a $100,000 check. He goes to retrieve the leg but it has already been picked up by a passing tramp, who is going around town trying to find someone willing to buy it. The husband manages, in the end, to track down the leg and obtain his check.

The Wooden Leg (1909), directed by D. W. Griffith, has to do with a father trying to force his daughter to give up her boyfriend and marry a rich businessman. The daughter borrows a wooden leg from a tramp and pretends, during a date with the businessman, that the leg is her own. This disgusts the businessman enough that he decides against marrying the young lady.

The concept is turned around to give the perspective of the suitor in the Roach comedy *His Wooden Wedding* (1925). Charley Chase is preparing to marry when he is informed by an anonymous note that his bride has a wooden leg. The note is from a disgruntled romantic rival trying to break up the wedding. Chase should know better, but this is where characterization rather than a funny concept drives the story. Chase established himself in films as a high-strung, self-conscious character who can be rankled fairly easily. It is understandable that the idea of his bride having this physical imperfection would make this status-conscious character unbearably squeamish. What would the neighbors think?

This is comparable to a storyline in a 1996 episode of *Seinfeld* in which a girlfriend's defective limb is grounds for Jerry Seinfeld to terminate their relationship. The difference, though, is that the woman's limb is neither missing nor damaged. The defect that repulses

Jerry is that this otherwise beautiful woman has masculine hands, or what Jerry bluntly terms "man hands."[2] Standards of attractiveness had definitely changed in 70 years. In many ways, Jerry represents the evolution of Chase's socially restricted character. Social anxiety has become heightened in today's busy and crowded world, where people are relentlessly exposed to strangers. Perhaps, this is enough to make a person neurotically fussy when it comes to sorting through the rank and file. This may justify Jerry once breaking up with a woman because it bothered him that she ate her peas one at a time.

The Snapping Crab

Lloyd Hamilton gets a job at a restaurant in *Waiting* (1925). He is supposed to compress a chicken inside a box-shaped kitchen device, but the chicken keeps on popping out. He attempts to hold the chicken inside the box only to have his hand crushed by the device. Hamilton bawls as he holds up his hand and sees that it is hugely swollen and visibly pulsating. After giving thought to the matter, he sticks his hand in the icebox to soothe the pain. He smiles in relief at first, but then a crab in the icebox snaps down on his finger. This is not an entirely original scene. Billy Bevan found himself in a similar situation in *Galloping Bungalows* (1924). In this two-reeler, Bevan hits his hand with a hammer while doing carpentry work on a beach house. His hand swells up to an enormous size, so he dips it into the ocean to cool it off. Just then, a crab latches onto his hand and he has to struggle to shake it loose. This is a typical Sennett scene, with its giant prop hand and prop crab, but Hamilton took this same material and made it more about his reactions than the props. The fact that Hamilton was willing to cry and smile made him significantly different than the more mechanical Bevan.

The Drenched Dog

In *The Simp* (1920), Lloyd Hamilton rescues a young lady's dog from a lake. He squeezes the dog's tail, which spurts an impossibly long stream of water. He then twists the dog's torso, which allows him to wring out substantially more water.

This routine was used by Billy Dooley in *Briny Boob* (1926). Dooley at first shakes the dog, which releases a large amount of water. He then squeezes the dog's stomach, which causes a stream of water to spray out of its mouth. The dog, a sponge-like facsimile created by the prop department, is able to withstand Dooley's rough handling. Dooley goes as far as to sing while playing the dog like an accordion. In the end, he squeezes the dog's backside, which triggers a powerful stream of water to shoot up into his face. Dooley's "go for broke" version of the routine takes a silly idea and makes it even sillier.

Shemp Howard later took on the drenched dog routine in the Three Stooges short *He Cooked His Goose* (1952).

Addiction

Cheech & Chong did not create the stoner comedy. A trend in films about characters addicted to drugs or alcohol started with the Selig short *A Turkish Cigarette* (1911). The comical consequences of smoking opium was something that could be appreciated internationally. Italy contributed the Cines comedy *Kri Kri Smokes Opium* (1913) while France came through with the Pathé Comica short *Bigorno Smokes Opium* (1914). In the latter film, René Lantini has an assortment of visions, which are achieved through inventive stop-motion effects. The 1916 Falstaff comedy *Theodore's Terrible Thirst* (1916) had to do with a father and son who must abstain from drinking to gain a large inheritance. The son, unable to trust his alcoholic father to abstain, kidnaps the old man and relocates him to a deserted island. In *Mystery of the Leaping Fish* (1916), Douglas Fairbanks plays Coke Ennyday, a brilliant detective who cannot start his day without a drink and an injection of cocaine. Janiss Garza noted in the All Movie Guide that the film had "a small cult revival in the early '70s because of its brazen displays of drug usage."[3] The Willis O'Brien claymation film *Morpheus Mike* (1917) features a hobo who smokes a hallucinogenic substance and dreams that he is a caveman in prehistoric times. The caveman visits a restaurant where the menu is a stone tablet with hieroglyphics, and the waiter is a mastodon. The mastodon responds to the caveman's order by sucking up soup in its trunk and spraying it into the caveman's face.

The Joker comedy *Some Nightmare* (1915) featured Ernie Shields and Eddie Boland as drug-addled layabouts less benign and affable than Cheech and Chong. The actors, billed as "The Dreamer and the Other Dreamer," spend their time obsessively smoking opium. The *Universal Weekly* specifically noted that Ernie, the leader of the pair, just "loves that dream-producing pie."[4] In this film, the addicts rob a poor blind man to buy their latest stash of opium from Chinatown drug dealer Hong Hee.

Police were raiding establishments that were selling liquor years before the Federal government initiated Prohibition under the 18th Amendment in 1919. The raids mostly occurred in the South, where prohibition had been enacted on a local level, and also occurred in "wet" jurisdictions as a way to assure that establishments had a liquor license. For a time, saloon owners were able to circumvent licensing requirements by claiming to charge patrons to see an attraction: serving liquor was solely on a complimentary basis. One popular attraction was a pig which had lost its sense of sight. In response, law enforcement came to refer to a business that sold alcohol unlawfully as a "blind pig." The L-KO company addressed the issue expressly in a two-reeler called *The Blind Pig* in 1918.

Prohibition comedies had become popular by 1920. Snub Pollard starred in a number of these, including *How Dry I Am* (1919) and *Drink Hearty* (1920). The latter film involved Pollard running a "blind pig" in his barn. Revenue officers raid the barn and chase Pollard and his young assistant (Ernie Morrison) through a haystack. *The Speakeasy* (1920), a Sennett comedy, centered on a hotel proprietor (Charlie Murray) who tries to run a speakeasy in the cellar. *Moving Picture World* praised Mack Sennett for the "up-to-date subject"[5] and for capturing "the humors of prohibition."[6] The Reelcraft two-reeler *Kick* (1920) showed Milburn Morante trying to cope with Prohibition by buying a home-brew kit. Morante brews up a potent batch of beer that unleashes the brute in him. His wife enjoys this new manly husband even after he gives her a black eye. *Moonshines and Jailbirds* (1920), a Universal Rainbow comedy, has Billy Engle employing turtles to smuggle bottles of liquor across the Mexican border. Even cartoon characters became involved in Prohibition. In the Fox cartoon *The Rum Runners* (1920), Mutt and Jeff visit a submarine café just outside the three-mile offshore limit and invite a school of mermaids to join them for a liquor-fueled soirée.

Psychoactive substances — which are able to alter perception, loosen inhibitions and confuse thinking — will always stand as an ideal device for creating wild and wacky comedy. The hallucinations were known as a "wild trip" or a "turn on" by the time Jackie Gleason fell under the influence of LSD in *Skidoo* (1968). This preceded a slew of drug-related humor in the 1970s, never more prominent than it was in the Cheech and Chong films.

Drug and alcohol humor has come to dominate big-budget studio comedies in recent years. Comedy fans have been exposed to an unprecedented amount of drug and alcohol humor from big-budget studio comedies such as *The Big Lebowski* (1998), *Scary Movie* (2000), *Jay and Silent Bob Strike Back* (2001), *Harold & Kumar Go to White Castle* (2004), *Wedding Crashers* (2005), *Talladega Nights: The Ballad of Ricky Bobby* (2006), *The Heartbreak Kid* (2007), *Knocked Up* (2007), *Superbad* (2007), *Tropic Thunder* (2008), *Pineapple Express* (2008), *Land of the Lost* (2009), *Hangover* (2009), and *Get Him to the Greek* (2010).

The Two Favorite Parts of the Anatomy in Silent Film Comedy

A scene in *Luncheon at Twelve* (1933) involves a table being painted by three workmen, played by Charley Chase, Billy Gilbert and Jimmie Adams. The painters, not looking at what they are doing, repeatedly get paint on each other. Chase, distracted by a pretty girl, continues with his paintbrush past the table and paints a thick line across Gilbert's backside. Gilbert becomes so preoccupied yelling at Chase that he fails to notice Adams kneeling down to paint a table leg and he applies a sloppy coat of paint to Adams's bald head. The two parts of the human anatomy that were most often the focus of abuse in early film comedy were the bald head and the backside. This scene manages, in skillful fashion, to cover both ends of the spectrum.

The bald head was a blank canvas to the slapstick artist, predating Jackson Pollock in using the "drip" technique, decorating bald heads with molasses, ink, pudding, eggs and jam. In *The Suitor* (1920), Larry Semon spills a bowl of unidentifiable goop (gravy? pudding?) onto a bald-headed man. In *The Guide* (1921), Clyde Cook pokes around inside a nest and drops eggs on Edgar Kennedy's bald head. Molasses spill on a bald man's head in *Free and Easy* (1921). *Dummies* (1928) opens with Semon doing a magic act. A monkey sitting offstage throws an egg at a bald man in the audience. The audience member assumes that it was Semon who hit him with the egg because Semon is performing a trick with white balls that look very much like eggs.

It was rare in a slapstick comedy not to have a character's backside injured in a funny way. The truth was that it was impossible to injure a backside in an *unfunny* way. A character was likely to get kicked in their backside, or shot in their backside, or get their backside burned with hot rivets. A man could sit on a gas torch, as demonstrated in *Step This Way* (1922), or a man could get a burning arrow in his backside, as in *Tenderfoot Luck* (1922). These injuries represented their very own comedy sub-genre. In *When Spirits Move* (1920), a horse kicks jockey Hank Mann out of his stable and leaves his horseshoes stuck on the jockey's backside. Billy Bevan gets a lobster latched onto his backside in *The Quack Doctor* (1920). In *A Submarine Pirate* (1915), Sydney Chaplin gets in the way of sailors loading a torpedo tube and gets a torpedo thrust into his backside. Injuries also came out of more elaborate routines. In *The Guide* (1921), Clyde Cook, leading a group of mountain climbers, has trouble with a woman who repeatedly hits him in the backside with her pick axe as she scales up the mountain behind him. Cook finally solves the problem by sticking a cork on the tip of her axe. In *Ship Ahoy* (1919), Billy West, trying to be helpful, retrieves a knife for a knife-thrower and hurls it back in the man's direction. The knife-thrower does not turn around fast enough to catch the knife, which ends up sticking in his backside. The knife-thrower, in a panic, runs up and down the hallway as West tries to catch up to him to render assistance. West finally gets hold of the man and gets him to bend over. He has to stick his foot on the knife-thrower's backside to gain leverage before he is able to yank out the deeply embedded blade.

Never were more backsides assaulted in a single film than in Our Gang's *The First Seven Years* (1930). A sword duel between two boys (Jackie Cooper and Donald Haines) migrates to a backyard where bed sheets are hanging out to dry. The duelers thrust their swords at every silhouette that appears on the sheets, whether the silhouette belongs to their opponent or an innocent bystander. The sword points are drawn like magnets straight to the gluteus maximus. A sword even pierces the posterior of Pete the dog, who immediately soothes the wound in a garden pond.

Cactus bushes provided the most common risk to backsides. A basic example can be found in *Ham's Strategy* (1916), when Bud Duncan takes a spill into a cactus bush and then runs around in excruciating pain, struggling to pluck spines out of his backside. Usually, it was only the means of propulsion that varied. In *A Twilight Baby* (1920), Virginia Rappé is on a swing when she unintentionally kicks Billie Ritchie into a cactus bush. In *Fast and Furious* (1924), it is the momentum created by a hand car crashing that catapults the hand car operator (Spencer Bell) into a cactus patch. Buster Keaton is tied to the back of an elephant while he is dragged through a field of cactus in *Three Ages* (1923). A mule kicks Larry Semon into a patch of cactus in *The Wizard of Oz* (1925).

Most of the time, the prop cacti were modeled after the saguaro cactus, the tall and upright cactus that shows up in picturesque desert scenes, but comedians were able to vary the cactus to suit their purposes. Semon, for example, preferred the prickly pear cactus, which had round spiny pads that could flop around as Semon ran in circles trying to pry them off his backside. Billy Bevan ran afoul of a cactus-like shrub called an agave in the Sennett comedy *Be Reasonable* (1921). Bevan is in flight from the police when he backs into the shrub. A long, prickly frond sticks the fugitive in the backside but he assumes that this is a police officer prodding him with the barrel of his rifle. Bevan raises his hands to surrender and, as he marches down the street, the frond protruding from his backside freely bounces up and down.

A particularly involved and gruesome cactus scene occurs in *Honest Injun* (1926). Johnny Arthur falls off his horse and lands directly onto a cactus bush. He springs to his feet, crying out in pain. Cactus spines, looking as thick and long as carpenter nails, are sticking out of his backside. Arthur, in the middle of chase, does not have time to remove the spines and simply jumps back on his horse. The horse, jabbed by the spines, becomes highly agitated. The animal charges down the trail and, within moments, Arthur gets knocked off by a low-hanging branch.

The cactus ended its reign as a comic staple in the early forties. Curly Howard gets a cactus in his backside in a Three Stooges short appropriately titled *Cactus Makes Perfect* (1942). Three years later, in *The Bullfighters* (1945), the cactus made its last prominent backside-injuring appearance when Laurel & Hardy stumble into a cactus patch.

In *Pineapple Express* (2008), Seth Rogen tries to force Danny McBride to divulge information by waving a potted cactus in his face. But nothing else is done with the cactus. It is not dropped down McBride's pants. No one sits on it. Modern comedians simply fail to appreciate the history of the comic cactus and recognize the powerful affinity that the cactus shares with the gluteus maximus.

Charlie Chaplin tended to engage in rude and sexually suggestive gags in relation to the backside. In *The New Janitor* (1914), Chaplin is not paying attention to what he is doing while dusting the office and accidentally dusts the well-rounded rump of a bent-over secretary. If a person were to bend over near Chaplin, the comedian would lean towards them to use their backside as an armrest, or he might even light a match against it. As a stagehand in *His New Job* (1915), Chaplin tries to stick a prop sword into its holder but misses, sticking an actress in her protruding posterior.

Andy Clyde, in the early days of sound comedy, proved that he could be more expressive than most comedians when it came to the backside. In *Alimony Aches* (1935), Clyde's ex-wife is helping him to recover from the measles so that he is able to pay her back alimony. She has him lie on his stomach so that she can massage his back. His backside slowly rises into the air as she rubs his shoulders, suggesting that he is getting aroused. His disgusted ex delivers a sharp smack to Clyde's saucy rump, causing Clyde to collapse flat on his stomach.

Backside injury was eventually replaced onscreen by groin injury, a phenomena that received an auspicious start in *Blazing Saddles* (1974). In a time when cactus spines in the backside were no longer standard, John Candy got slammed in the groin by a desert shrub in *Wagons East* (1994).

Brats

The English music hall had a tradition of comedians dressing up in schoolboy outfits and behaving like mischievous brats. The Little Lord Fauntleroy outfit played a prominent role in this sub-genre. Bobby Vernon wore the outfit, complete with a long blonde wig, to masquerade as a boy in *Second Childhood* (1923) and *Short Socks* (1927). Lupino Lane shamelessly strutted around in the outfit in *The Missing Link* (1917) and *Naughty Boy* (1927). Larry Semon is a model student wearing velvet knee pants, a white lace collar and frilly shirt cuffs in *School Days* (1920).

An equivalent outfit available for a comedienne to wear under similar circumstances was a high-waisted play dress. This was worn by Dorothy Devore when she posed as a mischievous little girl in *Kidding Katie* (1923). Devore proved that she could be just as bratty as the boys. It is no coincidence that Vernon, Lane and Devore all found themselves under the stern rule of Blanche Payson. Payson, by her large size and rough demeanor, was well-suited to disciplining rowdy, oversized children.

The Little Lord Fauntleroy outfit remained a popular costume for a time. When Laurel & Hardy assumed the role of mischievous children in *Brats* (1930), Hardy was dressed in a Little Lord Fauntleroy suit, including short pants, white ankle socks and black patent-leather strap shoes. Moe and Curly Howard were memorably dressed in Little Lord Fauntleroy outfits in *All the World's a Stooge* (1941). Of course, the ultimate grown man in a Little Lord Fauntleroy outfit was Joe Besser, who wore the outfit while playing overgrown mama's boy "Stinky" on *The Abbott and Costello Show* (1952–53).

Tramp, Tramp, Tramp (1926) concludes with Harry Langdon as a proud new papa, peeking into a nursery to see how his baby boy is doing. The baby is revealed to be Langdon himself dressed in a bonnet and gown and sitting in a crib, built large enough to make the comedian look, by comparison, to be the size of a baby. Baby Harry chews on a big ball as if he is teething. He playfully tosses away the ball, which hits the wall, bounces back, and hits him on the head.

The idea of increasing the size of furniture and props to make an actor look like a child

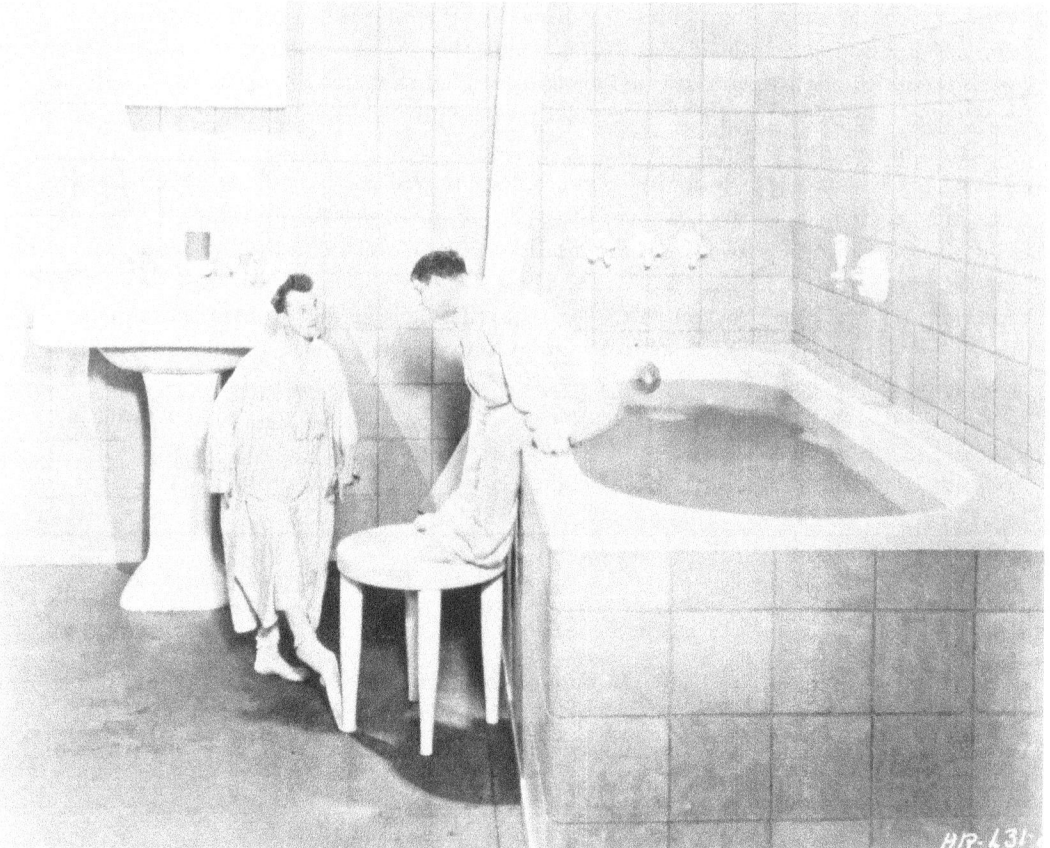

Laurel (left) and Hardy, playing their own children, prepare for a bath in *Brats* (1930) (courtesy Bruce Lawton Collection).

did not originate with *Tramp, Tramp, Tramp*. An unidentified still dating back at least five years earlier shows Roscoe Arbuckle costumed in a Little Lord Fauntleroy outfit while sitting on an enlarged garden bench beneath an enlarged window.

The clever design concept was later used more ambitiously, and more famously, by Laurel and Hardy in *Brats* (1930). Laurel and Hardy are the fathers of two small boys, also played by Laurel and Hardy. Split-screen utilized to show the interaction between the fathers and their offspring works ideally to maximize the illusion. Set designers constructed three elaborate sets (living room, bedroom and bathroom) in which the two "children" are able to run wild. A multitude of supersized props, as varied as a hairbrush, a popgun and a bottle of liniment, are available for their use. The comedians climb a 12-foot-tall dresser and play around in a bathtub large enough for them to swim laps. Neither Laurel nor Hardy were new to playing tykes. *Playmates* (1918), which featured Hardy and Billy West as an unruly pair of small boys, can be seen as a warm up to *Brats*. Laurel, portraying a baby in *Mother's Joy* (1923), was absurdly depicted laid out in an oversized baby basket and garbed in a bonnet and gown. But the elaborate set made all the difference.

Red Skelton combined elements of both *Tramp, Tramp, Tramp* and *Brats* when he portrayed infant twins in *The Yellow Cab Man* (1950). A big crib is now replaced by a big playpen. The two versions of Skelton, situated on either side of a split screen, are dressed in

Laurel (left) and Hardy enjoy a friendly game of checkers in *Brats* (1930) (courtesy Bruce Lawton Collection).

bonnets and gowns. Much like Laurel and Hardy's combative tykes, Skelton's infants get into a fight and one of the infants smashes the other infant in the head with an oversized bottle.

The simple (yet effective) illusion created by unusually large props became an irresistible device for comedians playing children. From 1969 to 1973, Lily Tomlin regularly sat in an oversized rocking chair to play five-year-old Edith Ann in a popular series of sketches for *Rowan & Martin's Laugh-In*. Even more recently, within the span of a single week, the effect was used by Tina Fey in a *30 Rock* episode ("Reaganing," 2010) and by Taylor Swift in a Target commercial ("Speak Now," 2010).

This effect was later used more extensively in science fiction and fantasy films. Included among the oversized props of *The Incredible Shrinking Man* (1957) were a 12-foot sewing needle and a 20-foot mousetrap. These extreme props bring to mind a scene in *He Came Up Smiling* (1918) where Douglas Fairbanks, a discontent teller toiling in a bank cage, has an absurd vision of himself locked up inside a giant bird cage. More recently, Peter Jackson was widely praised for his elaborate use of oversized props, along with false perspectives to turn normal-sized cast members into diminutive Hobbits for *The Lord of the Rings: The Fellowship of the Ring* (2001).

Is He Dead?

The constant stream of slapstick battles never resulted in onscreen death, but it was not uncommon for a person to beat someone into a lifeless state and then panic and try to hide the body. This was certainly the case in the Biograph comedy *Mr. Bragg, a Fugitive* (1911), in which Mr. Bragg (Dell Henderson) attacks a man for flirting with his wife and comes to believe that he has killed the man.

This plot turned up in much the same form at other studios. The Joker comedy *Fooling Father* (1915) gets under way with the ill-tempered Mr. Brown (Max Asher) striking his neighbor Tom (Billy Franey) with his cane. When Tom drops to the ground unconscious, Mr. Brown assumes that he has killed him and desperately flees the scene. Tom regains consciousness, but he decides to teach Mr. Brown a lesson about controlling his anger. He enlists the aid of a friendly cop (Ralph McComas) and Mrs. Brown (Gale Henry) to lead Mr. Brown to believe that he is, in fact, dead.

Other examples of this premise are plentiful. Billie Ritchie is left for dead in *Cupid in a Hospital* (1915); it takes someone coming along and giving Ritchie a whiff of gin to revive him. Ritchie finds himself on the other side of the situation when he thinks that he has beaten his girlfriend's father to death in *The Avenging Dentist* (1915). Lloyd Hamilton thinks that he has killed his partner, Bud Duncan, in *A Phoney Cannibal* (1915) and disposes the body by simply tossing it out of his bedroom window. In *Bill's New Pal* (1915), Henry Bergman, believing that he has stabbed Billie Ritchie to death, stuffs him inside a barrel. In *A Voice from the Deep* (1912), Fred Mace pushes Eddie Dillon off a pier and then panics, thinking that Dillon has drowned. Dillon, who has secretly swum to shore, returns, posing as a ghost to scare Mace. The film was remade the following year with Roscoe Arbuckle under the title *A Noise from the Deep*. A 1916 Vogue comedy *Ducking a Discord* found Rube Miller so maddened by his wife's constant accordion playing that he resorts to binding her up in a sack and tossing her into a river. The wife is rescued and returns home, pretending to be a ghost. The Three Stooges provided a rare reprise of the premise with *Love at First Bite* (1950), in which Moe and Larry think that they have killed Shemp and try to get rid of his body.

Food Spilled Down a Woman's Back

In *The Adventurer* (1917), Charlie Chaplin makes a *faux pas* at a fancy dinner party when he drops ice cream down the back of a matronly woman's dress. The cold and wet sensation of ice cream on her back sends the woman into a tizzy. Chaplin's rival (Eric Campbell) puts his hand down the woman's dress to remove the ice cream, which so upsets the woman that she slaps him. Comedians often played the clumsy dinner party guest who spilled pie or mashed potatoes down the back of a woman's gown, but it certainly made for a more dynamic scene for the food item that slipped down the woman's dress to be ice cream. It takes a genius to recognize the creativity of another genius, and that may be the reason Buster Keaton, in the role of a careless waiter, drops ice cream down the back of a woman's dress in *The Cook* (1918). Still, Keaton had not fully learned Chaplin's lesson. No one at the party had seen Chaplin drop the ice cream down the woman's back and Chaplin was too shrewd to step forward to take the blame. Keaton readily accepts blame for the mishap and is eager to make amends, but he only makes matters worse when he stretches his hand down the woman's dress to retrieve the ice cream. He is treated even more badly than Campbell.

Sometimes, something more disturbing can drop down the back of a woman's dress. This point is made clear in *The Suitor* (1920). Larry Semon arrives at a dinner party with flowers for his girlfriend (Lucille Carlisle). Carlisle is leaning forward to smell the flowers when a lizard jumps out and lands on her nose. Semon flicks off the lizard, sending it flying down the back of a matronly woman's dress. The woman is jiggling around as Semon, even less discreet than Campbell and Keaton, plunges his arm down the back of her dress to reclaim the lizard. Other guests, assuming that Semon is molesting the woman, give him a furious beating and throw him out of the party. Semon no doubt deserved the beating considering the delicacy of this situation. More subtlety could be found with Hank Mann. In *When Spirits Move* (1920), Mann bumps into a maturely dignified woman at a dinner party and spills food down the back of her dress. Mann annoys the woman as he tries to clean off her back, but he tries to be as careful as possible while making physical contact with the woman and he is not so coarse as to thrust his arm down the back of the woman's dress.

It is understandable for Semon, whose outlandish stunt-filled comedies frequently featured jump cuts which substituted a person for a dummy, to treat people as inanimate objects. Semon performed a similar routine the following year in *The Bakery* (1921). Semon is up on a ladder, retrieving a jar from a shelf, when a white mouse crawls up his sleeve. Semon, in a panic, kicks his leg to jerk the mouse loose. The mouse finally falls out of his pants leg and drops down a dress worn by yet another matronly woman. Semon is able to lure the mouse out with cheese. The mouse is on the woman's neck when Semon slams the woman with a sack of flour. The woman not only takes the brunt of the blow, but the sack bursts open and coats her in flour. The woman is hysterical. Semon's manager (Oliver Hardy) seeks to make amends, but it only makes the woman angrier when he hands her a complimentary sack of flour. Hardy, at least, tried to show the woman some courtesy. Semon had absolutely no consideration as to how painful it would be for this woman to be slammed with a sack of flour.

The Fake Musician

"All right!" is a popular Abbott & Costello routine that the team first performed in *Hit the Ice* (1943). The setup is simple. Costello hopes to fool a woman into thinking he can play the piano. He plans to do this by hiding a phonograph behind a piano and cueing Abbott to play a recording of a piano solo when he says the word "All right!" The plan goes awry when Costello unwittingly says the cue word at the wrong times. Eventually, Abbott gets so bored with the scam that he falls asleep and leaves the recording playing, even after Costello has turned his back to the keyboard.

Billy Quirk performed a similar routine in *Canned Harmony* (1912). Quirk wins over his girlfriend's father by pretending to play a violin, while it is actually his girlfriend playing the music on a phonograph. The father grants his consent for the couple to marry. The maid, however, plays the same violin recording at the wedding ceremony, and the father soon realizes he was duped. *Canned Harmony*, as a story, is cute, romantic and tidy. Abbott & Costello, in contrast, turned the situation into an enjoyably raucous mess. Improbably, their scheme carries on even though nothing goes right from the beginning. Costello spends much of the scene desperately banging on the keyboard while screaming "All right!" at the top of his lungs. No idyllic marriage ceremony is in the future for this fool.

Harold Lloyd performs a variation of this routine in *The Non-Stop Kid* (1918). Lloyd pretends to sing opera while Snub Pollard hides behind a curtain playing a record. Pollard breaks the record by mistake and has to quickly find a replacement, but the new record features a melody composed specifically for a burlesque "skirt dancer." Lloyd, having to alter his performance to suit the lively new music, is soon wiggling his hips and leaping across the parlor. Essentially the same premise was used by the Three Stooges in *Micro-Phonies* (1945). Again, everything goes well until the record breaks and a less than suitable replacement is produced. Moe, Larry and Curly give a *tour de force* performances as they lip sync to a sextet of singing voices.

The Case of the Growing Fruit

The "tree of truth" routine, in which a magical tree punishes people for lying by dropping acorns on their heads, was originally performed by Dan Leno in the 1891 Drury Lane pantomime "Humpty Dumpty." Leno continued to perform this routine throughout his career. He found in time that it made the routine funnier for the prop fruit that knocked him in the head to be apples, which could be designed to look fuller, heavier and more painful than acorns. Audiences responded enthusiastically when, at the climax of the sketch, buckets of apples dropped loudly on the comedian's head. Leno last performed the routine as part of a revival of "Humpty Dumpty," which was staged only a few months before his death in 1904.

The routine was in time exported to the United States, where it became the highlight of a 1903 Broadway musical comedy called "The Runaways." The show, which cast Alexander Clark as an irascible man who uses horse track winnings to buy his own private South Pacific island, featured a tropical tree that dumped overgrown oranges on Clark as he related a highly unlikely fishing story.

The earliest known film version of the routine was performed as a musical number by Bert Wheeler and Dorothy Lee in the RKO feature *The Rainmakers* (1935). Wheeler and Lee are being less than truthful as they proclaim romantic platitudes. Wheeler croons that he would not trade a million dollars for all the happiness that Lee brings him. *Plunk!* He is hit square on the head by a gargantuan orange. The comedian, determined to outwit the tree, bats away oranges with a polo mallet and, at one point, shoves Lee aside just in time to prevent a citrus missile from striking her.

It is a burlesque-style version of the routine from Abbott & Costello's *Pardon My Sarong* (1942) that remains the best known. Lou Costello isn't telling a fish story as he sits in the tree's shade. Instead, he somehow gets it into his head to treat a lovely island girl to a ribald "farmer's daughter" story. Tension in the scene comes from the fact that Costello will incur the wrath of his prudish partner, Bud Abbott, if he tells the story in unexpurgated detail and he will incur the wrath of the truth-seeking tree if he suppresses the risqué facts of the tale. Tell the truth and Abbott will slap him. Lie and the tree will drop concussive fruit on his head. The wrath of Abbott is indeed something to fear and Costello chooses to accept the tree's punishment. The fruit du jour, bigger and harder than all that came before, takes the form of plump and hard-shelled coconuts, a barrage of which rains down upon the hapless comedian.

The Cliff

A car was hung off the side of a cliff in many films, including *Special Delivery* (1922), *Built on a Bluff* (1923), *Wall Street Blues* (1924), *A Ten-Minute Egg* (1924), *Family Life* (1924), *Out Bound* (1924) and *Air-Tight* (1931). The 1970s British sitcom *Some Mothers Do 'Ave 'Em* was, in many ways, an homage to silent film comedy. A 1973 episode, appropriately titled "Cliffhanger," has Michael Crawford hanging from the bumper of his car over the side of a cliff.

Gratitude

Reliable old plots can turn up unexpectedly and achieve new success. In *Faithful* (1910), Arthur Johnson feels guilty when his chauffeur runs down a simple-minded rube (Mack Sennett). He takes the man into his home to feed him and later buys the man clothing. Sennett develops such gratitude towards his kind benefactor that he will not go away. This old plot turned up again in a 1964 episode of *The Andy Griffith Show* titled "Andy Saves Gomer." Andy walks into the office at Wally's Gas Station and finds Gomer sound asleep while the room is quickly filling up with smoke. Andy sees that the smoke is originating from a barrel where gas rags are smoldering. Gomer wakes up in time to see Andy pouring a bucket of water into the barrel to put out the fire. He is so grateful to Andy for saving his life that he devotes most of his waking hours doing favors for Andy. Andy is soon exhausted by Gomer's relentless favors and becomes desperate to get rid of him. Andy pretends to be in jeopardy, allowing Gomer to balance the scales by rescuing *him*.

This episode was so popular that it was recycled for a 1969 episode of *Gomer Pyle, U.S.M.C.*, entitled "To Save a Life," and a 1972 episode of *The Odd Couple*, "You Saved My Life."

Pie on the Ceiling

An innovative variation of the classic pie-in-the-face gag was central to the opening scene of an Andy Clyde two-reeler *In the Doghouse* (1934). Clyde's wife (Vivien Oakland) whacks her grandson on the backside, causing the child to toss a pie into the air. No one seems to notice or care that the pie has ended up sticking to the ceiling. Moments later, when Clyde bends Oakland backward to give her a kiss, the pie drops off the ceiling and smacks her in the face.

The gag will be familiar to fans of the Three Stooges. In *Movie Maniacs* (1936), Curly is trying to flip a pancake in a pan, but he strains too hard and the pancake flies into the air and gets stuck on the ceiling. Moe is unaware that he is standing directly beneath the pancake and, when the gooey cake comes loose, it drops off the ceiling and hits him squarely in the face. This became a popular gag for the Stooges, who repeated the gag a number of times: *Half Wits' Holiday* (1947), *Pest Man Wins* (1951), *Wham Bam Slam* (1955) and *Pies and Guys* (1958).

The *Half Wits' Holiday* version of the gag is the one that the fans like the best. This version, which is set at a fancy dinner party, has Moe needing to get rid of a custard pie that Curly swiped off a banquet table. He ends up tossing the pie against the ceiling, where it loosely takes hold. Moe tries to leave the area before the pie drops but he is interrupted by a society woman, who is interested in having a conversation with him. Moe desperately tries to excuse himself. "What's wrong?" the woman asks. "You act as though the Sword of Damocles is hanging over your head." "Lady," replies Moe, "you must be psychic." In this instance, the filmmakers have made a point to increase the stakes and prolong the action. The audience is shown that the pie is coming loose and know that, if Moe doesn't get away fast enough, he will become caught up in an embarrassing situation. It is Hitchcock's "Bomb Theory" used to comic purpose. Hitchcock acknowledged that it was dramatic to have two men sitting at a table and causally talking about baseball when a bomb planted under the table suddenly explodes. However, Hitchcock believed that it was more dramatic to build suspense by showing the audience beforehand that a bomb is under the table and it is set to go off in five minutes. A viewer watching this gag play out in *Half Wits' Holiday* is squirming in their seat and laughing well before the pie hits the woman in the face.

The gag was later revived, with a pizza replacing the custard pie, in *Dude, Where's My Car?* (2000).

A New Generation

Author Saul Austerlitz called the Three Stooges "silent comedians for the era of sound."[7] The Stooges, who worked with a talented crew of silent film comedy veterans, carried on the hard-won traditions of the medium unlike most other sound-era comedians, who were heavily dependent on the traditions of vaudeville, burlesque and Broadway. Their unrestrained silliness did much to recall the bygone years of silent comedy.

A memorable gag in the Three Stooges' two-reeler *Hoi Polloi* (1935) features Curly unwittingly getting a spring from a chair cushion caught on his backside. The spring hooks Curly to another man and, every time that he tries to move away, it keeps pulling him back towards the man. Curly cannot understand what is going on and becomes increasingly frustrated. In the process he is knocked down, falls on the spring, and bounces back to his feet. The routine was so well-received that Curly used it again in other films, including *Three Little Sew and Sews* (1939) and *An Ache in Every Stake* (1941). The routine may now be identified with Curly, but it originally showed up more than a decade earlier in the Sennett comedy *Asleep at the Switch* (1923), in which Ben Turpin was the one with a spring on his backside. The sight of Curly bouncing off the ground, as funny as it was, was not as blissful a sight as Turpin bouncing off the ground, as weightless as a cartoon character. This could have had to do with the unrivalled skill of Sennett's crack effects team, but it more likely had to do with the physics (and film speed) that ruled the absurd dream world of silent films. This is not to say that Curly needs a wildly surreal special effect to make the scene funny. Curly, with his natural comic vitality, is his *own* special effect. The comedian patented a special brand of comic frustration, which is on display in this scene as he grunts, squeals and slaps his own face. By demonstrating the full force of his frustration towards the freeloading chair spring, Curly comes across far funnier than Turpin, who expresses no emotion at all.

Time had passed before the Stooges freely picked through this toy chest of silent routines. By then, the recreation of these old routines fell into the category of revival or homage. It was not like the case of Billy West, who reprised the chair-spring routine less than a year after *Asleep at the Switch* for *Line's Busy* (1924). West, at one time a shameless Chaplin imitator, also manages in the same film to borrow gags from Keaton (a mud-puddle gag from *The Balloonatic*), Lloyd (a phone booth gag from *Number, Please?*), Arbuckle (a thermometer gag from *Goodnight, Nurse!*), and Chaplin (a bratty kid gag from *The Pilgrim*). Even by the standards of his day, West may have crossed the line from joke sharer to joke thief.

West greatly expanded the chair-spring routine with varying results. It was funny when the woman shoved Turpin to the ground and he sprang back up. West thought he could get laughs doing the same gag, and get even more laughs if he did it more than once. He did it, in total, 14 times. This occurs during an altercation with a burly police officer. West slams into the officer as he springs to his feet, and the officer (who assumes that West is putting up a fight) knocks him down again. This only leads West to vault into the officer again, repeating the process all over again. But this wasn't apparently enough for West, who was determined to fill out the remainder of the film with spring gags. West slips on a banana peel and bounces back up. A pretty girl offers to give him a ride in her convertible, but he no sooner leaps into the back seat than he launches into the air as if he was the victim of James Bond's ejector seat. At a park, he rushes onto a bridge to get to a man drowning in a lake, but the spring latches onto the railing and his brave dive into the lake ends with him being pulled into reverse and returned up onto the bridge. Even the Stooges could not have gotten away with this much silliness.

Lupino Lane does a number of pratfalls in *A Friendly Husband* (1923). He usually gets back up on his feet quickly, but in one instance he does something different — he takes the time to roll over on his side and then, by pivoting his weight on his shoulder, he is able to spin himself around in a complete circle. This bit of comic business is surely familiar to Stooges fans, who have seen it performed by Curly on countless occasions. The fans have even come up with an official name for the trick. The name, so eloquent in its simplicity, is the "Shoulder Spin." It is conceivable for Lane, who often came up with funny falls and tumbles, to have been the originator of this strange move, call it dance, stunt, schtick or outburst. Other comedians came to adopt it in the ensuing years. Buster Keaton can be seen performing the Shoulder Spin after being tackled during a football game in *Three Ages* (1923). But Curly's "spin" episodes differed in a key way. Lane and Keaton act as if they are dazed and confused about their circumstances. They are pumping their legs as if they assume they are moving forward on their feet. Curly, however, did this spin as an expression of enthusiasm. The rotund Stooge flopping around on the floor with his trademark "woo-woo-woo" cry was far funnier than either Lane or Keaton had been with this same silly trick.

Sadly, Curly's death (in 1952) occurred before the onset of the Stooges' renaissance, and the comedian never got the chance to talk about his influences. We will never know if it was Lupino Lane who introduced him to the Shoulder Spin, just as we will never know if Arbuckle introduced him to the Belly Butt. Yet it does not change the fact that Curly, for all his influences, will forever remain a true comedy legend.

The Stooges, as a team, specialized in a blunt, brisk, hard-sell comic style most often identified with the Sennett comedies. But the trio failed dismally when they tried to recreate routines originated by more subtle and patient comedians like Keaton, Lloyd, Langdon, or Laurel & Hardy. Laurel and Hardy were at their best in *Towed in a Hole* (1932). The duo is featured as fish peddlers, determined to catch their own fish as a way to increase their profits. The comedians spend most of the film renovating an old boat that they picked up at a junkyard. The Stooges, who remade this comedy in 1945 as *Booby Dupes*, lacked Laurel & Hardy's finesse to draw out laughs from a simple situation; they compressed the boat renovation into a three-minute scene. The rest of the film is devoted to pointless complications, including the Stooges' efforts to steal naval uniforms that they can wear on the boat. Is it really helpful to wear an admiral's uniform while fishing?

It was in revitalizing wildly extravagant comedy routines of the past that the Stooges came to excel. In *A Plumbing We Will Go* (1940), the Stooges are called out to a fancy home to repair some water pipes. After mistakenly unscrewing an electrical pipe, Curly determines that the water is not working because this particular pipe is, in his words, "plugged up with wires." He tears out the electrical wires and reattaches the pipe to a plumbing pipe. Soon, water is spraying out of a light fixture, a stove, and a telephone. A group of partygoers are gathered to watch a live broadcast of Niagara Falls on television, when water comes bursting through the screen. Gags from this film are derived from a number of early plumbing comedies, including *The Plumber* (1914), *Hearts and Flames* (1915) and *Bath Tub Perils* (1916). In *Hearts and Flames*, Billie Ritchie is attempting to fix a leak when he mistakenly fits plumbing pipes with electrical pipes. In the dining room, water pours in on dinner guests from an overhead light fixture. In *Bath Tub Perils*, a repairman's incompetence leads to water squirting out of gas jets and gas streaming out of faucets. Still, the Niagara Falls gag, the funniest gag derived from this premise, belongs entirely to the Stooges. The Stooges were in their glory with leaky pipes and hefty wrenches. *A Plumbing We Will Go* is the plumbing comedy to end all plumbing comedies. These clownish comedians may not have developed identities with great depth or intricacy, but their identities were clearly defined, indelible, and extremely funny.

Brats

Prior mention was made of a routine that Harold Lloyd performed in *Number, Please?* (1920). Lloyd has an urgent need to get into a phone booth to make a call, but a series of people cut ahead of him before he can make it inside the booth. At one point, a mother clasping a baby barges in front of him and expects him to hold the baby while she makes a call. The baby begins crying and Lloyd is unable to console him. In *Line's Busy* (1924), Billy West takes on the phone booth routine, except that he eliminates the crying baby and replaces him with a bratty little girl. After climbing into his lap, the girl repeatedly slaps West in the face, willfully ignoring his polite admonishments. It might look as if West was adding a new wrinkle to Lloyd's routine, but that is by no means the reality of the situation. West, who picked up bits and pieces from various sources, was consolidating this routine with another one, replacing Lloyd's crying baby with the type of slap-happy child on display in Chaplin's *The Pilgrim* (1923). But West, as usual, missed the point of the routine. Chaplin meets up with the child under awkward circumstances: he has recently escaped from prison and has taken up residence in a new town, posing as a minister. It is while he is sitting in a parlor with members of his congregation that he is approached by this little terror of a boy (Dean Riesner), who proceeds to slap and punch him with relentless enthusiasm. Chaplin must show patience and kindness to the boy or his cover will be blown. The scene ends with everyone exiting the parlor except for Chaplin and the boy. Chaplin is about to follow the others out when he finds the boy hanging off his coat tail. Chaplin pauses at the doorway just long enough to boot the boy to the floor. The scene thereby ends with the brat receiving an overdue and well-deserved punishment.

W. C. Fields, playing on his reputation as a loather of children, enacted a similar scene

Charlie Murray is overwhelmed with his babysitting duties. Children are unidentified (courtesy Robert Arkus).

with Baby LeRoy in *The Old Fashioned Way* (1934). LeRoy delivers a wider range of abuse: he violently pinches Fields's nose, he throws food at him, and he dips his watch in molasses. This is an improvement over the Chaplin scene, as Riesner's repeated blows become monotonous after awhile. Fields, while not concealing a criminal identity, is highly motivated to be polite — he is desperate to solicit money from the child's rich mother. And, as usual, Fields flavors the scene with his muttering asides. ("I don't know why he's behaving like this," his mother says. "You should see him when he's alone." Fields mutters under his breath, "Yes, I'd like to catch him when he's alone.") When he finally gets that chance, Fields gives the brat a swift kick in the backside. Chaplin may have performed the same wickedly funny business, and he may have done it first, but Fields just seems to enjoy this moment of triumph so much more and it is his performance, complete with a suitably devilish grin, that leaves the more lasting impression.

These scenes point up West's failings. West, who performs the routine unmoored from its original story and characterizations, has no real justification to tolerate this abuse. He, in the end, displays as much characterization and motivation as a Bobo doll being punched thoughtlessly by a child. Even worse, he fails to end the scene with the punch line — the brat's comeuppance. Fields improved the routine. West did not.

West at least navigated through the routine without falling victim to its one grave pitfall. No doubt, care is vital to assure that a routine climax with a man kicking a child does not turn coarse and mean-spirited. Even in an age when a so-called "supernanny" must be called upon to stop superbrats from tearing apart a home, a child should still evoke a natural sympathy from the big people on which they depend. But that concern was not at all evident when Robert Downey, Jr., undertook the routine in *Due Date* (2010). Downey, annoyed by an eight-year-old boy yanking on his tie and shoving a rubber snake in his face, takes control of the situation by grabbing the boy and punching him square in the stomach. The scene lacks a humorous dilemma, lacks a clever buildup, and lacks a nuanced characterization from its lead performer. Fields, as irritated or dismayed as he becomes, has to pretend to the other adults in the room that he has nothing but love for the boy. Downey, who has no other adults around, has no reason to feign affection or stifle his anger. His anger builds quickly and then he violently strikes out. The routine, stripped down of its comedic elements, becomes nothing more than bare assault. The Fields scene ends with a shot of LeRoy smiling so that the audience knows that the child was not hurt, but the Downey scene ends with the child doubled over and groaning in pain. The scene is strictly designed for shock appeal. Downey's action is so wildly inappropriate that a viewer is supposed to feel thrilled and express this sudden excitement with a howl of laughter. But the results prove to be less than amusing.

A more elaborate version of this routine is enacted by Red Skelton in *The Yellow Cab Man* (1950). Skelton, who plays a novice cabdriver, is asked by a woman to hold her little boy (Danny Richards Jr.) while she gets travel directions out of her purse. The bratty boy jams his lollipop into Skelton's mouth and then bawls to his mother that Skelton pilfered the sticky sucker. Skelton is reluctantly left with the child while the mother storms off to buy another lollipop. The boy is not yet through with his mischief. He snatches a watch away from Skelton, in the same way that Baby LeRoy once snatched a watch away from Fields, except the child doesn't drop the watch into a pitcher of molasses — he drops it into a mailbox. Skelton is trying to figure out how to retrieve his watch, which is a family heirloom, when a police officer forces him to move his cab. The mother is panicked when she returns and finds that the terrible lollipop-stealer has vanished with her child. The situation gets even worse when the police officer hears the watch ticking inside the mailbox and assumes that a terrorist has planted a bomb. Kidnapping. Bombs. Hysteria expectedly ensues. Police join together to hunt down the apparent kidnapper and fire trucks arrive to handle the supposed mailbox bomb. A crowd watches in morbid fascination as a workman slices open the mailbox with a blow-torch. Meanwhile, Skelton gets caught in traffic outside a hotel and has an amorous pair of newlyweds climb into the back seat of his cab as a mob of rice-tossing well-wishers swarm around the vehicle. Skelton is telling everyone that he has to get this boy back to his mother, but not a single person is willing to listen to what he has to say. Skelton circles the block to get back to where he started, at which time he is assailed by the police and manages in the confusion to crash his cab.

The routine is skillfully sustained for seven minutes as the situation escalates. This involves more than a bratty boy smacking a comedian in the face. Police have become involved. Firemen have become involved. An entire wedding party has become involved. In the end, the chaos and devastation is revealed in its totality by a sweeping crane shot.

The routine, whether performed by Chaplin, Fields or Skelton, mocks one of the great social taboos — an adult mistreating a child. A belief held strongly by the general public is that only a really bad person can be at odds with a child. It becomes a source of tension in these scenes for an adult to have to treat a child with good will despite the fact that the child does nothing to inspire good will. Chaplin and Fields maintained a pretense to avoid upsetting the community around them, but Skelton is not as successful and the result is moral panic and outrage.

The Beast That Sucks

The suction power of a vacuum cleaner is so great in *The Great Vacuum Robbery* (1915) that two bank robbers (Edgar Kennedy and Louise Fazenda) are able to use the household item to quickly clean the money out of a bank vault. This level of suction power was bound to make one of these campy vacuum cleaners hard to handle. A more common routine had a comedian struggling to control a vacuum cleaner while it sucked up a variety of items. The machine is so voracious that it removes the fur off a dog's back. The routine can be traced as far back as *The Vacuum Cleaner Nightmare* (1906), which showed a salesman being pulled inside a vacuum cleaner. This was a less than personal routine that comedians could enact interchangeably. The routine was performed at various times by Al St. John (*The Paper Hangers*, 1921), Billy Bevan (*Wall Street Blues*, 1924) and Lloyd Hamilton (*Breezing Along*, 1927).

Jerry Lewis manages the most expansive, the wildest and the funniest version of this routine in *Who's Minding the Store?* (1963). This vacuum cleaner, which has a far greater suction than its predecessors, is able to single-handedly destroy an entire department store. It doesn't just suck the fur off a dog — it devours the entire dog. The dust bag expands like a balloon and, when it explodes, showers debris down upon shoppers and stirs up strong enough winds to sweep a fat woman across the floor and toss a floorwalker out a window. The previous routines were slight in comparison to this one. The one problem with the scene is that the vacuum cleaner soon takes over and Lewis is left with little to do. But it was the prop-driven nature of the routine that now, as always, rendered it impersonal.

It seemed for awhile that every decade needed its own defining version of the routine. In *The Return of the Pink Panther* (1975), Peter Sellers has considerable trouble with a hotel's industrial-strength vacuum cleaner. No dogs are present this time, but the vacuum cleaner sucks a squawking parrot through the bars of its cage. The routine climaxes with Sellers trying to turn off the device and getting his head sucked into the canister drum. In *Mr. Mom* (1983), a family has given their cranky vacuum the ominous nickname of "Jaws." This version of the routine, despite a suspenseful build-up that includes the *Jaws* theme song, is less than dynamic. All the vacuum cleaner does is to snatch hold of a little boy's blanket. Michael Keaton, in one quick and decisive action, pounces on the beastly machine and plucks the blanket out of its carnivorous maw. The scene, which is cute at best, allowed the routine to die not with a high-powered drone, but with a mere whimper.

Trying to Get Arrested

O. Henry unintentionally provided the makings of an enduring comedy routine with his 1904 short story, "The Cop and the Anthem." For Soapy, a tramp feeling the chill of the coming winter, a prison with warm cells and regular meals looks to be an appealing haven. However, Soapy's efforts to get himself arrested are thwarted at every turn. He snatches an umbrella away from a well-dressed man, only to find that the item was not the man's to steal. He pretends to be a masher when approaching a young woman, but the woman turns out to be a prostitute and is cordial to his advances. In a key scene, Soapy consumes a large meal at a restaurant and confesses to the waiter that he does not have the money to pay his bill. Instead of the waiter calling a cop, he obtains the assistance of a second waiter to pitch the tramp out onto the sidewalk. Soapy experiences a spiritual epiphany while listening to a church organist play a Christmas hymn, the "anthem" of the title. He decides that he will "pull himself out of the mire" and "make a man of himself again." He will start to get his life right by seeking employment. A police officer abruptly interrupts this personal transformation to arrest the tramp for vagrancy. Proven, in the end, is the perversity of fate.

The earliest-known film adaptation of "The Cop and the Anthem" was *Trying to Get Arrested* (1909), directed by D. W. Griffith for American Mutoscope & Biograph. This film reduces the witty story to crude slapstick as the tramp sets out to get arrested by starting a street brawl. Thomas R. Mills, a British actor with a fondness for the writings of O. Henry, directed and starred in an adaptation for Vitagraph in 1917. Other direct adaptations were produced over the years in different countries, including France and Czechoslovakia.

In 1954, a version of "The Cop and the Anthem" was developed as a Christmas special for Red Skelton. Skelton's stock tramp character, Freddy the Freeloader, faithfully follows the action of the story, but never misses an opportunity to throw in a goofy wisecrack. A departure in this family-friendly show was to replace the streetwalker with a spinster, who reacts so amorously to Skelton's advances that she is the one who is arrested as a masher.

Lamar Trotti, an Oscar-winning screenwriter best known for his work on *The Ox-Bow Incident* (1943) and *Wilson* (1944), provided the finest adaptation of the story as part of an anthology film called *O. Henry's Full House* (1952). Charles Laughton, as Soapy, renders a performance as funny as it is poignant. Soapy, with his exquisite diction and florid vocabulary, is presented as a downtrodden aristocrat. The addition of a second tramp, an attentive sidekick named Horace (David Wayne), allows Soapy to amply express his views and schemes as the story progresses. In the restaurant scene, Soapy is insulting and haughty to the waiters to ensure that they will not treat him with sympathy. His response to being handed the check is to rudely tear it up.

Charlie Chaplin saw this story as a suitable vehicle for his own tramp character and incorporated a version of the story into *Modern Times* (1936). In this version, Chaplin helps himself to two trays of food at a cafeteria. It is not until he has gorged himself on every last speck of food that he informs the cashier that he doesn't have the money to pay the bill. A police officer leads him outside of the cafeteria and, while the officer is calling for a paddy wagon, Chaplin casually obtains a cigar from a cigar stand to indulge in an after-dinner smoke.

Fair Enough (1922) combined "The Cop and the Anthem" with another O. Henry classic, "The Gift of the Magi." Dorothy Devore plays a reckless heiress locked up in jail for speeding. She becomes enamored of a fellow inmate (Earle Rodney), an unjustly imprisoned man. After her father bails her out of jail, she is determined to get arrested again so that she can reunite with Rodney. She succeeds in getting arrested, but arrives at the jail just in time to see him being released. Rodney is so desperate to be with Devore that he sets out to commit a crime that will put him back behind bars. However, Dorothy's father has come back to the jail to bail out his daughter a second time. As in "The Gift of the Magi," the mutual sacrifices that lovers make for each other fail to bring about the intended outcome. This running routine is brought to an end when Devore becomes handcuffed to a dangerous criminal who seizes the first opportunity to break out of jail.

22. Other Variations 289

Charlie Chaplin (left), in the process of being arrested for failing to pay a restaurant bill, stops to have an after-dinner smoke in *Modern Times* (1936). The police officer is Pat Harmon; the cigar counterman is Buddy Messinger (courtesy Bruce Lawton Collection).

Other versions of the story also deviated from the idea of a tramp seeking a warm jail cell. *The Star Boarder* (1919) presents Larry Semon as a parolee determined to get arrested so that he can resume his romance with the warden's daughter. Wallace Reid plans to go to jail to escape an insanely jealous romantic rival in *Thirty Days* (1922). Charlie Ruggles seeks refuge in prison to avoid gangsters in *The Girl Habit* (1931). Lou Costello hopes to acquire prison stripes to be eligible for free dental treatment in a 1952 episode of *The Abbott & Costello Show* entitled "The Dentist Office." Abbott and Costello, more than the others, put their own personal stamp on the routine, turning the classic O. Henry tale into a raucous burlesque sketch. This time, the streetwalker has been replaced by a gangster's moll. The moll, on edge because she is "on the lam," becomes infuriated that Costello happened to call to her by her underworld nickname "Toots." She grabs hold of Costello and gives him a thrashing. Next, Costello sets out to trigger a false alarm, but his action allows the fire trucks to arrive just in time to put out an actual fire that has broken out. A lovely woman, grateful to Costello for saving her life, lavishes Costello with kisses.

Dentistry also entered into a version of the routine featured in a 1966 episode of *Get Smart* entitled "The Whole Tooth and...." The task falls to secret agent Maxwell Smart (Don Adams) to get into prison to extract a prisoner's tooth that contains top-secret microfilm. In an attempt to get arrested, he dines on a extravagant meal at a restaurant and then tells the waiter that he doesn't have the money to pay. The manager of the restaurant takes sympathy on Max, whom he assumes is having financial problems, and takes up a collection among the diners to give him money to help him out. Max next attempts to mug a man in an alleyway. The man, who turns out to be a psychiatrist, explains to Max the reasons for his anti-social behavior and concludes their encounter by handing Max his business card. Max tosses away the card, which gets him arrested for littering.

Christmas folk stories have a tendency to blend together. This is the reason that "The Cop and the Anthem" was brought together with Charles Dickens's *A Christmas Carol* in a 1960 episode of *The Andy Griffith Show* called "Christmas Story." A Scrooge-like old man (Will Wright) commits petty crimes (stealing a city bench, parking in front of a fire hydrant) to join a Christmas party that Andy is hosting at the jailhouse.

An episode of *Seinfeld* ("The Millennium," 1997) provided a fresh update of this over-used premise. George (Jason Alexander) is looking to get fired from his job with the Yankees so that he can take a better job with the Mets. He performs a series of infractions, including vandalizing a souvenir Babe Ruth jersey, streaking across the field in the middle of a game, and hitching a World Series Trophy to his car and dragging it through the parking lot. The last stunt nearly gets him fired until his supervisor steps forward to take the blame because he, too, wants the job with the Mets.

Trading Places

The Scandinavian folk tale "The Man Who Kept House" involves a bad-tempered farmer who regularly complains to his wife that, compared to him, she does little work. The wife, exhausted by the complaints, offers to go out to work on the farm if her husband is willing to stay home and handle the domestic chores. He happily agrees. The wife does well harvesting crops, but the husband is less successful in his domestic duties and suffers a series of calamities, including getting stuck in the chimney. The wife returns home in time to rescue her husband.

The idea of a husband and wife trading jobs for a day became the premise of a number of film comedies. The earliest-known example is a Charley Chase vehicle titled *The Poor Fish* (1924). Chase and his wife (Katherine Grant) are feeling harried by their daily responsibilities and bicker with each other over which of them has the more demanding job. The couple decides to resolve the debate by trading jobs.

Chase, under taunts of his mother-in-law, struggles through the household work. Washing dishes should be simple task, but Chase is interrupted by a door-to-door salesman and neglects to shut off the faucet before leaving the kitchen. It takes little time for the sink to overflow and the floor to become flooded. Chase finishes cleaning up the mess in time to start dinner. He pours rice into a pot, but doubts that he put in enough rice. He scoops up more and adds it to the pot, but he still does not think that it is enough. He ends up pouring the entire contents of a gallon canister of rice into the pot before being interrupted by yet another salesman at the door. By the time that Chase has returned to the kitchen, a mountain of rice has sprung up inside the pot and he needs to pull out buckets to contain it all.

Chase comes to feel emasculated by the experience. This point is underscored when a salesman makes an effeminate hand gesture in response to seeing Chase in a dust cap and apron. However, Chase should feel that he has been spared considering the indignities that would be inflicted on his successors.

In *The Chaser* (1928), a husband and wife do not elect to change places on their own. Their situation beings with a heated argument that lands Harry Langdon and his wife (Gladys McConnell) into court. The instigator of the argument was Harry's mother-in-law, who was angry at Harry for staying out late at his lodge. She even went so far as to threaten Harry with a gun, forcing Harry and his wife to wrestle the weapon away from her. However, the mother-in-law tells a different story in court, and succeeds in convincing the judge that Harry assaulted her with a knife. The judge says that he could sentence Harry to six months in prison but he will, instead, order him to switch places with his wife for 30 days so that he might "realize his responsibilities."

Wearing a cap and apron was emasculating enough for Chase, but Harry goes considerably further by wearing a skirt. In accordance with the role reversal, McConnell dresses for work in a masculine business suit and acts even more bossy towards Harry than usual. The newly obedient husband brushes off his wife's jacket before she departs for work. Later, Harry's skirt gives the wrong impression to visiting tradesmen. A furniture salesman makes a pass at him. A leering ice man sneaks up behind him and plants a kiss on his cheek.

Harry, too, proves inept in the kitchen. He nearly blows up the house in a simple effort to light the oven. He is careful, after opening the oven door, to step back and toss in a match. The stove bucks violently, after which a giant flame shoots out. This went on to become a stock gag for the Three Stooges.

In 1937, Edgar Kennedy starred in a virtual remake of *The Poor Fish* entitled *Bad Housekeeping*. The extended running time of *Bad Housekeeping* (18 minutes compared to *The Poor Fish*'s eight minutes) allows the story to be further developed, and grants Kennedy the opportunity to get into a greater amount of trouble. In *The Poor Fish*, the husband and wife were simply shown snapping at each other, the exact details of their altercation being left to the viewer's imagination. But Kennedy and his wife (Vivien Oakland) engage in a pointed debate as to whether housekeeping duties could be accomplished in a short amount of time if a well thought-out system were applied.

The meddlesome mother-in-law is replaced by a meddlesome piano tuner (Franklin Pangborn), who has dropped in for a service call. A running gag in *The Poor Fish* involved a sign that read "What is a Home without a Mother?" That sign has now been replaced by a "Home Sweet Home" sign, which falls off the wall at inopportune moments. The piano tuner blanches at the sight of Kennedy in an apron and dust cap. Kennedy possesses neither Chase's willowy form nor Langdon's tender face. It would take more than a cap and apron to have this burly Irishman convey a suggestion of femininity.

Kennedy is, in the end, outdone by his own ham-handedness and quick-temperedness. He breaks everything that he touches and then allows his mishaps to spin out of control by losing his temper. A simple effort to change the sheets on his bed ends up with the bed breaking apart and Kennedy trapped beneath the box spring. He manages, with his indelicate fingers, to split open a pillow case, which fills the air with a storm of feathers. He is depositing laundry into the washing machine when he gets his tie caught in the clothes ringer. He rushes to the stove to remove a pot of rice that is boiling over, but the handle is too hot for him to hold and the pot crashes to the floor. The mishap causes the floor to become covered in rice and hot water. Kennedy, finding himself in a desperate state, hires professional housekeepers to clean up the mess before his wife returns home.

In *Turnabout* (1940), a party even more powerful than a judge intervenes in the lives of a bickering husband and wife (John Hubbard and Carole Landis). It is through the magical powers of a Buddha statue that the couple find themselves inhabiting each other's bodies.

Hal Erickson wrote in the All Movie Guide, "As a result, Sally awakens with a deep voice and dons Tim's business suit, while Tim speaks in a falsetto and favors Sally's frilly frocks."[8] It is during the course of the spiritual displacement that the husband gets pregnant and gives birth. The tagline used to promote the film read, "The man's had a baby instead of the lady." Nothing in the other films approached this level of gender-switching, although it was suggested in an odd way by a scene in *The Chaser*. Kevin Brownlow, described this scene in *The Parade's Gone By...*: "[Langdon] shuffles out to the chicken house with a frying pan and tries to induce a hen to lay an egg. He holds the hen over the pan, hoping for the eggs to drop straight in. When nothing happens, he looks curiously at the sleepy chicken, puts it to his ear, and shakes it like a defective alarm clock. Meanwhile, another hen has crawled under his skirt, deposited an egg, and crawled out again. When Harry lets the chicken go, he steps back and is startled to discover an egg that he has apparently produced himself."[9]

Turnabout came along decades before *Freaky Friday* (1976) started a trend of body-swapping comedies, or movies like *Rabbit Test* (1978) and *Junior* (1994) tried to mine laughs from the idea of a man giving birth. This is a perfect example of an idea that built through repeated use, but it is possible for some ideas to be taken further than they need to go.

The role-reversal premise was revived by television sitcoms, including *I Love Lucy* ("Job Switching," 1952) and *The Flintstones* ("Operation Switchover," 1964). In the *I Love Lucy* episode, neither husband nor wife does well at their respective jobs. Lucy (Lucille Ball) does not have the success of the previous wives as the series depended on her klutzy housewife character to make a mess of situations. This is the famous episode wherein Lucy and Ethel (Vivian Vance) are employed at a candy factory wrapping chocolates that come down a conveyor belt. The pair is unable to keep up and take to hiding chocolates down their blouses, under their caps and, finally, inside their mouths. Ricky (Desi Arnaz) seems at first to be having an easier time at home. This husband, although presented wearing an apron with a large Valentine heart embroidered on one side, has no problem retaining his natural manliness. He mounts a newspaper on a vacuum cleaner so that he can read the sports page while vacuuming. He keeps a pack of cigarettes rolled up in his shirt sleeve so he always has a smoke at the ready. He may be doing housework, but he is still a man. But then everything goes wrong. While ironing, Ricky burns his shirt. Then, he has a problem boiling rice, much like Chase had twenty-eight years earlier. It was a vital element of these stories that the husband make a mess while preparing dinner. The farmer of the Scandinavian folk tale takes a break from churning butter to drink beer, and it is at this moment that a pig comes along and knocks over the churn. The kitchen floor immediately becomes covered with cream. It is not much different than what happens to Ricky. He washes a chicken in the sink unaware that a volcanic eruption of rice is occurring behind him. When he finally does see the rice, he frantically runs around the kitchen, grabbing bowls and pans to contain the spillage before it ends up on the floor. The task proves futile, and the rice is soon spread across the floor, which makes the floor slick and causes Ricky to slip and fall. This is a rare instance where a television sitcom has more wildly energetic activity than a silent film comedy. Arnaz, underrated for his comic skills, provides an exceptionally funny performance.

Arnaz's rice scene (an exaggeration of Chase's rice scene) was taken directly from an episode of Ball's radio show, *My Favorite Husband* ("Women's Rights, Part 2," 1950). Richard Denning (who played Lucy's husband) phones his neighbor (Gale Gordon) to express his concern that the rice is beginning to swell up. ("Hey, hey, what a minute!" he cries suddenly. "Something's pushing the kitchen door open. Holy cow, it's the rice!") Gags can be exaggerated to a cartoonish extent on radio, which brings us directly to the animated series *The Flintstones*. The gags were certainly exaggerated in this interpretation of the story. The iron burns a huge steaming hole in an outfit. The rice expands to a size greater than the house can hold and comes bursting through the front door. It takes a shovel to clean up the mess.

A sitcom adaptation of *Turnabout* starring John Schuck and Sharon Gless was broadcast on CBS in 1979. The new aspect of the story was that neither husband nor wife works in the home. The husband makes a living as a sportswriter and the wife is a cosmetics executive. The professions were no doubt expected to create comical complications as a man is bound to be baffled by lipstick and a woman has to be nervous inside a football locker room. The husband does not get pregnant in the series, but he does panic when his period is late. This bizarre series never threatened to unseat the sex-driven, men-are-men-and-women-are-women sitcom champ *Three's Company*, and was unceremoniously canceled after seven episodes.

Still, *Turnabout* lives on. Pivotal elements of the story have found their way into *Dating the Enemy* (1996), *A Saintly Switch* (1999), *The Hot Chick* (2002) and *It's a Boy Girl Thing* (2006). *A Saintly Switch* took the professional sports element of the *Turnabout* series further by making the husband, played by David Alan Grier, into an NFL quarterback.

The premise in its original, magic-free form was used most recently by the Fox sitcom *Running Wilde* ("It's a Trade-off," 2010).

The Tricky Statue and the Kicking Scarecrow

A Commedia dell'Arte routine called "Lazzi of the Statue," which is believed to have originated in Paris in 1670, had the mischievous Arlecchino posing as a statue and playing tricks on people while their backs were turned. Arlecchino was nimble enough to instantly revert to the pose of the statue whenever a person turned around to face him.

A faithful version of this routine was performed by Stan Laurel in *White Wings* (1923). Laurel pretends to be part of a statue in an effort to evade a belligerent police officer (Marvin Loback). At first, Laurel assumes a variety of silly poses. Then, while Loback's back is turned, Laurel decides to have fun with the officer by tilting the officer's hat and sticking a finger in his ear. This has all of the elements of the original Commedia dell'Arte routine — the comedian pretends to be a statue, the comedian strikes a series of poses, and the comedian plays tricks on passersby.

Lupino Lane, a member of a longstanding theatrical family, was well-versed in Commedia dell'Arte routines. In *Roaming Romeo* (1928), Lane and his brother Wallace Lupino pose as statues to elude Roman soldiers. When the soldiers' backs are turned, the two break their poses to argue about what to do. Every time the soldiers turn towards them, they assume an entirely new and somewhat preposterous pose. Music hall reviews suggest that this routine shares similarities with a statue routine that Lane's uncle, George Lupino, Jr., performed in "The Spider and the Fly" music hall pantomime in 1890. Other screen duos performed this routine. Ham and Bud provided an early version of the routine in *The Toilers* (1915). Abbott & Costello did an exceptionally funny version of the routine in *Pardon My Sarong* (1942). A similar variation of the routine was employed in the 1913 Éclair comedy *Gavroche Sculpteur Pour Rire* (known in America as *Gavroche, a Sculptor for a Laugh*), in which a ne'er-do-well (Paul Bertho) has two friends pose as statues to fool his uncle into thinking he has become a great sculptor.

Buster Keaton in disguise in *The Scarecrow* (1920) (courtesy www.doctormacro.com).

The version of the routine seen most often in films was not faithful to the original Commedia dell'Arte routine. In fact, it did not even include a statue. In *Happy Jack, a Hero* (1910), servants break the stand holding up a suit of armor and, fearful of their boss finding out, hire a tramp (Mack Sennett) to stand inside the armor while they have the stand repaired. The mischievous tramp acts up during a party, kicking guests when their backs

22. Other Variations   295

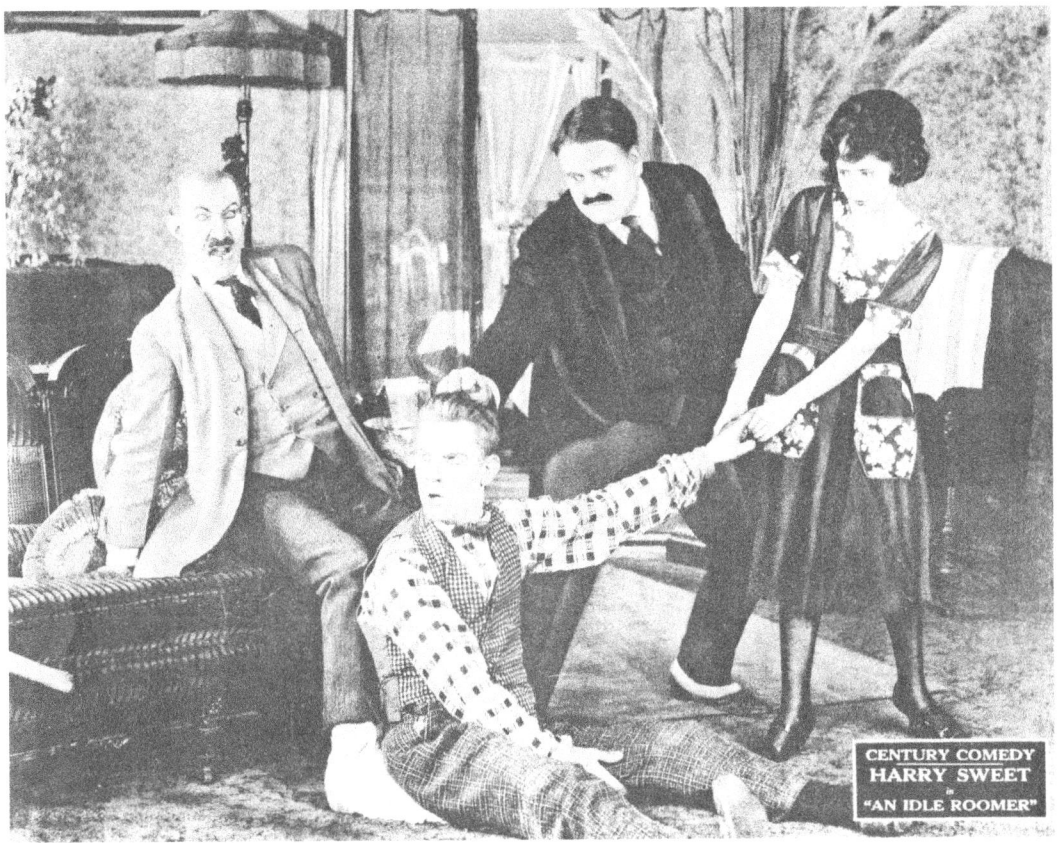

Bud Jamison (second from right) and an unidentified actress struggle to lift Harry Sweet off Jimmy Finlayson's gout-ridden foot in *An Idle Roomer* (1922). A man with gout was always vulnerable to harm in a slapstick comedy. Gout victims were exploited by a number of comedians, including Charlie Chaplin (*The Cure*, 1917), Laurel & Hardy (*Perfect Day*, 1929) and Charley Chase (*The Tabasco Kid*, 1932) (courtesy Cole Johnson Collection).

are turned. Guests, blaming each other for their sore backsides, fight among themselves. A suit of armor makes clanking and creaking noises in the real world, but it is an ideally surreptitious disguise in the context of a silent film.

Sennett remade this comedy as *Love in Armor* (1915). This time, Sennett gave the man in the armor, Charley Chase, motivation for his actions. Chase is in love with Mae Busch, but Busch's father regards Fritz Schade as a more appropriate suitor. Chase hides inside the suit of armor to get into a party at Busch's home. He kicks guests when no one is around to blame except for Schade. This, however, is not enough to discredit his romantic rival. When Schade's back is turned, Chase plants the hostess's valuable necklace into his pocket to make the family think that *he* is a thief.

Sennett's version of the routine set the standard. It was repeated in a number of films, including *Her Birthday Knight* (1917), *Reilly's Wash Day* (1919) and *Beware of the Bride* (1920).

The Commedia dell'Arte routine drew laughs from the statue's shifting poses and the varied pranks, but most film versions restricted the action to people being kicked in the backside. A good example of this is in the one-reeler *Fresh Paint* (1920), in which Snub Pollard poses as the statue of a Roman soldier in order to escape from an irate husband (Noah

(Left to right) Ena Gregory, Robert McKenzie, Lee Moran, and Blanche Payson are embroiled in hostile domestic relations in *Foolish Lives* (1922). The routine of bickering cohabitants using masking tape to divide a house down the middle was used on a variety of sitcoms in the 1950s and 1960s. It can be found in *I Love Lucy* ("Men Are Messy," 1951), *The Munsters* ("A House Divided," 1966), *The Monkees* ("Monkees Get Out More Dirt," 1967) and *Steptoe and Son* ("Divided We Stand," 1972) (courtesy Cole Johnson Collection).

Young). When Young turns his back, Pollard gives him a swift kick in the backside. A maid comes along and applies her feather duster to Pollard, whom she assumes is no more than stone. This proves a problem as the duster's bristles tickle Pollard's nose and cause him to sneeze. Young, now wise to the ruse, is even more determined to capture Pollard as he resumes the chase. Laurel's tricks were harmless compared to all of this unrestrained kicking.

Elements of this routine can be traced back as far as 1900, when a similar routine showed up in the Edison short *Uncle Josh in a Spooky Hotel*. Uncle Josh (Charles Manley), a guest at the aforementioned "spooky hotel," is speaking to a friend when a ghost suddenly appears behind him and knocks off his hat. The ghost disappears before Uncle Josh is able to see him and Uncle Josh has no one else to blame for his toppled hat except for his friend. The two men get into a fistfight. Once the men calm down, the mischievous ghost reappears, smacks the friend in the face, and promptly disappears again. This incites another battle between the men. The men soon become exhausted and sit down. The ghost returns and, this time, taps the friend on the shoulder. The friend turns, sees the ghost, and flees the room. This allows the ghost to take the friend's place in the chair next to Uncle John. Unaware of the change, Uncle John jokes, laughs and slaps the ghost's knee. The existing print abruptly ends just as Uncle John is turning his head toward the ghost. The routine was later performed by Ham and Bud in *Lotta Coin's Ghost* (1915) and Laurel and Hardy in *A Chump at Oxford* (1940). An ad for *Lotta Coin's Ghost* featured the headline "What would YOU do if a ghost sat down right beside you?"

In the end, it was established by *Uncle Josh in a Spooky Hotel* that a ghost is free to attack a man without the need for a disguise. This is the reason that, while playing a ghost in *The Time of Their Lives* (1945), Lou Costello found that he was finally able to kick the abusive Bud Abbott with impunity.

Scarecrows proved to be even more violent than statues, men in armor, or ghosts. In *The Country Lovers* (1911), two farm boys want to prove their manliness to a girl by getting rid of a tramp trespassing on their property. They use a scarecrow to pose as the tramp and beat the scarecrow mercilessly while the girl watches. But, then, the real tramp takes the scarecrow's place and gives the farm boys a beating.

Buster Keaton engaged in similar mischief as a scarecrow in a comedy titled, simply, *The Scarecrow* (1920). And, once again, Keaton gives the routine his own unique twist. He is slumped over a stake with a big floppy hat obscuring his face. The hat, which only periodically conceals his face during the scene, is a better costuming choice than the creepy

Betty Boyd and Jackie Levine (right) provide dubious assistance to Wallace Lupino (center) in *Hard Work* (1928). The film involved a family's nightmare renovating an old home, a premise later used in *Mr. Blandings Builds His Dream House* (1948), *The Money Pit* (1986) and *Are We Done Yet?* (2007) (courtesy Cole Johnson Collection).

cloth mask that Max Linder wore when he recreated the routine in *Be My Wife* (1921). Keaton chooses not to merely swing out a leg to drive a foot into someone's backside, which is the way Larry Semon was to handle the routine in his 1925 version of *The Wizard of Oz*. Keaton makes his version of the routine more intricate and energetic than that. Keaton disguises himself as a scarecrow to outwit a couple of men. He has to unhitch himself from the stake and climb to the ground before he can kick the men and then, afterwards, he has to climb back on the stake and reattach himself. He has to be quick, careful and precise to pull off these sneak attacks. Keaton makes his most daring move when he leaps high into the air with both legs raised to kick both men simultaneously. He then jumps back onto the stake, which promptly collapses under his weight. He is swinging his limbs wildly as he hits the ground, which allows the men to see that he is actually a living person.

The silent film comedian rarely executed a routine in a simple way. Keaton and his contemporaries remain appreciated today for their unyielding inventiveness and their unsurpassed work ethic.

Chapter Notes

Introduction

1. Gerald Nachman, *Seriously Funny: The Rebel Comedians of the 1950s and 1960s* (New York: Pantheon, 2003).

Chapter 1

1. Steve Massa, "Alice Howell & Gale Henry: Queens of Eccentric Comedy," *Griffithiana* 73/74 (2003).
2. Plot summary for *Les débuts d'un chauffeur* (1906), http://www.imdb.com/title/tt0000509/plotsummary.
3. Richard Abel, *The Ciné Goes to Town: French Cinema, 1896–1914* (Berkeley: University of California Press, 1994), p. 111.

Chapter 2

1. James L. Neibaur, Review of *Lost and Found: The Harry Langdon Collection*, *Cineaste*, January 2008. Retrieved from http://www.cineaste.com/articles/lost-and-found.htm.
2. Abel, *The Ciné Goes to Town*, p. 216.
3. Dave Karger, "Ogre and Out," *Entertainment Weekly*, No. #1104, May 28, 2010.

Chapter 3

1. Anthony Slide, "Dorothy Devore: Interview by Anthony Slide," *The Silent Picture*, #15, Summer 1972.
2. Diana Serra Cary, *What Ever Happened to Baby Peggy?* (Albany, GA: BearManor, 2009), p.44.
3. *Ibid.*
4. *Ibid.*, p. 26.
5. "Lillian Peacock Rides an Ostrich," *Moving Picture Weekly*, February 1916.
6. Cary, *What Ever Happened to Baby Peggy?*, p 36.
7. *Ibid.*
8. Edison Catalog, as cited by the Internet Movie Database, http://www.imdb.com/title/tt0379720/plotsummary.
9. *Moving Picture World* 18, no. 12, December 20, 1913.
10. *Ibid.*, no. 8, November 22, 1913.
11. Charlotte Spratt, "Hugh Grant and Sarah Jessica Parker have a hairy run-in with a grizzly bear named Bart," *Daily Mail Online*, August 18, 2009. Retrieved from http://www.dailymail.co.uk/tvshowbiz/article-1207179/Hugh-Grant-Sarah-Jessica-Parker-hairy-run-grizzly-bear-named-Bart.html.
12. Edison Catalog, as cited by the Internet Movie Database, http://www.imdb.com/title/tt0231524/plotsummary.
13. Jon C. Mirsalis, Lon Chaney Filmography. Retrieved from http://www.lonchaney.org/filmography/8.html.
14. *Moving Picture World* 16, no. 1, April 5, 1913.
15. Cole Johnson, e-mail correspondence to author, November 20, 2009.
16. Richard Abel, *The Ciné Goes to Town: French Cinema, 1896–1914* (Berkeley: University of California Press, 1994), p. 391.

17. *Moving Picture World* 16, no. 10, June 7, 1913.
18. Jim Kline, *The Complete Films of Buster Keaton* (New York: Citadel Press, 1993), p. 108.
19. Director commentary, *Year One* (DVD), Sony Pictures, 2009.
20. Production Notes to *The Hangover*, as provided by Warner Bros., 2009.
21. *Ibid.*
22. *Ibid.*
23. *Moving Picture World*, April 17, 1920, p. 462.
24. Storyline of *Billy Whiskers* (1920), as provided by the Internet Movie Database, http://www.imdb.com/title/tt0473135/.
25. *Moving Picture World* 16, no. 1, April 19, 1913, p. 310.
26. *Ibid.*
27. American Humane Association's Film & Television Unit, Report on *Cats & Dogs* (2001), http://www.ahafilm.info/movies/moviereviews.phtml?fid=7171.
28. Gorilla Men blog, http://www.members.shaw.ca/gorillagallery2/gorillamenclassic/emil_van_horn.htm.
29. Steven Jay Schneider and Daniel Shaw, *Dark Thoughts: Philosophic Reflections on Cinematic Horror* (Lanham, MD: Scarecrow Press, 2003).

Chapter 4

1. The *Moving Picture World*. December 23, 1916. p. 1819.
2. L. Frank Baum, *Queen Zixi of Ix* (Mineola, NY: Dover, 1971).
3. Joyce Milton, *Tramp: The Life of Charlie Chaplin* (New York: Da Capo Press, 1998), pp. 245–246.
4. "Those Friendly Enemies," *New York Times*, April 17, 1933.

Chapter 6

1. David P. Hayes, Citations and Case Summaries, Copyright Registration and Renewal Information Chart and Web Site, http://chart.copyrightdata.com/c13A.html.
2. *Ibid.*
3. Annette D'Agostino Lloyd, *Harold Lloyd: Magic in a Pair of Horn-Rimmed Glasses* (Albany, GA: BearManor, 2009), p. 221.
4. Donald W. McCaffrey, *Three Classic Silent Screen Comedies Starring Harold Lloyd* (Cranbury, NJ: Associated University Press, 1976), p. 255.
5. Hayes, Citations and Case Summaries, Copyright Registration and Renewal Information.
6. *Ibid.*
7. "Silent Star Heir Sues Disney," BBC News, October 31, 2000, http://news.bbc.co.uk/2/hi/entertainment/999973.stm.
8. *Ibid.*
9. *Ibid.*

Chapter 7

1. Gerald Nachman, *Seriously Funny: The Rebel Comedians of the 1950s and 1960s* (New York: Pantheon, 2003).
2. S. D. Travalanche blog, http://travsd.wordpress.com/2009/05/22/stars-of-vaudeville-12-13-nazimova-and-the-ritz-brothers/.
3. Bruce G. Hallenbeck, *Comedy-Horror Films: A Chronological History, 1914–2008* (Jefferson, NC: McFarland, 2009).
4. *Ibid.*
5. Helen G. Scott and François Truffaut, *Hitchcock* (New York: Simon & Schuster, 1985), p. 103.

Chapter 8

1. Biograph Catalog, as cited on the Internet Movie Database. Plot summary for *Hooligan as a Safe Robber* (1903). Retrieved from http://www.imdb.com/title/tt0490147/plotsummary.
2. *Ibid.*
3. *Moving Picture World*, December 17, 1916, p. 1866.
4. Lubin Catalog, as cited on the Internet Movie Database. Plot Summary for *Burglar and the Old Maid* (1903). Retrieved from http://www.imdb.com/title/tt0406613/plotsummary.

Chapter 10

1. Press sheet for *Joy Land* (July 1929).
2. Lupino Lane, "The Royal Family of Greasepaint," http://www.arthurlloyd.co.uk/Hammersmith/Lupino.htm.

Chapter 11

1. Kalton C. Lahue and Sam Gill, *Clown Princes and Court Jesters* (South Brunswick, NJ: A. S. Barnes, 1970).
2. Kage Baker, "Ancient Rockets: The Mechanical Man," March 16, 2009, http://www.tor.com/index.php?option=com_content&view=blog&id=17664.
3. *Ibid.*
4. Paghat the Ratgirl, http://www.weirdwildrealm.com/f-mechanical-man.html.
5. Mark Bourne, Review of *Charley Bowers: The Rediscovery of an American Comic Genius*, DVD Journal, http://www.dvdjournal.com/quickreviews/c/charleybowers.q.shtml.
6. *Ibid.*
7. Paul Brenner, Review of *Charley Bowers—The Rediscovery of An American Comic Genius*, Media Screen, http://www.mediascreen.com/c/completecharleybowers.htm.
8. William Morrow, IMDb user reviews for *There It Is* (1928), http://www.imdb.com/title/tt0019466/usercomments.

Chapter 12

1. *Universal Weekly*, February 27, 1915, p. 18.
2. Hal Erickson, Plot synopsis of *Avenging Dentist* (1910), All Movie Guide, http://www.allmovie.com/work/avenging-dentist-236530.

Chapter 13

1. Gerald Martin Bordman, *American Musical Theatre: A Chronicle* (New York: Oxford University Press, 1978), p. 335.
2. Ivo Blom, "All the Same or Strategies of Difference: Early Italian Comedy in International Perspective" (Amsterdam: University of Amsterdam, 2003), iivoblom.files.wordpress.com/2009/05/all-the-same-final.pdf.
3. David Kalat, "Evolution of a Gag," *Becoming Charley Chase* (DVD), VCI Entertainment, 2009.
4. Adamson, Joe. Groucho, Harpo, Chico and Sometimes Zeppo. New York: Simon & Schuster, 1973.

Chapter 14

1. "Murphy Beds Are Making a Comeback!" Murphy Wall Beds blog, May 5, 2008, http://murphywallbeds.blogspot.com/2008_05_01_archive.html.

Chapter 17

1. Kline, *The Complete Films of Buster Keaton*, p. 104.
2. *The Film Daily*. October 23, 1927. p. 7. No prints of *New Wrinkles* are known to exist, which makes a comprehensive analysis of the hat-changing scene impossible. However, the scene was described with great affection in a review published in *The Film Daily*. The reviewer pointed out that the humor of the sequence mostly came from Hamilton's reactions, including "pained surprise" and "injured dignity," as he carefully examined his appearance in each new hat. It also amused the critic to see Hamilton employing "his peculiar walk as he pose[d] up and down before the mirror." Hamilton, who had become fickle about wearing his trademark checkered cap, may have been making a statement when he tried to toss away his checkered cap and it kept flying back to him like a boomerang. Keaton does not have the same problem when he is trying on hats and comes across his old porkpie hat. The comedian stares at the hat apprehensively for moment and then tosses it out of sight for good.
3. William K. Everson, *The Films of Laurel and Hardy* (Secaucus, NJ: Citadel, Press, 1967).
4. Herb Feinstein, "Buster Keaton: An Interview," *Massachusetts Review* 4, no. 2, October 6, 1960, pp. 392–407.
5. *Ibid.*
6. Pat Cashin, e-mail correspondence to author, May 25, 2010.

7. Jackie Chan, *I Am Jackie Chan: My Life in Action* (New York: Ballantine, 1998).
8. "Knoxville Almost Killed Recreating Keaton Stunt," November 9, 2006. Retrieved from http://www.contactmusic.com/news.nsf/story/knoxville-almost-killed-recreating-keaton-stunt_1013217.
9. Kevin Brownlow and David Gill, *Buster Keaton — A Hard Act to Follow*, Thames Television, 1987.
10. "Roi Cooper Megrue Writes Another One," *New York Times*, August 9, 1916.
11. Lisa Schwarzbaum, Movie Review: *The Bachelor*, *Entertainment Weekly*, no. 512, November 12, 1999.
12. Edith Sorenson, "On Location with Boy Rifkin," *Houston Press*, March 10, 1994. Retrieved from http://www.houstonpress.com/content/printVersion/215999/.

Chapter 18

1. David B. Pearson, "Lloyd vs. Keaton," Hello, Harold Lloyd website, 1999, http://www.haroldlloyd.us/index.php?id=9&option=com_content&task=view.
2. *Ibid.*

Chapter 19

1. User Reviews for *A Connecticut Yankee in King Arthur's Court* (1921), http://www.imdb.com/title/tt0012067/.
2. Ron Schuler, "The Good Badman," *Ron Schuler's Parlour Tricks* (blog), December 6, 2005, http://rsparlourtricks.blogspot.com/2005/12/good-badman.html.
3. Kline, *The Complete Films of Buster Keaton*, p. 97.
4. *Ibid.*, p. 114.
5. *Ibid.*, p. 115.
6. Alan Parker, Interview with Michael Palin, *Monty Python: Almost the Truth: The Lawyers Cut* (DVD), Vivendi Entertainment, 2009.
7. *Ibid.*, Interview with Terry Gilliam.
8. *Ibid.*, Interview with Eric Idle.

Chapter 20

1. Barry Grantham, *Commedia Plays: Scenarios — Scripts — Lazzi* (London: Nick Hern, 2007), p. 214.

Chapter 21

1. *Moving Picture World*, May 15, 1920, p. 985.
2. Herb Feinsten, "Buster Keaton: An Interview," *Massachusetts Review*, vol. 4, no. 2, pp. 392–407 (October 6, 1960).
3. David N. Bruskin, *The White Brothers: Jack, Jules, and Sam White* (Lanham, MD: Scarecrow Press, 1990).
4. Steve Massa, "Race Riots: Beyond Black and White," Cruel and Unusual Comedy Blog, May 1, 2009. Retrieved from http://www.cruelandunusualcomedy.com/2009/05/may-27-at-4pm-race-riots.html.
5. *Moving Picture World*, October 21, 1916, p. 444.
6. Marc Singer, "Beating a Dead Man's Chest," July 10, 2006, http://notthebeastmaster.typepad.com/weblog/2006/07/beating_a_dead_.html.

Chapter 22

1. Steve Massa, "Gender Benders: Masculine Women/Feminine Men," Cruel and Unusual Comedy Blog, October, 2010. Retrieved from http://www.cruelandunusualcomedy.com/2010/10/gender-benders-masculine-womenfeminine_04.html.
2. David Mandel, "The Bizarro Jerry," *Seinfeld*, Season 8, Episode #137. Original airdate: October 3, 1996.
3. Janiss Garza, Plot synopsis of *The Mystery of the Leaping Fish*, All Movie Guide, http://www.allmovie.com/work/the-mystery-of-the-leaping-fish-175526.
4. *Universal Weekly*, February 27, 1915, p. 20.
5. *Moving Picture World*, January 17, 1920, p. 471.
6. *Ibid.*
7. Saul Austerlitz, *Another Fine Mess: A History of American Film Comedy* (Chicago: Chicago Review Press, 2010), p. 467.
8. Hal Erickson, Review of *Turnabout*, All Movie Guide, http://www.allmovie.com/work/turnabout-114675.
9. Kevin Brownlow, *The Parade's Gone By...* (Berkeley: University of California Press, 1976), p. 40.

Bibliography

Books

Abel, Richard. *The Ciné Goes to Town: French Cinema, 1896–1914*. Berkeley: University of California Press, 1994.
Austerlitz, Saul. *Another Fine Mess: A History of American Film Comedy*. Chicago: Chicago Review Press, 2010.
Baum, L. Frank. *Queen Zixi of Ix*. Mineola, NY: Dover, 1971.
Bordman, Gerald Martin. *American Musical Theatre: A Chronicle*. New York: Oxford University Press, 1978.
Bruskin, David N. *The White Brothers: Jack, Jules, and Sam White*. Lanham, MD: Scarecrow, 1990.
Cary, Diana Serra. *What Ever Happened to Baby Peggy?* Albany, GA: BearManor, 2009.
Chan, Jackie. *I Am Jackie Chan: My Life in Action*. New York: Ballantine, 1998.
Everson, William K. *The Complete Films of Laurel & Hardy*. Secaucus, NJ: Citadel Press, 1967.
Grantham, Barry. *Commedia Plays: Scenarios — Scripts — Lazzi*. London: Nick Hern Books, 2007.
Hallenbeck, Bruce G. *Comedy-Horror Films: A Chronological History, 1914–2008*. Jefferson, NC: McFarland, 2009.
Kline, Jim. *The Complete Films of Buster Keaton*. New York: Citadel Press, 1993.
Lahue, Kalton C., and Sam Gill, *Clown Princes and Court Jesters*. South Brunswick, NJ: A. S. Barnes, 1970.
Lloyd, Annette D'Agostino. *Harold Lloyd: Magic in a Pair of Horn-Rimmed Glasses*. Albany, GA: BearManor, 2009.
Milton, Joyce. *Tramp: The Life of Charlie Chaplin*. New York: Da Capo Press, 1998.
Nachman, Gerald. *Seriously Funny: The Rebel Comedians of the 1950s and 1960s*. New York: Pantheon, 2003.
Schleier, Merrill. *Skyscraper Cinema: Architecture and Gender in American Film*. Minneapolis: University of Minnesota Press, 2009.
Schneider, Steven Jay, and Daniel Shaw, *Dark Thoughts: Philosophic Reflections on Cinematic Horror*. Lanham, MD: Scarecrow, 2003.
Scott, Helen G., and François Truffaut, *Hitchcock*. New York: Simon & Schuster, 1985.
Towsen, John. *Clowns*. New York: E. P. Dutton, 1976.
Walker, Brent. *Mack Sennett's Fun Factory*. Jefferson, NC: McFarland, 2009.

Articles

Blom, Ivo. "All the Same or Strategies of Difference: Early Italian Comedy in International Perspective." University of Amsterdam, 2003.
Bourne, Mark. Review of *Charley Bowers: The Rediscovery of an American Comic Genius*. *DVD Journal*, 2004.
Feinstein, Herb. "Buster Keaton: An Interview." *Massachusetts Review*, October 6, 1960.
Karger, Dave. "Ogre and Out." *Entertainment Weekly*. no. 1104, May 28, 2010.
Massa, Steve. "Alice Howell & Gale Henry: Queens of Eccentric Comedy." *Griffithiana* 73/74 (2003).
_____. "Gender Benders: Masculine Women/Feminine Men." Cruel and Unusual Comedy Blog October 2010.
_____. "Race Riots: Beyond Black and White." Cruel and Unusual Comedy Blog, May 1, 2009.
Neibaur, James L. Review of *Lost and Found: The Harry Langdon Collection*. *Cineaste*, January 2008.
Pearson, David B. "Lloyd vs. Keaton." Hello, Harold Lloyd (website). 1999.
Schuler, Ron. "The Good Badman." Ron Schuler's Parlour Tricks blog. December 6, 2005.
Schwarzbaum, Lisa. Movie Review: *The Bachelor*. *Entertainment Weekly*. No. 512, November 12, 1999.
Singer, Marc. "Beating a Dead Man's Chest." *I am NOT the Beastmaster* (website). July 10, 2006.
Sorenson, Edith. "On Location with Boy Rifkin." *The Houston Press*, March 10, 1994.
Slide, Anthony. "Dorothy Devore: Interview by Anthony Slide." *The Silent Picture* no. 15, Summer 1972.

Spratt, Charlotte. "Hugh Grant and Sarah Jessica Parker have a hairy run-in with a grizzly bear named Bart." *Daily Mail Online*, August 18, 2009.
Warner Bros. Production Notes to *The Hangover*. 2009.

DVDs

Brownlow, Kevin, and David Gill, dirs. *Buster Keaton — A Hard Act to Follow*. Thames Television, 1987.
Kalat, David, dir. "Evolution of a Gag." *Becoming Charley Chase*. VCI Entertainment, 2009.
Parker, Alan, dir. *Monty Python: Almost the Truth: The Lawyers Cut*. Vivendi Entertainment, 2009.
Ramis, Harold, dir. *Year One*. Sony Pictures, 2009.

Websites

All Movie Guide
American Humane's Film & Television Unit
DVD Journal
Gorilla Men Blog
Internet Movie Database
Kansas Board of Review Movie Index
Media Screen
New York Times
The Three Stooges Online Filmography
TV Tropes
Weird Wild Realm Blog
Wikipedia

Periodicals

Moving Picture World
Universal Weekly (also known as *Moving Picture Weekly*)

Index

Page numbers in **_bold italics_** indicate photographs.

Abbott & Costello 8, 22, 28, 36, 51, 63, 73, 74, 83, 84, 90, 93–96, 105, 106, 116, 120, 132, 137, 156, 161, 165, 171, 173, 176, 183, 185, 190, 221, 258, 275, 279, 280, 289, 293, 297
An Ache in Every Stake (1941) 79, 189, 263, 282
Adams, Jimmie 67, 81, 121, 137, 267, 273
Adler, Felix 94, 116
The Adventurer (1917) 9, 138, 203, 278
The Adventures of Baron Munchausen (1988) 217
An Adventurous Automobile Trip (1905) 11
Africa F.O.B. (1925) 81
Alexander, Frank **108**, 136, **_233_**, 250
Alexander, Jason 41, 290
Alice Cans the Cannibals (1925) 256
Alice in Society (1916) 8
All Cooked Up (1915) 130
All the World's a Stooge (1941) 275
All Wet (1922) 68
Allen, Woody 9, 26, 74, 83, 95, 166, 185, 230, 234, 238
Always a Gentleman (1928) 175, 262
Ambrose's Little Hatchet (1915) 26
American Pie 2 (1999) 267
An American Werewolf in London (1981) 75
Among the Mourners (1914) 9
Among Those Present (1921) 62, 86, 112, 138, 222
Andy Griffith Show 139, 281, 290
Animal Crackers (1930) 31, 104
The Animated Poster (1903) 141
Another Name Was Maude (1906) 130

Arbuckle, Roscoe 7, 8, 9, 13, **_35_**, 48, 49, 67, 68, 77, 78, 81, 83, 87, 107, 112, 131, 168, 175, 179, 192, 207, 210, 212, 247, 260, 261, 276, 278, 283
Ardath, Fred 23
Arnaz, Desi 292
Arthur, Johnny 52, 54, 81, 90, 243, 274
Astor, Gertrude 26, 101, 217
Aubrey, Jimmy **89**, **_108_**, 159
Aunt Jane and the Tabasco Sauce (1902) 96
The Avenging Dentist (1915) 160, 278

Babe (1995) 69
Baby Peggy (aka Diana Serra Cary) 40, 44, 232, 252
Back to the Future (1985) 106, 157, 228
Bacon, Lloyd 162
Bad Housekeeping 291
The Bakery (1921) 211, 212, 279
Ball, Lucille 25, 32, 219, 292
The Balloonatic (1923) 49
Banks, Monty 19, 70, 81, 243, 250
Bara, Theda 99
Barrett, Harry 197
Bart the Bear 52
Bataille, Lucien 23, 46
The Bath Chair Man 12
Battling Sisters (1929) 13, 102
Baum, L. Frank 86, 213
Be Big (1931) 182
Be My Wife (1921) 122, 298
Be Reasonable (1921) 23, 183, 204, 274
A Bear Affair (1915) 48
Beard, Matthew "Stymie" 83
Bell, Spencer 50, **_235_**, 249–250, 274
The Bell Hop (1922) 136

Bergman, Henry 78, 259, 278
Besser, Joe 73, 170, 172, 275
Bevan, Billy 18, 23, 60, **_66_**, 67, 69, 92, **_104_**, 123, 138, 179, 183, **_184_**, 187, 194, 204, 257, 271, 273, 274, 287
The Bewitched Inn (1897) 118, 137
Big Business (1988) 167
The Big Noise (1944) 199
Biggs, Jason 267
Billy Blazes, Esq. (1919) 231, 247
Billy Madison (1995) 9
Biograph 9, 46, 48, 96, 112, 130, 133, 168, 172, 173, 178, 213, 235, 246, 261, 278, 288
A Bird in the Head (1946) 73, 122
Black Eyes (1915) 180
Black Sheep (1996) 14
The Blacksmith (1922) 153
Blazing Saddles (1974) 9, 275
Bletcher, Billy 248
Bloch, Robert 126
Blood and Bosh (1913) 32
Blue, Ben 26, 31, 83, 121, 124, 263
The Boat (1921) 144, 202
Bostock Animal and Jungle Show 57
Bourbon, Ernest 164
Bowers, Charley 92, 143, 152–156, 309
Brats (1930) 275, 276
The Brave Hunter (1912) 46, 48
Brideless Groom (1947) 215, 262
Bringing Up Baby (1938) 67, 115
Bromo and Juliet (1926) 143
Brooks, Mel 170, 235, 237
Bruckman, Clyde 115, 124, 197, 215
Bugs Bunny 90, 165
A Bullet-proof Bed (1900) 168
Bungles Lands a Job (1916) 211
Busch, Mae 217, 225, 295
Byrne Brothers 194, 200

305

Index

Caddyshack (1980) 90
Caesar, Sid 86, 122
The Cameraman (1928) 37, 110, 150, 197, 201, 220
Campbell, Eric 9, 138, 263, 278
Campbell, William 40
The Candid Camera (1932) 179
Candy, John 52, 275
Cantor, Eddie 69, *105*, 233
Capra, Frank 217
Carrey, Jim 41, 53, 74, 86
Catlett, Walter 73, 103
Chan, Jackie 194, 208, 308
Chaplin, Charlie 5, 8, 9, 15, 17, 18, 20, 24, 30, 39, 45, 49, 49, 61, 76, 80, 81, 83, 85–89, 123, 138, 146, 153, 158, 162, 169, 170, 187, 195–197, 203, *214*, 219, 222, 223, 244, 254, 259, 263, 274, 278, 282, 284, 285, 287, 288, **289**
Chaplin, Sydney 44, 89, 132, *147*, 273
Chapman, Graham 114, 216
Chase, Charley 10, 13, 17, 18, 30, 64, 69, 72, 113, 123, 133, 134, 143, 146, 164, 168, 171, 175, 180, *196*, 226, 254, 260, 270, 273, 290, 295
Chase, Chevy 267
The Chaser (1928) 291
Cheech & Chong 271–273
The Chef's Revenge (1915) 77
Chickens Come Home (1931) 218
Chinese Laundry Scene (1895) 12
Christie, Al 54
The Christie Film Company 48, 54, 72
A Chump at Oxford (1940) 120, 297
The Circus (1928) 24, 39, 61, 244
Cleese John 74, 80, 108, 183, 240
Cline, Eddie 148, 205
Clyde, Andy 14, 31, 44, 51, 55, 72, 74, 99, 125, 137, 140, 142, 165, 172, 173, 176, 237, 248, 251, 257, 275, 281
The Coal Strike (1905) 9
Cockeyed Cavaliers (1934) 233
Cogley, Nick 9, 246
Cold Hearts and Hot Flames (1916) 141, 241
Cold Turkey (1925) 123
College (1927) 210, 252
Colvig, Pinto 96
Commedia dell'arte 9, 18, 26, 30, 31, 77, 83, 86, 88, 120, 135, 137, 139, 158, 183, 184, 185, 210, 211, 241, 243, 245, 250, 270, 293, 294, 295
Confessions of a Shopaholic (2009) 33
Conklin, Chester 77, 131, 263

Conklin, Heinie *47*, 194, ***230***, ***261***
Conley, Lige 7, 13, 28, 49, 50, 64, 69, 81, 134, 152, 164, ***205***, 227, 243, 250
A Connecticut Yankee in King Arthur's Court (1921) 229
Consul the Great 36
Convict 13 (1920) 94, 148, 204, 220, 252
The Cook (1918) 79, 81, 82, 192, 210, 278
Cook, Clyde 25, 70, 90, 92, 175, 185, 273
Cooper, Jack 30, 125, ***131***, 161, 237
"The Cop and the Anthem" (short story) 287
Cops (1922) 129, 194, 203, 222
A Cork Leg Legacy (1909) 270
Costello, Lou *see* Abbott & Costello.
The Court Jester (1955) 26, 225, 235
The Courtship of Miles Sandwich (1923) 229
The Covered Schooner (1923) 70, 243
Cramer, Rychard 84
Creeps (1926) 29, 51, 121, 123, 250, 265
Crosby, Bing 70, 73, 138
Crushed (1924) 242
Cumpson, John R 112, 133
Cupid in a Dental Parlor (1913) 160
Cupid in a Hospital (1915) 278

Dames and Dentists (1920) 158
Dance of the Rolls (comedy routine) 87, 88
Daniels, Bebe 232, 247
Daniels, Mickey 30, 185, 258
The Daredevil (1923) 21, 138, 143, 267
David, Larry 114
"David After Dentist" 159
Davidson, Max 31, 58, 108
Davis, Joan 115
The Deadwood Sleeper (1905) 173
Deed, André 12, 25, 56, 136, 140, 151, 194, 211
Deep Sea Panic (1924) 7, 263
Dent, Vernon 253, 267
The Dentist (1919) 161
The Dentist (1932) 161
Desperate Poaching Affair (1903) 12
Devore, Dorothy 40, 46, 48, 275, 288, 309, 311
Dickerson, Dudley 31, 97, 140, 250, 253
"Dippy Doo-Dads" series 42
Dizzy Detectives (1943) 29, 73, 124

A Dog's Life (1918) 30, 80, 146, 223
Dome Doctor (1924) 123, 154
Don't Throw That Knife (1951) 137
Dooley, Billy 14, 20–21, 31, 64, 104, 173, 224, 271
Dopey Dicks (1950) 139
Downey, Robert, Jr. 248
Drink Hearty (1920) 247, 272
Duchovny, David 167
Due Date (2010) 248, 286
Dummies (1928) 25, 28, 273
Dunston Checks In (1996) 41
Durante, Jimmy 97

Easy Curves (1927) 20
The Edison Company 9, 12, 16, 30, 46, 54, 133, 142, 158, 168, 180, 185, 213, 243, 245, 252, 260, 296, 311
Edwards, Blake 131, 159, 191
Edwards, Harry 103
"Eight Bells" (stage routine) 194
The Electric House (1922) 153
Elephants on His Hands (1920) 54
Ella Cinders (1926) 14, 59, 64, 242
Étaix, Pierre 24, 55, 144, 216, 218

Fair Enough (1922) 288
Fairbanks, Douglas 37, 232, 238, 243, 272, 277
The Famous Box Trick (1898) 23
Farina (aka Allen Hoskins) 71, 72
Farley, Chris 9, 14, 15, 174
Farley, Dot 55, 232
Fast and Furious (1924) 7, 274
The Fatal Dress Suit (1914) 112
Fatal Footsteps (1926) 155
Feet of Mud (1924) 18, 125, 267, 268
Feldman, Marty 225
Felix Dopes It Out (1925) 256
Ferrell, Will 65, 114, 177
Dix Femmes pour un mari 213
Fey, Tina 115, 142, 277
Fields, W.C. 42, 73, 82, 109, 161, 174, 243, 262, 284, 286, 287
Fighting Fluid (1925) 18
Fine, Larry *see* The Three Stooges
Finlayson, Jimmy *15*, 34, 82, 84, 133, 210, 217, 225, 243, ***295***
The First Execution (1913) 13
The Flintstones (television series) 292, 293
The Flirts (1919) 67, 137
The Floorwalker (1916) 162
The Flower Girl (1924) 44

A Flyer in Flapjacks (1917) 79, 260
For Heaven's Sake (1926) 9, 85, 245
Forgetting Sarah Marshall (2008) 107
Fox, Michael J. 106
The Fox Chimps 36, 37
Fraidy Cat (1924) 17
Franey, Billy 19, 146, 211, 255, 278
Freaky Friday (1976) 292
Free and Easy (1921) 49, 81, 273
Fresh Paint (1920) 139, 295
The Freshman (1925) 23, 110
From Hand to Mouth (1919) 203, 222
Frozen Hearts (1923) 99, 232
The Frozen North (1922) 143, 230
The Fuller Brush Man (1948) 106, 208
Furry Vengeance (2010) 53, 70

Gay's Lion Farm 57, 62
Gemora, Charles 71
The General (1926) 50
Get Along Little Zombie (1946) 251
Getting Evidence (1906) 9, 252
Gilbert, Billy 26, 121, 185, 187, **190**, 273
Gilliam, Terry 73, 144, 192, 240
Go West (1925) 55, 65
Go West (1940) 208
The Goat (1921) 22, 23, 116, 219, 222, 250, 259
The Gold Ghost (1934) 31, 108, 194, 207
The Gold Rush (1925) 15, 49, 86
Good Night, Nurse! (1918) 8, 83
The Gown Shop (1923) 21, 123, 211
Grant, Cary 67, 115
Grant, Hugh 47, 52, 309, 311
Grant, John 95
The Great Alexander 36
The Great Vacuum Robbery (1915) 287
Gremlins (1984) 76
Gribbon, Harry 64, 68, 152, 160, 243
Grief in Bagdad (1925) 36, 148
Grips, Grunts and Groans (1937) 18
Guinness, Alec 113, 197
Guy-Blaché, Alice 162

Half Wits' Holiday (1947) 281
The Halfback of Notre Dame (1924) 160
Hall, Huntz 83, 94, 106, 139
The Hall Room Boys 32, 254
Ham and Bud 119, 187, 260, 293, 297
Hamilton, Lloyd 9, 13, 37, 59, 75, 76, 79, 80, **82**, 86, 90, 91, 95, 101, 113, 116, 121, 132, 164, 173, 174, 180, 183, 194, 197, 210, 213, 225, 226, **242**, 247, 252, **254**, 262, 263, 269, 271, 278, 287, 301, 302
Hammock Over Water (1903) 172
The Hangover (2009) 65–67
Hanneford, Poodles 189, 202, 241
Happy Jack, a Hero (1910) 235, 294
Hardy, Oliver (solo) 21, 30, 211, 249, 257, 279
Hart, William S. 231
The Haunted Hat (1909) 123, 135
The Haunted House (1921) 121, 137, 192, 265
The Haunted Lounge (1909) 135
Haunted Spooks (1920) 122, 211
He Comes Up Smiling (1918) 243, 277
He Done His Best (1926) 92, 153, 154
He Wouldn't Stay Down (1915) 168
Healthy, Wealthy, and Dumb (1938) 267
Hello, Hollywood (1925) 164
Help! (1924) 28, 121, 137
Henderson, Dell 96, 112, 278
Henry, Gale 48, 91, 214, 256, 278, 309, 311
Hepworth, Cecil 11, 32
Her Dummy Husband (1915) 29
Herbert, Hugh 29, 73, 97, 104, 248, 251, 253
Heuzé, André 12
Hey Doctor! (1918) 7
High Sign (1921) 147
The Hilarious Posters (1906) 23, 142
Hill, Benny 166
His Bridal Fright (1940) 69, 183
His First Flame (1927) 18
His Lucky Day (1909) 134
His Marriage Wow (1925) 183
His Musical Career (1914) 187
His Musical Sneeze (1919) 64, 90, 116
His New Mamma (1924) 124
His Silent Racket (1933) 133, 254
His Wooden Wedding (1925) 270
Hit the Ice (1943) 8, 51, 105, 123, 171, 187, 279
Hitchcock, Alfred 75, 126
The Holy Terror (1929) 70
Home Alone (1990) 30
Homer Joins the Force (1920) 23
Hope, Bob 70, 104, 137, 138, 171, 230, 237
Horseshoes (1923) 197
Hot Water (1924) 95, 123, **175**, 267, 268
How Cretinetti Paid His Debts (1909) 136

How Rastus Gets His Turkey (1910) 246
Howard, Curly *see* The Three Stooges
Howard, Moe *see* The Three Stooges
Howard, Shemp *see* The Three Stooges
Howell, Alice 7, 130, 248, 309, 311
Hughes, John 30, 267

I Do (1921) 125
I Dood It (1943) 218
I Love Lucy (television series) 25, 32, 166, 292, 296
Ice Cold Cocos (1926) 187
An Impossible Balancing Feat (1902) 141
In God We Tru$t (1980) 225
In the Grease (1925) 243
The Inconsistencies of Boireau (1912) 141
It's a Gift (1923) 152

Jackass Number Two (2006) 65
Jackson, Mar Ann 55, 70
A Jersey Skeeter (1900) 241
Jim Hensen Creature Shop 66
Jungle Jitters (1938) 256

Kaye, Danny 26, 225, 235, 238, **239**
Keaton, Buster 5, 14, 15, 22–24, 26, **27**, 31, 36–38, 41, 49, 50, 55, 59, 65, 73, 81–83, 94, 108, **109**, 110, 115, 116, 121, 123, 128, 129, 137, 140–144, 147, 148, 150, 153, 155, 161, 171, 174, 185, 192–222, 230, 231, 238, 240, 243, 247, 250, 252, **253**, 259, 260, 263, 265, **266**, 274, 278, 279, 283, 287, **294**, 297, 298, 308–310
Keep 'Em Flying (1941) 96, 132
Kennedy, Edgar 11, 69, 73, **147**, 159, 168, 173, 189, 253, 265, 273, 287, 291
The Keystone Film Company 5, 7, 9, 12, 17, 22, 42, 47, 48, 57, 58, 59, 68, 77, 95, 99, 131, 158, 160, 168, 169, 179, 187, 229, 246, 263
Kick (1920) 272
The Kid from Borneo (1933) 258
The Kid from Spain (1932) 69
Kidding Katie (1923) 275
Kiser, Terry 217, 219
Knoxville, Johnny 208
Kri Kri Smokes Opium (1913) 164, 272

The Ladykillers (2004) 144
Lane, Lupino 13, 18, 23, 26, 27, 29, 32, 50, 65, 68, 101, 102,

103, 123, 128, 145, 151, 185, 196, 201, 212, 217, 222, 233, 234, 237, 263, 275, 283, 293
Langdon, Harry 8, 14, 15, 18, 20, 21, 22, 26, 28, 31, 68, 85, 99, 101, 102, 103, 105, 124, 125, 126, *128*, 174, 183, 206, 217, 218, 243, 244, 245, 261, 262, 263, 268, 270, 275, 283, 291, 292, 309, 311
Lasser, Louise 225
Laughing Gas (1914) 158
Laurel, Stan (solo) *15*, 34, 53, 66, 69, 90, 99, 185, 201, 218, 224, 225, 232, 235, 259, 293
Laurel & Hardy *10*, *11*, *38*, 51, 64, *71*, 72, 73, 81, 84, *89*, 95–97, 101, *120*, 126, *127*, *132*, 134, 137, *159*, 171, 172, 174, 178–182, 185, *186*, 187, *188*, 189, 190–192, 198, 218, 233, 260, 265, 274–276, *277*, 283, 295, 297
Laurel-Hardy Murder Case (1930) 126–127
"Lazzi of Arlecchino's Portrait" 139
"Lazzi of Hunger" 86
"Lazzi of Spilling No Wine" 210
"Lazzi of the Ghost" 120
"Lazzi of the Nightfall" 120
"Lazzi of the Stones" 83
"Lazzi of the Waiter" 77, 83
"Lazzo of Hiding" 137
"Lazzo of the Fly" 241
"Lazzo of the Hands Behind the Back" 30
"Lazzo of the Living Corpse" 31, 120
"Lazzo of the Multiple Thief" 120
The Leaking Glue Pot (1908) 265
Leave 'Em Laughing (1928) 159
Lee & Moran 118
Legend of Ponchinella (1906) 22
Lester, Richard 131
Lewis, Jerry 64, 76, 122, 287
Life of Brian (1979) 114, 231, 240
Linder, Max 13, 22, 28, 55, 59, 107, 108, 111, 113, 121, 122, 134, 137, 155, 162, 163, 201, 203, 213, 230, 232, 234, 237, 242, 252, 259, 260, 265, 298
Line's Busy (1924) 99, 223, 282, 284
Little Shop of Horrors (1986) 156, 161
The Living Doll (1913) 16
The Living Posters (1903) 142
Lloyd, Harold 5, 7, 9, 23, 24, 29, 30, *39*, 62, 65, 81, 85, 86, 95, 101, 110, *111*, 114–117, 122, 123, *124*, 125, 129, 130, 138, 139, 146, 152, 162, 174, 175, 203, 211, 222–229, 231, *236*,

237, 245, 247, 259, 268, *269*, 280, 284
"Load! Unload!" (circus routine) 185
Loco Boy Makes Good (1942) 115
Long Pants (1927) 20, 68, 99
Lord, Del 92, 124, 187
Love 'Em and Weep (1927) 217, 225
Love in Armor (1915) 295
Loves Me, He Loves Me Not (1903) 243
Luck o' the Foolish (1924) 174
Luke's Fireworks Fizzle (1916) 130
Lupino, George 145, 146, 150, 293

Mace, Fred 48, 160, 169, 179, 229, 246, 278
Machin, Alfred 56
Mack, Hughie 54, 56
The Magic Book (1900) 142
The Man in White Suit (1951) 113
"The Man Who Kept House" (folk tale) 290
Mann, Hank 13, 82, 83, 130, 139, 140, 146, 194, 210, 226, 267, 273, 279
Martin, Joe 40, 41, 46
Martin, Steve 161
The Marx Brothers 5, 9, 73, 164, 199, *200*, 201, 208
McCarey, Leo 164, 165
McIntyre, Christine 106
McKee, Raymond 51
The Mechanical Man (1921) 151
Méliès, Georges 11, 16, 17, 23, 25, 33, 45, 118, 135, 137, 141, 142, 144, 146, 155, 192, 194, 195, 205, 206, 237, 245
Midler, Bette 167
Midnight at the Old Mill (1916) 120
The Mighty Boosh (television series) 74
Mighty Like a Moose (1926) 13
Mind the Baby (1924) 42
Missing Link (1917) 275
Mr. Jinks Buys a Dress (1913) 18
Monks a la Mode (1923) 36
Monsieur Beaucaire (1946) 137, 230, 237, 239
Monty Python 63, 73, 80, 90, 183, 192, 216, 229, 235, 239, 240
Moonshines and Jailbirds (1920) 272
Moony Mariner (1927) 224
Moore, Colleen 14, 59, 64, 99, 242
Moran, Lee 139, 174
Moran & Mack 253
Morante, Milburn 255, 272
Morrison, Ernest (aka "Sunshine Sammy") 247

Mother's Joy (1923) 276
Movie Crazy (1932) 115
Movieland (1926) 23, 26
Murray, Bill 54, 161
Murray, Charlie *119*, 121, 131, 161, 168, 229, *230*, *238*, 272, *285*
The Music Box (1932) 187, 189
My Pants Ripped (1908) 111
Myers, Harry C. 229
Myers, Michael 109, 143, 225

Naked Gun 2½ (1991) 133
National Lampoon's Christmas Vacation (1989) 267
Naughty Boy (1927) 217, 275
The Naughty Nineties (1945) 51, 84, 90, 116, 165, 176, 221
The Navigator (1924) 37, 41, *169*, 192, *193*, 202
Nerve Tonic (1924) 121, 137
Never Give a Sucker an Even Break (1941) 82, 174, 243, 263
Never Weaken (1921) 7, 227
The New Janitor (1914) 274
Nielsen, Leslie 33, 106, 172
Night at the Museum (2006) 28, 33, 41, 44, 70
A Night at the Opera (1935) 199, *200*
A Night in the Show (1915) 195
Night Owls (1930) 134
A Noise from the Deep (1913) 9
North By Northwest (1959) 128
Norton, Jack 199
Nothing But Pleasure (1940) 171
Now or Never (1921) 174, 227
Now You Tell One (1926) 154
Numa 60–62
Number, Please? (1920) 222, 223, 225, 284

O. Henry 52, 287, 288, 289
O. Henry's Full House (1952) 52, 288
Oakley, Frank "Slivers" 220
O'Brien, Conan 33
O'Brien, Willis 154, 272
Off to Bloomingdale Asylum (1901) 245
Oh, Doctor (1917) 7
One Shivery Night (1950) 140, 251
One Track Minds (1933) 69
One Week (1920) 206, 208, 211, 212
Onésime contre Onésime (1912) 164
Only Me (1929) 18, 32, 196
Our Gang 8, 48, 52, 70, 72, 83, 174, 225, 237, 243, 250, 258, 274
Our Hospitality 5, 115, 231
Out of Place (1922) 10
Out West (1918) 148, 247, 260
Over and Back (1915) 194

"Pack/Unpack" 187
Painless Pain (1926) 160
Pal the Dog 42
Pangborn, Franklin 179, 291
Parker, Sarah Jessica 47, 52, 309, 311
Parrott, Paul 7, 263, **264**
Pasha, Kalla 7, 263, **264**
The Passing of a Grouch (1910) 8–9
Pathé Frères 12, 13, 46, 70, 118, 130, 138, 142, 151, 194, 235, 246, 261, 264, 265
Pay or Move (1924) 19
Peacock, Lillian 42, 255, 311
Pee Wee's Big Adventure (1985) 152
Peg o' Movies (1923) 232
Pegg, Simon 16
Perez Marcel 22, 25, 211
Picking Peaches (1924) 28, 85
The Pilgrim (1923) 284
Pineapple Express (2008) 273, 274
The Pink Panther Strikes Again (1976) 106, 159, 234
The Pirates (1922) 68, 123
Pirates of the Caribbean (2003) 41
Pitts, ZaSu 31, 63, 83, 260
The Playhouse (1921) 36, 192, 195
Playmates (1918) 276
A Plumbing We Will Go (1940) 22, 284
"Pokes and Jabbs" (series) 137, 246
Pollard, Snub 91, 139, 152, 154, 158, 206, 210, 229, **236**, 247, 255, 257, 272, 280, 295
Polycarpe Wants to Shoot at Targets (1912) 25
The Poor Fish (1924) 290
Poor Simp (1920) 26
Prohibition 40, 272
Project A (1983) 194
Psycho (1960) 126
The Purple Rose of Cairo (1985) 142
Purviance, Edna 138

A Quiet Little Wedding (1913) 9, 45
Quiet Please! (1933) 173

Ray, Bobby 130, 134, 248
A Reckless Romeo (1917) 179
Reilly, John C. 114, 177
Return of Pink Panther (1975) 287
Reuben, Reuben (1983) 160
Ride 'Em Cowboy (1942) 51
Ritchie, Billie 14, 42, 44, 45, 78, 159, 226, 241, 274, 278, 284
Ritz, Harry 122
The Ritz Brothers 73, 122

Roach, Hal 34, 42, 44, 225
Roaming Romeo (1928) 29, 293
Roaring Lions and Wedding Bells 44, 45, 48, 58, 65, 70, 75
Roars and Uproars (1922) 44, 64, 75, 247
Robert Macaire and Bertrand (1907) 17, 205
Roberts, Joe 161, 189, 252
Rock, Joe 18, 44, 142, **233**
Rolling Stone (1919) 82, 143, 162
Rooney, Mickey 133, 202
Rowan and Martin 65
Rub, Chris 58
Rube's Visit to the Studio (1902) 16
Run, Fat Boy, Run (2007) 16

Safety Last! (1923) 24, 128, 129, 226–228
St. Clair, Malcolm 32
St. John, Al 7, 10, 59, 68, 77, 227, **228**, 260, 287
Sandler, Adam 117
Saps at Sea (1940) 84
The Scarecrow (1920) 153, 161, 297
Scared Stiff (1926) 70
Schade, Fritz 295
Schneider's Anti-Noise Crusade (1909) 134
School Days (1920) 275
Sebastian, Dorothy 217
Segel, Jason 107
Selig, William 57
Sellers, Peter 86, 106, 108, 174, 219, 234, 235, 287
Semon, Larry 2, 3, 13, 14, 21, 25, 26, 28, 48, 59, 81, 84, 88, 90, 96, 99, 123, 146, 154, 155, 195, 197, 206, 211, 222, 226, 232, 244, 247, 249, 251, 273, 274, 275, 279, 289, 298
Sennett, Mack 9, 46, 48, **60**, 112, 178, 213, 253, 272, 281, 294
Sennett Comedies 12, 14, 44, 48, 60, 62, 63, 72, 85, 92, 96, 97, 102, 112, 121, 123, 124, 143, 153, 161, 179, 183, 187, 264, 271, 272, 274, 281, 282, 283, 295
Servaès, Charles 25
Seven Chances (1925) 14, 26, 212, 247, 252
Seven Years Bad Luck (1921) 55, 59, 162, 201, 203, 237, 252, 265
Shaun of the Dead (2004) 129
The Sheik (1921) 232
Ship Ahoy (1919) 146, 273
Shivering Sherlocks (1948) 29, 93, 122, 124
Should Married Men Go Home? (1928) 11, 95

Should Sailors Marry? (1925) 175
The Show (1922) 13, 84, 195, 212
The Sin of Harold Diddlebock (1947) 62, 67
Sinatra, Frank 217
Sitka, Emil 73
Skelton, Red 106, 138, 201, 208, 212, 218, 238, 252, 276, 286–288
Skylarking (1923) 64, 68, 152
Smith, Sid 9, 78, **170**, 185, **231**
Smith Family's Candy Shop (1927) 55
Smith's Vacation (1926) 51
Snitch in Time (1950) 267
Snooky the Chimp 40, 44
Some More of Samoa (1941) 68
Sons of the Desert (1933) 84, 178–182
Sorcellerie culinaire 146
Le Soupirant (1962) 24, 216, 218
A Southern Yankee (1948) 138, 212
Speedy (1928) 29, 95, **224**
Spencer, Fred 42, 183
"The Spider and the Fly" (stage play) 293
The Spiritualistic Photographer (1903) 142
The Star Boarder (1919) 146, 289
Steamboat Bill, Jr. (1928) 26, 143, 197, **199**, 205, 208, 222
Stecker, Curly 40
Step This Way (1922) 142, 273
Sterling, Ford 7, 48, 68, 168
Stiller, Ben 28, 41, 44, 70, 114, 143
Stone, Arthur 59, 62, 164
Stop Thief! (1901) 12
The Strong Man (1926) 18, 101, 217
The Stunt Man (1927) 21, 251
Sturges, Preston 67
A Submarine Pirate (1915) 89, 123, 132, 273
Sugar Daddies (1927) 218
Le Suicide de Boireau (1909) 211
The Suitor (1920) 13, 212, 273, 279
Super-Hooper-Dyne Lizzies (1925) 123, 251
A Surgeon's Revenge (1916) 160
Swain, Mack 15, 26, 42, 49, 87, 89, 181, 187, 229, 248
Sword Points (1928) 145, 233

Tall, Dark and Gruesome (1948) 73, 251, 253
Talladega Nights (2006) 65
Temple, Shirley 43, 258
Ten Wives for One Husband 213
A Terrible Night (1896) 241
That's the Spirit (1924) 123, 248
30 Rock (television series) 5, 115, 142, 277

Three Ages (1923) 59, 230, 243, 252, 274, 283
Three Little Maids 10
The Three Must-Get-Theres (1922) 230, 232
Three Pests in a Mess (1945) 31, 106, 124
The Three Stooges 8, 10, 18, 22, 29, 31, 41, 51, 63, 68, 73, 77, 79, 83–85, 86, 88, 90, 92–94, 97, 106, 115, 116, 122–125, 132, 137, 139, 143, 159, 160, 161, 165, 171–174, 189, 197, 211, 215, 237, 241, 251, 262, 263, 267, 271, 274, 275, 278, 280–284, 291
Todd, Thelma 63, 71, 83
Tomlin, Lily 277
Toto 99
Tramp, Tramp, Tramp (1926) 14, 206, 275, 276
A Troublesome Satchel (1909) 134
Turnabout (1940) 291
Turpin, Ben **8**, 21, 23, **47**, 56, 77, 90, 99, 113, 135, 138, 143, 153, 161, 232, ***261***, 264, 267, 282

Uncle Josh in a Spooky Hotel (1900) 118, 296

Van Dyke, Dick 82
Vernon, Bobby 72, 203, 232, 275
Voice from the Deep (1912) 278

The Waif and the Statue (1907) 16
A Waiters' Ball (1916) 67
Waiting (1925) 9, 210, 247, 271
Wandering Willie (1924) 92
Watch the Birdie (1950) 201
The Water Plug (1920) 19, 146
The Waterboy (1998) 117
The Watermelon Patch (1905) 245
Way Out West (1937) 84, 101, 260
We Faw Down (1928) 11, 182
Weber and Fields 9
Weekend at Bernie's (1989) 217, 219

West, Billy 82, 99, 143, 146, 162, 164, 223, 273, 276, 282, 284
Wheeler & Woolsey 210, 233, **234**, 280
White, Jack 250
White Wings (1923) 224, 293
Who's Afraid? (1927) 27, 201
Who's Minding the Store? (1963) 287
Wild Roomer (1927) 152
Williams, Bert 246, 248
Wistful Widow of Wagon Gap (1947) 93
Witwer, H.C. 110
The Wooden Leg (1909) 270
A Wreath in Time (1909) 178

The Yellow Cab Man (1950) 276, 286, 287
Young, Noah 139, 175, ***236***
YouTube 159

Zigoto à la fête (1912) 23
Zombieland (2009) 5, 76

www.ingramcontent.com/pod-product-compliance
Lightning Source LLC
Chambersburg PA
CBHW080759300426
44114CB00020B/2763